Taxis – Licensing Law and Practice

D1343438

Taxis – Licensing Law and Practice

James T.H. Button

BA, Solicitor, ACIArb

Butterworths
London, Dublin, Edinburgh
1999

United Kingdom	Butterworths, a Division of Reed Elsevier (UK) Ltd, Halsbury House, 35 Chancery Lane, LONDON WC2A 1EL and 4 Hill Street, EDINBURGH EH2 3JZ
Australia	Butterworths, a Division of Reed International Books Australia Pty Ltd, CHATSWOOD, New South Wales
Canada	Butterworths Canada Ltd, MARKHAM, Ontario
Hong Kong	Butterworths Asia (Hong Kong), HONG KONG
India	Butterworths India, NEW DELHI
Ireland	Butterworth (Ireland) Ltd, DUBLIN
Malaysia	Malayan Law Journal Sdn Bhd, KUALA LUMPUR
New Zealand	Butterworths of New Zealand Ltd, WELLINGTON
Singapore	Butterworths Asia, SINGAPORE
South Africa	Butterworths Publishers (Pty) Ltd, DURBAN
USA	Lexis Law Publishing, CHARLOTTESVILLE, Virginia

A CIP Catalogue record for this book is available from the British Library.

ISBN 0 406 90012 4

Typeset by M Rules, London
Printed by Butler & Tanner, Frome and London

Visit us at our website: http://www.butterworths.co.uk

I'm Tootles the Taxi,
I'll give you a ride.
Put up your hand,
Then jump inside.
Just watch the meter,
You'll see the fare—
Distance no object—
Go anywhere!

For Daniel and Eleanor

Preface

This book covers all aspects of legislation and practice relating to hackney carriage and private hire licensing in England and Wales.

These are two distinct licensing regimes with some overlap of provisions but it must be borne in mind that the licensing controls on hackney carriages are distinct and in some cases quite different from, those which apply to private hire vehicles.

It used to be possible to use the expression 'taxi' to refer generically to the hackney carriage and private hire trades collectively, but recent legislation has started to use 'taxi' to mean 'hackney carriage'. The result of this development is to deprive us of a generic term.

This means that throughout this book references will be to hackney carriages or private hire vehicles specifically and the word 'taxi' will now be reserved for its specific legislative meaning.

The book is a practical day-to-day guide for all those involved in hackney carriage and private hire licensing, whether they are local authority lawyers, enforcement officers, administrators, local authority members, members of the hackney carriage and private hire trades or lawyers in private practice and it will not assume any prior knowledge to explain and amplify certain points. Where applicable and possible, procedures are illustrated by the use of flow charts which experience has shown are a valuable tool for assisting in understanding complex administrative processes.

In this field, as in many other local authority fields, case law is extremely important and there are a number of High Court decisions on aspects of hackney carriage and private hire licensing which have an important bearing on the way the operations are undertaken by local authorities and which do in certain cases refine the legislation quite considerably. Again, where possible, digests of these cases together with a commentary on their impact have been included. As there are statutory rights of appeal against local authority decisions to the lower courts (the magistrates' court and thereafter to the Crown Court), there has been a plethora of decisions by various magistrates' courts and Crown Courts up and down the country. These will probably have had a significant impact upon the ways in which those local authorities conduct their operations in relation to hackney carriage and private hire licensing. However, except in one or two cases these are not referred to or contained in this book, as they are of no assistance to other authorities in terms of precedent and indeed reference to them can be quite misleading. The exceptions are where there is no High Court decision and a Crown Court decision with a reasonable transcript of the judgment is better than nothing.

As this is intended to be a practical user's guide, footnotes have been kept to a minimum. The view is that if the reader needs to know about it, it should be in the body of the text and if the reader does not need to know it will not be included at all. Footnotes are therefore confined to case references and other reference material or occasionally to point the reader in the direction for further reading or research.

The layout and arrangement of the book follows a logical pattern with an initial exploration of the way in which the local authority operates both generally and specifically in relation to licensing, including matters that can and cannot be taken into account when reaching decisions, the way in which that decision is reached, and methods of challenging those decisions.

This book would not have been written without the encouragement and help of a great many people. I cannot name them all, as the list would probably be longer than the book itself, but to everyone who has asked a question, made a suggestion or told me of an experience, I am very grateful. The members of the Local Government Licensing Forum have helped enormously, as has Sue Bate, Law Librarian at Manchester University. Sue Leigh undertook the bulk of the typing, and a number of people waded through earlier drafts and gave me the benefit of their wisdom. Butterworths placed a lot of faith in me, and I hope I have repaid it. Finally, without the support of my family and friends, I would still be looking at a sheet of paper headed 'Chapter 1'.

It is customary to say it, but in this case it is all too true – any mistakes are mine!

James T.H. Button
July 1999

James Button & Co, Solicitors
Public Health Legal Information Unit
The Granary
Catton
Walton on Trent
Derbyshire DE12 8LN
Tel: 01283 711533
Fax: 01283 711544

Acknowledgement

Illustration of 'Tootles the Taxi' and verse (by Joyce B. Clegg) from *TOOTLES THE TAXI and Other Rhymes* (Ladybird, 1954) © Ladybird Books Ltd, 1954. Reprinted by permission of Ladybird Books Ltd.

Contents

Contents

Table of Statutes

Paragraph numbers printed in **bold** type indicate where Statutes have been set out in part or in full.

Table of Statutory Instruments

Table of Cases

Chapter 1

Hackney carriage and private hire licensing

A BRIEF OVERVIEW

It is true to say that while there are hackney carriages in most parts of the country (the licensing of hackney carriages or private hire vehicles in the Metropolitan Area is not being examined in this work), there are also private hire vehicles. There are two separate and distinct licensing regimes dealing with these two types of vehicles, both of which are administered by local authorities. There are some considerable similarities, but there are also some important distinctions. One of the main similarities between the two types of vehicle (and, therefore, those who drive them and control them) is that both transport members of the public to a specific destination upon request, in exchange for payment of a fare.

The 'public' are not a homogeneous mass, but are comprised of many individuals with different needs, abilities and, in some cases, disabilities. It is important that the service provided by hackney carriages and private hire vehicles is able to cope with this variety. The rationale behind a licensing regime covering this important part of the public transport of the country is the provision of a service to the public that is accessible and safe, and seen to be so. Public safety is paramount in the licensing regimes that govern these vehicles, their drivers and operators, whether it is to prevent direct danger to the passenger from the driver of the vehicle themselves or a slightly less direct danger to the passenger and other members of society from the vehicle itself or the way in which the vehicle is driven. In addition, it must not be overlooked that the hackney carriage and private hire trades employ a great many people who also have a right to expect a fair and reasonable licensing regime to govern their activities.

Parliament has, for the last one hundred and sixty years, passed legislation covering hackney carriages and private hire vehicles, but the actual day-to-day implementation of that legislation falls to local authorities, who have the complex and, at times, extremely difficult task of reconciling the needs and expectations of the public with the needs and expectations of those involved in the two trades.

Local authorities are democratically elected bodies who are able to respond to the needs of their electorate and the issues which affect the area that they

1.1

1.2

1.3

1.4

1

represent. Due to the vast range of activities which they undertake, licensing, in general, and hackney carriage and private hire licensing, in particular, are unlikely to be the priority of either an individual councillor, or that of the local electorate, but it is undoubtedly true that, on occasions, hackney carriage and private hire licensing can cause a great deal of concern.

1.5   Although this is a sweeping generalisation, it appears to be the case that most of the public do not understand the distinction between hackney carriages and private hire vehicles. The public simply believe that both types are 'taxis', which will serve the purpose that they require. These purposes range from pre-booking a service to take them to a specific place through to transporting people when they are out and need to go somewhere else. In addition, hackney carriages and private hire vehicles fulfil a vital late-night role in emptying the many town and city centres of people who have gone out to be entertained for the evening and need to be taken home. When the many other uses of 'taxis' are taken into account (school contracts being one of the most important), it starts to become more apparent that there is no one perfect or ideal use of a 'taxi'.

1.6   In trying to balance all of these conflicting needs and expectations, local authorities are placed in an unenviable position and may face both political and legal challenges to their decisions.

The right to challenge, however, should not simply be seen as an irritant from the local authority's point of view. It is an important method of checking and controlling the activities of local authorities and of protecting the interests of those involved in the trade who are directly affected by decisions councils make. Without such methods, the only brake on local government decision-making in this field would be the use of the democratic process at local government elections and although the numbers of people involved in the trade across the country are significant, in any individual local authority it is unlikely this number would be sufficient to seriously affect the outcome of an election.

Hackney carriages

1.7   Hackney carriages are the oldest form of hire vehicle that is recognised in England and Wales. They have been in existence in one form or another for at least two hundred years and they have been regulated in some areas for one hundred and fifty years.

The principal features of a hackney carriage are: it can carry passengers for hire or reward; it can be hailed by a prospective passenger; and it can also park on a rank to await the approach of passengers. It must be driven by a driver, who holds a hackney carriage driver's licence, and cannot be driven by anyone who does not hold such a licence, whether the vehicle is actually working or not (except for a specific statutory exemption in relation to testing). The philosophy behind this licensing is that each hackney carriage is individually controlled and is available for public hire. In practice, however, in a great many parts of the country, most hackney carriage activities are more akin to private hire vehicle activities than this traditional view of the hackney carriage would suggest.

The local authority can lay down conditions as to the type of vehicle that can **1.8** be used for hackney carriage work. These can cover the size, appearance, methods of access and egress, colour, number of seats, number of doors and such specific matters as turning circle and luggage space of the vehicle.

The local authority has the power to limit the number of hackney carriages **1.9** within its area, but only if it is satisfied that there is no significant unmet demand for hackney carriage services. A number of local authorities do limit numbers, whilst others rely on a more *laissez-faire* approach, allowing market forces to determine the number of hackney carriages within the locality.

In relation to a hackney carriage driver, there are statutory tests that have to **1.10** be complied with before a person can be granted a licence. These are primarily concerned with the fitness and propriety of the individual (which, in itself, covers a wide range of areas) and the length of time that they have been driving under a full Driver and Vehicle Licensing Agency (DVLA) licence. Again, there are mechanisms which allow the local authority to impose their own tests and conditions. A great many do so through such means as medical tests, driving tests, testing knowledge of the locality and checking on any criminal convictions that the driver may have.

Most local authorities also prescribe the fares that the hackney carriage **1.11** proprietor can charge for his services. These range from a simple charge per unit of distance travelled to complex, multi-tiered fare structures which take account of: the time of the hiring (and, in some cases, the date, eg, Christmas Day); the number of people carried; the number of items of luggage carried; time spent stationary (eg, at traffic lights or in traffic jams); and, in some cases, a fixed charge for cleaning the vehicle should it become soiled.

Once a hackney carriage is plying for hire (whether cruising the streets or **1.12** waiting on a rank), there are only a few reasons the driver can use to refuse to take a passenger and, once the vehicle has been hired, the hirer is then contractually bound to pay the fare.

It is, therefore, both in theory and generally in practice, an extremely satisfactory, reliable, safe and acceptable form of transport, with safeguards for both hirer and driver.

Private hire vehicles

Private hire vehicles are a more recent development. National legislation **1.13** (excluding the Metropolitan Area) was not introduced until 1976. It has not developed in the intervening two decades to any great extent.

Private hire vehicles are not 'mini-cabs'. This term referred to non-hackney carriages which provided services for hire and reward within the Metropolitan Area before legislation was introduced to control them. Under the provisions of the Private Hire Vehicles (London) Act 1998, a licensing regime will be applied to the Metropolitan Area, in respect of private hire vehicles, which is similar to that already existing in the rest of the country.

3

1.14 A private hire vehicle cannot ply for hire or stand in a rank. It must be pre-booked with a private hire operator.

The private hire operator is the linch-pin of the private hire vehicle licensing regime. He takes the booking for a private hire vehicle and despatches the vehicle (which must be driven by a private hire driver) to fulfil that request. A private hire vehicle cannot operate independently from a private hire operator. The legislation places considerable duties on private hire operators to ensure that the vehicles and drivers which they operate are properly licensed.

1.15 Local authorities have various powers in relation to private hire vehicles, drivers and operators. Once again, they can consider the fitness and propriety of persons applying for a driver's or operator's licence and, in the case of drivers, how long they have held a DVLA licence. In relation to vehicles, they can impose conditions on the size, number of doors, passenger space, seats, luggage space, condition, etc of the vehicle. They also have the power to impose conditions upon operators' and drivers' licences, in order to govern their behaviour and conduct.

1.16 The main difference between hackney carriages and private hire vehicles is in their fares. The local authority has no power to prescribe fares for private hire vehicles. This will, therefore, be a matter for arrangement between the operator and the hirer. It has been argued that this allows for negotiation between the two parties, but, in general, the price is determined by the operator.

1.17 The local authority has no power to prescribe a maximum number of private hire vehicles within its area. Market forces, therefore, determine the number of private hire vehicles that operate within a district.

1.18 The local authority not only grants licences for hackney carriages and hackney carriage drivers, private hire vehicles, drivers and operators, but it also enforces the provisions that apply to them. This means that they must ensure that licensees comply with both the legislation and any conditions that they may impose upon them. The local authority will also take action against those who are unlicensed. Whilst the former action arguably only protects the travelling public, action against the latter protects both the public and the trade itself.

Present and future law

1.19 There have been a number of calls in recent years for a review of 'taxi' legislation, with arguments ranging from concern about the confusion caused by having two types of vehicle undertaking what are extremely similar activities, through to the feeling that 150-year-old legislation is too outdated to control an important area of transportation in the approach to the next millennium. It remains to be seen whether new legislation will be forthcoming, but, in the meantime, it is worth acknowledging that, generally, the current old legislation works well and has the advantage of consistency and certainty. This is a tribute to all those involved in hackney carriage and private hire licensing, as is the fact that legislation, which was designed for horse-drawn vehicles, is as effectively applied to modes of transport would have been beyond the wildest dreams of those who drafted the legislation in 1847.

The remainder of this book will examine in detail the law and practice of the licensing of hackney carriage vehicles (proprietors' licences), hackney carriage drivers, private hire operators, private hire vehicles and private hire drivers. It will explore the interaction between these licences and other areas of transportation and will aim to demonstrate how the law is being, and can be, used to fulfil the overriding aim of public safety.

Chapter 2

Licensing within local government

INTRODUCTION

This chapter is intended to provide a brief overview of how licensing fits **2.1** within the local government framework. For a more detailed study, or to take further any of the points made here, please consult *Butterworths Local Government Law*.

Local authorities have a large number of licensing and registration functions. **2.2** These are generally the responsibility of district councils, metropolitan district councils, unitary authorities, London borough councils and the Common Council of the City of London in England, and county councils and county borough councils in Wales. There are some licensing and registration functions which fall to county councils in England to discharge.

Hackney carriage and private hire licensing is the function of a district **2.3** council, unitary council or metropolitan district council in England outside the Metropolitan Area and a county or county borough council function in Wales. Every authority has its own structure and procedures. This is also true where hackney carriage and private hire licensing is concerned. As a result, it is impossible to state one preferred method when there are a number of acceptable systems in operation across the two countries.

However, there are some fundamental points which remain constant, notwithstanding the particular administrative and organisational set-up the council has adopted. These are explored in this chapter, together with specific points concerned with the licensing of hackney carriages and private hire vehicles.

THE LOCAL AUTHORITY ITSELF

Power to act

Local authorities are statutory creations and the basis of local authority **2.4** legislation is the Local Government Act 1972. This Act has been amended considerably since it brought the, then, new authorities into existence on 1 April 1974. In terms of local authority structure, the most important subsequent legislation has been the Local Government Act 1985 (which

7

abolished the metropolitan county councils in England and the Greater London Council), the Local Government Act 1992 (which paved the way for the creation of unitary authorities in certain parts of England (which included the abolition of the 'created' counties from the 1974 reforms – Avon, Cleveland and Humberside)) and the Local Government (Wales) Act 1994 (which fundamentally altered local government in Wales, replacing the former two-tier system with a Principality-wide single-tier system of unitary authorities).

2.5 Due to the statutory nature of the existence of local authorities, it is only possible for a local authority to undertake activities for which it is statutorily empowered. This means that, for every function and action that a local authority undertakes, it must be able to show that there is either a specific statutory power for it to do so, as it is acting to discharge a specific statutory duty, or that the activity is authorised because it is incidental to another specific statutory function.

In relation to hackney carriage and private hire licensing, this point is not of enormous importance in relation to day-to-day activities, as there are specific powers contained in section 37 of the Town Police Clauses Act 1847, allied to section 15 of the Transport Act 1985 and section 45 of the Local Government (Miscellaneous Provisions) Act 1976.

Discharge of functions

2.6 Once the local authority has established that it has a power or duty to undertake the function, it is then for the local authority to decide how it is going to discharge these particular functions. In the absence of any other specific statutory power (eg giving duties or powers to specified officers of the authority or to statutory committees), the power lies with the council (that is, at a meeting of the full council).

Obviously, it is impracticable to expect full council meetings to decide upon all the activities of a local authority, irrespective of the size of the authority, and, accordingly, every local authority adopts a system and structure of committees and sub-committees.

2.7 Section 101 of the Local Government Act 1972 allows the local authority to:

> ' ". . . arrange for the discharge of any of their functions": by a committee, sub-committee or an officer of the authority.'

There is no one particular way in which this is set up, although there are a number of models which are in use around the country.

Once the committee or sub-committee has been set up it is then necessary for the council itself to decide how the committee discharges the functions for which it has been created. This is usually exercised in two ways, either by a delegation of powers or through an investigative role. Both are an arrangement for the discharge of functions, but are materially different.

Delegation of powers means that the power or duty which lies with the council is delegated to that committee. This means that a decision of the committee is a decision of the council and no approval by any other body is required. The alternative is that the committee is asked to investigate matters and then to report its findings to the council in order to enable the council to make a decision on the basis of the information obtained by the committee.

It should be noted that powers can also be delegated to sub-committees or to officers, as, indeed, can a request for investigation. In those circumstances, the effect is exactly the same as that outlined above[1].

1 Local Government Act 1972, s 101(1)(*a*).

Such mechanisms are laid down by the council and are contained in a document approved by the council. This tends to be called either a Scheme of Delegations or a Schedule of Delegations. This will have been passed by the council and is used in conjunction with the Standing Orders of the Council, which, again, are adopted by the council by means of resolution. These control the procedural aspects of the local authority's activities. In any proceedings, there should be evidence in the form of a certified copy of the resolution, to show that the Scheme of Delegations and Standing Orders are the current ones in force[1].

2.8

1 Local Government Act 1972, s 234.

The Scheme of Delegations will state that a certain committee (and department created to support the committee) have responsibility for the licensing of hackney carriages and private hire vehicles. As stated earlier, there is no one model, and hackney carriage and private hire licensing is undertaken by a wide range of different committees and departments. These include: environmental health departments; legal departments, chief executive's departments; engineers departments; planning departments; and town clerk's departments. Some authorities have licensing departments, which may be autonomous, or divisions of other departments, and these undertake the whole range of licensing functions applicable to that authority, whereas others tend to scatter their varying licensing functions across a number of departments. However, hackney carriage and private hire licensing do tend to stay together.

2.9

In relation to the Scheme of Delegations, it is vital to ensure that it fully covers all matters which are likely to be encountered in relation to hackney carriage and private hire licensing. Specific reference should be made to each of the pieces of legislation which cover this field[1].

1 See Appendix I.

In relation to hackney carriage and private hire vehicle licensing, the more common models employed are either a sub-committee, which undertakes all functions, or a sub-committee, which will have power to deal with all functions, but which has delegated the power to grant licences in certain specified situations (usually where there are no grounds for refusal) to officers. Some authorities have delegated the entire licensing regime to officers, with the power to both grant and refuse, and there are other authorities where the entire regime is discharged by committee or sub-committee, with no officer-delegated power.

2.10

The question as to which model is adopted is a matter for local decision, bearing in mind the need to balance the conflicting requirements of member involvement and time involved. Provided that the personnel involved understand the nature of their role and the extent of their power, it is difficult to say whether one system is more effective or efficient than any other.

2.11   What is clear, however, is that it is highly desirable for the committee or officer who considers the application for a licence to have the delegated power
to deal with that application. If the findings of the officer or committee
have to then be reported to another body, it is extremely difficult to ensure
that every fact and furthermore every nuance is accurately and adequately
reported.

There is a well-known passage from the judgment given by Woolf J in the
case of *R v Chester City Council, ex p Quietlynn Ltd*[1] in relation to the licensing of a sex establishment. Paragraph 10(19) of Schedule 3 to the Local
Government (Miscellaneous Provisions) Act 1982 requires the local authority to give an applicant for a sex establishment licence an opportunity to be
heard, which is not the case in hackney carriage and private hire licensing.
However, the principle raised is an important one, and the following extract
from *R v Chester City Council* is worth considering. Woolf J stated:

> 'Although I fully accept the importance of the use of committees and
> sub-committees in local government and accept that, in respect of purely
> administrative matters, it is quite proper for committees to act on the rec-
> ommendations of other committees, it does not follow that the position is
> the same when the authority is performing the sort of function involved in
> considering applications for the grant of a licence. Such applications must
> be considered fairly and, in many cases it may be necessary for the deter-
> mining body to have at least a summary of the representations of the
> applicant, whether they have been made in writing or at a hearing before
> another committee.'

1   (1983) Times, 19 October.

2.12   Notwithstanding these sentiments, the High Court decided at first instance
in that case that there was no unfairness to the applicants. On appeal, the
Court of Appeal did not agree and allowed one of the four appeals.
However, they approved the approach outlined above by Woolf J in the
High Court. Giving his judgment in the Court of Appeal, Stephen Brown LJ
said[1]:

> 'It is submitted on behalf of the local authority that in this case it was not
> necessary that anything should be said by way of a report by the licensing
> panel because the decision was one which was based on locality, the char-
> acteristics of which would be known to all the members of the committee
> and that the five members of the licensing panel were present as members
> of the committee and could have given any information about the hearing
> and (sic) which had taken place if they had been asked. Accordingly, since
> the schedule provides that the hearing may be made by a sub-committee,
> there would be no breach of any procedural requirement such as would
> entitle the court to intervene in the conclusion that was reached.
>
> It seems to me that this raises a very narrow point in this instance. I
> accept that the administrative functions of local authorities cover a very
> wide spectrum. They include the various licensing functions which fall
> upon local authorities. There is however an element of the judicial process
> in this particular function. That is made clear by paragraph 10, sub-
> paragraph (19) of Schedule 3 to the Act of 1982. [His Lordship read the
> sub-paragraph and continued].
>
> The principle, which is expressed in the maxim *audi alterem partem*, there-
> fore is relevant and does apply, in my judgment, to this particular
> function.

On this occasion the uncontested facts show that no report of any kind was made to the decision-making committee. It may be that a report could have been a very short report indeed, but in my view it is a requisite of the sub-paragraph that the applicants' representations should be considered by the committee making the decision. In this case no report of any kind was made. For that reason, I take the view that there was a procedural irregularity which cannot be cured by the fact that the members of the committee could probably be expected to have known of the characteristics of the locality and could have asked, if they had wished, for details of the hearing before the panel from their members who had actually heard the applicants' representative. In my judgment this was a breach of the procedural rules which does vitiate the decision arrived at.'

1 *R v Preston Borough Council, ex p Quietlynn* (1984) 83 LGR 308, CA at 315.

From both legal and practical points of view, it therefore makes sense for the person or body who hears the application to have the power to make the decision on that application. Obviously, if reporting further has to be undertaken this will waste both time and effort on the part of all concerned. This allied to the risk of judicial unhappiness at such a procedure, reinforces the point that it is not the approach to take. **2.13**

The decision itself

Once it has been established who or which body is empowered to make decisions relating to licensing, the actual mechanics of the decision-making process can be considered. The grant or refusal of a licence is not a criminal matter, nor is it a purely civil matter. It is an administrative matter and, accordingly, the rules which govern the operation and undertaking of that procedure are not the rules of criminal or civil evidence. This has major implications upon the way in which the decision is arrived at, and the evidence, both of type and, indeed, in some cases, quantity, that is adduced and can be considered by the decision-maker. **2.14**

Quasi-judicial body

It is frequently stated that a local authority licensing committee (whether this is a sub-committee, committee or an officer) is a quasi-judicial body. That has found judicial favour in a number of cases. The Court of Appeal agreed in *R v Liverpool Corpn, ex p Liverpool Taxi Fleet Operators' Association*[1] when Lord Denning MR stated (at 391): **2.15**

'It is perhaps putting it a little high to say that they are exercising judicial functions. They may be said to be exercising an administrative function. But even so, in our modern approach, they must act fairly: and the court will see that they do so.'

What then is the practical effect of a having a quasi-judicial body making these decisions? The most important effect is that the rules of natural justice must be observed, in its simplest form this means that the applicant must be treated fairly, and be seen to be treated fairly. The rules themselves are quite clear and fall neatly into two specific rules.

1 [1972] 2 QB 299.

A right to be heard before a decision is reached

2.16   The first rule of natural justice is *audi alteram partum*: any person who is going to be affected by the decision that is to be made has a right to be heard before the decision is reached. In relation to hackney carriage and private hire licensing, this will generally mean the applicant, although there are exceptions, eg a proposal to increase the number of hackney carriage proprietors' licences. Obviously, if the application is uncontested, ie the applicant satisfies all the criteria that the local authority have laid down, then it is unnecessary for the applicant to attend a hearing and be given a chance to speak when there are no objections against which he has to speak. However, the situation is quite different where there are prima facie grounds for refusing the licence. In those circumstances, the applicant must be given the chance to make representations.

2.17   There is no statutory requirement that the applicant should be given the opportunity to make oral representations, but many local authorities do allow such a course of action. However, the case law supports the view that the local authority can set its own procedures and it is, therefore, open to a local authority to allow only written representations.

2.18   This view was supported by Lord Denning MR in *Selvarajan v Race Relations Board*[1]. This case concerned an investigation into allegations of racial discrimination. These allegations were investigated by a conciliation committee of the Race Relations Board, which found discrimination, but failed to achieve a settlement. The matter was then referred to the Board itself. They found no evidence of racial discrimination. The applicant for judicial review argued that the Board had failed in its duty to act fairly. He failed in that assertion. Lord Denning MR stated (at 19B):

> 'In all these cases it has been held that the investigating body is under a duty to act fairly: but that which fairness requires depends upon the nature of the investigation and the consequences which it may have on persons affected by it. The fundamental rule is that, if a person may be subjected to pains or penalties, or be exposed to prosecution or proceedings, or deprived of remedies or redress, or in some such way adversely afflicted by the investigation and report, then he should be told the case made against him and be afforded a fair opportunity of answering it. The investigating body is, however, the master of its own procedure. It need not hold a hearing. It can do everything in writing. It need not allow lawyers. It need not put every detail of the case against a man. Suffice if the broad grounds are given. It need not name its informants. It can give the substance only. Moreover, it need not do everything itself. It can employ secretaries and assistants to do all the preliminary work and leave much to them. But, in the end, the investigating body itself must come to its own decision and make its own report.'

1   [1976] 1 All ER 12, CA.

2.19   This approach has been supported in subsequent cases, especially in relation to oral hearings. In *R v North Yorkshire County Council, ex p M (No 2)*[1] Ewbank J, in relation to an application before an adoption panel, stated:

> 'There is no provision for oral submissions to be made by a guardian *ad litem* in court proceedings or by any other person. Although the guardian *ad litem* may think it desirable to attend the adoption panel and put her

submissions orally, this is essentially a matter for the adoption panel themselves to decide. There is no reason to suppose that the guardian *ad litem*'s views cannot be adequately expressed in the report written by her, nor adequately conveyed by the meeting she had with the principal officer and the social worker. In my view, the suggestion that the decision not to allow her to attend the adoption panel was contrary to the law is unarguable. Indeed, in my judgment, I would have thought it was good practice to come to the decision that the authority came to in this case.

Although it is incumbent on a local authority when there is a court case in train to listen to the guardian *ad litem*'s views, that does not imply the guardian *ad litem* is entitled to decide how the adoption panel, or any other branch of the local authority, should conduct its affairs, nor is she entitled to insist on attending meetings.'

1 [1989] 2 FLR 79, QBD.

2.20 In fact, many authorities do allow persons to speak in support of (or if the situation warrants it) against an application, but these cases (and others) show that there is no right, either under statute law or common law to require this. It is, therefore, a matter for the discretion of the authority as to whether oral representations will be allowed. If they are, it is then a matter for the further discretion of the local authority as to whether such persons making oral representations are open to cross-examination.

If oral representations are allowed, consideration should be given to allowing the applicant the opportunity to be represented. This does not need to be by a legally qualified representative, but can be by somebody simply acting on the applicant's behalf. However, oral representations and representatives may increase the time taken for each application, and it is for the local authority to decide on its procedures and to communicate their decision to applicants and others in advance.

2.21 Another important consideration is the need for the person concerned to know what the allegations against him are. In *R v Assistant Metropolitan Police Comr, ex p Howell*[1], this point arose. Mr Howell had held a hackney carriage driver's licence in London for 12 years. At the age of 50, he had to have a medical to renew his licence, and went to his own doctor. His own doctor reported that Mr Howell had a past history of epilepsy, but that he was currently fit to drive. As a result of this, a second medical report was obtained, which concluded that Mr Howell had indeed suffered from epilepsy, but was not affected at the present time. As a consequence of this second report, the licence was not renewed. However, Mr Howell was not allowed to see the second report, nor was he told what it contained.

Ackner LJ stated (at 59H):

'The power of the assistant commissioner is to be exercised – and only to be exercised – after due consideration and determination of Mr Howell's [the applicant] fitness to drive. It is not a discretion that may be exercised arbitrarily and without accountability. The consideration must, therefore, be a fair consideration of Mr Howell's fitness to drive. The duty is, therefore to act fairly.'

The Court of Appeal held that Mr Howell had a justifiable grievance because he was not told of the contents of the report nor allowed to make representations about its contents. In addition, the decision was based on scanty and unreliable information. Ackner LJ continued (at 60H):

'In my judgment it was defective. It was defective because it did not provide Mr Howell with any indication of what were the objections which the assistant commissioner thought disentitled Mr Howell from receiving a renewal of the licence and he was thereby denied an opportunity of meeting those objections in such manner as was available. This was unfair.

I do not in any way seek to criticise the assistant commissioner for feeling anxious when he received the [second] report . . . What I do criticise is his reaching his decision without communicating to Mr Howell what it was that was causing him anxiety and concern and was likely to be the operative reason for refusing to extend the licence, so as to give Mr Howell an opportunity to meet and satisfy that concern and anxiety if he could.'

This decision-making process was defective and unfair, and the matter should be reconsidered by the Assistant Commissioner. This decision was supported by both the other judges, Slade and Purchas JJ.

1 [1986] RTR 52, CA.

No person should be a judge in his own cause

2.22   The second rule of natural justice is *nemo judex in causa sua potest*: that no person should be a judge in their own cause. In practice this means that if there is anybody who has any vested interest or any other interest, beyond a pecuniary interest which would fall within ss 94–97 of the Local Government Act 1972[1], then they must not take a part in the decision-making process. The rule in fact is slightly wider than that. It is not sufficient merely not to take part, one has to be seen not to be taking part. It is important that a member, who has this type of interest, distances themself from the decision-making and makes it quite clear, publicly and openly, that they are not taking part in the decision.

1 For further details see *Butterworths Local Government Law*.

2.23   This is well illustrated by the case of *Hannam v Bradford City Council*[1]. In this case, a teacher was dismissed by the governors of a school and, under the then current legislation and articles of government of the school, the local education authority had the power to prevent that dismissal. It was agreed that the staff sub-committee of the education authority, which considered whether or not to exercise that power, was sitting in a quasi-judicial capacity. On that sub-committee, which, on the day of the decision, consisted of ten members, were three people who were governors of the school from which the teacher had been dismissed, although they had not been present at the governors' meeting when the dismissal was approved. It was alleged that there was a risk of bias in the findings of the committee. Lord Sachs LJ said (at 942D):

'. . . it was abundantly clear that the staff sub-committee decision could not stand. No man can be a judge in his own cause. The governors did not, upon donning their sub-committee hats, cease to be an integral part of the body whose action was being impugned, and it made no difference that they did not personally attend the governors meeting [where the decision to dismiss was taken].'

Lord Widgery LJ added (at 946A):

'I am much impressed by the fact that when the sub-committee sat down to consider what the plaintiff would regard as an appeal, the chairman was a member of the governors against whose decision this so-called appeal was being brought. I think that if it had been disclosed at the outset that no less a person than the chairman of the sub-committee was a member of the governors in question, the immediate reaction of everyone would have been that some real likelihood of bias existed. I say that with every respect to the distinguished gentleman who chaired the sub-committee on this occasion; but when one is used to working with other people in a group or on a committee, there must be a built-in tendency to support the decision of that committee, even though one tries to fight against it, and this is so even though the chairman was not sitting on the occasion when the decision complained about was reached.'

Finally, Lord Cross LJ put forward the following suggested test for assessing whether there was any possible bias in such circumstances (at 949C):

'If a reasonable person who has no knowledge of the matter beyond knowledge of the relationship which subsists between some members of the tribunal and one of the parties would think that there might well be bias, then there is in his opinion a real likelihood of bias. Of course, someone else with inside knowledge of the characters of the members in question might say: "Although things don't look very well, in fact there is no real likelihood of bias." That, however, would be beside the point, because the question is not whether the tribunal will in fact be biased, but whether a reasonable man with no inside knowledge might well think that it might be biased.'

1 [1970] 1 WLR 937, CA.

In the case of *R v Barnsley Metropolitan Borough Council, ex p Hook*[1], it was **2.24** the presence of an officer, who was directly involved in the situation in question, which rendered the decision unsatisfactory. The markets manager who terminated the licence of a person to trade in the market (for urinating in an alley) then took part in the decision on the subsequent internal appeals heard by the council. Lord Scarman LJ said (at 1060D):

'In my judgment, the local authority was in breach of one rule of natural justice which is so old that it can be put in the Latin language: *nemo debet esse judex in causa propria* . . .

When the authority came to file its evidence, then it seems to me it did appear that Mr Fretwell, the market manager, and the chairman of the committee had participated, first, in the decision to revoke the licence; secondly, in the first appeal . . . and, lastly, in the final appeal . . . There can be no doubt upon the affidavit of Mr Fretwell himself that he and the chairman were parties to the original decision to revoke the licence. It seems to me an inescapable inference from the way in which Mr Fretwell has described what was then done. There can be no doubt that the two of them were both members of the first appeal committee. There can be no doubt that one of them, namely, the chairman, was a party to the final appeal, and it is clear from the evidence that, whether or not he participated in the decision, Mr Fretwell, the market manager, was present with the committee throughout the discussion, hearing, and determination of the final appeal.

. . . the evidence of Mr Fretwell indicates plainly his presence throughout, his participation in the first appeal, and the participation of the chairman throughout.

. . . In the present case the corporation was considering something very like dismissing a man from his office, very like depriving him of his property, and they were charging him with doing something wrong. It was the revocation of a licence because of misconduct that they had under consideration – not merely the man's fitness or capacity for the grant of a licence. There was, therefore, a situation here in which (using the terms broadly) Mr Hook was on trial, and on trial for his livelihood. There was a complainant, the market manager. The market manager had a professional interest in the matter since he was concerned to protect his employees, or the employees for whom he was responsible, from abuse and misconduct by stallholders in the market. Mr Fretwell was a prosecutor, a complainant; Mr Hook was a man, albeit in an administrative field, who was on trial not for his life but for his livelihood.

If ever there was a case in which it was imperative that the complainant or the prosecutor should not participate in the adjudication, I should have thought it was this one; . . . most certainly the rule of *nemo debet esse judex in causa propria* should have been rigorously observed throughout the whole appellate process.'

1 [1976] 1 WLR 1052, CA.

2.25   In reality, there will be a number of occasions where local politicians, as members of the local authority, will have expressed opinions on certain subjects or even campaigned for or against matters that are now before them in the licensing committee. How does this affect their decision-making, or presence on the committee?

2.26   In the case of *R v Reading Borough Council, ex p Quietlynn Ltd*[1] this question arose. An application was made for a sex establishment licence, and the matter was considered by a three-member Sex Establishment Licensing Panel, itself a sub-committee of the Environment Committee. Two of those members belonged to a political group which had, some months previously, decided that it was not in favour of sex establishments. However, no whip or party ruling was applied to those members. In addition, one of those two members had, over a year before the meeting at which the applications were considered, written to the local press in his role as a local councillor, stating his personal opposition to sex establishments and his support for the view that they should be prohibited completely.

The question before the court was whether the presence of these councillors, for slightly different reasons, had rendered the panel biased or capable of bias, thereby conflicting with the *nemo judex in causa sua potest* rule. Kennedy J, after due consideration, said (at 399):

'. . . has this council acted in such a way that it is clear that when the panel came to consider these applications for licences it could not exercise proper discretion? That question would clearly be answered in the affirmative if, for example, the council appointed to the panel councillors from a group which had agreed that no member of the group would be a party to the grant of any licence, or appointed to the panel a councillor who had a financial interest in the grant or refusal of a licence but it should not, in my judgment, be answered in the affirmative simply because the council appointed to the panel a councillor who held and expressed views about whether or not in general licences ought to be granted . . . every councillor is to some extent a communicator, a man or a woman whose function it is to formulate and to express views on subjects of local interest such as the licensing of sex establishments. It would be astonishing if by doing his job as a communicator he were to disqualify himself from taking any part in deciding something which Parliament has left to local authorities to decide. Indeed, the astute applicant for a licence could easily improve his chances by getting any councillor he suspected to be unsympathetic to express his views in public.

. . . Of course, it would have been better if the council had refrained from appointing to this small panel a councillor who had been particularly vocal in relation to the issue with which the panel was to deal, but his mere presence as a member of the panel would not, in my judgment, have led any independent and informed observer to suspect that a fair decision was not possible.'

This approach was followed in two subsequent cases, both concerning sex establishments.

1 (1986) 85 LGR 387, QBD.

In *Darker Enterprises v Dacorum Borough Council*[1], the question raised was   **2.27**
whether a councillor, who had sat on a committee which previously had refused an application for a sex establishment at particular premises, could sit on a subsequent application for a licence at the same premises. It was held, following the *Reading* approach[2], that there was no evidence that the councillor could not exercise his discretion in the correct manner.

1 [1992] COD 465, DC.
2 *R v Reading Borough Council, ex p Quietlynn Ltd* (1986) 85 LGR 387, QBD.

In *R v Chesterfield Borough Council, ex p Darker Enterprises Ltd*[1], one of the   **2.28**
members of the sub-committee, which considered the application for a sex establishment licence, had taken part in a demonstration against the sex shop. Again, it was held that 'whatever the views of individual councillors may be, provided that they are prepared to listen to the argument, the requirements of the law are fulfilled'. In that case, a second ground of appeal was successful, as another sub-committee member was a director of the local Co-operative Society, which owned the premises next door to the sex shop, and he should not have taken part in the decision.

1 [1992] COD 466, DC.

It can be seen that, notwithstanding the rulings in the *Hannam* case[1], the   **2.29**
courts recognise the difficulties placed on local councillors in such cases. However, it is worth repeating the words of Kennedy J in the *Reading* case:

'Of course, it would have been better if the council had refrained from appointing to this small panel a councillor who had been particularly vocal in relation to the issue with which the panel was to deal.'

In such circumstances local authorities should do their utmost to create sub-committees or panels that have sufficient numbers of members so as to allow a member with such strong and well-documented views to exclude themselves from a decision, whilst at the same time allowing the sub-committee to remain quorate, so it can continue to discharge its functions.

1 *Hannam v Bradford City Council* [1970] 1 WLR 937, CA.

Procedure

The hearing

2.30 To enable the applicant to be given a fair hearing, it is necessary for him to know what the rules are by which his application will be considered; if the council has approved any policies or general conditions which apply, then these should be brought to the attention of the applicant before his application is made. They should be available, in full and in time, to enable the applicant to fully appreciate their implications and to formulate his arguments against them, if need be.

2.31 In relation to the hearing itself, it is important to recognise that, although it is quasi-judicial in nature, it is not judicial. It is not a criminal hearing, nor is it a civil hearing, and the admissibility or otherwise of evidence is a frequent question. Should the criminal or civil rules governing admissibility be relied upon?

2.32 The case of *Kavanagh v Chief Constable of Devon and Cornwall*[1] is useful in respect of this question. This concerned an appeal against a refusal by the Chief Constable to grant a shotgun certificate to the appellant and to register the appellant as a firearms dealer under the provisions of the Firearms Act 1968. Such licences and registrations could only be granted if the Chief Constable was 'satisfied' of certain matters. The Chief Constable considered hearsay material in discharging his duty. The question to be determined by the Court of Appeal was whether the Crown Court could consider hearsay evidence in determining a subsequent appeal against refusal to grant such registrations and certificates. Lord Denning stated (at 698G):

> '. . . I think [the Crown Court] should act on the same lines as any administrative body which is charged with an enquiry. They may receive any material which is logically probative even though it is not evidence in a court of law. Hearsay can be permitted where it can be fairly regarded as reliable. No doubt they must act fairly. They should give the party concerned an opportunity of correcting or contradicting what is put against him. But it does not mean that he has to be given a chance to cross examine. It is enough if they hear what he has to say . . . In an appeal under the Firearms Act 1968, it seems to me essential that the Crown Court should have before it all the material which was before the chief officer of police . . . If he refuses [the application] and the applicant appeals to the Crown Court, then the Crown Court must see whether or not the chief officer was right in refusing. For that purpose the Crown Court ought to know the material that was before him and what were the reasons which operated on his mind. It can also consider any other material which may be placed before it. In the end it must come to its own decision whether a firearm certificate should be granted or refused, or whether a person should be registered as a firearms dealer.'

1 [1974] 2 All ER 697.

2.33 In the case of *Westminster City Council v Zestfair*[1], the reasoning in *Kavanagh*[2] was followed. The *Zestfair* case concerned a refusal to grant a night café licence under the Greater London Council (General Powers) Act 1968. At the subsequent appeal to the magistrates' court, the stipendiary magistrate had ruled that hearsay evidence was not admissible and, as a consequence, granted a licence. The council appealed and the High Court granted the appeal.

Pill J stated (at 291):

'It is common ground that the court should rehear the application on the merits and not simply decide whether the council were wrong in law. At the hearing of the complainants' complaint before the magistrates' court oral evidence was given by four witnesses for the council and one witness for the complainants. The council then sought to put in evidence all of the matters that had been placed before the licensing sub-committee.

The practical question, as appears from counsel's submissions, was whether an officer or officers of the council could give evidence to the court of complaints made to them as to nuisance alleged to have been caused by reason of the conduct of the premises. It is common ground that the licensing sub-committee, provided they act fairly, are entitled to have regard to material which would not ordinarily be admissible in a civil proceeding in a court of law.'

He went on to conclude (at 294):

'The two tribunals should approach the issue in section 49(2) [of the Greater London Council (General Powers) Act 1968] on the same evidential basis and the parties should have the opportunity to call evidence on the same basis.'

Accordingly, it is quite clear that hearsay evidence can be admitted, but caution must be exercised with regard to the weight that is attached to any such evidence.

1 (1990) 88 LGR 288, DC.
2 *Kavanagh v Chief Constable of Devon and Cornwall* [1974] 2 All ER 697.

This view has been supported in the case of *McCool v Rushcliffe Borough Council*[1]. In this case, a private hire driver was prosecuted for committing an indecent assault on a passenger. At the first trial, the jury failed to reach a verdict. At the retrial, the complainant did not appear because she could not face the trauma of giving evidence again. As a result Mr McCool was acquitted. Rushcliffe Borough Council refused to renew his licence, as they did not feel he was a fit and proper person. That decision was upheld by the magistrates' court on appeal. Mr McCool appealed by way of case stated. On the question of the admissibility of hearsay evidence, Bingham LCJ said (at 893F):

2.34

'It is common ground that in reaching their decision the justices were entitled to rely on hearsay evidence. That is in my judgment clear from section 51(1)(*a*) of the Act [of 1976] and also from *Kavanagh v Chief Constable of Devon and Cornwall*, . . . It is also in my judgment plain from the judgment of Pill J in *Westminster City Council v Zestfair*. I conclude that, in reaching their respective decisions, the Borough Council and the justices were entitled to rely on evidential material which might reasonably and possible influence the making of a responsible judgment in good faith on the question in issue. Some evidence such as gossip, speculation and unsubstantiated innuendo would rightly be disregarded. Other evidence, even if hearsay, might by its source, nature and inherent probability carry a greater degree of credibility. All would depend on the particular facts and circumstances.'

1 [1998] 3 All ER 889, QBD.

2.35 When considering an application most local authorities have standard procedures which they follow, covering such matters as: is there to be an oral hearing? if so, can the applicant be accompanied and by whom? can the applicant bring witnesses? can witnesses be cross-examined? can the applicant ask questions of officers or other witnesses? are there any time limits placed on the presentation that an applicant, objector or witnesses can make? and so on.

2.36 Assuming that this is a decision being made by a committee or sub-committee, there will be a considerable number of people in the room, who will be not only the members of the committee, but also officers who are there to advise the committee. It must be made clear to all concerned and then made demonstrably clear by their actions that the officers do not take part in the decision-making, they merely advise the members as to their powers. This should be emphasised by the fact that officers withdraw for the decision. The only exception to this could be the lawyer advising the committee, who can remain, not to influence the committee or take any part in the decision, but merely to advise them on points of law and procedure that may arise.

In some authorities, the procedure is for all officers to withdraw and the committee calls the legal adviser back, if they need legal advice. In others, the lawyer remains, but then withdraws after any such points have been raised.

In all cases, the decision must be made solely by members, unless the power is delegated to an officer. In this case, the officer must place himself in the same position as the members.

2.37 Another important matter to consider is whether such hearings are in public or in private. If the matter is being decided by an officer, then there is no problem, because that can quite properly and legitimately be decided in private, but if the matter takes the form of a committee meeting, then the provisions of Part VA of the Local Government Act 1972 applies with regard to access to both information and the meeting.

2.38 Section 100A of the Local Government Act 1972 states that 'a meeting of a principal council shall be open to the public except to the extent that they are excluded . . .'. The grounds for exclusion are either that confidential information would be disclosed (section 100A(2)) or that exempt information would be disclosed (section 100A(4)). Exempt information is information which falls into one of the categories contained in Schedule 12A of the Local Government Act 1972.

2.39 A number of authorities exclude the public and the press from matters concerning applications for various licences (including hackney carriage and private hire licences) through section 100A(4) and Schedule 12A, paragraph 7, which allows exclusion on the grounds that 'information relating to the financial or business affairs of any particular person (other than the authority)' would be revealed. However, some authorities do conduct the entire proceedings in public.

If these proceedings involve a consideration of, or, discussion about, the business of the applicant, then it would appear to be correct that they should be conducted in private session (part B or part 2 of the agenda, depending on the terminology used by the council in question). However, if it is resolved to exclude the press and public because criminal convictions recorded against an individual may be revealed, this is harder to justify, as there is no category of exempt information which covers such matters. It seems that this alone cannot be used as a ground for conducting the meeting in private and there must be information which legitimately falls into paragraph 7 to enable this to happen.

Two alternative approaches involve the use of paragraph 4 or paragraph 12 of Schedule 12A. **2.40**

Paragraph 4 approach Paragraph 4 allows the exclusion of the press and public **2.41** because the committee will be considering 'information relating to any particular applicant for, or recipient or former recipient of, any service provided by the authority'. This requires an acceptance that the granting of a licence to an applicant equates to the receipt of a service.

Paragraph 12 approach Paragraph 12 allows exclusion of the press and public **2.42** in relation to:

> '. . . any advice received, information obtained or action to be taken in connection with:
>
> (a) any legal proceedings by or against the authority, or
> (b) the determination of any matter, affecting the authority,
>
> (whether in either case, proceedings have been commenced or are in contemplation).'

This requires the acceptance that, in relation to any licence application, legal proceedings are being contemplated. This may be true, but only if the licence is refused, and, at the time the decision to exclude is made, that will not be clear.

It seems that local authorities are rarely, if ever, challenged on the matter of **2.43** conducting hackney carriage and private hire licensing matters in private, but it is an area where the authority should be satisfied as to its powers to exclude the press and public. It must not merely take it for granted that such considerations will automatically be heard in private.

It is not clear, however, what sanction, if any, can be applied to the local authority if it can be shown that they exceeded their powers by excluding the press and public wrongly.

The committee meeting

Turning to the procedure that is adopted at the committee meeting, again, **2.44** this is a matter for each local authority to decide upon. However, some basic points are important and must be considered.

Firstly, the procedure should be agreed in advance and it makes sense to have one standard procedure, which is always used. This has the advantage of allowing the applicant and the applicant's representative to be given it in advance, so that they know what to expect. There is also certainty for officers and members of the authority, as they will always be following the same procedure. Finally, it should have been approved by the local authority lawyers to ensure that it is an acceptable procedure.

2.45   The applicant should be called and asked to confirm his name and address. It may be helpful to identify the members of the committee (although it is not necessary to do so by name, this is merely to differentiate them from officers) and the officers who are advising the committee. If the applicant has a representative, they should also introduce themselves.

2.46   The matter under consideration should be outlined. In some authorities, this is done by the Chair of the Committee. In others, either the clerk to the committee, the lawyer advising the committee or the licensing officer outline the matter in question.

2.47   *'Fit and proper person'* If the hearing concerns the granting of a licence to a driver (either hackney carriage or private hire) or a private hire operator, the grounds for objecting to the application should be made clear. This is likely to concern previous convictions, which may prevent the applicant being considered a 'fit and proper person'[1].

It will not be necessary to read out the previous convictions (if this is an open meeting that approach should be treated with caution), as it is sufficient to have them printed and distributed. The applicant should be asked whether he agrees with the list of previous convictions and, if the answer is in the negative, the matter should be adjourned to clarify the position. Assuming, however, that the applicant does agree that the list is accurate, the spokesperson for the council should explain why these convictions would lead to the refusal of the application, referring to any policy guidelines that the council may have adopted. The applicant should then be given a chance to explain the circumstances surrounding the convictions in question and any other relevant information. Following this, officers and councillors may ask questions to clarify the situation and establish to their satisfaction whether or not this person is a fit and proper person to be granted a licence. Thereafter, the applicant should be asked whether or not there is anything else they wish to add and then all interested parties should withdraw (applicant and applicant's representative, officers of the local authority and, if they are present, any members of the public).

1 See Chapter 5 in relation to 'spent' convictions.

The decision

2.48   The members will then make their decision. It should be noted that only members who have heard the entire application are able to consider the decision. This prevents a member taking part if they arrived late for the item in question or left for part of the matter, returning before the decision was made.

2.49   Most authorities invite the applicant back in to the meeting to verbally inform them whether or not they have been successful, but some will only impart that information later in writing. Even if the decision is given verbally, it must be confirmed in writing as soon as possible.

2.50   Whilst the usual and most common method of challenge to a decision of the licensing committee is by way of one of the statutory appeals which lie to the magistrates' court (or, in one particular circumstance, direct to the Crown Court), there is also the wider application of judicial control of the decision-making process itself. This is by means of the judicial review procedure which allows the High Court to consider the approach to the decision which the local authority has made.

Reasonableness

Assuming that the decision-making body had the power to make the decision, that is to say, the delegated powers were in place and standing orders were followed, a judicial review will concern itself with the reasonableness, or otherwise, of the decision that was reached and also whether the rules of natural justice were followed. In relation to local government decision-making (and indeed other public body decision-making), the test of reasonableness is not the 'Clapham omnibus' test, but the rather more refined test originating in the case of *Associated Provincial Picture Houses Ltd v Wednesbury Corpn*[1]. Lord Green MR laid down the following principles (at 228–230):

2.51

> 'When discretion . . . is granted the law recognises certain principles upon which that discretion must be exercised . . . What then are those principles?
>
> . . . The exercise of such a discretion must be a real exercise of the discretion. If, in the statute conferring the discretion, there is to be found expressly or by implication matters which the authority exercising the discretion ought to have regard to, then in exercising the discretion it must have regard to those matters. Conversely, if the nature of the subject-matter and the general interpretation of the Act make it clear that certain matters would not be germane to the matter in question, the authority must disregard those irrelevant collateral matters . . .
>
> It is true the discretion must be exercised reasonably. Now what does that mean? Lawyers familiar with the phraseology commonly used in relation to exercise of statutory discretions often use the word "unreasonable" in a rather comprehensive sense. It has frequently been used and is frequently used as a general description of the things that must not be done. For instance, a person entrusted with a discretion must, so to speak, direct himself properly in law. He must call his own attention to the matters which he is bound to consider. He must exclude from his consideration matters which are irrelevant to what he has to consider. If he does not obey those rules, he may truly be said, and often is said, to be acting "unreasonably". Similarly, there may be something so absurd that no sensible person could ever dream that it lay within the powers of the authority . . .
>
> . . . It is true to say that, if a decision on a competent matter is so unreasonable that no reasonable authority could ever have come to it, then the courts can interfere. That, I think, is quite right; but to prove a case of that kind would require something overwhelming . . .'

1 [1948] 1 KB 223.

This test has itself been re-addressed frequently in the last 50 years. In *Council of Civil Service Unions v Minister for the Civil Service*[1], Lord Diplock used the expression 'irrationality'. He said:

2.52

> 'By "irrationality" I mean what can by now be succinctly referred to as "*Wednesbury* unreasonableness". It applies to a decision which is so outrageous in its defiance of logic or of accepted moral standards that no sensible person who applied his mind to the question to be decided could have arrived at it.'

This term is now widely accepted as being interchangeable with '*Wednesbury* unreasonableness'. It is imperative that a decision is not unreasonable in '*Wednesbury*' terms if it is to remain unchallenged.

1 [1985] AC 374.

2.53 The courts have made it quite clear that the judicial review process is available when it is the reasonableness of the decision-making process, or a question over the exercise of powers or duties or application of the law, which is open to challenge, rather than the decision itself. If the decision leads to a statutory ground of appeal, then those should be exhausted before any judicial review is considered, unless exceptional circumstances exist.

Reasons

2.54 There is some debate over whether reasons should be given for the decision and then, if reasons are given, how detailed they should be.

There is no statutory requirement to give reasons for any decision in relation to any matter connected with hackney carriage or private hire licensing. This can be contrasted with sex establishment licensing, where the applicant can request a written statement of the reasons for refusal to renew a sex establishment licence.

A number of cases also make it clear that there is no general common law right to be informed of the reasons for refusal, either. However, there have been occasions where the courts have decided that reasons should be given in relation to planning decisions (eg *Sir George Grenfell-Baines v Secretary of State for the Environment*[1]), and other occasions where the courts have decided that there is no requirement to give reasons at all (eg *R v Secretary of State for Social Services, ex p Connolly*[2]).

1 [1985] JPL 256, DC.
2 [1986] 1 All ER 998, CA.

2.55 There are, however, a number of cases which follow the line that, in the interests of fairness, reasons should be given for a decision, even if there is no statutory requirement to do so.

In *R v Civil Service Appeal Board, ex p Cunningham*[1], a prison officer sought judicial review of the decision of the Civil Service Appeal Board. The Board refused to give reasons for various aspects of its decision. The Court of Appeal decided that the Board should have given reasons because it was a quasi-judicial body. Procedural fairness required sufficient reasons to be given to enable the parties to be satisfied that the correct issues had been addressed and that it had acted lawfully.

1 [1991] IRLR 297, CA.

2.56 This approach was endorsed by the House of Lords in *R v Secretary of State for the Home Department, ex p Doody*[1]. It was held that prisoners serving mandatory life sentences for murder were entitled to be given reasons by the Secretary of State if he departed from the minimum period recommended by the judge, before a review of their case for release on licence would be given. Lord Mustill specifically approved the decision in *Ex p Cunningham*, and went on to say (at 564H):

'. . . the Secretary of State ought to implement the scheme as fairly as he can. The giving of reasons may be inconvenient, but I can see no ground at all why it should be against the public interest; indeed, rather the reverse. This being so, I would ask simply: Is refusal to give reasons fair? I would answer without hesitation that it is not.'

1 [1994] 1 AC 531, HL.

The Privy Council recently considered the need to give reasons in *Stefan v* **2.57**
General Medical Council[1]. They took the view that, although there was still no common law duty to give reasons:

'The trend of the law had been towards an increased recognition of the duty upon decision-makers of many kinds to give reasons. That trend was consistent with current developments towards an increased openness in matters of government and administration.'

But the trend was proceeding on a case-by-case basis and had not lost sight of the established position of the common law that there was no general duty, universally imposed on all decision-makers.

There was certainly a strong argument for the view that, what were once seen as exceptions to a rule, may now become examples of the norm and the cases, where reasons were not required, might be taking on the appearance of exceptions.

1 (1999) 143 Sol Jo LB 112, PC.

A recent case has considered the position in relation to private hire licences. **2.58**
In *R v Burton-upon-Trent Justices, ex p Hussain*[1] judicial review was sought of the failure by the magistrates to give reasons for their decision, on an appeal against a refusal to grant a private hire driver's licence and operator's licence by the local authority.

In relation to drivers' licences, the provisions of section 61(1) and (2) of the Local Government (Miscellaneous Provisions) Act 1976 apply and in relation to the private hire operator's licence section 62(1) and (2) (of the 1976 Act) apply. In both those sections sub-section 2 states:

'Where a district council suspend, revoke or refuse to renew any licence under this section they shall give to the driver (61(2)(*a*) [or] operator 62(2)) notice of the grounds of which the licence has been suspended or revoked or on which they have refused to renew such licence . . .'

Those grounds are in each case contained in sub-section 1 of the relevant section.

1 (1996) 9 Admin LR 233.

In the *Burton-upon-Trent* case[1], it was argued that it was insufficient to **2.59**
simply state that the reason for the refusal to renew the licence in question was one of the grounds contained in either section 61(1)(*a*) or (*b*) or section 62(1)(*a*)–(*d*).

Potts J stated (at 236H):

'Mr Storey [for the applicant] submits that the expression "notice of the grounds" has the effect of requiring the licensing authority to give reasons for reaching its decision.'

He went on (at 237A):

'The licensing authority in the present case . . . simply informs the applicant that his driver's licence was revoked under s 62(1)(b) and his operator's licence revoked under s 62(1)(a), (b), (c) and (d), but failed to specify what the applicant had done or failed to do in order to justify revocation.

In my judgment, there is force in this submission. The decision letter did not sufficiently inform the applicant of the ground or grounds on which the licensing authority had concluded that revocation was appropriate.

This failure could not be decisive of this application since the decision under review is that of the justices. But, as I have sought to indicate, the justices made no findings of fact and gave no reasons for their decision. In my judgment, they ought to have done both. Had they made findings of fact, the court may well not have been faced with the problem identified above in relation to the first ground of application, namely, conflicting accounts on affidavit as to what occurred in court.

Furthermore, the applicant would have been informed of the basis upon which the court reached its decision. In my judgment, the applicant was entitled to be so informed.

In any event, I am satisfied that the justices ought to have had in mind the provisions of ss 61 and 62 of the 1976 Act, as they were concerned (as Mr Hibbert pointed out in his affidavit) with a rehearing of the original panel meeting.

Therefore the justices ought to have related their findings of fact to the provisions of s 62(1)(b) (reasonable cause) and of s 62(1) and identified the reasons and ground in respect of which revocation of the applicant's licence was thought appropriate. For example, under s 61(1)(b), the applicant was entitled to know what the "reasonable cause" was. The failure to make findings of fact and to give reasons relating to s 61(1)(b) and s 62(1) of the Act, in my judgment, amounted to a denial of natural justice[2].'

1 *R v Burton-upon-Trent Justices, ex p Hussain* (1996) 9 Admin LR 233.
2 See *R v Harrow Crown Court, ex p Dave* [1994] 1 WLR 98, 158 JP 250.

2.60 This case is interesting in that the legislation requires notice of the grounds for the refusal (or revocation or suspension) to be given and specifically states what grounds are available for such action to be taken. It would appear that the court, in this case, has extended the requirement from simply stating which ground has been relied upon to actually requiring the magistrates' court and, by logical extension, the local authority to give reasons for such action over and above the statutory requirement.

2.61 The argument in favour of giving detailed reasons is that, the more the applicant knows as to why they were unsuccessful, the less likely they are to indulge in an appeal which would be both fruitless for them and a waste of time and effort for the council. The counter-argument is that, the more detailed reasons that are given, the greater opportunity there is for the applicant to find one which they believe is spurious, which they can then use as the basis of their appeal.

The arguments for giving no reasons or extremely sketchy reasons are really the converse of the above, that is to say, if there are very few reasons the applicant will not know what to appeal against, but, equally, this may act as a springboard for a great many appeals which have, in themselves, very little merit.

The case law on this point is not mandatory. Lord Mustill, in his judgment in *Ex p Doody* stated 'I accept without hesitation, and mention it only to avoid misunderstanding, that the law does not at present recognise a general duty to give reasons for an administrative decision.' **2.62**

However, it is suggested that, in relation to hackney carriage and private hire licensing in light of the decision in *R v Burton on Trent Justices, ex p Hussain*, it is better to give reasons than not to. The advantages appear to outweigh the disadvantages and it should help unsuccessful applicants either to re-apply, in the light of the reasons that led to initial failure or to accept defeat and not waste time and money on appeals that are unlikely to succeed. **2.63**

This in turn leads to the difficulty that some authorities face, namely their members are less than keen to actually formulate the reasons for refusing to grant the licence. It is essential that the reasons cited are the actual reasons which led to the refusal and not some spurious afterthought designed to justify an, otherwise, insupportable decision. Likewise, the reasons must be the reasons that the committee (or other decision-making body) actually formulate, rather than reasons created by officers to support the decision. **2.64**

Making decisions on a licensing sub-committee or committee is an onerous duty; the livelihoods of the applicants are at stake and this has to be balanced by risk to the safety of both the travelling public and the public at large. Members of such committees should not approach the task lightly (very few do) and they must appreciate the gravity of the situation in which they find themselves acting as a quasi-judicial body. **2.65**

The local authority can set policies, but must be careful not to fetter its discretion. It is important that the policies are both worded initially and then subsequently approached in such a way as to enable deviation from them to be undertaken in appropriate circumstances, when justice demands.

It is this application of discretion which is a fundamental part of the local authority licensing process; it allows for a human element in what would, otherwise, simply be a box-ticking, rubber-stamping exercise. However, like all things, it must be exercised judiciously and should not be used simply as a method of ignoring or avoiding policies which have previously been approved.

It will be appreciated that the licensing committees' deliberations are important from a number of perspectives. Whilst it is impossible to guarantee that any decision will be completely watertight legally, it is important from the local authority's point of view that the correct considerations are applied to any decision – appeals and judicial reviews are costly and should be avoided, if at all possible. **2.66**

From the applicant's perspective, it is equally important that the hearing is conducted correctly and fairly, and the decision is communicated in such a way as to explain to the applicant where there are grounds for improvement in their approach or why they will find it extremely difficult to obtain a licence from that authority for the foreseeable future.

Having said that, it is equally important that those involved in this decision-making are not over-awed by such considerations and are prepared to undertake the function that is imposed upon them.

Consequences of mistakes made by the local authority

2.67   If the local authority make a mistake, their decision is capable of challenge, either by judicial review or appeal[1]. If the challenge is upheld, the effects of the decision will be reversed in some way. However, one important question in relation to the local authority's decision-making process is if there is any right to compensation should the council make some mistake, either in the interpretation of the law or in their procedures.

1 See Chapter 3.

2.68   This was the question that was considered in the case of *R v Knowsley Metropolitan Borough Council, ex p Maguire*[1]. The claim arose out of an application for hackney carriage proprietors' licences, after the passing of section 16 of the Transport Act 1985 (which removed the absolute discretion that the local authority had to limit the number of hackney carriage proprietors' licences that it would grant)[2]. A procedure was adopted by Knowsley Metropolitan Borough Council whereby licences would be granted to all who applied and met specified criteria, until such time as the results of surveys to assess demand were known. Letters were sent to applicants explaining this and detailing the criteria. One element of the criteria was that a suitable vehicle (in this case, a purpose-built hackney carriage – FX4) should be presented.

Following the ruling in *R v Reading Borough Council, ex p Egan*[3] Knowsley Metropolitan Borough Council revised its decision, as it appeared that their policy was unlawful. As a consequence, the local authority refused to grant the applicants their licences, notwithstanding the fact that they had purchased vehicles. Although that decision was quashed and the applicants received the licences they had applied for, they maintained that they had suffered damage as a result of the local authority's illegal action. They claimed compensation under a number of heads: first, that the local authority was in breach of its statutory duty, secondly, that the local authority had been negligent; thirdly, that the local authority was in breach of contract; and, finally on the grounds that the local authority should be estopped (that is to say prevented) from effectively changing its mind.

Schiemann J dismissed the claim under each head.

1 (1992) 90 LGR 653.
2 See Appendix I.
3 (1987) [1990] RTR 399n. See Chapter 8, para 8.111.

2.69   In relation to breach of statutory duty, he stated (at 660):

> 'In the present case, there is no indication at all in the legislative provisions that they were passed for the benefit of would-be cab drivers rather than the public at large. A refusal of a licence gives rise to a right of appeal to the crown court. The imposition of a condition alleged to be unlawful gives rise to a right of appeal to the magistrates' court. I am not persuaded that Parliament intended anyone to have a private right of action in respect of any failure by a licensing authority to exercise its powers lawfully. In consequence the claim fails under this head.'

In relation to negligence he stated (at 661):

> 'I am entitled to form my own view as to whether or no[t] what the local authority did amounted to negligence and I do not think it did.

"As is well-known, anybody, even a judge, can be capable of miscon-
struing a statute; and such misconstruction, when it occurs, can be
severely criticised without attracting the epithet 'negligent'. Obviously,
this simple fact points rather to the extreme unlikelihood of a breach of
duty being established in these cases[1]."

Mr Braithwaite [for the council] submits that the local authority found
themselves overwhelmed with applications at a time when they had not
done a demand survey, that the local authority were in principle entitled
to balance supply and demand for cabs and were not negligent during the
interim period in which they were establishing the demand position in
adopting a policy of excluding those who had had the benefit of one
licensed cab and had chosen to sell it. I think there is force in this submission and that he is entitled to make it, notwithstanding the judgment
of Otton J.

Since I do not find the local authority negligent I do not need to consider
the difficult question of law of whether the local authority were under a
duty of care owed to the applicants not to be negligent in their construction of the statute. As appears from *Takaro (supra)*, the answer is not
self-evident.'

1 See *Rowling v Takaro Properties Ltd* [1988] AC 473 at 502.

On the argument that the local authority were in breach of contract **2.70**
Schiemann J found that they were not and that the correspondence that had
been entered into did not amount to a contract. He stated (at 663):

'He [Mr Braithwaite] submits that we are not here in the field of contract
at all but rather in the field of local government administration. Local
authorities are always adumbrating policy documents but those are not to
be construed as offers to the world at large and that the same applies to
letters setting out policy.

In my judgment this submission is well founded. There is no reason to
suppose that neither the local authority nor the applicants ever thought in
terms of contract. That is not conclusive and I accept that there are cases
where courts will after considering the relevant documentation and actions
find that the parties have entered into a contract notwithstanding the fact
that they may never have applied their minds consciously to doing so. A
good example is *Carlill v Carbolic Smoke Ball Co*. But it will be remembered that in that case the defendants offered their reward in order to
persuade people to buy their product.

"If the vendor of an article . . . with a view to increase its sale or use,
thinks fit publicly to promise to all who buy or use it that, to those who
shall not find it as surely efficacious as it is represented by him to be he
will pay a substantial sum of money, he must not be surprised if occasionally he is held to his promise[1]."

In the present case to construe the letter of 18 May as a contractual offer
seems to me to be to lose touch with reality and to insert the law of contract into an inapposite situation.'

1 *Carlill v Carbolic Smoke Ball Co* [1892] 2 QB 484 at 489 per Hawkins.

The last claim was that of estoppel which was dealt with in the following way **2.71**
(at 664):

'Finally, Mr Davies [for the applicants] sought to mount a submission on the basis of estoppel of convention. In substance this was a submission that, although in truth the local authority were not contractually liable to the applicants, the local authority had acted as though there was such a contract and the local authority are now estopped from contending the contrary. It is true that the local authority – rightly in my view – perceived those who had acted on the indication given in the letter of 18 May as having a strong claim to a licence, but there is no indication before me that the local authority ever represented that they ever thought of such a claim as a *contractual* claim as opposed to a claim based on a desire to administer well and fairly.'

2.72 Although the court found against the claimants on all heads, the decision is extremely important as an indication of the way in which the law may develop[1]. The conclusion drawn by the judge was (at 664):

'It follows that the applicants' claims fail. They fail because we do not have in our law a general right to damages for maladministration.'

and at 665:

'The arguments ingeniously advanced by Mr Davies are an attempt to remedy what from the point of view of his clients are shortcomings of our administrative law by extending the concepts of negligence, contract and estoppel. While I have considerable sympathy with his clients I do not think that I am at liberty to extend the law in the way he suggests. The applications fail.'

1 Reference was made to the findings of two investigations, the Law Commission in 1969 and the Committee of the Justice – All Souls Review of the Administrative Law of the United Kingdom – *Administrative Justice; some necessary reforms.*

2.73 It remains to be seen whether the *Knowsley* case[1] marks the beginning of new developments in this field, which will ultimately lead to the right to damages for those affected by administrative decisions, or whether matters will remain as they are. Either way, it will be an interesting area and one which will undoubtedly lead to more litigation before the questions are finally settled. In the meantime, it appears that local authorities are reasonably well protected from the financial consequences of any mistakes that they may make in statutory interpretation or application of the general law.

1 *R v Knowsley Metropolitan Borough Council, ex p Maguire* (1992) 90 LGR 653.

Human Rights Act 1998

2.74 At some point during the year 2000, the Human Rights Act 1998 will come into force. This will have a fundamental impact on the way in which local authorities have to approach their decision-making in a number of areas[1].

1 For a full consideration of the impact of the Human Rights Act, please see Lester and Pannick: *Human Rights – Law and Practice* 1999.

2.75 In relation to hackney carriage and private hire licensing, it seems that the most direct impact will be as a result of the right contained in Article 6, paragraph 1 of Part I to Schedule 1 of the Act. This states:

'In the determination of his civil rights and obligations or of any criminal charge against him, everyone is entitled to a fair and public hearing within a reasonable time by an independent and impartial tribunal established by law. Judgment shall be pronounced publicly but the press and public may be excluded from all or part of the trial in the interest of morals, public order or national security in a democratic society, where the interests of juveniles or the protection of the private life of the parties so require, or to the extent strictly necessary in the opinion of the court in special circumstances where publicity would prejudice the interests of justice.'

Although it seems unlikely that a local authority sub-committee (or even a officer) making a decision on the question as to whether or not to grant a licence fulfils the requirement for a hearing before 'an independent and impartial tribunal', the fact that there is, in relation to every licence relating to hackney carriage and private hire matters, a statutory right of appeal to an independent tribunal (either a magistrates' court or Crown Court), should prevent a successful challenge being launched against the procedure which is currently in place. **2.76**

That is not to say, however, that local authorities should not be fully aware of the Human Rights Act 1998 and its potential impact upon their decision-making, and they should take steps to ensure that, so far as possible, their procedures are not incompatible with the rights that the Act grants.

This will undoubtedly be an area of law which will develop at a rapid pace over the next few years. At the moment, it is difficult to see what, if any, impact it will ultimately have upon hackney carriage and private hire licensing, but there is little doubt that Human Rights Act arguments will be used in these areas. **2.77**

One case in particular concerning European taxi licensing should be noted, *Sigurour A Sigurjonsson v Iceland*[1]. One of the requirements of the Icelandic taxi legislation was that a driver's licence could only be granted to a person who was a member of a specified trade union. In this case, when the applicant failed to pay his membership subscriptions to that union, his taxi driver's licence was revoked. He successfully challenged this on the grounds that it was unlawful under the European Convention of Human Rights (which the Human Rights Act 1998 incorporated into English law) because it contravened his right to freedom of association, as enshrined in Article 11. **2.78**

As a result of this case, it can be seen that any condition which requires an applicant for a licence to be a member of a specified body would be unlawful after the introduction of the Human Rights Act 1998. It seems unlikely that any local authority uses such a condition, but clearly any such condition would need to be removed, if it did exist.

1   (1993) 16 EHRR 462.

Chapter 3
Appeals

Decisions made by local authorities are open to challenge. That can be by way of a statutory right of appeal or by judicial review.

3.1

STATUTORY RIGHTS OF APPEAL

There are two different approaches to statutory appeals, depending upon whether the Local Government (Miscellaneous Provisions) Act 1976 (hereinafter 'the 1976 Act') has been adopted or not.

3.2

Districts where the Local Government (Miscellaneous Provisions) Act 1976 has been adopted

If the 1976 Act has been adopted, then, in relation to four of the five licences which are covered by hackney carriage and private hire licensing:

3.3

- hackney carriage drivers' licences;
- private hire operators' licences;
- private hire drivers; and
- private hire vehicle licences;

there are statutory rights of appeal to the magistrates' court. These are available, both against a refusal to grant or renew a licence and a decision to suspend or revoke a licence that is in existence, as well as a right to appeal against any conditions which may have been imposed on any such licence by the local authority.

The exception is that of an appeal against a refusal to grant a hackney carriage proprietor's licence, which lies directly to the Crown Court. However, an appeal against a failure to renew, or to suspend or revoke, a hackney carriage proprietor's licence is to the magistrates' court.

3.4

The following rights of appeal are to be found in the 1976 Act:

3.5

- Appeal against conditions imposed on a hackney carriage proprietor's licence: section 47.

- Appeal against refusal to grant a private hire vehicle licence, or conditions imposed on such a licence: section 48.
- Appeal against refusal to grant a private hire driver's licence, or conditions imposed on such a licence: section 52.
- Appeal against refusal to grant a private hire operators' licence, or conditions imposed on such a licence: section 55.
- Appeal against refusal to grant a hackney carriage driver's licence: section 59.
- Appeal against suspension, revocation or refusal to renew a hackney carriage or private hire vehicle licence: section 60.
- Appeal against suspension, revocation or refusal to renew a hackney carriage or private hire driver's licence: section 61.
- Appeal against suspension, revocation or refusal to renew a private hire operators' licence: section 62.

3.6 Section 77 of the 1976 Act states:

> **'Appeals**
>
> 77–(1) Sections 300 to 302 of the Act of 1936, which relate to appeals, shall have effect as if this Part of this Act were part of that Act.
>
> (2) If any requirement, refusal or other decision of a district council against which a right of appeal is conferred by this Act:
>
> (a) involves the execution of any work or the taking of any action; or
> (b) makes it unlawful for any person to carry on a business which he was lawfully carrying on up to the time of the requirement, refusal or decision;
>
> then, until the time for appealing has expired, or, when an appeal is lodged, until the appeal is disposed of or withdrawn or fails for want of prosecution:
>
> (i) no proceedings shall be taken in respect of any failure to execute the work, or take the action; and
> (ii) that person may carry on that business.'

The reference to 'the Act of 1936' is to the Public Health Act 1936. The provisions of sections 300–302 of the 1936 Act are a well-known, workable method of seeking an appeal against a decision of a local authority. They can be found in Appendix I. By virtue of section 301 of the Public Health Act 1936, there is then a further appeal, as of right, to the Crown Court from the decision of the magistrates' court.

3.7 The effect of section 77(2) of the 1976 Act is to stay any action pending the determination of an appeal. In practice, this means that, if the appeal is against a refusal to renew a licence or a decision to suspend or revoke a licence, the licence is deemed to remain in force, pending the determination of the appeal. However, if it is an application for a new licence, then, as there is no licence already in force, the mechanism does not work and the licence will not be deemed to come into existence until the court overturns the decision of the local authority or, if it is an appeal to the Crown Court from the decision at the magistrates' court, the decision of the magistrates.

3.8 Where the 1976 Act has been adopted, the only licence which carries a right of appeal directly to the Crown Court on refusal is a hackney carriage proprietor's (vehicle) licence. The reasons for this are as follows:

Originally, the Town Police Clauses Act 1847 had to be incorporated by a special (local) Act. Then section 171(4) of the Public Health Act 1875 incorporated all the 1847 Act powers in relation to hackney carriages for urban districts. The Local Government Act 1972 did not extend those powers to all areas of England and Wales (Schedule 14, paragraph 24(b)), but this was done by the Transport Act 1985, section 15, which extended the provisions of the Town Police Clauses Acts 1847 and 1889 (both deemed to be incorporated in the Public Health Act 1875) to all areas of England and Wales.

For some inexplicable reason, the 1976 Act did not grant a specific right of appeal to the magistrates' court against a refusal to grant a hackney carriage proprietor's licence. Accordingly, the appeal lies under the pre-1976 regime. It is covered by section 7 of the Public Health Acts Amendment Act 1907, which, by virtue of section 2(1), is construed as one with the Public Health Act 1875. Section 7 states: **3.9**

'Appeals to Crown Court, etc

7–(1) Except where this Act otherwise expressly provides any person aggrieved:

(*a*) By any order, judgment, determination, or requirement of a local authority under this Act;

(*b*) By the withholding of any order, certificate, licence, consent or approval, which may be made, granted, or given by a local authority under this Act;

(*c*) By any conviction or order of a court of summary jurisdiction under any provision of this Act;

may appeal to the Crown Court.'

Districts where the 1976 Act has not been adopted

In districts where the 1976 Act has not been adopted, there is no private hire licensing, so any considerations will concern hackney carriages. **3.10**

The appeal against a refusal to grant or renew a hackney carriage proprietor's licence lies to the Crown Court as outlined in para 3.9 above. Similarly, a refusal to grant a hackney carriage driver's licence would carry the same right of appeal, as would a decision to revoke either such licence under the powers contained in section 50 of the 1847 Act. **3.11**

All appeals

Such hearings are neither criminal nor civil. They are a repeat of the exercise that was conducted in front of the local authority and, as such, the court exercises the same quasi-judicial functions as the local authority. **3.12**

It is quite clear that such hearings are hearings de novo (which is to say, that they are a completely fresh hearing). The court places itself in the position of the body whose decision is being appealed against, whether that is the local authority or the magistrates' court. The appeal court has to substitute **3.13** its decision for the decision of the local authority and must satisfy itself on the same principles as the local authority must have satisfied itself to start with.

The case of *Stepney Borough Council v Joffe*[1] supports this proposition and the reasoning was followed by the Court of Appeal in *Sagnata Investments Ltd v Norwich Corpn*[2].

What then is the practical effect of this? The appeal is a completely fresh hearing and, as a result, if there are any new developments or if any new information is obtained between the date of the local authority hearing decision and the date of the appeal being determined, that can be adduced before the appeal court. This, of course, works both ways and is open for the appellant and the respondent to produce any new material which may be relevant to their appeal.

However, the local authority have come to a position and they have been given the power to adjudicate on such applications and other matters. What then is the impact of their decision on a subsequent appeal? Is the court hearing the appeal entitled to disregard the decision being appealed, or must it take it into account? If it is to be taken into account, how much weight must it be given?

1 [1949] 1 KB 599, DC.
2 [1971] 2 QB 614.

3.14   In the *Stepney* case[1], this matter was considered. The case concerned a decision by the council to revoke street trading licences which had been granted to three traders, under the provisions of the London County Council (General Powers) Act 1947. The argument had been put forward that the magistrate on an appeal was not entitled to substitute his decision for that of the local authority. That view was not accepted by the Divisional Court. Lord Goddard CJ stated (at 602):

> 'It is said that, on an appeal . . . the magistrate is not entitled to substitute his opinion for the opinion of the borough council; that all he can decide is whether there was evidence upon which the council could come to that conclusion. I find myself quite unable to accept that argument. If that argument be right, the right of appeal . . . would be purely illusory. Such an appeal would . . . really be only an appeal on the question of law whether there was any evidence upon which the borough council could have formed an opinion. If their decision were a mere matter of opinion and that opinion were to be conclusive, I do not know that the borough council would be obliged to have any evidence. They could simply say "In our opinion this person is unsuitable to hold a licence". It is true that they must give a sufficient reason, but they could give any reason they liked and say: "That is sufficient in our opinion". I do not know how a court could then say on appeal that that was not a sufficient reason. If the reason need only be one which is sufficient in the opinion of the borough council, it is difficult to see how any court of appeal could set aside their decision. It seems to me that [s 25(1)] gives an unrestricted right of appeal, and if there is an unrestricted right of appeal it is for the court of appeal to substitute its opinion for the opinion of the borough council.'

In relation to the question of the relevance of the previous decision by the local authority, Lord Goddard CJ said this (at 602):

'That does not mean to say that the court of appeal, in this case the metropolitan magistrate, ought not pay great attention to the fact that the duly constituted and elected local authority have come to an opinion on the matter, and it ought not lightly to reverse their opinion. It is constantly said (although I am not sure that it is always sufficiently remembered) that the function of a court of appeal is to exercise its powers when it is satisfied that the judgment below was wrong, not merely because it is not satisfied that the judgment was right.'

1 *Stepney Borough Council v Joffe* [1949] 1 KB 599, DC.

In the *Sagnata* case[1] the Court of Appeal upheld both elements of the   **3.15**
Stepney judgment: that such an appeal is a hearing de novo, a completely fresh hearing; and that the court should take account of and give considerable, but not overwhelming, weight to the fact that the local authority came to the decision that it did. Edmund Davies LJ cited with approval the judgment of Lord Goddard CJ in the *Stepney* case (at 149G and 150G).

It is therefore clear that an appeal is a rehearing. What then can the court take into account? The cases of *Kavanagh v Chief Constable of Devon and Cornwall*[2], *Westminster City Council v Zestfair*[3] and *McCool v Rushcliffe Borough Council*[4] make it clear that hearsay evidence is admissible.

1 *Sagnata Investments Ltd v Norwich Corpn* [1971] 2 QB 614.
2 [1974] 2 All ER 697. See Chapter 2, para 2.32.
3 (1989) 88 LGR 288, DC. See Chapter 2, para 2.33.
4 [1998] 3 All ER 889, QBD. See Chapter 2, para 2.34.

As the appeal is quasi-judicial, as opposed to judicial, the normal rules of   **3.16**
procedure and evidence, either criminal or civil, do not strictly apply and most local authorities and magistrates' courts have evolved their own procedure.

The most striking part of this procedure is that it is generally agreed that the respondent local authority should present their case, as to why the licence should not be granted (or renewed or, it should be revoked or suspended) first and the appellant should then respond to that. The thinking behind this is to enable the court to understand what the appellant is appealing against, rather than having the rather bizarre situation of the appellant explaining his reasons for appeal, followed by the respondent explaining why the appeal should not be granted.

If this approach is undertaken, it is important that the respondent local authority should reserve their right to address the court as the last matter before the court makes its decision.

It is open to the appeal court to substitute its decision for the decision   **3.17**
which is being appealed against. In certain circumstances, it can modify or vary the decision which is being appealed against. This depends on the way in which the complaint is worded. This process is governed by Rule 14 of the Magistrates Court Rules 1981. It is obviously important to word the complaint in the correct way so as to enable the court to make any variation which is requested. The court also has the discretion to award costs.

3.18   The wording of most of the appeal provisions is that an appeal is available to any 'person aggrieved'. This is usually taken as meaning a person who is not granted a licence or is granted a licence subject to conditions which they find unacceptable. Since the case of *Cook v Southend Borough Council*[1] it has become clear that a local authority can be a 'person aggrieved' for the purposes of such appeals.

In this case, the Court of Appeal considered whether it was possible for a local authority to be a 'person aggrieved' after a decision by a magistrates' court, following an appeal against the local authority's decision in relation to hackney carriage and private hire licensing.

In a comprehensive judgment, Woolf LJ stated as follows (at 7B):

'In these circumstances it is, I hope, useful if I set out certain general propositions which I would expect to apply where the expression "a person aggrieved" is used in relation to a right of appeal in the absence of a clear contrary intention in a particular statutory context. (1) A body corporate including a local authority is just as capable of being a person aggrieved as an individual. (2) Any person who has a decision decided against him (particularly in adversarial proceedings) will be a person aggrieved for the purposes of appealing against that decision unless the decision amounts to an acquittal of a purely criminal offence. In the latter case the statutory context will be all important. (3) The fact that the decision against which the person wishes to appeal reverses a decision which was originally taken by that person and does not otherwise adversely affect that person does not prevent that person being aggrieved. On the contrary it indicates that he is a person aggrieved who is entitled to exercise the right of appeal in order to have the original decision restored.

Turning to the circumstances giving rise to this appeal, in the absence of authority I would have no hesitation in coming to the conclusion that irrespective of whether or not the justices had made an order for costs, the council had a right of appeal under section 301.'

1   [1990] 2 QB 1.

3.19   There had been a number of earlier cases which his Lordship considered at length, most of which made a distinction between the position of a council which had had costs awarded against it by the magistrates' court and those where no such costs were awarded against a council. This had led to the anomalous situation whereby a council was actually in a better position if it had had costs awarded against it, because it had a right of appeal, as opposed to a council where no costs had been awarded against it and had no right of appeal. His Lordship took the view that this was absurd and that the question of costs was irrelevant. The grievance felt by the local authority was in losing the appeal, rather than in having costs awarded against it, and he concluded (at 18H):

'I would therefore dismiss this appeal on the basis that the council was a person aggrieved by the decision of the Southend justices quite apart from the order for costs which was made against the council. However, even if this is not the position, the effect of the order for costs is to make this case indistinguishable from the decision of the House of Lords in *Jennings v Kelly* [1940] AC 206.

It follows in my view this appeal must be dismissed.'

This has wide-ranging implications, as it allows the local authority to appeal   **3.20**
when the local authority feels that the decision of the magistrates, on
overturning the local authority's decision, was wrongly made and enables it
to then appeal to the Crown Court. This ability has been used on a number
of occasions since 1990 with varying success.

The time-scales involved in an appeal to the magistrates' court are contained   **3.21**
within section 300 of the Public Health Act 1936. This requires any appeal
to be brought within 21 days 'from the date on which notice of the council's
requirement, refusal or other decision was served upon the person desiring
to appeal'. Such an appeal is by way of complaint.

Most local authorities communicate their decision to the applicant in writ-   **3.22**
ing and the 21 days to make an appeal takes effect from the date on which
that letter is deemed to have been received by the unsuccessful applicant.
By virtue of section 7 of the Interpretation Act 1978, service is deemed to
be effected 'at the time at which the letter would be delivered in the ordinary course of post', so, for a letter sent 1st class, it will be the day after
posting and approximately two days after posting, if sent 2nd class. This is
notwithstanding the fact that the applicant may well have been told of the
decision in person at the determination of the hearing. This simply gives
the applicant slightly longer to get his appeal lodged and it would appear
difficult to argue successfully that such verbal notice is the date from
which time runs.

Section 300(3) of the Public Health Act 1936 states: **3.23**

> 'in any case where such an appeal lies, the document notifying to the
> person concerned the decision of the council in the matter shall state the
> right of appeal to a court of summary jurisdiction and the time within
> which such an appeal may be brought.'

It is therefore vital that the letter or notice informing the applicant of the
decision contains details of his right of appeal and the time-scales involved.

A further right of appeal lies to the Crown Court by virtue of section 301 of the   **3.24**
1936 Act. In this situation, the Crown Court sits as an appeal court against
the decision of the magistrates' court below. The method of commencing
such an appeal is laid down in Part III of the Crown Court Rules 1982.

The procedure in the Crown Court is much the same as the procedure in
the magistrates' court, the principle difference being that, as solicitors
employed by the local authority do not (yet) have rights of audience in the
Crown Court, it is necessary for counsel to be instructed. The Crown Court
sits with a judge and two magistrates from jurisdictions other than that
which heard the appeal to the magistrates' court. In the case of an appeal
against a refusal to grant a hackney carriage proprietor's licence, or in areas
where the 1976 Act has not been adopted, magistrates should be from a
jurisdiction other than that which covers the authority against whom the
decision is being made.

Once again, the Crown Court has a discretion to award costs and can   **3.25**
substitute its decision for that of the magistrates' court or local authority.
Evidential and procedural matters remain as for the magistrates' court.

Further appeals

3.26 The magistrate's court and Crown Court are the only venues for statutory rights of appeal, but it is possible to appeal further, on a point of law, against the decision of either the magistrates' court or Crown Court, by way of 'case stated'.

3.27 In the case of an appeal from the Crown Court, this is an appeal to the High Court under the provisions of section 28 of the Supreme Court Act 1981 and is available on the grounds that the 'order, judgment or other decision' was 'wrong in law, or is in excess of the jurisdiction'.

3.28 If the appeal is from the magistrates' court, the provisions of section 111 of the Magistrates' Courts Act 1980 apply to any 'conviction order, determination or other proceeding of the Court' on the grounds that it was 'wrong in law, or is in excess of the jurisdiction'.

3.29 The procedure for both applications is contained in Order 56 of the Rules of the Supreme Court.

3.30 In *R v Reading Crown Court, ex p Reading Borough Council*[1], the Crown Court judge refused to state a case at the request of the local authority. The local authority had refused to renew a private hire driver's licence because of his previous convictions. In 1993, the first check was made of his criminal record by the local authority and the full extent of his record was revealed – this included an assault, when acting as a taxi driver (which would appear to be an early example of road rage), an offence of driving without due care and attention and a conviction for theft as a result of shop-lifting. There were numerous other convictions which had taken place over previous years. The applicant appealed to the magistrates' court, who dismissed his appeal. He then appealed to the Crown Court, which upheld his appeal. The local authority sought a judicial review of the judge's decision not to state a case. This was dismissed. The High Court decided that there were no grounds on which a case could be stated and, even though the decision to allow the appeal may have been surprising, it was not so extraordinary that no reasonable judge could have reached it. Collins J concluded:

> 'It may be that this was an unexpected decision. But the test is not whether I would have reached the same decision or whether another court would have reached the same decision. The test is whether this decision is such that no reasonable body could have reached it. In my judgment, it cannot be so described. It seems to me that it was a decision to which the learned judge and his colleagues were entitled to come on the material before them. In those circumstances, there were no grounds upon which a case could properly be stated. Even if the case should have been stated, the inevitable result would have been that the appeal would be dismissed. Accordingly, it seems to me that both these applications must be refused.'

This case provides a salutory lesson that, occasionally, decisions seem wrong, but that this has to be accepted by the losing party. Sometimes, there is nothing that can be done about an appeal result.

1 [1996] COD 90.

JUDICIAL REVIEW

There are occasions when it is the decision-making process of the local **3.31** authority which is open to challenge and, when that is the case, the method of challenge is by way of judicial review of the local authority's decision.

Before that can done, however, a decision has to have been made. This was demonstrated in the case of *R v Halton Borough Council, ex p Poynton*[1]. Halton Borough Council had a policy of only granting private hire drivers' licences to people who would work as full-time private hire drivers. Mr Poynton completed an application form and stated he was already in full-time employment and intended to drive a private hire vehicle on a part-time basis. He was told by the local authority that it would not be able to accept his application. The local authority subsequently accepted that it was wrong to refuse to accept his application and that it would consider his case on its merits. Correspondence took place between the local authority and the solicitors acting for Mr Poynton, however, no application was actually received by the local authority. An application for leave to seek judicial review was therefore made. This was unsuccessful, for the reasons given by Otton J:

'In my judgment in the absence of any decision on the application made by this applicant this court does not have jurisdiction or power to order mandamus against the council to act or refrain from acting in a situation where the appropriate committee has had no opportunity to consider the matter at all. It is manifest from the correspondence that the council has been ready and willing to consider the application and to determine it on its merits.

It is thus open to the applicant to argue that the policy is ultra vires or that he falls outside it or that the only power the council has to limit his activities is to attach to the grant of a licence such conditions as they consider reasonably necessary under subsection (2) of section 51.

I am satisfied that it would be wrong for this court to attempt to deal with this application *in vacuo* and in the absence of any decision one way or the other. In reality, I consider that this application is an attempt to obtain from judicial review a writ of certiorari to bring up and quash a policy as it exists and which has been in existence for three years. This in my judgment is an inappropriate use of judicial review powers and procedures.

In arriving at this conclusion I also bear in mind that there is an alternative remedy open to the applicant in the event of an adverse finding by the council. He would be free to go to the magistrates and he may . . . succeed either before the justices or before the Crown Court. I see nothing oppressive or unjust in requiring Mr Poynton to pursue this remedy.

This application is therefore refused.'

1 (1989) 1 Admin LR 83.

However, judicial review is not appropriate when there is a statutory right of **3.32** appeal against a decision or action of the local authority. This view was upheld by Judge J in *R v Blackpool Borough Council, ex p Red Cab Taxis*[1], where judicial review was sought relating to the imposition of conditions on private hire vehicle licences. As there was a statutory right of appeal to the magistrates' court and subsequently, to the Crown Court, that route had to be used in preference to judicial review. Judge J said (at 410E):

> 'In exercising my discretion I have attempted to balance the very many dif-
> fering factors, some of which stand together and weigh down on one side,
> and some of which of course are diametrically opposed. Having reflected
> on the matter, my conclusion is that, notwithstanding that the decision-
> making process was flawed, the main issue in the case, the condition, in
> the overall interests of everyone – the council, the applicants, the drivers
> of taxis and the people living locally – should have been, and still could be
> best considered and decided by the justices in Blackpool in accordance
> with their statutory procedures. Such proceedings would have been more
> rapid and cheaper and ultimately of greater practical value to all those
> involved, including the applicants themselves.'

1 [1994] RTR 402, QBD.

3.33 There may be some situations where there is an overlap, with some elements
of a decision, which could be subject to judicial review (in the following
case, over the vires or power of a policy), and other elements, which could
be appealed to the magistrates' court. In those situations, judicial review
could be launched as well, as the magistrates could not reasonably consider
the question of vires.

3.34 This was considered in *R v Leeds City Council, ex p Hendry*[1]. In this case, a
private hire vehicle licence was refused by the council because, it was
alleged, a policy had been adopted whereby any vehicle which was presented for a new licence (and, in this case, the vehicle had previously been
licensed as a private hire vehicle, but the licence has lapsed prior to the
application, so it was a new application, rather than a renewal) should not be
granted one unless (441B):

> 'the vehicle was first registered on or after April 1st 1987 and was fitted
> with inertia reel seat belts of the three point type to all rear seats.'

The applicant sought a judicial review of his refusal, as he felt that the
statement was not an accurate statement of the policy which had been
adopted by Leeds City Council. On investigation, that proved to be true and
the policy in fact was that (441G):

> 'The council shall not grant a hackney carriage or private hire vehicle
> licence, unless the vehicle was manufactured on or after April 1st 1987, or
> already fitted with only inertia reel seat belts of the three point belt type to
> all outboard rear seats.'

Latham J considered whether the judicial review was the appropriate
means of seeking relief, when an appeal was available by virtue of section
48(7) of the 1976 Act, and whether such appeal procedures should be
exhausted before judicial review is contemplated. He stated (at 443C):

> 'In general terms that principle is correct and has been repeatedly
> affirmed, in particular recently in the case of *R v Birmingham City Council,
> ex p Ferrero Ltd* [1993] 1 All ER 530. The Court of Appeal once again said
> that where there is an alternative remedy, and especially where Parliament
> has provided a statutory appeal procedure, it is only exceptionally that
> judicial review should be granted. However, the question which has to be
> asked in every case such as this is not simply whether or not there is an
> alternative statutory appeal procedure but whether in the context of that
> procedure the real issue to be determined can sensibly be determined by
> that means. If it can, then clearly the statutory procedure should prevail

and should be the route adopted by any person aggrieved. If on the other hand the statutory appeal procedure is not apt to deal with the question that is raised in the given case, then there is nothing to prevent an applicant from seeking relief by way of judicial review.

In the present case, although Mr Straker on behalf of the council made a valiant attempt to say that the real issue was whether or not a vehicle was (if I can put it this way) safe for the purposes of hiring on the roads, it seems to me that this is not essentially the question in this case. The question in this case is very simply whether or not the officer purporting to refuse the application made by Mr Hendry, the applicant, was acting in accordance with the policy of the council or not. If he was not and therefore acting outside the authority that he had, it does not seem to me that the magistrates' court is the appropriate forum in which to ventilate that in order to come to any conclusion about it.

In the circumstances I decline to say that it was inappropriate for judicial review proceedings to have been bought in this case. I say and repeat "in this case". It may be that there would be circumstances where there is an overlap between the issues of vires and the issue which can be resolved by the magistrates such as to make it sensible to say that it is the magistrates' court which should in fact deal with the matter. That does not apply here.'

1 (1994) 6 Admin LR 439, QBD.

As the time limits for launching a judicial review are tight, it is important to decide at an early stage what the grounds for any judicial challenge are to be. It is then important to decide on the forum for such challenge and, if necessary, to pursue it. **3.35**

Accordingly, it is important for potential litigants to stage a challenge to the local authority in the correct manner. Obviously, appeals to magistrates' courts are much more straightforward, faster and, perhaps above all, cheaper than embarking upon a judicial review. It is difficult to see why, if an appeal procedure is available, judicial review would seem to be a preferable approach. However, there are occasions when judicial review is the only remedy available. **3.36**

Judicial review is in fact a two-stage process. The first stage is to seek leave to apply for a judicial review and, only if this is successful, is the second stage, the judicial review itself, undertaken. **3.37**

Judicial review is governed by Order 53 of the Rules of the Supreme Court. In the context of judicial review, it is important to be aware of the ability of the parties to bring proceedings. It is important that any judicial review is brought by a person, or incorporated association (ie a limited company). Some older cases were brought by Taxi Associations[1]. This was clearly demonstrated as not being possible in *R v Darlington Borough Council, ex p Association of Darlington Taxi Owners and Darlington Owner Drivers Association*[2]. This case concerned an application for judicial review of the decision of Darlington Borough Council to remove the limit on the number of hackney carriages which would be licensed and also to end a concessionary fare scheme for wheelchair-accessible vehicles. **3.38**

However, the case did not consider the merits of that point and instead addressed a far more important and useful question: whether an unincorporated association (that is, a group of individuals, rather than one individual or a limited company) is able to issue legal proceedings against a local authority in order to challenge a decision of that local authority.

It was decided by Auld J that an unincorporated association was not able to bring proceedings in such a case, as it lacked the legal capacity to do so. As a result, the application for judicial review was dismissed and the merits of the case were not considered.

1 See, eg *R v Liverpool Corpn, ex p Liverpool Taxi Fleet Operators Association*.
2 [1994] COD 424.

3.39 This led, however, to a second case, *R v Darlington Borough Council, ex p Association of Darlington Taxi Owners and Darlington Owner Drivers Association (No 2)*[1]. This was an application brought by the local authority, seeking the costs of the original hearing from the unincorporated associations (the Association of Darlington Taxi Owners and the Darlington Owner Drivers Association). This was challenged by the two Associations on the grounds that, as they had no standing to bring proceedings, they therefore had no liability in costs. However, this view was rejected again by Auld J, who held that, notwithstanding the fact that the proceedings were struck out, proceedings had been issued and, therefore, liability and costs accrued. In fact, the costs order was made against all the members of the two Associations at the time of the application for leave to apply for judicial review and that order was enforceable jointly and severally.

1 [1995] COD 128.

3.40 These cases make it clear that only an individual or a limited company can bring proceedings in hackney carriage and private hire licensing matters and that, if an unincorporated association brings proceedings, not only will they fail, but they will also incur a liability for costs.

THE OMBUDSMAN

3.41 In addition, in certain circumstances there is the possibility of a challenge to a local authority via the Ombudsman. The Ombudsman (correctly termed the Commissioner for Local Administration) was created, and is controlled by, Part III of the Local Government Act 1974[1].

1 For a full consideration of the role of the commissioner for local administration, please see *Butterworths Local Government Law*, Division A, Chapter 4.

3.42 The Ombudsman can investigate complaints made by members of the public that they have suffered injustice due to maladministration on the part of a local authority. 'Maladministration' is not defined in the 1974 Act. However, reference is often made to the 'Crossman catalogue' which includes 'bias, neglect, inattention, delay, incompetence, ineptitude, perversity, turpitude, arbitrariness and so on'.

3.43 In relation to hackney carriage and private hire licensing matters, the role of the Ombudsman appears to be limited by virtue of section 256(6) of the

Local Government Act 1974, which states:

> 'A local commissioner shall not conduct an investigation under this Part of this Act in respect of any of the following matters, that is to say:
>
> (*a*) any action in respect of which the person aggrieved has or had a right of appeal, reference or review to or before a tribunal constituted by or under any enactment;
>
> (*b*) any action in respect of which the person aggrieved has or had a right of appeal to a Minister of the Crown; or the National Assembly for Wales or
>
> (*c*) any action in respect of which the person aggrieved has or had a remedy by way of proceedings in any court of law.'

3.44 Obviously, in most situations, in relation to hackney carriage or private hire matters, there is a right of appeal, if it is the applicant who is affected by the decision of the local authority. The role of the Ombudsman is probably more relevant in relation to a complaint by a member of the public concerning the method or manner in which a local authority has exercised its powers with regard to hackney carriage and private hire licensing.

3.45 It should not be overlooked, however, that the findings of the Ombudsman are not binding on the local authority, although certain actions, including advertising the findings of the Ombudsman, are required.

It is a matter for individual local authorities as to how they react to an Ombudsman's investigation. Some authorities take the view that an investigation is merely an exercise in time wasting and clearly have no intention in complying with any findings that the Ombudsman may make, whilst other authorities at the other extreme react with such speed to any suggestion that the Ombudsman might be involved, so as to almost make a mockery of any suggestion of corporate independence.

It will be realised that neither approach is correct and the rational view of the Ombudsman is that it provides a cost-effective alternative method of addressing peoples' grievances which might result from the actions of local authorities.

Chapter 4

Fees for licences

Each of the licences outlined in Chapter 3: hackney carriage drivers' and **4.1** hackney carriage proprietors' (vehicle) licences, private hire operators' licences, private hire drivers, and private hire vehicle licences attracts a fee payable to the local authority.

AREAS WHERE THE LOCAL GOVERNMENT (MISCELLANEOUS PROVISIONS) ACT 1976 HAS BEEN ADOPTED

In areas where the Local Government (Miscellaneous Provisions) Act 1976 **4.2** (hereinafter 'the 1976 Act') has been adopted, the provisions controlling the levying of these fees are:

- section 53(2) of the 1976 Act, in respect of drivers' licences for both hackney carriages or private hire vehicles; and
- section 70 of the 1976 Act, for hackney carriage proprietors' licences, private hire vehicle licences and private hire operators' licences.

AREAS WHERE THE LOCAL GOVERNMENT (MISCELLANEOUS PROVISIONS) ACT 1976 HAS NOT BEEN ADOPTED

In areas where the 1976 Act has not been adopted, the provisions relating to **4.3** fees for hackney carriage proprietors' licences and drivers' licences are contained in:

- section 46 of the Town Police Clauses Act 1847, in respect of hackney carriage drivers' licences; and
- section 35 of the Transport Act 1981, in relation to hackney carriage proprietors' licences.

WHETHER THE LOCAL GOVERNMENT (MISCELLANEOUS PROVISIONS) ACT 1976 APPLIES OR NOT

The provisions of the 1976 Act, whether applicable or not to the local **4.4** authority, do not allow the authority discretion to charge whatever it likes for the grant of a licence. The cost of a licence has to be related to the cost of the licensing scheme itself. That is apparent from the wording used, as will be seen below, but the question of the level of fee is also governed by the decision in the case of *R v Manchester City Council, ex p King*[1]. Although this was a case concerning the street trading provisions of the Local Government (Miscellaneous Provisions) Act 1982 (hereinafter 'the 1982 Act'), the judgment has relevance to all local authority licensing fees.

1   (1991) 89 LGR 696, DC.

4.5   In the *King* case, Manchester City Council argued that the wording of the 1982 Act allowed them to set fees for street trading licences that reflected the commercial nature of the sites on which traders traded and that they did not have to be related to the cost of the street trading licensing and registration scheme. The High Court disagreed. Roch J stated (at 709):

> '. . . it would be surprising if Parliament had intended to include a general revenue-raising provision in a schedule which deals solely with street trading. The purpose of that part of the Act is to establish a general scheme for street trading which local authorities may adopt if they so desire . . .

> The fees charged, in my judgment, must be related to the street trading scheme operated by the district council and the costs of operating that scheme. The district council may charge such fees as they reasonably consider will cover the total cost of operating the street trading scheme or such lesser part of the cost of operating the street trading scheme as they consider reasonable. One consequence of the wording used is that, if the fees levied in the event exceed the cost of operating the scheme, the original decision will remain valid provided it can be said that the district council reasonably considered such fees would be required to meet the total cost of operating the scheme.'

Notwithstanding the difference in wording between the 1982 Act and the 1976 Act, this is an important decision.

WHERE THE LOCAL GOVERNMENT (MISCELLANEOUS PROVISIONS) ACT 1976 APPLIES

Driver's licence fees

4.6   Section 53(2) of the 1976 Act states:

> '**53**–(2) Notwithstanding the provisions of the Act of 1847, a district council may demand and recover for the grant to any person of a licence to drive a hackney carriage, or a private hire vehicle, as the case may be, such a fee as they consider reasonable with a view to recovering the costs of issue and administration and may remit the whole or part of the fee in respect of a private hire vehicle in any case in which they think it appropriate to do so.'

It is clear that the fees for drivers' licences for both hackney carriages or private hire vehicles, when covered by these provisions have to be both reasonable and imposed 'with a view to recovering the costs of issue and administration'. This will cover the costs of assessing the suitability of the applicant, including a police check and driving and knowledge tests. It will also include the costs of the issue of the badge and other associated administrative tasks. However, no provision can be made for the costs of enforcement undertaken by the authority against unlicensed drivers, unless that can legitimately be included in the term 'administration'. This would appear to be pushing the accepted meaning of 'administration' a little too far, although there seems to be no case law on this point.

Vehicle and operators' licences

In relation to the fees for both hackney carriage and private hire vehicle   **4.7**
licences and private hire operators' licences, section 70 of the 1976 Act
states:

'Fees for vehicle and operators' licences

70–(1) Subject to the provisions of subsection (2) of this section, a district council may charge such fees for the grant of vehicle and operators' licences as may be resolved by them from time to time and as may be sufficient in the aggregate to cover in whole or in part—

(a) the reasonable cost of the carrying out by or on behalf of the district council of inspections of hackney carriages and private hire vehicles for the purpose of determining whether any such licence should be granted or renewed;

(b) the reasonable cost of providing hackney carriage stands; and

(c) any reasonable administrative or other costs in connection with the foregoing and with the control and supervision of hackney carriages and private hire vehicles.

(2) The fees chargeable under this section shall not exceed—

(a) for the grant of a vehicle licence in respect of a hackney carriage, twenty-five pounds;

(b) for the grant of a vehicle licence in respect of a private hire vehicle, twenty-five pounds; and

(c) for the grant of an operator's licence, twenty-five pounds per annum;

or, in any such case, such other sums as a district council may, subject to the following provisions of this section, from time to time determine.

(3)(a) If a district council determine that the maximum fees specified in subsection (2) of this section should be varied they shall publish in at least one local newspaper circulating in the district a notice setting out the variation proposed, drawing attention to the provisions of paragraph (b) of this subsection and specifying the period, which shall not be less than twenty-eight days from the date of the first publication of the notice, within which and the manner in which objections to the variation can be made.

(b) A copy of the notice referred to in paragraph (a) of this subsection shall for the period of twenty-eight days from the date of the first publication thereof be deposited at the offices of the council which published the notice and shall at all reasonable hours be open to public inspection without payment.

(4) If no objection to a variation is duly made within the period specified in the notice referred to in subsection (3) of this section, or if all objections so made are withdrawn, the variation shall come into operation on the date of the expiration of the period specified in the notice or the date of withdrawal of the objection or, if more than one, of the last objection, whichever date is the later.

(5) If objection is duly made as aforesaid and is not withdrawn, the district council shall set a further date, not later than two months after the first specified date, on which the variation shall come into force with or without modification as decided by the district council after consideration of the objections.

(6) A district council may remit the whole or part of any fee chargeable in pursuance of this section for the grant of a licence under section 48 or 55 of this Act in any case in which they think it appropriate to do so.'

The wording of section 70(1), '. . . as may be sufficient in the aggregate to cover in whole or in part', suggests that the matters contained within paragraphs (*a*), (*b*), and (*c*) of section 70(1) can be grouped together for the purposes of calculating the cost. This includes initial inspection of the vehicle, the cost of providing taxi ranks (referred to in the legislation as hackney carriage stands), and then by virtue of paragraph (*c*) everything else that is connected with the administration and enforcement of the entire hackney carriage vehicle and private hire vehicle operation. This will include vehicle inspections, administration of vehicle records, random checks, hackney carriage demand surveys etc.

The wording of section 70(1)(*c*) clearly envisages the inclusion of the costs of enforcement, and subsequent legal proceedings as being part of the costs relating to the vehicles themselves. This will cover both enforcement of the provisions against licensed vehicles and also against unlicensed vehicles.

It is considerably less clear whether the costs of enforcement, in relation to operators' licences, can be included in the fee, as the wording of section 70(1)(*c*) appears to limit the use of that section to the vehicles themselves. Although private hire operators' licences are referred to in section 70(1), nowhere else within the section is there any reference to operators' licences, apart from the standard fee of £25 per year contained in section 70(2)(*c*).

4.8   The overall effect of the provisions contained within the 1976 Act, in respect of fees for licences, would appear to be, therefore, that, in relation to drivers, the costs of issue and administration can be recovered; in relation to vehicles, the costs of inspection, ranks, control and supervision (including enforcement), and the administration connected with it, can be recovered; and, in relation to operators' licences, it is difficult to see what can be recovered at all.

In order to be able to justify a fee levied under either section 53 or 70, it will be necessary to be able to differentiate between the two provisions. This will mean that there must be at least two identifiable accounts relating to the fees levied under each section.

Notice provisions

4.9   Under section 53(2) of the 1976 Act, the fee for hackney carriage and driving licences simply has to be reasonable and there are no statutory requirements for advertisements, notices, consultation or representations. In addition, there is no restriction on the number of times that the local authority can increase the fees. However, their actions must be reasonable, in accordance with the *Wednesbury* principles.

The provisions of section 53(2) can be contrasted with the requirements **4.10**
under section 70 of the 1976 Act in relation to:

* Hackney carriage proprietors' licences;
* Private hire vehicle licences; and
* Private hire operators' licences.

The district council can charge more than the fees laid down in section 70(2). **4.11**
If the fees are to be greater, then the following procedure must be followed:

1. A notice must be published in a local newspaper, stating the proposed fees which exceed those laid down in section 70(2).
2. This must give not less than 28 days for objections to be lodged.
3. It must also state where objections should be addressed and how they can be made. Obviously, it is desirable for such objections to be lodged in writing, as opposed to any other method (although an objection by a fax or e-mail should be acceptable).
4. A copy of the notice must be available at the council offices for inspection, free of charge, 'at all reasonable hours' (section 70(3)(*b*)).
5. Once the objection period (usually 28 days) has expired, if there have been no objections received or those received have subsequently been withdrawn, then the new fees take effect, either at the end of the objection period, or when the last objection is withdrawn (section 70(4)).
6. However, if objections are made and are not withdrawn, then the council must consider the objections.
7. In the light of those objections (although it must consider them, it does not have to vary the proposal as a result of them) the council then sets a second date, which cannot be more than two months after the first date specified, when the new fees come into force. [**see flow chart on p 52**]

Although section 53 of the 1976 Act contains no requirement for consulta- **4.12**
tion, a local authority would be ill-advised not to embark upon some
element of consultation with those persons who would be affected by an
increase in fees (eg the drivers of both hackney carriages and private hire
vehicles).

Although it is not a statutory requirement, it would seem sensible for local
authorities to follow the same procedure as contained in section 70 for
increases in fees under section 53, so as to provide the consultation which is
required and to demonstrate that they are approaching the matter in a reasonable fashion.

FEES FOR HACKNEY CARRIAGE PROPRIETORS' AND DRIVERS' LICENCES IN AREAS WHERE THE 1976 ACT HAS NOT BEEN ADOPTED

In those areas of England and Wales where the 1976 Act has not been **4.13**
adopted in relation to private hire vehicles, the mechanism for setting fees
for hackney carriage proprietors' and drivers' licences are contained in section 35 of the Transport Act 1981 (in relation to proprietors' licences) and
section 46 of the Town Police Clauses Act 1847 (in relation to drivers'
licences).

FLOW CHART FOR FEES SET UNDER SECTION 70 OF THE LOCAL GOVERNMENT (MISCELLANEOUS PROVISIONS) ACT 1976

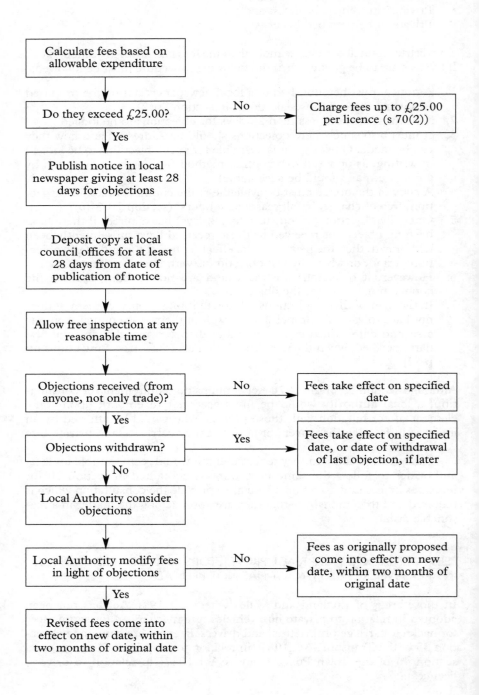

Calculate fees based on allowable expenditure

Do they exceed £25.00? — No → Charge fees up to £25.00 per licence (s 70(2))

Yes

Publish notice in local newspaper giving at least 28 days for objections

Deposit copy at local council offices for at least 28 days from date of publication of notice

Allow free inspection at any reasonable time

Objections received (from anyone, not only trade)? — No → Fees take effect on specified date

Yes

Objections withdrawn? — Yes → Fees take effect on specified date, or date of withdrawal of last objection, if later

No

Local Authority consider objections

Local Authority modify fees in light of objections — No → Fees as originally proposed come into effect on new date, within two months of original date

Yes

Revised fees come into effect on new date, within two months of original date

Section 35 of the Transport Act 1981

Section 35(3) and (3A) of the Transport Act 1981 states: **4.14**

'**Charges for licensing of cabs and cab drivers**

35–(3) Where section 70 of the Local Government (Miscellaneous Provisions) Act 1976 (fees for vehicle and operator's licences) is not in force in the area of a district council, the sums to be paid for a licence granted by the council under section 37 of the Town Police Clauses Act 1847 (licensing of cabs outside London) shall be such as the council may determine, and different sums may be so determined with respect to different descriptions of vehicle; and the sums so determined shall be such as appear to the council to be sufficient in the aggregate to cover in whole or in part—

(*a*) the reasonable cost of the carrying out by or on behalf of the district council of inspections of hackney carriages for the purpose of determining whether any such licence should be granted or renewed;

(*b*) the reasonable cost of providing hackney carriage stands; and

(*c*) any reasonable administrative or other costs in connection with the foregoing and with the control and supervision of hackney carriages.

[(3A) In subsection (3) above, references to a district council shall be read, in relation to Wales, as references to a county council or a county borough council.]'

It can be seen that the wording of section 35(3) is extremely similar to the wording of section 70 of the 1976 Act and the same considerations would appear to apply.

The interesting point is the expression contained in section 35(3), 'and different sums may be so determined with respect to different descriptions of vehicles'. This means that, for example, the fee for a purpose-built London style taxi could be higher than the fee for a saloon car hackney carriage or vice versa. This would appear to be reasonable within the framework of the legislation, provided that, in aggregate, the fees levied do not exceed the cost of those areas of activity covered in section 35(3)(*a*)–(*c*).   **4.15**

Another interesting distinction between section 35(3) and section 70 is the absence of any prescribed fee or advertising mechanism for publicising the proposed fees.   **4.16**

Once again, it would appear sensible for a local authority to follow the mechanism laid down in section 70 of the 1976 Act (notwithstanding the fact that it has not been adopted), as a suitable and satisfactory method of ensuring that consultation with interested parties has taken place before any increase in fees is levied.

Section 46 of the Town Police Clauses Act 1847

Turning to the question of hackney carriage drivers' licences, section 46 of the Town Police Clauses Act 1847 states: **4.17**

'**Drivers not to act without first obtaining a licence**

46 No person shall act as driver of any hackney carriage licensed in pursuance of this or the special Act to ply for hire within the prescribed distance without first obtaining a licence from the commissioners, which

licence shall be registered by the clerk to the commissioners, [and such fee as the commissioners may determine shall be paid] for the same; and every such licence shall be in force until the same is revoked except during the time that the same may be suspended as after mentioned.'

Again, this is not dissimilar in approach to the wording of section 53(2) of the 1976 Act, with no indication as to the fee that can be levied or the mechanism for announcing an increase. The comments in relation to hackney carriage proprietors' licences under section 35 of the Transport Act 1981 apply equally to this area.

FEES IN GENERAL

4.18 It is important to appreciate that a statutory power to levy a fee does not give a local authority an absolutely free hand in relation to the scale of the fee that is levied. The impact of any increase upon the livelihood of those affected has to be taken into account, as does the scale of the increase itself. Consultation must take place with interested parties, whether this is a statutory requirement or not, and results of that consultation must be considered by the local authority before the decision is finally made. It is important that any such consultation is undertaken fairly and that the results are then considered properly by the local authority. Any suggestion that the consultation process is a sham would be grounds for an application for leave to seek a judicial review of the final decision.

4.19 It must also be borne in mind that, when Parliament has given a local authority power to raise money to pay for an activity, then that power should not be rejected lightly. The control of hackney carriage and private hire vehicles, and associated drivers and operators, is a time-consuming and costly exercise, and it is quite legitimate for a local authority to recover as much of their costs as they are able to in relation to this. Those involved in the hackney carriage and private hire trades are in a business and it would be difficult to justify an approach whereby a local authority subsidises private enterprise by refusing to recover as much of the costs associated with its statutory duties as it is able to do so. Such a subsidy would be at the expense of the other services the council could provide to its council tax payers, if full cost recovery was undertaken.

This is obviously a matter of politics and, as ever, it will be for the elected members to make the final decision. However, the overriding aim must be to protect the public and, within the statutory mechanisms, to provide an efficient and effective service for all concerned: those involved in the trade, the council itself and those who elect the council and pay for its activities, the council tax payers.

Chapter 5

Rehabilitation of Offenders Act 1974

INTRODUCTION

The Rehabilitation of Offenders Act 1974 ('the 1974 Act') introduced a   5.1
mechanism whereby a person could 'lose' their criminal record in certain
circumstances. This was designed to remove what were regarded by many as
unfair consequences for people who had, perhaps, only committed one
crime, possibly in their youth, which affected the rest of their lives in a dis-
proportionate way. For example, they might not be able to obtain
employment or, at best, be discriminated against by prospective employers
and, likewise, obtaining insurance or consumer credit might be difficult in
some cases, and so on. It was felt that such persons should not be treated in
the same fashion as 'hardened' criminals with lengthy criminal records. The
result of this was the Rehabilitation of Offenders Act 1974.

THE WORKINGS OF THE REHABILITATION OF OFFENDERS ACT 1974

The consequence of the 1974 Act is that certain 'less serious' offences   5.2
become spent after a certain period of time and, once spent, for many purposes, a person is quite entitled to deny that they were ever convicted of such
an offence.

'Rehabilitated persons and spent convictions

1 – (1) Subject to subsection (2) below, where an individual has been convicted, whether before or after the commencement of this Act, of any
offence or offences, and the following conditions are satisfied, that is to
say—
  (a) he did not have imposed on him in respect of that conviction a sen-
      tence which is excluded from rehabilitation under this Act; and
  (b) he has not had imposed on him in respect of a subsequent conviction
      during the rehabilitation period applicable to the first-mentioned
      conviction in accordance with section 6 below a sentence which is
      excluded from rehabilitation under this Act;

then, after the end of the rehabilitation period so applicable (including,
where appropriate, any extension under section 6(4) below of the period
originally applicable to the first-mentioned conviction) or, where that
rehabilitation period ended before the commencement of this Act, after
the commencement of this Act, that individual shall for the purposes of

this Act be treated as a rehabilitated person in respect of the first-mentioned conviction and that conviction shall for those purposes be treated as spent.'

There are certain sentences which, when imposed, mean that a conviction can never become spent, as defined in section 5(1), but, other than those, the theory is that any other conviction can in due course become spent for the purposes of the Act.

5.3 The length of the period that has to elapse before a conviction becomes spent depends on the sentence imposed, rather than the crime committed, and these are contained in Table A to section 5(2) of the Act.

TABLE A
REHABILITATION PERIODS SUBJECT TO REDUCTION BY HALF FOR PERSONS [UNDER 18]

Sentence	Rehabilitation period
A sentence of imprisonment [detention in a young offender institution] [or youth custody] or corrective training for a term exceeding six months but not exceeding thirty months.	Ten years.
A sentence of cashiering, discharge with ignominy or dismissal with disgrace from Her Majesty's service.	Ten years.
A sentence of imprisonment [detention in a young offender institution] [or youth custody] for a term not exceeding six months.	Seven years.
A sentence of dismissal from Her Majesty's service.	Seven years.
Any sentence of detention in respect of a conviction in service disciplinary proceedings.	Five Years.
A fine or any other sentence subject to rehabilitation under this Act, not being a sentence to which Table B below or any of subsections (3)[, (4A)] or (8) below applies.	Five years.

In relation to persons under 18, these periods are halved, and Table B contains rehabilitation periods for sentences that can only be imposed on young offenders.

TABLE B
REHABILITATION PERIODS FOR CERTAIN SENTENCES
CONFINED TO YOUNG OFFENDERS

Sentence	**Rehabilitation period**
A sentence of Borstal training.	Seven years.
[A custodial order under Schedule 5A to the Army Act 1955 or the Air Force Act 1955, or under Schedule 4A to the Naval Discipline Act 1957, where the maximum period of detention specified in the order is more than six months.	Seven years.]
[A custodial order under section 71AA of the Army Act 1955 or the Air Force Act 1955, or under section 43AA of the Naval Discipline Act 1957, where the maximum period of detention specified in the order is more than six months.	Seven years.]
A sentence of detention for a term exceeding six months but not exceeding thirty months passed under section 53 of the said Act of 1933 or under section [206 of the Criminal Procedure (Scotland) Act 1975].	Seven years.]
A sentence of detention for a term not exceeding six months passed under either of those provisions.	Five years.
An order for detention in a detention centre made under [section 4 of the Criminal Justice Act 1982,] section 4 of the Criminal Justice Act 1961.	Three years.
[A custodial order under any of the Schedules to the said Acts of 1955 and 1957 mentioned above, where the maximum period of detention specified in the order is six months or less.	Three years.]
[A custodial order under section 71AA of the said Acts of 1955, or section 43AA of the said Act of 1957, where the maximum period of detention specified in the order is six months or less.	Three years.]

Note Table A amended by the Criminal Justice Act 1982, s 77, Sch 14, para 37, the Criminal Justice Act 1988, s 123(6), Sch 8, para 9(*b*) and the Criminal Justice and the Public Order Act 1994, s 168(1), Sch 9, para 11(1)(*a*), (2). Table B amended by the Armed Forces Act 1976, s 22, Sch 9, para 21(1), the Criminal Justice (Scotland) Act 1980, s 82(2), Sch 7, para 24, the Armed Forces Act 1981, s 28, Sch 4, para 2 and the Criminal Justice Act 1982, s 77, Sch 14, para 37.

The effects of re-offending

5.4   If a person commits another offence during the rehabilitation period for the first offence, then the rehabilitation period for the earlier offence is extended until the rehabilitation period for the subsequent offence has expired. Section 6(4) of the 1974 Act states:

> '**6**–(4) Subject to subsection (5) below, where during the rehabilitation period applicable to a conviction—
>
> (*a*)   the person convicted is convicted of a further offence; and
>
> (*b*)   no sentence excluded from rehabilitation under this Act is imposed on him in respect of the later conviction;
>
> if the rehabilitation period applicable in accordance with this section to either of the convictions would end earlier than the period so applicable in relation to the other, the rehabilitation period which would (apart from this subsection) end the earlier shall be extended so as to end at the same time as the other rehabilitation period.'

In reality, this means that many recidivists are never rehabilitated, and their convictions will never be spent.

5.5   In relation to the relevance of a criminal conviction to the holder of a licence relating to hackney carriage or private hire matters, it is worth considering the following. Criminal offences fall into one of six categories:

1.   Offences of dishonesty.
2.   Offences of violence (including sexual violence).
3.   Motoring offences.
4.   Offences involving substance abuse (both drink and drugs).
5.   Offences involving obscene materials.
6.   Offences involving consensual but under age sex.

It is suggested that there are no other categories and that all criminal offences fall into one of the above. When any of the licensed roles relating to hackney carriages and private hire vehicles are considered, it would be extremely difficult to argue, therefore, that any criminal conviction is irrelevant for those purposes.

5.6   The public needs to be protected and it is only too easy to foresee the temptations that could be put in the way of an habitually dishonest licence holder involved in the hackney carriage or private hire trade.

This ranges from a driver simply over-charging or wrongly changing through to drivers and operators taking advantage of the knowledge that a person is away from their property for a period. There have been incidents reported around the country, where people used a hackney carriage or private hire vehicle to take them to an airport for a holiday and who have returned to find their house burgled. In one incident, a spate of such crimes was directly linked to the drivers working for a particular private hire operator.

5.7   Likewise, a driver with violent tendencies, whether it is aggression towards men or women or sexual aggression, may not be a suitable person to drive the public around, bearing in mind that, on occasions, the public can be difficult and unco-operative, and, on other occasions, the driver will be dealing with people who are travelling on their own and may be extremely vulnerable for whatever reason.

Motoring offences are equally important in relation to somebody who intends to earn their living driving the public or providing vehicles in which the public will be conveyed. **5.8**

Offences involving substance abuse may indicate an inability to control the use of such substances, with a potentially highly detrimental effect upon passengers. Any tendency towards drinking and driving or towards abuse of controlled drugs, which may impair a driver's ability, should be viewed with extreme caution. **5.9**

Any convictions in relation to obscene materials should be viewed with concern, although it is accepted that such convictions do not necessarily indicate violent tendencies. **5.10**

Finally, convictions are obtained against people for having consensual sex with others under the age of consent, whether heterosexual or homosexual. Although these do not involve violence, they do indicate a disregard for the law. **5.11**

Implications for licensing

The purpose of hackney carriage and private hire licensing is to protect the public. As a consequence, there are many licences and permits that it would be inappropriate to grant to criminals. **5.12**

Notwithstanding this, the term 'criminal' tends to be a sliding one and it is important that the nature of a person's convictions, and possible threat that they may pose to the public, is balanced against the potential loss of livelihood, if the application is refused. **5.13**

As a result, the implications of the 1974 Act, in relation to spent and unspent convictions, are important. **5.14**

The effects of rehabilitation

Once a person has been rehabilitated, the provisions contained in section 4(1) of the 1974 Act come into effect: **5.15**

> '4–(1) Subject to sections 7 and 8 below, a person who has become a rehabilitated person for the purposes of this Act in respect of a conviction shall be treated for all purposes in law as a person who has not committed or been charged with or prosecuted for or convicted of or sentenced for the offence or offences which were the subject of that conviction; and, notwithstanding the provisions of any other enactment or rule of law to the contrary, but subject as aforesaid—
>
> (a) no evidence shall be admissible in any proceedings before a judicial authority exercising its jurisdiction or functions in Great Britain to prove that any such person has committed or been charged with or

> prosecuted for or convicted of or sentenced for any offence which was the subject of a spent conviction; and
>
> (*b*)   a person shall not, in any such proceedings, be asked, and, if asked, shall not be required to answer, any question relating to his past which cannot be answered without acknowledging or referring to a spent conviction or spent convictions or any circumstances ancillary thereto.'

On the face of it, this would prevent a local authority, in the discharge of its hackney carriage and private hire licensing functions, from enquiring about any spent convictions.

5.16   Under the Rehabilitation of Offenders Act 1974 (Exceptions) Order 1975 made under section 4(4) of the 1976 Act, there are certain defined occupations which are exempted from these provisions, but no hackney carriage or private hire licensing matter is contained amongst them.

5.17   However, as it was recognised that there was a danger to the public in certain situations where a person with undesirable convictions could seek the grant of a licence, the provisions of section 7(3) were enacted.

Using 'spent' convictions

5.18   Section 7(3) of the 1974 Act states:

> '7–(3) If at any stage in any proceedings before a judicial authority in Great Britain (not being proceedings to which, by virtue of any of paragraphs (*a*) to (*e*) of subsection (2) above or of any order for the time being in force under subsection (4) below, section 4(1) above has no application, or proceedings to which section 8 below applies) the authority is satisfied, in the light of any considerations which appear to it to be relevant (including any evidence which has been or may thereafter be put before it), that justice cannot be done in the case except by admitting or requiring evidence relating to a person's spent convictions or to circumstances ancillary thereto, that authority may admit or, as the case may be, require the evidence in question notwithstanding the provisions of subsection (1) of section 4 above, and may determine any issue to which the evidence relates in disregard, so far as necessary, of those provisions.'

5.19   The question is whether a hearing by a local authority licensing committee constitutes 'proceedings before a judicial authority'? This is defined in section 4(6) of the 1974 Act:

> '4–(6) For the purposes of this section and section 7 below "proceedings before a judicial authority" includes, in addition to proceedings before any of the ordinary courts of law, proceedings before any tribunal, body or person having power—
>
> (*a*)   by virtue of any enactment, law, custom or practice;
>
> (*b*)   under the rules governing any association, institution, profession, occupation or employment; or
>
> (*c*)   under any provision of an agreement providing for arbitration with respect to questions arising thereunder;
>
> to determine any question affecting the rights, privileges, obligations or liabilities of any person, or to receive evidence affecting the determination of any such question.'

This definition is less than clear and, for some time, it was by no means certain whether a licensing application fell within the definition. The only authorities which supported the view that section 7(3) did apply were Scottish[1], and therefore only persuasive. Whilst a number of local authorities were persuaded, many were not.

1 See *Morton v City of Dundee District Council* (1991) 1992 SLT (Sh Ct) 2 and *Francy v Cunninghame District Council* 1987 SCLR 6.

However, the situation as to whether section 7(3) of the 1974 Act covers **5.20** licensing applications has now been clarified by the case of *Adamson v Waveney District Council*[1]. The judgment in this case was delivered by Sedley J.

On the specific question as to whether section 7(3) applied to a decision to grant a hackney carriage driver's licence, Sedley J said (at 900F):

> 'It is common ground in this case that the initial consideration by the local authority of an application under section 59 of the Act of 1976 for a hackney carriage driver's licence is a proceeding before a judicial authority within this provision.'

It is difficult to see any argument that would prevent this principle being applied to all the hackney carriage and private hire licences, not just hackney carriage drivers. As such, it is an extremely useful statement.

1 [1997] 2 All ER 898.

At the time of the case, sections 51(1A) (in relation to private hire drivers) **5.21** and 59(1A) (in relation to hackney carriage drivers) of the Local Government (Miscellaneous Provisions) Act 1976 ('the 1976 Act') allowed for the observations of the chief officer of police to be sought by the local authority. This was usually done by means of a print-out of the person's record from the Police National Computer. These provisions have subsequently been repealed, but that does not affect the principles in this judgment[1].

The judgment of Sedley J continues (at 900G):

> 'It appears to follow that by virtue of section 4(2) [of the 1974 Act] the chief constable may treat the question put to him by the local authority as relating to spent as well as to unspent convictions . . . It poses an immediate problem if the recipient local authority is to receive the whole of a previous offender's record, spent and unspent, relevant or irrelevant.'

He then attempts judicial assistance with the problem that he has identified:

> 'It may be that what I have to say shortly will help to resolve the problem that this, on the face of it, poses.'

1 See para 5.28.

The judgment is well reasoned. However, the judge requires local authori- **5.22** ties to seek and obtain a high level of co-operation from chief constables. His suggestion is that the chief constable, in framing his response to the request for his observations, should (at 904C):

> '. . . give careful consideration to what spent convictions, if any, are capable of relating to the issue which the local authority will have to decide,

and to ensure that his disclosure (which is, after all, in the form of observations, according to the statutory language) is limited to what is capable
of being relevant.'

5.23 This would (in the judge's view) allow the following procedure (which he
suggests for appeals from the local authority) to apply to decisions of the
local authority itself. His suggested procedure is as follows (at 904A):

'. . . it seems to me that the following stages have to be gone through in
any application such as that with which the justices were here concerned.
First, with the help of the advocates before them, they have to identify
what the issue is to which any spent convictions must relate if they are to
be admitted. The issue here was the fitness of the applicant to hold the
material licence. Secondly, those responsible for presenting material to
the court must give their own objective, professional consideration to the
question whether any or all of the spent convictions on the record are
capable of having a real relevance to the issue which has been identified.
When the matter is before justices, it will be the advocate for the local
authority who must consider that. When the matter is before the
local authority, it will be the chief constable who must consider it.'

Once that has been accomplished, the following should occur (at 904E):

'Next, the "judicial authority", as the Act calls it, has to consider whether
it should admit the convictions in the light of the issue before it. Inevitably
there will be procedural differences between what can happen before a
local authority committee and what will happen before justices. These
may, however, be able to be brought satisfactorily into line in the following way. Before justices I have no doubt that the right course is for the
local authority advocate to indicate what is the class of offence, the age of
the offence and perhaps, in broad terms, the apparent seriousness (gauged
by penalty) of the offence shown by the record before him. That is the best
that can be done, without pre-empting the very decision that the justices
have to take, to enable the justices to decide (having heard anything the
applicant wishes to say to the contrary) whether to admit any spent convictions. They may decide that some but not others in the list ought to be
put before them.'

5.24 To assist the local authority at what might be termed 'first instance', Sedley J
adds (at 904G):

'Translating this back to the stage where the matter is before the local
authority, it may very well be that the chief constable should correspond-
ingly be invited to provide a covering letter giving the same broad
indications, but no more, so that the committee can decide whether it
needs to go into some or all of those offences, the existence of which has
been indicated to them. That indication will of course, as I have said,
already have been pruned of those which are clearly not relevant and
should not be considered under any circumstances.'

5.25 Assuming that there are some relevant convictions (whether spent or not),
this is the next stage (at 904H):

'Once some or all of the spent convictions are admitted in evidence, either
before the local authority committee or before justices, the applicant is
then entitled naturally to be heard, not by way of suggesting that the convictions were incorrectly arrived at but in order to persuade the judicial
authority that they are either, in truth, irrelevant or such, by reason of

their age, circumstances or lack of seriousness, that they should not jeop-
ardise his application. All of that is simple natural justice.'

And then, finally (at 904J):

'The judicial authority must then come to its own dispassionate conclusion, having in mind not only the interests of the applicant as a person
with spent convictions but also the interests of the public in whose interests these exceptional powers are being exercised.'

Practical implications

The difficulty with this is that a great deal of reliance is placed on the chief   **5.26**
constable and it is not clear how willing they are to accommodate such
requirements. It seems that some forces are very helpful, but others are less
so. It would seem prudent for the local authority to ascertain, in advance,
the chief constable's response to such a request in writing. If the chief constable agrees to this procedure, all well and good, but if he does not, then it
will be necessary for the local authority to put mechanisms in place, which
will best achieve the procedures outlined by Sedley J. In addition, the
response from the chief constable, stating that he cannot or will not assist in
the process suggested, can then be used to explain the local authority's
enforced departure from the Sedley J principles.

It is suggested that all criminal convictions will be relevant for the purposes   **5.27**
of considering whether an applicant is a suitable person to be granted a
licence or not, and the only question, in relation to these, that the committee should consider is the amount of time that has elapsed since the
offence was committed. In many cases, one offence committed many years
ago should not, on its own, bar a person from driving, but a more recent
offence or a pattern of repeat offending would legitimately give cause for
concern.

PRACTICAL EFFECT OF CRIMINAL CONVICTIONS ON APPLICANTS AND LICENCE HOLDERS

Government guidelines

Many authorities have adopted policies in relation to criminal convictions.   **5.28**
In 1992, sections 51(1A) and 59(1A) were inserted into the 1976 Act.
These enabled a local authority to seek the views of the police in relation to
an applicant for a hackney carriage or private hire driver's licence. A joint
Department of Transport and Home Office circular[1] was issued to local
authorities which included (at Annex D) some suggested guidelines for
dealing with criminal convictions[2]. These provisions have now been repealed
by section 134 and Schedule 9, paragraph 34 of the Police Act 1997 with
effect from 1 April 1998[3]. This means that there is no longer any statutory
power to seek the views of the police and if the police were to respond to a
request from a local authority, they would appear to be acting ultra vires
their powers if they provided a print out of the records held on the Police
National Computer (PNC). This retrograde step seems to be due to a

Home Office oversight, as the provisions of Part V of the Police Act 1997 which will allow individuals to obtain criminal conviction certificates have not been brought into force at the same time as the repeal of the earlier provisions. At the time of writing, there is no indication as to when Part V of the Police Act 1997 will be implemented. However, the Home Secretary stated in December 1998 that the Criminal Records Bureau, which will implement the scheme, would be run by the Passport Agency. At the time, the Home Office indicated that the Bureau would take two years to set up.

1   DoT circular 2/92, HO circular 13/92.
2   The circular is reproduced at Appendix II.
3   Police Act 1997 (Commencement No 5 and Transitional Provisions) Order 1998, SI 1998/354.

5.29   Many local authorities have adopted the guidelines contained in the 1992 circular wholesale, whilst others have used them as the basis for their own modified policy. Provided such a policy is used as a policy and not as hard and fast rules, this is quite acceptable, notwithstanding the repeal of the provisions which the circular referred to. It makes it easier for applicants, who will then know what considerations will be taken into account in relation to their application. All applicants should be given a copy of the policy guidelines adopted by the local authority when they are given their application form and other information.

Statutory declarations

5.30   After the repeal of sections 51(1A) and 59(1A) of the 1976 Act local authorities must once again depend upon statutory declarations sworn by applicants. It is open to the local authority, in addition to the statutory declaration, to require an applicant to provide a copy of the reocrds held by the police, which the applicant can obtain personally under the provisions of the Data Protection Act 1984. It should therefore be the practice of local authorities to require applicants to complete a statutory declaration[1].

1   See model forms in Appendix IV.

5.31   Motoring offences do not automatically appear on the police national computer (and therefore on records obtained by the applicant under the Data Protection Act 1984[1]) and to check for these, a search of the DVLA records can be made. Although this can be useful, it should be recognised that, if a driver has received a period of disqualification, for whatever reason, the DVLA records are cleared. As a result, there are occasions when such a search could be useful, but it should not be seen as either an automatic requirement or foolproof.

1   See para 5.50.

5.32   In addition to obtaining a copy of the records held by the police via the applicant under the Data Protection Act 1984[1], many authorities still require a statutory declaration to be completed in relation to driver applications. This has the advantage of revealing (assuming that it is completed correctly) any convictions that do not appear on the police national computer. It must be remembered that, in relation to other licences (hackney carriage proprietors' and private hire operators' and vehicle licences), there has never been a power to seek the observations of the police, so a statutory declaration is essential.

1 See para 5.50.

There are, in fact, a number of such convictions, where a body other than the Crown Prosecution Service or the police (prior to 1 January 1986) brought the prosecution. These include prosecutions by the DSS, in relation to benefit fraud; by local authorities, in relation to housing benefit fraud, hackney carriage and private hire matters, other licensing matters, trading standards offences (which include matters relating to motor cars, such as safety), environmental and planning offences and, possibly, matters such as harassment of tenants; and by the Inland Revenue, in relation to tax matters and Customs and Excise (which covers both VAT offences and also smuggling matters). **5.33**

Importance of statutory declaration's truthfulness

It can be seen that these can be extremely serious offences, which any local authority would wish to know about. These should be revealed on a statutory declaration. Although there is no method of checking the accuracy of a statutory declaration, most authorities retain applications from previous years and many have a policy of checking the offences revealed on each year's statutory declaration against those of former years. If there is a discrepancy, the applicant can be asked to explain it. This may be a simple oversight or mistake, or a more serious matter of intentionally not revealing criminal convictions. In those cases, a number of authorities have a policy of passing the file through to the police, with a view to a prosecution for perjury being instigated under section 5 of the Perjury Act 1911. Alternatively, it is possible for the local authority to prosecute the person under section 57(3) of the 1976 Act, provided the local authority have asked about previous convictions on the application form. A statutory declaration would appear to satisfy this requirement. **5.34**

Section 57(3) states:

> '57–(3) If any person knowingly or recklessly makes a false statement or omits any material particular in giving information under this section, he shall be guilty of an offence.'

When the local authority can make the request to the police, the application is actually 'a request for the chief officer's observations' and the chief officer is then under a duty to 'respond to the request'. Most police authorities do so by returning a copy of a print-out from the police national computer, in relation to the applicant. In those cases, it is important that local authorities do all they can to ensure that the applicant has submitted their correct and full names: omitting a middle name or adding a middle name can, on occasions, produce a print-out which relates to a different person. Print-outs should be checked against current DVLA driving licences to ensure that the names given are the same. This, in itself, is not infallible: if a person was prepared to sit a second driving test in a different name, then that would render all such checks meaningless. Although such an action would be an **5.35** offence under a variety of provisions[1] it is possible that a person with a long and serious list of previous convictions might consider taking such action. From a local authority perspective, such an approach would be extremely difficult to detect.

1 Road Traffic Act 1988 – obtaining a driving licence whilst disqualified; Theft Act 1968 – deception contrary to s 15 or dishonestly obtaining a pecuniary advantage contrary to s 16; Theft Act 1978 – obtaining services by deception.

5.36 If the police check reveals offences which do not correspond with offences revealed on the applicant's statutory declaration, it is good practice for the local authority to interview the person to establish why other offences have been revealed. It may be that there is a mistake on the records held by the police or that they may have omitted to reveal all of their offences on the statutory declaration. Either way, it is important that the position is clarified, so that the local authority knows exactly what offences do comprise the person's record.

He's paid his price; he's done his time

5.37 An argument often put forward against the use of previous convictions is that, once a person has served their sentence, their 'debt to society' has been paid and it is wrong to keep bringing a matter up and punishing them again for the same offence, eg by revoking a licence or refusing to grant or renew, thereby depriving them of their livelihood. However, the licensing committee is not punishing them, it is protecting the public from a person who has demonstrated a propensity towards wrongdoing. Accordingly, it is both correct and, arguably, essential that convictions, both current and spent, are considered.

Chapter 6

Enforcement

INTRODUCTION

Any legal requirements are meaningless and pointless unless they are   **6.1**
enforced. If there is no sanction applied for breach of the law, the law is
worthless. This is true of hackney carriage and private hire licensing, just as
much as it is true of any other area of law.

Enforcement of hackney carriage and private hire matters falls to local
authorities. In March 1998, the Better Regulation Unit of the Cabinet
Office produced the Enforcement Concordat. This is a framework, within
which local authorities should undertake enforcement, and is reproduced at
Appendix III. If the local authority has adopted the principles contained
within the Concordat, they should have regard to them, in relation to any
enforcement action they undertake.

The duties to implement hackney carriage legislation are applied to local   **6.2**
authorities by virtue of the Town Police Clauses Act 1847, the Public Health
Act 1875, the Local Government Act 1972 and the Transport Act 1985[1].

1 See Chapter 7, para 7.2 for full details of the chain of legislation that has led to local
   authorities being in the position that they are currently in.

In relation to the Local Government (Miscellaneous Provisions) Act 1976   **6.3**
('the 1976 Act'), which applies to both hackney carriages and private hire
vehicles, this is enforced by the local authority, but only after it has been
adopted by the local authority under the provisions of section 45 of the
1976 Act.

If enforcement involves prosecution for offences, it is essential that the local   **6.4**
authority can demonstrate they can fulfil two prerequisites.

1. In all cases, they must be able to show that they have authority to bring
    proceedings. This will be a decision by the council or the committee,
    sub-committee or officer who has the delegated power to make the
    decision to prosecute in this particular case.
2. If the prosecution is for an offence committed under the 1976 Act, it
    must be demonstrated that the Act has been adopted. Again by this will
    be means of a certified copy of a resolution adopting the Act. If, since
    the adoption of the Act, reorganisation of local government has taken

place within the area, it will also be necessary to demonstrate how and why an adoption by an authority, which has since been reorganised, still applies to the new authority bringing the proceedings.

These points are often overlooked, but are fundamental to the question of a prosecution.

6.5 The point was actually considered in the case of *Kingston-upon-Hull City Council v Wilson*[1]. Although this was a case primarily concerned with other points, the question of failing to demonstrate adoption would have been fatal in other circumstances. In that case, Buxton J stated the following:

> 'A question, however, arises as to how the matter should be resolved. Towards the end of his argument Mr Neish drew our attention to the fact that it was nowhere below proved, on behalf of the local authority, that a resolution has, in fact, been passed under section 45 of the Act, applying that Act to the district of the City of Hull. Therefore, the fact at the basis of all this law that this is a controlled district was never proved. Mr Sampson [for the local authority], who has dealt with this matter very fairly on behalf of the prosecutor, accepted that it was incumbent upon the local authority to prove (no doubt as a formal matter, but it was not done) that the Act applied to the Hull district and therefore the necessary pre-condition of all these offences, that Mr Wilson [the defendant in the original prosecution] was acting in a controlled district, had not been made out.
>
> I see no answer to this objection. It may be regarded as a technical, and even unattractive, point but it is properly taken. That means that there would be no point in remitting this case to the Magistrates because even if it were remitted there would be a fatal gap in the evidence that was before them on the first occasion, which could not now be filled; as I put to Mr Sampson in argument, and he properly accepted, if Mr Wilson has been represented below, and that representative has properly waited until the end of the prosecution case and then submitted there was no case to answer because of this defect in the prosecution evidence, it would have been extremely difficult for the prosecutor to argue that he should be allowed to reopen his case.
>
> For that reason, therefore, I would not remit this case to the Magistrates.'

1   (1995) Times, 25 July, see further Chapter 13, para 13.38.

ENFORCEMENT UNDER THE TOWN POLICE CLAUSES ACT 1847

6.6 Under the hackney carriage provisions of the Town Police Clauses 1847 ('the 1847 Act'), there is no specific reference to a particular officer empowered to enforce the provisions of the Act. This means that the power to enforce lies with the local authority itself, rather than a specific statutorily designated officer, and it will be for the local authority to delegate its powers of enforcement to whichever department and officers it sees fit.

6.7 If the 1976 Act has not been adopted by the district council, the local authority is given no powers to enter or inspect records in relation to its enforcement of hackney carriage matters.

There are, however, a number of offences contained within the provisions of the 1847 Act which fall to the local authority to enforce, although the police could take action, if they wished, as they are no longer prevented from doing so. Until the passing of section 27 of the 1976 Act, the police were prevented from prosecuting by section 253 of the Public Health Act 1975, unless specifically authorised to do so by the relevant section. **6.8**

Table 6.1 gives a brief outline of the offences under the 1847 Act. **6.9**
These are all summary offences as a consequence of section 251 of the Public Health Act 1875. This was repealed for all purposes, except for the prosecution of offences under the Town Police Clauses Act 1847, by section 346 and Schedule 3, Part I of the Public Health Act 1936.

ENFORCEMENT WHERE THE LOCAL GOVERNMENT (MISCELLANEOUS PROVISIONS) ACT 1976 HAS BEEN ADOPTED

Under the 1976 Act, there are a number of offences relating to both hackney carriages and private hire vehicles. Again, enforcement falls to the local authority, but the 1976 Act introduces the concept of an authorised officer. These is defined in section 80 as: **6.10**

> '"authorised officer" means any officer of a district council authorised in writing by the council for the purposes of this Part of this Act;'

There is also a specific offence of obstruction of authorised officers contained in section 73 of the 1976 Act:

> '73–(1) Any person who—
>
> (a) wilfully obstructs an authorised officer or constable acting in pursuance of this Part of this Act or the Act of 1847; or
>
> (b) without reasonable excuse fails to comply with any requirement properly made to him by such officer or constable under this Part of this Act; or
>
> (c) without reasonable cause fails to give such an officer or constable so acting any other assistance or information which he may reasonably require of such person for the purpose of the performance of his functions under this Part of this Act or the Act of 1847;
>
> shall be guilty of an offence.
>
> (2) If any person, in giving any such information as is mentioned in the preceding subsection, makes any statement which he knows to be false, he shall be guilty of an offence.'

It can be seen that an authorised officer is a person appointed by the district council to act on their behalf, in relation to enforcement activities under the 1976 and 1847 Acts. It will be necessary for such an officer to demonstrate his authorisation, if required, and that authorisation must be in writing to satisfy the requirements of section 80. **6.11**
Table 6.2 outlines the hackney carriage offences under the 1976 Act and Tables 6.3 and 6.4 outline the private hire offences. Again, these are all summary offences by virtue of either section 76:

TABLE 6.1
ENFORCEMENT TABLE – TOWN POLICE CLAUSES ACT 1847

Section	Offence	Enforcement – Local Authority/Police	Maximum Penalty
40	Giving false information on application for hackney carriage proprietor's licence	Local authority/Police	Level 1
44	Failure to notify change of address of hackney carriage proprietor	Local authority/Police	Level 1
45	Plying for hire without a hackney carriage proprietor's licence	Local authority/Police	Level 4
47	Driving a hackney carriage without a hackney carriage driver's licence	Local authority/Police	Level 3
47	Lending or parting with a hackney carriage driver's licence	Local authority/Police	Level 3
47	Hackney carriage proprietor employing unlicensed driver	Local authority/Police	Level 3
48	Failure by hackney carriage proprietor to hold hackney carriage driver's licence	Local authority/Police	Level 1
48	Failure by hackney carriage proprietor to produce hackney carriage driver's licence	Magistrates' Court	Level 1
52	Failure to display hackney carriage plate	Local authority/Police	Level 1
53	Refusal to take a fare	Local authority/Police	Level 2
54	Charging more than the agreed fare	Local authority/Police	Level 1
55	Obtaining more than the legal fare	Local authority/Police	Level 3 and 1 month imprisonment until the excess is refunded
56	Travelling less than the lawful distance for an agreed fare	Local authority/Police	Level 1
57	Failing to wait after a deposit to wait has been paid	Local authority/Police	Level 1
58	Charging more than the legal fare	Local authority/Police	Level 3
59	Carrying other person than the hirer without consent	Local authority/Police	Level 1
60	Driving a hackney carriage without proprietors consent	Local authority/Police	Level 1
60	Person allowing another to drive a hackney carriage without proprietors consent	Local authority/Police	Level 1
61	Drunken driving of hackney carriage	Local authority/Police	Level 1
61	Wanton or furious driving or wilful misconduct leading to injury or danger	Local authority/Police	Level 1
62	Driver leaving hackney carriage unattended	Police	Level 1
64	Hackney carriage driver obstructing other hackney carriages	Local authority/Police	Level 1

Note The penalty for breach of byelaws made under section 68 of this Act or section 6 of the Town Police Clauses Act 1889 is a fine not exceeding level 2 by virtue of section 183 of the Public Health Act 1875.

TABLE 6.2
ENFORCEMENT TABLE – HACKNEY CARRIAGE PROVISIONS – LOCAL GOVERNMENT (MISCELLANEOUS PROVISIONS) ACT 1976

Section	Offence	Enforcement – Local Authority/Police	Maximum Penalty
49	Failure to notify transfer of hackney carriage proprietor's licence	Local authority/Police	Level 3 (by virtue of section 76)
50(1)	Failure to present hackney carriage for inspection as required	Local authority/Police	Level 3 (by virtue of section 76)
50(2)	Failure to inform Local Authority where hackneycarriage is stored if requested	Local authority/Police	Level 3 (by virtue of section 76)
50(3)	Failure to report an accident to Local Authority	Local authority/Police	Level 3 (by virtue of section 76)
50(4)	Failure to produce hackney carriage proprietor's licence and insurance certificate	Local authority/Police	Level 3 (by virtue of section 76)
53(3)	Failure to produce hackney carriage driver's licence	Local authority/Police	Level 3 (by virtue of section 76)
57	Making false statement or withholding information to obtain hackney carriage driver's licence	Local authority/Police	Level 3 (by virtue of section 76)
58(2)	Failure to return plate after notice given after expiry, revocation or suspension of hackney carriage proprietor's licence	Local authority/Police	Level 3 plus daily fine of £10
61(2)	Failure to surrender drivers licence after suspension, revocation or refusal to renew	Local authority/Police	Level 3 (by virtue of section 76)
64	Permitting any vehicle other than hackney carriage to wait on a hackney carriage stand	Local authority/Police	Level 3 (by virtue of section 76)
66	Charging more than the meter fare for a journey ending outside the district, without prior agreement	Local authority/Police	Level 3 (by virtue of section 76)
67	Charging more than the meter fare when hackney carriage used as private hire vehicle	Local authority/Police	Level 3 (by virtue of section 76)
69	Unnecessarily prolonging a journey	Local authority/Police	Level 3 (by virtue of section 76)
71	Interfering with a taximeter	Local authority/Police	Level 3 (by virtue of section 76)
73(1)(*a*)	Obstruction of authorised officer or constable	Local authority/Police	Level 3 (by virtue of section 76)
73(1)(*b*)	Failure to comply with requirement of authorised officer or constable	Local authority/Police	Level 3 (by virtue of section 76)
73(1)(*c*)	Failure to give information or assistance to authorised officer or constable	Local authority/Police	Level 3 (by virtue of section 76)

TABLE 6.3
ENFORCEMENT TABLE – PRIVATE HIRE PROVISIONS – LOCAL
GOVERNMENT (MISCELLANEOUS PROVISIONS) ACT 1976

Section	Offence	Enforcement – Local Authority/Police	Maximum Penalty
46(1)(*a*)	Using an unlicensed private hire vehicle	Local authority/Police	Level 3 (by virtue of section 76)
46(1)(*b*)	Driving a private hire vehicle without a private hire drivers licence	Local authority/Police	Level 3 (by virtue of section 76)
46(1)(*c*)	Proprietor of a private hire vehicle using an unlicensed driver	Local authority/Police	Level 3 (by virtue of section 76)
46(1)(*d*)	Operating a private hire vehicle without a private hire operator's licence	Local authority/Police	Level 3 (by virtue of section 76)
46(1)(*e*)	Operating a vehicle as a private hire vehicle when the vehicle is not licensed as a private hire vehicle	Local authority/Police	Level 3 (by virtue of section 76)
46(1)(*e*)	Operating a private hire vehicle when the driver is not licensed as a private hire driver	Local authority/Police	Level 3 (by virtue of section 76)
48(6)	Failure to display private hire vehicle plate	Local authority/Police	Level 3 (by virtue of section 76)
49	Failure to notify transfer of private hire vehicle licence	Local authority/Police	Level 3 (by virtue of section 76)
50(1)	Failure to present private hire vehicle for inspection as required	Local authority/Police	Level 3 (by virtue of section 76)
50(2)	Failure to inform local authority where private hire vehicle is stored if requested	Local authority/Police	Level 3 (by virtue of section 76)
50(3)	Failure to report an accident to local authority	Local authority/Police	Level 3 (by virtue of section 76)
50(4)	Failure to produce private hire vehicle licence and insurance certificate	Local authority/Police	Level 3 (by virtue of section 76)
53(3)	Failure to produce private hire driver's licence	Local authority/Police	Level 3 (by virtue of section 76)
54(2)	Failure to wear private hire driver's badge	Local authority/Police	Level 3 (by virtue of section 76)
56(2)	Failure by private hire operator to keep records of bookings	Local authority/Police	Level 3 (by virtue of section 76)
56(3)	Failure by private hire operator to keep records of private hire vehicles operated by him	Local authority/Police	Level 3 (by virtue of section 76)

TABLE 6.3 *cont.*

Section	Offence	Enforcement – Local Authority/Police	Maximum Penalty
56(4)	Failure to produce private hire operator's licence on request	Local authority/Police	Level 3 (by virtue of section 76)
57	Making false statement or withholding information to obtain private hire drivers or operator's licence	Local authority/Police	Level 3 (by virtue of section 76)
58(2)	Failure to return plate after notice given after expiry, revocation or suspension of private hire vehicle licence	Local authority/Police	Level 3 plus daily fine of £10
61(2)	Failure to surrender drivers licence after suspension, revocation or refusal to renew	Local authority/Police	Level 3 (by virtue of section 76)
67	Charging more than the meter fare when hackney carriage used as private hire vehicle	Local authority/Police	Level 3 (by virtue of section 76)
69	Unnecessarily prolonging a journey	Local authority/Police	Level 3 (by virtue of section 76)
71	Interfering with a taximeter	Local authority/Police	Level 3 (by virtue of section 76)
73(1)(*a*)	Obstruction of authorised officer or constable	Local authority/Police	Level 3 (by virtue of section 76)
73(1)(*b*)	Failure to comply with requirement of authorised officer or constable	Local authority/Police	Level 3 (by virtue of section 76)
73(1)(*c*)	Failure to give information or assistance to authorised officer or constable	Local authority/Police	Level 3 (by virtue of section 76)

TABLE 6.4
ENFORCEMENT TABLE – PRIVATE HIRE PROVISIONS – TRANSPORT ACT 1980

Section	Offence	Enforcement – Local Authority/Police	Maximum Penalty
64(2)(*a*)	Driving a private hire vehicle with a roof sign which contravenes section 64(1)	Local authority/Police	Level 3
64(2)(*b*)	Causing or permitting a private hire vehicle to be driven with a roof sign which contravenes section 64(1)	Local authority/Police	Level 3

'Penalties

76 Any person who commits an offence against any of the provisions of this Part of this Act in respect of which no penalty is expressly provided shall be liable on summary conviction to a fine not exceeding [level 3 on the standard scale].'

or the relevant section which defines the offence.

PROSECUTING UNDER BYELAWS

6.12 All pre-1974 local authorities were abolished on 21 March 1974 and new authorities came into existence on 1 April 1974. Many local authorities use hackney carriage byelaws, which were made before 31 March 1974, by local authorities whose area is now part of the 'new' authority.

Pre-1974 byelaws remain in force for the 'new' authorities by virtue of article 9(3) of the Local Authorities Etc (Miscellaneous Provisions) Order 1974 and section 238 of the Local Government Act 1972 and prosecution is possible under these provisions. It will again be for the local authority to demonstrate its ability to prosecute in any criminal proceedings brought for contravention of those byelaws.

6.13 The case of *Boddington v British Transport Police*[1] should be noted in relation to prosecution for breach of byelaws. In this case, the House of Lords decided that it was possible for a defendant, being prosecuted for breach of byelaws, to raise the validity of the byelaws, particularly whether they were intra vires (within the powers) the byelaw-making power.

1 [1998] 2 All ER 203, HL.

CAUTIONS

6.14 A number of authorities use formal cautions as a method of dealing with less serious cases[1]. Briefly, a formal caution is not a conviction, but can be cited before a court on a subsequent conviction, but it should be kept separate from any list of previous convictions. Two preconditions are required before a formal caution can be offered:

- there has to be sufficient evidence to have lead to a prosecution; and
- the offender must admit his guilt.

In addition, the offender must agree to accept a formal caution. There is currently no maximum length of time that a formal caution remains on file, but police forces tend to use a minimum period of five years from the date the formal caution was administered.

1 Guidance on the use of formal cautions is contained in Home Office circulars 1990/59 and 1994/18.

DEFENCES

Apart from technical defences (eg failure to demonstrate adoption of the **6.15** 1976 Act) there are some points worth mentioning here, in relation to prosecution for non-compliance with certain provisions.

In relation to any offence under section 46 of the 1976 Act, it is necessary to show 'knowledge' on the part of the defendant. Quite why this is the case is unclear, as most other offences in relation to hackney carriage and private hire licensing are strict liability offences. However, that is the situation.

The case of *Reading Borough Council v Ahmad*[1] reinforces this point. In this **6.16** case, a prosecution was brought for driving a private hire vehicle without holding a private hire driver's licence. The High Court held that the offence contained in sections 46(1)(*b*) and 46(2) of the 1976 Act, requires knowledge, on the part of the person driving without a driver's licence, that he was in a controlled district (that is, a district which has adopted the provisions of the 1976 Act), was driving a licensed private hire vehicle and did not hold a private hire vehicle driver's licence. It is immaterial whether or not money changed hands at the time of the offence or, indeed, whether any passengers had been carried at the time. The ruling in *Benson v Boyce*[2] makes it clear that a private hire vehicle is always a private hire vehicle.

1 (1998) Times, 4 December, QBD.
2 [1997] RTR 226.

Another case relating to 'knowledge' is that of *Latif v Middlesbrough Borough* **6.17** *Council*[1], where a private hire operator was prosecuted under section 46(1)(*e*) of the 1976 Act for operating a vehicle when the driver did not hold a private hire driver's licence. His conviction was quashed, as he had provided the driver with the money to obtain a licence and had not turned a blind eye to the situation.

1 [1997] COD 486. See Chapter 12, para 12.42.

A very different defence was used successfully in the case of *Eden District* **6.18** *Council v Braid*[1]. In this case, a defence of duress was pleaded against a charge of carrying more passengers than the byelaw allowed. The situation arose at the Appleby Horse Fair, when a booking was made for a customer. When the customer emerged from the premises, he got into the front seat of the hackney carriage and, a few moments later, four more adults, one teenager and four children also emerged from the premises and got into the hackney carriage. The carriage was licensed to carry six people, including the driver, but was now carrying 11. The driver refused to drive until some of them got out, but they refused to leave the vehicle and said that the driver would have to remove them physically, if he wanted them out. The driver was aware that they were smelling of drink and he feared physical harm to himself and damage to his vehicle. Accordingly, he drove them to where they wanted to go. This had been observed by an enforcement officer from the local authority, although, when he approached the driver and passengers at the end of the journey, there was a great potential for violence and the enforcement officer retreated. The magistrates found that a plea of duress had been established and acquitted the driver. The local authority appealed, by way of case stated, on the grounds: first, that duress was not available for an offence of strict liability and, secondly, whether it was open to the magistrates to find that the defence had been made out on the facts.

In relation to the first question, Bingham LCJ giving judgment said:

'In challenging the justices' decision on behalf of the local authority Mr Dutchman-Smith first submits in his skeleton argument that a defence of duress is not available where the alleged offence is one of strict liability. That is a proposition which he has not sought to pursue in argument and for which no authority is cited. It appears to me to run counter to the clear understanding of the defence of duress as described, for example, in Smith and Hogan "Criminal Law" (8th edition) 238 and 240; Blackstone's Criminal Practice 1998 at paras. A3.20 and A3.23; and Archbold at s 17–119. It would also seem to me to be wrong in principle. Even in an offence of strict liability there must be an intention to do the act which the law proscribes. If the only reason why the defendant does the act which the law proscribes is because he is subjected to a threat of serious personal injury which he reasonably thinks will be carried out in circumstances where a reasonable person of ordinary firmness with the same apprehension might act in the same way, I can for my part see no reason why the defence of duress should not be available.'

On the second point his judgment was as follows:

'The appellant's more substantial ground is an argument that there was no evidence upon which a reasonable bench could have concluded that on the facts the defence of duress was tenable. In making that submission Mr Dutchman-Smith relies in particular on the acceptance by the respondent that he could have got out of the vehicle, gone into the club and rung the police, and could have dialled 999 and could have left the car. Those are, of course, matters which the justices had fully in mind. It was, however, very much a matter for them as to what the respondent could or should reasonably have done in the circumstances. Our attention has been drawn to *R v Hudson and Taylor* [1971] 2 QB 202, [1971] 2 All ER 244 in which a judgment prepared by Widgery LJ was read by Parker LCJ. At page 207G the court said:

"In the opinion of this court it is always open to the Crown to prove that the accused failed to avail himself of some opportunity which was reasonably open to him to render the threat ineffective, and that upon this being established the threat in question can no longer be relied upon by the defence. In deciding whether such an opportunity was reasonably open to the accused the jury should have regard to his age and circumstances, and to any risks to him which may be involved in the course of action relied upon."

The justices plainly had this matter in mind and they made findings that no other viable options were available to the respondent at the time; and that he had every reason to believe that he would be set upon and suffer serious physical injury as a result of the gypsies' threat if he did not do as they asked. Plainly the justices were not of the opinion that the respondent could, without fear of being attacked, have simply left the vehicle with the passengers in it and gone into the club.

Reliance is also placed by the appellant on the statement by the respondent that he feared damage being caused to his car. That, counsel submits, does not support a plea of duress. It is, however, to be noted that the respondent quite plainly feared injury to himself as well as damage to his vehicle, and a threat of injury to himself certainly does support a plea of duress, even if a threat of damage to the vehicle does not.

In my judgment, whether or not I would myself have reached the same decision as the justices, this is not an appeal which should be allowed. The justices were correctly advised in law and there is no hint in the case that they misapplied the law in any way. They made findings of fact which were in my judgment open to them. These findings may to some extent be regarded as surprising, but one should be very slow to think that the Divisional Court sitting in London is better placed than Appleby Justices to understand the factual situation prevailing in Kirkby Stephen during the Appleby Horse Fair. It is true that this is a defence which can very rarely succeed and its bounds should not be widened. It is not, however, irrelevant in my judgment that the byelaw in question here was one made for the safety of persons to be carried in this taxi; that the very persons to be carried were those who were coercing the respondent to act as he did; and that the offence which he committed was one for which the maximum penalty was £50. It would not of course be the wish of this court in any way to encourage breaches of any law or byelaw, but it is perhaps right to point out that the criminal act which the respondent performed, even in the absence of duress, was one ranking relatively low in any scale of criminal heinousness. In my judgment the justices reached a sustainable conclusion. I would dismiss this appeal.'

1 [1998] COD 259.

NON-CRIMINAL ENFORCEMENT

Enforcement of the hackney carriage and private hire provisions can also be effected by means of action taken against the licence held by the person who has transgressed. That transgression may be evidenced by a criminal conviction, but it need not be[1].   **6.19**

1 For example, the cases of *R v Maidstone Crown Court, ex p Olson* [1992] COD 496 (see Chapter 10, para 10.70) and *McCool v Rushcliffe Borough Council* [1998] 3 All ER 889, QBD (see Chapter 10, para 10.72) clearly demonstrates that action can be taken against a licence where no criminal conviction was ultimately obtained.

Under section 50 of the 1847 Act, the council can revoke a hackney carriage proprietors' or hackney carriage driver's licence, if the licence holder has been convicted of two offences under the 1847 Act.   **6.20**

Under the 1976 Act, suspension or revocation of hackney carriage or private hire vehicle licences (proprietors, in the case of hackney carriage) is possible under section 60:   **6.21**

'Suspension and revocation of vehicle licences

60–(1) Notwithstanding anything in the Act of 1847 or in this Part of this Act, a district council may suspend or revoke, or (on application therefor under section 40 of the Act of 1847 or section 48 of this Act, as the case may be) refuse to renew a vehicle licence on any of the following grounds—
(*a*) that the hackney carriage or private hire vehicle is unfit for use as a hackney carriage or private hire vehicle;
(*b*) any offence under, or non-compliance with, the provisions of the Act of 1847 or of this Part of this Act by the operator or driver; or
(*c*) any other reasonable cause.

(2) Where a district council suspend, revoke or refuse to renew any licence under this section they shall give to the proprietor of the vehicle notice of

the grounds on which the licence has been suspended or revoked or on which they have refused to renew the licence within fourteen days of such suspension, revocation or refusal.

(3) Any proprietor aggrieved by a decision of a district council under this section may appeal to a magistrates' court.'

6.22   Similar sanctions are available against drivers' licences (for both hackney carriages and private hire vehicles) under the provisions of section 61 of the 1976 Act:

'Suspension and revocation of drivers' licences

61–(1) Notwithstanding anything in the Act of 1847 or in this Part of this Act, a district council may suspend or revoke or (on application therefor under section 46 of the Act of 1847 or section 51 of this Act, as the case may be) refuse to renew the licence of a driver of a hackney carriage or a private hire vehicle on any of the following grounds—
(*a*)   that he has since the grant of the licence—
  (i)   been convicted of an offence involving dishonesty, indecency or violence; or
  (ii) been convicted of an offence under or has failed to comply with the provisions of the Act of 1847 or of this Part of this Act; or

(*b*)   any other reasonable cause.

(2)
(*a*)   Where a district council suspend, revoke or refuse to renew any licence under this section they shall give to the driver notice of the grounds on which the licence has been suspended or revoked or on which they have refused to renew such licence within fourteen days of such suspension, revocation or refusal and the driver shall on demand return to the district council the driver's badge issued to him in accordance with section 54 of this Act.
(*b*)   If any person without reasonable excuse contravenes the provisions of this section he shall be guilty of an offence and liable on summary conviction to a fine not exceeding [level 1 on the standard scale].

(3) Any driver aggrieved by a decision of a district council under this section may appeal to a magistrates' court.'

6.23   Finally, in relation to private hire operators' licences only, section 62 of the 1976 Act allows suspension and revocation:

'Suspension and revocation of operators' licences

62–(1) Notwithstanding anything in this Part of this Act a district council may suspend or revoke, or (on application therefor under section 55 of this Act) refuse to renew an operator's licence on any of the following grounds—
(*a*)   any offence under, or non-compliance with, the provisions of this Part of this Act;
(*b*)   any conduct on the part of the operator which appears to the district council to render him unfit to hold an operator's licence;
(*c*)   any material change since the licence was granted in any of the circumstances of the operator on the basis of which the licence was granted; or
(*d*)   any other reasonable cause.

(2) Where a district council suspend, revoke or refuse to renew any licence

under this section they shall give to the operator notice of the grounds on which the licence has been suspended or revoked or on which they have refused to renew such licence within fourteen days of such suspension, revocation or refusal.

(3) Any operator aggrieved by a decision of a district council under this section may appeal to a magistrates' court.'

The question of suspension of any licence raises an interesting point. Such **6.24** action is often used by local authorities as a method of punishing a licence holder for a transgression, which is viewed as being serious, but not serious enough to warrant revocation of the licence. The problem arises in relation to the rationale behind a suspension.

In relation to vehicle licences (section 60), suspension certainly makes sense **6.25** when the vehicle is unsatisfactory or dangerous for some reason. Suspending the vehicle licence removes the danger to the public until the problem is rectified.

However, in relation to private hire operators' licences (where the power is **6.26** contained in section 62) and both hackney carriage and private hire drivers' licences (section 61), the difficulty arises in relation to the fitness and propriety of the licence holder.

In all these cases, the local authority cannot grant (or renew) a licence, **6.27** unless they are satisfied that the applicant is a 'fit and proper person' to hold the licence[1].

The power contained in sections 61 and 62 of the 1976 Act to suspend, revoke or refuse to renew must therefore, be based upon that concept of fitness and propriety, as any breach, which would lead to action being taken under that section must ultimately affect the fitness of the applicant to hold the licence.

If that is the case, the person is either fit and proper to hold a licence or they are not, depending upon the situation in question and any policy guidelines, in relation to criminal offences, that the local authority may have adopted.

1 See the 1976 Act: s 55 in relation to operators, and ss 51–59 in relation to drivers.

The concept of a suspension is, therefore, difficult to sustain, as the argu- **6.28** ment appears to run that a period of inactivity as a licensed private hire operator, driver or hackney carriage driver will enable a person to regain their fitness and propriety and that such a period will enable them to effectively to purge their wrongdoings.

Whilst it is fully accepted that the impact of wrongdoing (whether criminal or otherwise) fades over time – that, in itself, is the entire rationale behind the Rehabilitation of Offenders Act 1974 – it is difficult to see how a transgression which is so serious that the local authority decide to take away a person's livelihood, can be purged in such a short time as to make a suspension a reasonable penalty. Notwithstanding these reservations, suspension of a licence is used by a great many authorities across England and Wales as a means of re-enforcing their enforcement powers.

CONCLUSIONS

6.29 It was stated at the commencement of this chapter that it is only through enforcement that any laws have effect and this is true of hackney carriage and private hire legislation, just as much as it is of other areas. Vigorous enforcement of hackney carriage and private hire provisions is essential if the ultimate aim of the licensing regime, to protect the travelling public, is to be achieved. There is no doubt that enforcement is expensive in terms of both the staff and legal costs involved, but, unless it is undertaken, the licensing of hackney carriages and private hire vehicles becomes a merely administrative exercise. That is of benefit to no one, except unscrupulous persons who do not comply with the requirements.

6.30 Licensees who pay licence fees are entitled to expect an enforcement regime which aims, not only to protect the public, but also to protect themselves from those who do not comply with the requirements. Indeed, this is one of the justifications for levying a fee for the grant of licences. As a result, those authorities without effective enforcement policies and procedures are, not only letting down their population and anyone who visits their district, but also letting down the vast majority of people involved in the hackney carriage and private hire trades who abide by the rules and work hard to provide a good, safe and reliable service to the public.

Chapter 7

Hackney carriages: an introduction

LEGISLATION

The Town Police Clauses Act 1847

Hackney carriages are an extremely old form of public transport and are   **7.1**
governed primarily by the provisions of the Town Police Clauses Act 1847
('the 1847 Act').

'Clauses Acts' were popular in the last century and were intended as a set
of acceptable sections which could be adopted and incorporated into local
Acts of Parliament promoted by local authorities.

The Town Police Clauses Act 1847 no longer needs specific adoption by   **7.2**
a local authority and stands as a complete Act in its own right, in relation
to hackney carriages. It was incorporated (together with the Town Police
Clauses Act 1889) into the Public Health Act 1875 by section 171 of the
1875 Act and then applied to the whole of England and Wales by section
15 of the Transport Act 1985. If any local authority which had adopted
the provisions of the 1847 Act had powers which exempted them from the
hackney carriage provisions within the 1847 Act, those powers were also
repealed by section 15 of the Transport Act 1985.

The net effect of this is that the 1847 Act applies throughout England and
Wales and provides the bed-rock of the legislation relating to hackney
carriages.

This Act has been modified and amended over the last one hundred and   **7.3**
fifty years and it appears that, in the absence of new 'taxi' legislation, it will
continue to be amended as new ideas emerge and new problems need to be
solved.

A hackney carriage is a vehicle licensed by the district council in the area in   **7.4**
which it undertakes its business, is driven by a person who holds a hackney
carriage driver's licence granted by the same local authority and which falls
within the definition contained in section 38 of the 1847 Act. To fall within
this definition, the vehicle must seat fewer than nine passengers, but other
than that, it can be of any type or description. In 1847, the internal combustion engine had not been invented and, accordingly, it is not a
requirement that a hackney carriage is powered by an internal combustion

81

engine. The licensing regime can apply to horse-drawn vehicles and to human-propelled vehicles just as effectively.

7.5   A hackney carriage can ply for hire and also wait at a hackney carriage stand (generally referred to as a taxi rank).

7.6   Once a hackney carriage has either been hailed or approached on a stand, the driver must take the person to the destination requested, provided it is within the 'prescribed distance' (which is defined as the area of the district council in question)[1].

1 See the Town Police Clauses Act 1847, s 53.

7.7   In exchange for carrying that passenger or passengers, the driver is entitled to charge a fare which may be regulated by the local authority. If it is regulated, then the driver cannot charge more than the fare, but can charge less; if the local authority do not set the fares, then the fare must be reasonable.

7.8   The district council can impose conditions upon the grant of a hackney carriage proprietor's licence and can make byelaws to control the conduct of both the proprietors and the drivers.

7.9   The vehicles themselves must be inspected by the local authority, who must be satisfied that they are mechanically sound and comply with any particular conditions before the proprietor's licence can be granted. Records of licences granted must be kept by the local authority.

The 1847 Act contains considerably more provisions than those mentioned here but they will be considered in detail in the subsequent chapters which relate to hackney carriage vehicles and hackney carriage drivers.

The Town Police Clauses Act 1889

7.10   The Town Police Clauses Act 1889 allows proprietors' and drivers' licences to be granted for less than a year (section 5) and extends the range of topics which can be covered by byelaws made by the local authority (section 6).

The Local Government (Miscellaneous Provisions) Act 1976

7.11   The Local Government (Miscellaneous Provisions) Act 1976 ('the 1976 Act') has considerable impact on hackney carriages, notwithstanding its overriding aim being to regulate private hire vehicles. This includes:

- power to attach conditions to hackney carriage proprietors' licences;
- transfer of hackney carriages;
- testing of hackney carriage vehicles;
- various provisions relating to drivers' licences, badges etc;
- powers for suspension and revocation of drivers and vehicle licences; and

• has considerable impact on the provision of hackney carriage stands.

In addition, section 65 of the 1976 Act provides an alternative method of fixing fares to that contained within the byelaws procedure and also includes provisions, whereby obstruction of authorised officers is an offence (section 73).

7.12 The 1976 Act is adoptive and it is for local authorities to adopt its provisions if they wish. Such adoption is wholesale: that is to say the district council must adopt the whole of Part II of the 1976 Act and cannot pick specific sections that they wish to adopt.

7.13 The process of adoption is contained in section 45 of the 1976 Act and the process is straightforward. However, cases in relation to sex establishment licensing under the adoptive provisions of the Local Government (Miscellaneous Provisions) Act 1982 demonstrate that it is imperative that the procedures laid down in the statute are followed exactly, and there is no room for variation or flexibility[1].

1   This is illustrated by cases such as *R v Birmingham City Council, ex p Quietlynn Ltd* (1985) 83 LGR 461 and *R v Swansea City Council* (1983) Times, 19 October.

7.14 Other primary legislation also affecting hackney carriages includes the Transport Acts of 1981 and 1985 and the Disability Discrimination Act 1995.

The Transport Act 1985

7.15 After 1976, the next significant impact on hackney carriage licensing was the Transport Act 1985. This introduced the idea of hackney carriages being hired to more than one person at a time, with each person paying separate fares. The hire of the carriage could be either immediately or by booking in advance and could also be used to provide local services under a restricted Public Service Vehicle operator's licence. As already seen, it extended the impact of the 1847 Act to the whole of England and Wales.

7.16 However, by far and away the most important alteration resulting from the introduction of Transport Act 1985 was the abolition of the ability of the district council to set a maximum number of licences which they would grant for hackney carriage proprietors or vehicles. After 6 January 1986, the district council could only limit the numbers of hackney carriage proprietors' licences that they would grant, if they were satisfied that, at that time, 'there is no significant demand for the services of hackney carriages (within the area to which the licence would apply), which is unmet'. The effect of this was that a refusal to grant a hackney carriage proprietor's licence, on the grounds of the numbers of hackney carriages within the area, could only be satisfied if the district council could demonstrate that there was no significant demand which remained unmet for hackney carriage services. This has led to a new industry which conducts surveys for local authorities so as to support these decisions[1].

1   This area is looked at in further detail in Chapter 8, para 8.99ff.

The Disability Discrimination Act 1995

7.17   The Disability Discrimination Act 1995 will also fundamentally affect hackney carriages. Regulations may be passed under section 32, which will require vehicles to be accessible for persons in wheelchairs. Licences for hackney carriages must not be granted to a vehicle which is not accessible for such people (sections 32 and 34). Local authorities will be able, in certain circumstances, to apply for exemption from this requirement under section 35, but, if such exemption is granted, the Secretary of State can still impose 'swivel seat regulations' to enable some sections of the travelling public to use hackney carriages.

7.18   The impact of these regulations and requirements will be enormous, although it may be felt more in areas where there is currently no provision of disabled-accessible hackney carriages.

7.19   At the time of writing, there is still no indication from the government as to when the draft regulations concerning wheelchair accessibility will be published for consultation, when implementation is proposed. Indeed it remains to be seen whether the regulations are, in fact, ever introduced.

BYELAWS

7.20   Finally, consideration must be given to byelaws. These can be made under either section 68 of the 1847 Act or section 6 of the Town Police Clauses Act 1889. They require the approval of the Home Secretary, but the Home Office is reluctant to approve any byelaws which depart from the model byelaws which they provide.

The model byelaws, which were revised in 1974, are reproduced at Appendix II as an annex to Department of Transport Circular 8/86 and the procedure for making byelaws is contained in section 236 of the Local Government Act 1972[1].

1   See *Butterworths Local Government Law*.

Chapter 8

Hackney carriage vehicles: definition and demand

WHAT IS A HACKNEY CARRIAGE?

The definition of a hackney carriage is contained in section 38 of the Town Police Clauses Act 1847 ('the 1847 Act'): **8.1**

> **'What vehicles to be deemed hackney carriages**
>
> **38** Every wheeled carriage, whatever may be its form or construction, used in standing or plying for hire in any street within the prescribed distance, and every carriage standing upon any street within the prescribed distance, having thereon any numbered plate required by this or the special Act to be fixed upon a hackney carriage, or having thereon any plate resembling or intended to resemble any such plate as aforesaid, shall be deemed to be a hackney carriage within the meaning of this Act; and in all proceedings at law or otherwise the term "hackney carriage" shall be sufficient to describe any such carriage: Provided always, that no stage coach used for the purpose of standing or plying for passengers to be carried for hire at separate fares, and duly licensed for that purpose, and having thereon the proper numbered plates required by law to be placed on such stage coaches, shall be deemed to be a hackney carriage within the meaning of this Act.'

It is interesting to note that, in all subsequent acts, the above definition is used for a hackney carriage[1] and, even where the legislation has started to use the word 'taxi', it is made clear that a 'taxi' means a hackney carriage, eg:

- section 64(3) of the Transport Act 1980;
- section 13(3) of the Transport Act 1985; and
- section 32(5) of the Disability Discrimination Act 1995.

1 See the Local Government (Miscellaneous Provisions) Act 1976, s 80.

The maximum number of passengers that can be carried in a vehicle for it to be capable of being licensed as a hackney carriage is eight. Any vehicle which carries more than eight will be classified as a Public Service Vehicle (PSV) under the Public Passenger Vehicles Act 1981. **8.2**

STATUS OF A HACKNEY CARRIAGE

Hawkins v Edwards

8.3   In the case of *Hawkins v Edwards*[1], the question of whether a hackney carriage was always a hackney carriage was considered. Mr Hawkins held a hackney carriage proprietor's licence and was prosecuted for failing to display the plate correctly. He argued that, at the time, the vehicle was not acting as a hackney carriage, was therefore not a hackney carriage and, therefore, he did not need to display the plate. The matter was considered in the High Court and Alverstone LCJ gave the judgment of the court (supported by Lawrance J). He stated (at 172):

> 'The point raised in this case is one of some nicety, and requires consideration. I confess I was at first struck with the hardship which, it was said, might arise through holding that a person could not employ his carriage, if it was licensed as a hackney carriage, in any other way than as a hackney carriage. But upon consideration I think the grievance is one which we need not take into account. The general purview of the by-law is to protect the public: the object is to provide for a proper supervision of carriages which are licensed to stand or ply for hire as hackney carriages. I think that if a man elects to have the privilege of keeping a carriage which is licensed, he elects to devote that carriage to the services indicated in the by-law. The words of the by-law, "while such carriage may stand, ply, or be driven for hire", in my view, are merely meant to indicate a period during which the hackney carriage is a thing which must have its number shewn, and we ought not to accede to the argument of the appellant's counsel that the by-law only applies whilst the carriage is actually standing, plying, or being driven for hire. I think the right view is that the carriage is licensed for a period, and if used during that period in standing or plying for hire the number must be shewn for the whole period. The language of s 38 of the Town Police Clauses Act 1847, means, I think, that every wheeled carriage which is in fact from time to time used in standing or plying for hire is to be deemed to be a hackney carriage for the whole period during which it is so from time to time used, and the language of the section does not limit the period to the time during which the carriage is in fact used for standing or plying for hire in a street.'

1   [1901] 2 KB 169.

Yates v Gates

8.4   The question of the status of a hackney carriage was reconsidered by the High Court in the case of *Yates v Gates*[1]. In fact, this was a second question in relation to the case, the primary point concerning the necessity to obtain positive consent from a passenger hiring a hackney carriage to the carrying of another person[2].

1   [1970] 1 All ER 754, QBD.
2   See Chapter 10, para 10.53.

8.5   However, the question as to whether a hackney carriage was always a hackney carriage, and therefore whether anyone driving a vehicle, which was licensed as a hackney carriage, needed a hackney carriage driver's licence, irrespective of whether or not the vehicle was working at the time, was raised. Parker LCJ gave the judgment of the court and he stated (at 756B):

> 'The second information charged the respondent that on the same day he drove a hackney carriage which was duly licensed to ply for hire not having obtained a licence to act as such driver. The justices took the view that since on the occasion in question the sign "For Hire" was not illuminated, and in the circumstances that the respondent was not driving the vehicle for hire, therefore did not require a licence, and dismissed the information. In regard to that, s 46 of the Act [of 1847] in question provides:
>
> > "No person shall act as driver of any hackney carriage licensed in pursuance of this or the special Act to ply for hire . . .without first obtaining a licence from the commissioners. . . ."
>
> Section 47 provides the penalty: "If any person acts as such driver as aforesaid without having obtained such licence . . ." he shall be guilty of an offence.
>
> Pausing there, it is undoubtedly true that the respondent did not have the necessary licence, and that the vehicle in question was itself licensed to ply for hire. The justices, however, took the view that unless the vehicle was plying for hire it would not be a hackney carriage the driver of which would require a licence. That of course envisages that a vehicle licensed as a hackney carriage as defined in s 38 of the 1847 Act must change its character from moment to moment; when it is not plying for hire it is not a hackney carriage, and when it is plying for hire it is a hackney carriage.
>
> In my judgment s 46 is perfectly plain. No person shall drive any vehicle which is licensed as a hackney carriage, whatever it may be doing at that particular moment unless he himself has a licence as required by s 46. Support for this view may be found in *Hawkins v Edwards*, where the argument which apparently found favour with the justices in this case was not acceded to in the Divisional Court.'

PLYING AND STANDING FOR HIRE

The question of what is meant by plying or standing for hire is fundamen- **8.6**
tal to both hackney carriage and private hire activities. Only hackney carriages can ply for hire and private hire vehicles cannot. As a result, this question has been a major source of contention over a long time. The right to ply for hire is jealously guarded by hackney carriage proprietors, rightly so, as this is, to a large extent, the most important distinction between the two different types of vehicle. As a result, this area has been the subject of considerable litigation over the last century or so, and a large body of case law has built up. Unfortunately, that is not perhaps as helpful as it might at first appear. Parker LCJ observed in *Cogley v Sherwood*[1] (at 323):

> 'The court has been referred to a number of cases from 1869 down to the present day dealing with hackney carriages and stage carriages. Those decisions are not easy to reconcile, and . . . I have been unable to extract from them a comprehensive and authoritative definition of "plying for hire".'

and since that case, no complete definition has emerged.

1 [1959] 2 QB 311.

8.7   One of the difficulties which has lead to this is the age of the legislation. As has been stated elsewhere, the 1847 Act was passed at a time when the internal combustion engine had not been invented and the current road transport, traffic and social situations could not even have been imagined. As a result, the legislation addresses itself to horse-drawn vehicles from another era, and the case law has struggled to apply that to an ever-changing reality.

Case law

Cogley v Sherwood

8.8   In *Cogley v Sherwood*[1], the court considered and reviewed a lot of the older cases. This case concerned an operation at London airport. There was a desk that was staffed at the airport, where cars could be booked or hired for immediate transport. The vehicles that were supplied were not hackney carriages and also, crucially, were not visible at the time the booking or hiring was made. They were prosecuted for unlawful plying for hire, contrary to section 7 of the Metropolitan Public Carriage Act 1869. The wording is slightly different from the wording of the 1847 Act, but the question which was central to this case was whether by this mechanism the vehicles were plying for hire. Parker LCJ, in a lengthy judgment, considered a large number of previous cases. He stated (at 323):

> 'The court has been referred to a number of cases from 1869 down to the present day dealing with hackney carriages and stage carriages. Those decisions are not easy to reconcile, and like the justices, with whom I have great sympathy, I have been unable to extract from them a comprehensive and authoritative definition of "plying for hire." One reason, of course, is that these cases all come before the court on case stated, and the question whether a particular vehicle is plying for hire, being largely one of degree and therefore of fact, has to be approached by considering whether there was evidence to support the justices' finding.'

1   [1959] 2 QB 311.

8.9   Parker LCJ considered that the cases of *Allen v Tunbridge*[1], *Armstrong v Ogle*[2], *Case v Storey*[3] and *Clarke v Stanford*[4] all indicated that the vehicle in question must be exhibited in order for there to be a plying for hire. He continued (at 325):

> 'In the ordinary way, therefore, I should, apart from authority, have felt that it was of the essence of plying for hire that the vehicle in question should be on view, that the owner or driver should expressly or impliedly invite the public to use it, and that the member of the public should be able to use that vehicle if he wanted to.'

He took the view that *Gilbert v McKay*[5] and *Cavill v Amos*[6] did not apply because, in those cases, there was an exhibition of vehicle. He considered the case of *Griffin v Grey Coaches Ltd*[7] as distinguishable on its facts, as it concerned stage carriages. His conclusion was that, in this circumstance, there was no plying for hire as there was no exhibition of the vehicles themselves.

1   (1871) LR 6 CP 481.
2   [1926] 2 KB 438.

3 (1869) LR 4 Exch 319.
4 (1871) LR 6 QB 357.
5 [1946] 1 All ER 458.
6 (1899) 16 TLR 156.
7 (1928) 45 TLR 109.

That judgment was supported by Donavan J who stated (at 328):   **8.10**

> 'The expression "ply for hire" is not defined in the statute, and I would
> respectfully concur in the justices' finding that no comprehensive defi-
> nition is to be found in the decided cases. But the term does connote in
> my view some exhibition of the vehicle to potential hirers as a vehicle
> which may be hired. One can perhaps best explain the reason by taking
> an example. It is a fairly common sight today to see in smaller towns
> and villages a notice in the window of a private house "Car for Hire".
> If the car in question is locked up in the owner's garage adjacent to the
> house, it could not in my view reasonably be said that at that moment
> the car was "plying for hire". If a customer wishes to hire it, he comes
> and makes his terms with the owner. On the return journey the owner
> might exhibit a sign on its windscreen, as some of them do, "Taxi" and
> then clearly he would be plying for hire. Similarly, if he left the car out-
> side his house, the same notice on the car would involve, I think, that
> the car was then plying for hire, and the notice in the window might
> also then have the same effect.'

He took the view that both *Gilbert v McKay* and *Griffin v Grey Coaches Ltd*
were distinguishable: *Gilbert* on its facts; and *Griffin* because it was a stage
carriage. He concluded that the vehicles which were the subject of the bookings in this situation, were not plying for hire.

The final judgment was given by Salmon J who agreed with the views   **8.11**
expressed by the two previous judges (at 330):

> 'I also agree, although not without some doubt, that, for the reasons
> stated by my Lord, this appeal should be allowed. Such doubt as I feel
> springs not from the words of the statute, which appear to me to be rea-
> sonably plain, but from the multifarious decisions upon it. If the matter
> were *res integra*, I should have thought that it was obvious that the words
> "plying for hire" have a meaning different from and narrower than "letting
> for hire" or "carrying on a private hire business". But for authority, I
> should have thought that a vehicle plies for hire if the person in control of
> the vehicle exhibits the vehicle and makes a present open offer to the
> public, an offer which can be accepted, for example, by the member of the
> public stepping into the vehicle.

> But from time to time in the past people owning vehicles which were
> plying for hire have exercised their ingenuity for circumventing the provi-
> sions of the Act of 1869, and on a large number of occasions this court has
> had to consider those attempts. During the course of the years, observa-
> tions have been made which deal with the particular circumstances of a
> case, and these have been adopted and expanded in other cases; and so we
> have dome to a position where, on the authorities, it is possible, . . . to
> make a powerful argument, . . . for holding that this Act means something
> quite different from what any ordinary man would think that it meant on
> reading it.

> Indeed, this court, to my mind, is driven to the very brink of saying that
> whenever a private hire firm has a fleet of motor-cars in its garage and
> advertises for customers, those motor-cars are plying for hire. That seems

to me to be quite wrong. It was never within the contemplation of the leg-islature that the job-master (who was the counterpart in 1869 of the car hire service of 1959), should be within the Act, as was pointed out by Montague Smith J, in *Allen v Tunbridge* as long ago as 1871. I do not feel that we are constrained by authority to cross the brink. Although author-ity precludes a finding that the making of a present open offer is a necessary part of "plying for hire", I do not feel compelled by any author-ity to find that a vehicle plies for hire unless it is exhibited. In this case the vehicles were not, as my Lords have pointed out, exhibited, and for that reason I agree that this appeal should be allowed.'

8.12   As *Cogley v Sherwood*[1] provide a comprehensive assessment of the cases which had been decided prior to that date, there seems little point in con-sidering them at length. From 1959 (the date of *Cogley v Sherwood*), it has been quite clear that, for there to be a plying for hire, there has to be an exhi-bition of the vehicle in question. That view has been clearly supported by *Rose v Welbeck Motors Ltd*[2], *Newman v Vincent*[3] and *Vant v Cripps*[4].

1   [1959] 2 QB 311.
2   [1962] 1 WLR 1010.
3   [1962] 1 WLR 1017.
4   (1963) 62 LGR 88.

Rose v Welbeck Motors Ltd

8.13   *Rose v Welbeck Motors Ltd*[1] concerned a prosecution for plying for hire under the Metropolitan Carriage Act 1869. As noted above, the wording of that Act is slightly different from the wording in the 1847 Act. In *Rose*, a mini-cab was parked on a bus standby, an area where buses turn round. When a bus came along, the mini-cab moved some ten yards further along the road. In total, it was there for 50 minutes. The question was whether the driver of the mini-cab was plying for hire. Parker LCJ gave the principal judgment of the court. He considered the case of *Cogley v Sherwood*[2] and then stated (at 1014):

'That the vehicle in the present case was on exhibition in the sense that it was on view to the public is undoubted. The real question, as it seems to me, is whether a prima facie case was made out that the vehicle in ques-tion was impliedly inviting the public to use it. Whether in any case such a prima facie case is made out must, of course, depend upon the exact cir-cumstances, and I certainly do not intend anything I say in this judgment to apply to any facts other than those here. What are the facts here? One starts with the fact that this vehicle was of a distinctive appearance, regard-ing its colour, its inscriptions, its equipment in the form of radio communication, and its type. Secondly – and this is equally important – it was standing with the driver at the steering wheel for some fifty minutes in a public place on public view and at a place where buses turned round: in other words, at a place where many members of the public would be get-ting off the buses and where many members of the public would forgather to board the buses. Moreover, when requested to leave, the driver drove away only to return immediately almost to the same place.'

He concluded (at 1015):

'In my judgment, there is no real difference between the expression, "taxi" and "cab" and, in the particular circumstances of this case, it seems to me that any tribunal would be bound to hold that this vehicle was exhibiting itself as a vehicle for hire. Therefore, this case ought to be remitted to the justices with the direction that there was a case to answer and that they should continue the hearing of the case. I deliberately refrain from saying what, in my judgment, might amount to a defence.'

1   [1962] 1 WLR 1010
2   [1959] 2 QB 311.

Newman v Vincent

On the same day the same court gave a similar ruling in the case of *Newman v Vincent*[1]. The facts were very similar to those in *Rose v Welbeck Motors Ltd*[2], except that the vehicle was only parked for some 20 minutes. However, it did have a notice attached to the passenger side sun visor, which read 'Mini-cab Booking'. The matter of the notice on the sun visor seemed extremely important in the mind of Parker LCJ, who gave judgment (at 1019):   **8.14**

> 'It is quite true that in some respects this is a weaker case than the case of *Rose v Welbeck Motors Ltd*, in which we have just given judgment, because the period of time in the present case was 20 minutes and, although the vehicle was on a public street, it was not at a bus turn-round, and may well have given the appearance of waiting outside a private house. On the other hand, it has the exceptional feature of the sun visor but, more important to my mind, the evidence that its appearance and conduct was such that two members of the public came up and asked if it was for hire. For my part I find it quite impossible in those circumstances to say that there was not a prima facie case of the vehicle's plying for hire in the sense of being on view to the public and inviting the public to use it.'

1   [1962] 1 WLR 1017.
2   [1962] 1 WLR 1010.

Vant v Cripps

Vant v Cripps[1] concerned a private hire vehicle (although it was not licensed as this case dates from 1963, some period before the introduction of the Local Government (Miscellaneous Provisions) Act 1976) which was parked outside a house on one occasion, and was parked on the driveway of the same house on another occasion. On the rear of the vehicle was a sign, measuring eight inches by six inches, which read 'Barry's Taxis, Moortown' and gave a telephone number. On the house, itself, was an electric light with a rectangular globe which had the word 'Taxi' on it and the same telephone number. The driver was prosecuted for unlawfully plying for hire and both he and the proprietor were prosecuted for not having the relevant insurance.   **8.15**

1   (1963) 62 LGR 88.

Parker LCJ gave the judgment of the court and stated (at 92):   **8.16**

> 'Their real trouble here is that albeit they are running, or said to be running, a genuine private hire business, they kept this vehicle outside their house with a great sign on it at the back, "Barry's Taxis", and a telephone number. On top of that, at the corner of the house was an electric light fitting with a rectangular globe on which appeared the word "Taxi" and the telephone number.

> Accordingly, anyone walking up the street and seeing the car outside the house and the sign at the corner of the house would say "Here is a car waiting to be hired" – not a private car but what is known as a taxi, a cab.'

He continued, explaining that a police officer had interviewed both defendants (at 92):

'. . . it appeared that while he [the police officer] was there, in the kitchen of the house, somebody came along who had seen the car outside and the two signs, the one on the car, and the one on the house, and came in and attempted to hire the car, and was refused. The relevance of that is that it appeared at any rate to one member of the public that the car was outside plying for hire.

The magistrate found – and this must be almost entirely a question of fact – that this vehicle with this sign and standing under the electric sign on the house could do no other than cause a member of the public to assume that the vehicle was available in the business for hire without a previous contract being made, and, as I have said, he found the defendants guilty on these charges.'

He concluded (at 93):

'In my judgment, the defendant, Barry Vant, was properly convicted here. On the facts it is perfectly clear that this vehicle was plying for hire. I say that bearing in mind the cases which have been decided under section 7 of the Act of 1867, and in particular *Rose v Welbeck Motors Ltd* [1962] 1 WLR 1010, 60 LGR 423. That is the position with regard to the vehicle. So far as Barry Vant is concerned, he was clearly the person in charge of the vehicle in the sense that he was in the house; he was the person who would drive the vehicle if it was used; and he knew that the vehicle was outside with this sign on it and standing under the sign that was on the house, and, accordingly plying for hire. In those circumstances, it seems to me quite impossible to contend that he himself was not plying for hire in the sense of being in charge of a vehicle which was itself plying for hire.'

8.17 Ashworth J agreed and quoted from *Cogley v Sherwood*[1]. He stated (at 93):

'In my view this passage precisely fits the present case. Donovan J said (at 328–9):

"The expression 'plying for hire' is not defined in the statute, and I would respectively concur in the justices' finding that no comprehensive definition is to be found in the decided cases. But the term does connote in my view some exhibition of the vehicle to potential hirers as a vehicle which may be hired. One can perhaps best explain the reason by taking an example. It is a fairly common sight today to see in smaller towns and villages a notice in the window of a private house 'Car for Hire'. If the car in question is locked up in the owner's garage adjacent to the house, it could not in my view reasonably be said that at that moment the car was 'plying for hire'. If a customer wishes to hire it, he comes and makes his terms with the owner. On the return journey the owner might exhibit a sign on its windscreen, as some of them do, 'Taxi' and then clearly he would be plying for hire. Similarly, if he left the car outside his house, the same notice on the car would involve, I think, that the car was then plying for hire, and the notice in the window might also then have the same effect."

If one substitutes for the notice in the window the lettering on the electric light globe, that passage precisely fits this case.'

1 [1959] 2QB 311.

The approach shown in *Cogley v Sherwood*[1], *Rose v Welbeck Motors Ltd*[2],   **8.18**
Newman v Vincent[3] and *Vant v Cripps*[4] was clearly a sensible approach before
there was regulation of private hire vehicles under the 1976 Act. Once this
had occurred, a greater difficulty arose because there were other licensed
vehicles: private hire vehicles, which could provide a transport service to the
public, but which could quite clearly not ply for hire. When this is considered, it makes sense for the original test to have been developed in the light
of modern circumstances. Unless every private hire vehicle could be hidden
in a garage when not carrying out a hiring, it would appear possible to
argue that it was plying for hire.

1 [1959] 2 QB 311.
2 [1962] 1 WLR 1010.
3 [1962] 1 WLR 1017.
4 (1963) 62 LGR 88.

Eldridge v British Airport Authority: the expression 'standing'

Eldridge v British Airport Authority[1] is a useful case as it concerned the   **8.19**
meaning of the expression of 'standing in any street' which is contained in
section 35 of the London Hackney Carriage Act 1831. As the London legislation is different from the 1847 Act, the case itself is not of enormous
importance, but it contains a useful statement by Donaldson J (at 396E):

> 'In my judgment "standing" in the context of that section means some-
> thing akin to waiting or parking. It does not mean being stationary. Were
> it otherwise, the licensed driver in an ordinary taxi cab who was stopped
> at traffic lights would be at the mercy of everyone who wished to hire a
> cab. A similar problem would confront a driver who stopped momentar-
> ily whilst seeking a petrol pump on his way home. This would be an
> intolerable situation for taxi-cab drivers.'

This shows a very sensible and practical approach to the question of
'standing'.

1 [1970] 2 QB 387.

Ogwr Borough Council v Baker

In relation to 'plying', the approach in *Cogley v Sherwood*[1], *Rose v Welbeck*   **8.20**
Motors Ltd[2], *Newman v Vincent*[3] and *Vant v Cripps*[4] was apparently followed
very strictly in the case of *Ogwr Borough Council v Baker*[5]. In this case, it was
held that a private hire vehicle, which was parked near a hot-dog van, was
plying for hire. There was no visible invitation to the public to use the vehicle, but it was parked near to a hackney carriage stand. The driver
maintained that he was parking there because he sometimes bought a hot-
dog, although he had not done so on this occasion. When a couple from a
nearby night club approached the vehicle and asked if he was there to fulfil
their booking, he radioed through to his operator and ascertained that his
was not the vehicle provided for the booking. The report does not say
whether he took the couple, but suggests that he did not. He was acquitted
of plying for hire contrary to section 45 of the 1847 Act, but the local
authority appealed by way of case stated. The appeal was upheld, with the
High Court taking the view that parking by a hot-dog stand was an absurd
excuse and that the driver was clearly plying for hire.

Unfortunately, there is only a report of this case in the *Crown Office Digest* and full details of the judgment are not reported.

1   [1959] 2 QB 311.
2   [1962] 1 WLR 1010.
3   [1962] 1 WLR 1017.
4   (1963) 62 LGR 88.
5   [1989] COD 489.

Nottingham City Council v Woodings

8.21   However, in *Nottingham City Council v Woodings*[1], the approach differed significantly. This is the most recent case to date on the question of what is meant by 'plying for hire'. The case concerned a private hire car licensed by Nottingham City Council parked in Nottingham city centre. The driver, who was a licensed private hire driver, was sitting in the car. The driver got out of the car and went to some nearby public toilets. When he returned to the car, he was approached by two plain clothes police officers. The defendant was asked 'are you free?', to which he replied 'yes'. He was then asked if he could take the two men to a destination and, when asked how much it was going to be, the driver replied 'depends on where you are going'. The two plain-clothed officers then got in to the car and revealed their identity. Woodings was prosecuted for unlawfully plying for hire, contrary to section 45 of the Town Police Clauses Act 1847. He was convicted by the magistrates' court, but appealed successfully to the Crown Court. The local authority appealed to the Divisional Court by way of case stated. The specific question raised was:

> 'does the driver of a marked minicab whose vehicle is not a licensed hackney carriage ply for hire, within the meaning of the Town Police Clauses Act 1847, if he, without more, is approached by a member of the public and then enters into and/or concludes negotiations for the hire of the vehicle?'

1   [1994] RTR 72.

8.22   Judgment was given by Rose LJ. He referred to a number of cases, including *Cavill v Amos*[1], *Sales v Lake*[2], *Cogley v Sherwood*[3], *Rose v Welbeck Motors Ltd*[4], and *Vant v Cripps*[5], and then stated (at 78D):

> 'In my judgment, when the defendant parked the marked car in the street, for the purpose of going to the toilet, he was not plying for hire, and when he came out of the toilet, he was not plying for hire. But when, having sat in the driver's seat, he told the prospective passengers that he was free to carry them, at that stage he was, bearing in mind where the car was and what the car looked like, plying for hire.'

He concluded (at 78G):

> 'For my part, I accept Mr Lewis's submission [for the local authority] that it is not a necessary ingredient of this offence under section 45, as distinct from an offence under section 7 of the Metropolitan Public Carriage Act 1869, for the car to be exhibited. Clearly, if a car is exhibited as a taxi and the driver is sitting in it, those are highly material circumstances when one comes to consider the question of whether he is plying for hire with a carriage. But it does not seem to me that it is a necessary ingredient in this offence that the vehicle should be exhibited in the way which was a necessary requirement in *Cogley v Sherwood* and *Rose v Welbeck Motors Ltd*.

The vehicle must, of course, be with the accused driver because that is what section 45 requires. No doubt, that will normally mean it is somewhere very near, but whether or not the vehicle is itself plying for hire within *Cogley v Sherwood* and *Rose v Welbeck Motors Ltd* is not, in my view, determinative of whether or not the driver is plying for hire with a carriage.'

As this case postdates *Ogwr Borough Council v Baker*[6], the ruling in *Woodings* appears to be a reasonable, accurate, up-to-date and sensible interpretation of the law.

1 (1900) 16 TLR 156.
2 [1922] 1 KB 553.
3 [1959] 2 QB 311.
4 [1962] 1 WLR 1010.
5 (1963) 62 LGR 88.
6 [1989] COD 489.

The current view

What conclusions can be drawn about 'plying for hire' from these cases? As they are all High Court decisions, there is no obvious precedent to follow, so a chronological approach is a good way of deciding which is the correct view. The decision in *Woodings*[1] is the most recent and, as it took account of most of the other important cases (although *Ogwr Borough Council v Baker*[2] was not referred to), it seems to represent the current view. Certainly, it has provided a much more workable test, when the existance of private hire vehicles has to be taken into account. As a result, the simple question of where the vehicle is parked is too crude an indicator as to whether or not it is plying for hire. It will ultimately be a matter of fact and degree as to whether a vehicle is plying for hire. This will need to take into account its appearance, whether it is visible, where it is parked, whether the driver is present and also, if there is a conversation between the driver and a prospective passenger, the content of that exchange. What is clear is that merely parking or stopping a non-hackney carriage, even in company with other vehicles, whether they are hackney carriages or not, is not sufficient to constitute plying for hire.

8.23

1 *Nottingham City Council v Woodings* [1994] RTR 72.
2 [1989] COD 489.

Young v Scampion

The decision in *Young v Scampion*[1] is also of considerable interest. It concerned a prosecution brought by Solihull Metropolitan Borough Council, relating to the user of hackney carriages licensed by Birmingham City Council at Birmingham International Airport, which lies within the metropolitan district of Solihull. There was a private road, known as Airport Way, at the airport where there was a hackney carriage stand. That road was not a public highway, although it was a continuation of the public highway. At the demarcation point of the public highway and private road there was, in fact, a barrier, although this was apparently only ever closed on Christmas Day. To all intents and purposes, traffic could pass and re-pass over the private road, despite a sign that indicated that parking was not allowed, apart from in specified authorised areas. The defendants in the case were hackney carriage drivers licensed by Birmingham City Council, driving hackney

8.24

carriage vehicles licensed by Birmingham City Council. They stood on the rank at Birmingham airport on Airport Way and, when they got to the front, they took passengers to destinations within Solihull. They were convicted of standing, plying for hire and driving a hackney carriage at Airport Way and also of driving in the street in Solihull when they had no licence to ply for hire in Solihull. They appealed by way of case stated. The matter was heard by Mann LJ and Auld J.

1   (1988) 87 LGR 240, QBD.

8.25   There were four questions raised by the magistrates in their stated case. First:

> 'whether the words "any carriage" in the second limb of section 45 means "any hackney carriage".'

Auld J found that they did and stated (at 251):

> 'In my view no offence is committed under either limb of section 45 unless the vehicle is a hackney carriage within the meaning of the Act.'

8.26   The second question was:

> 'Whether the justices were entitled to find, as they did, that the defendants' vehicles were hackney carriages, and thus subject to the control in section 45, because they were designed and/or normally used as hackney carriages, or whether they should have been constrained by section 38 only so to find if the vehicles were "used in standing or plying for hire in any street" within the Solihull area.'

This turned upon:

> 'the status of . . . a [hackney carriage] vehicle outside its own licensing area where it was not licensed and not required to carry . . . a [hackney carriage] plate, and where there is no evidence that it had stood or plied for hire in any street over which the public had a legal right of standing or passage. As counsel for the defendants in this case put it, a Birmingham licensed taxi does not lose its character as a Birmingham taxi when it enters Solihull, but it does not thereby become, in addition, a Solihull taxi.' (per Auld J at 253)

He continued:

> 'In considering this question it is important to remember that in every case the use of a vehicle in question is that in the area of the local authority seeking to enforce their licensing control. Before that authority can mount a prosecution under section 45 they must be in a position to prove that the taxi in question is a hackney carriage in their own area. The need for such local control arises out of the local *use* [Auld J's emphasis] of a vehicle, in the words of section 38, "whatever may be its form or construction" as a hackney carriage or, in today's language, as a taxi.

> A vehicle's design or normal use in some other local authority area must be irrelevant to a local authority's control if the vehicle does not stand or ply for hire within their area, but only passes through it with fares taken up in some other area. If that were not the case, no taxi driver could pick up a fare in one area and convey him to any other area unless he was licensed there; and if on a long journey and passing through several local areas of control, he would require a licence for each area through which he passes. The absurdity of such interpretation is reflected in a comparatively recent

provision introduced in the Local Government (Miscellaneous Provisions) Act 1976, which consolidated a number of provisions found in a number of local Acts concerning the control of hackney carriages and private hire vehicles, and provided for their adoption by local authorities in whose areas the Act of 1847 was already in force. Section 75(1)(*a*), referring to *its* [Auld J's emphasis] provisions in the Act of 1976, not those of the Act of 1847, set out the following saying:

> "Nothing in this Part of this Act shall – (*a*) apply to a vehicle used for bringing passengers or goods within a controlled district in pursuance of a contract for the hire of the vehicle made outside the district if the vehicle is not made available for hire within the district."

In my view, it would be absurd for there to be a saving for vehicles coming into a controlled area applicable to supplemental provisions gathered together in the Act of 1976 if the basic provisions in the Act of 1847 applied to vehicles across local authority boundaries whether or not they stand or ply for hire outside the area for which they are licensed.'

At 254, he continued:

> 'The horse-drawn carriage has given way to the taxi cab, which itself has evolved over recent years, ranging in design from the London black cab to ordinary saloon cars distinguishable as taxis only by their licence plates. It follows that the only constant and sensible definition of a hackney carriage within the meaning of the Act of 1847 is by reference to its use, not its design.
>
> In my view, the legislature, in section 38, has defined and territorially limited that use to standing or plying for hire in any street in the area of the borough seeking to enforce their control.'

The next question concerned the meaning of 'street' in section 38 and   **8.27**
whether that meant only a street to which the public have a legal right of access, or any street irrespective of the right of access. Auld J took the view that the definition in section 3 of the 1847 Act only referred to public streets. He stated (at 255):

> 'If I had been looking at this question without the benefit of authority, I would have had little difficulty in concluding that what Parliament intended to refer to here was a public street in the sense of a street where a carriage was entitled as of right to ply for hire (subject to the licensing provisions of the Act of 1847) and where the public were entitled as of right to go. I say that, not only because of the clear purpose of the legislation to which I have referred, but also because of the definition of the word "street" in section 3, the interpretation section, of the Act of 1847. As I have already noted, it provides that the word "shall extend to and include any road, square, court, alley and thoroughfare, or *public passage* within" the borough (my emphasis). In my view, the qualification of word "passage" with the word "public" was clearly not intended to distinguish between it and other listed locations. It cannot have been intended that plying for hire on public or private streets and roads etc qualified for control, whereas plying for hire in private passages did not. The introduction of the qualifying word "public" for the word "passage" is, in my view, a clear indication that the public nature of the place, obvious in the other locations listed, but not so obvious in the case of a passage, should be underlined.

My view is supported by authority. *Curtis v Embery* (1872) LR 7 Exch 369 and *Jones v Short* (1900) 69 LJQB 473.'

He concluded on this point by saying (at 258):

'The restriction of the control of the Act of 1847 to vehicles standing or plying for hire on public property has been recognised by Parliament in that in 1925 it specifically extended that control to railway premises: see section 76 of the Public Health Act 1925.'

8.28 This then led on to the next question. Was Airport Way a street? Auld J concluded that it was not a street. He found that the earlier cases of *Birmingham and Midland Motor Omnibus Co v Thompson*[1] and *White v Cubitt*[2] were distinguishable, as, in those cases, vehicles were parked, albeit on private land, but in order to draw custom from the general public in the adjoining street. He followed the rulings in *Curtis v Embery*[3] and *Jones v Short*[4], which had concerned carriages parked on railway property. He stated (at 260):

'In *Curtis v Embery* and *Jones v Short*, the railway cases, the carriages were parked on railway land to draw custom from those members of the public using the railway, that is people on the railway company's private property. Both the carriages and the behaviour of the railway travellers using them were, when on that land, subject to the control of the railway company.

Here, the defendants were parked on the airport authority's private property in order to draw custom from those using the airport. They were not soliciting custom from those using the public streets of Solihull, and, whilst there, were physically separated from such general custom more completely than were the vehicles in the railway cases or those relied upon by Solihull Council. Whilst there, they and their potential customers were subject to the control of the airport authority as expressed in its byelaws and as exercisable by it as owner of the land.

The various matters relied upon by the justices in the case stated going to the lack of any physical restriction or sign of change at the boundary between the public highway and the start of Airport Way are no more relevant than the lack of physical divide between the road and hackney carriage stand in the railway cases. The principle applied in those cases, with which, as I have said, I agree, is that land is not a "street" for the purpose of section 38 unless the public, including taxi drivers in their taxis, have a legal right of access to it. The fact that the public, including taxi drivers, in fact resort to a particular location in large numbers, as they do to modern railway stations, airports and hotel entrances, and the like, cannot of itself make such a location a street for this purpose.'

Accordingly, it was concluded that a hackney carriage did not have to be licensed by the borough in which it was standing at a rank, if that rank was on a private road for the purposes of people who were not generally passing on public streets.

1 [1918] 2 KB 105.
2 [1930] 1 KB 443.
3 (1872) LR 7 Exch 369.
4 (1900) 69 LJQB 473.

8.29 The final question was, once having picked up a passenger could a hackney carriage drive on roads within the area of a council with which it was not licensed? In relation to that question Auld J stated (at 261):

'. . . the mere driving by the defendants of their taxis through the streets of Solihull could not make them so. The functional definition in section 38 refers only to standing or plying for hire. They are in no different position from a licensed Birmingham taxi, or a taxi licensed in any other local authority area, conveying a passenger taken up within their own area into the Solihull area.

In short, a vehicle licensed in one area does not need a licence from any other authority into whose area it is driven or in which it solicits or accepts passengers from private land.'

Although considerable emphasis was placed on the fact that Airport Way at Birmingham airport was not only a private road but was in control of Birmingham airport and was subject to byelaws made by the airport authority, it would appear from this ruling that hackney carriages from another district could park on private land provided they have the permission of the land owner to do so, and if it could be argued that they are not plying or standing for hire for the benefit of persons moving along a public highway but for persons who are on private land. An obvious example of this would be a rank created at a large shopping centre for the purposes of persons using the shopping centre, which due to its geographical location would be unlikely to attract pedestrians from other public roads. It remains to be seen whether this would be possible in practice.

Hulin v Cook

A slightly different point was raised in *Hulin v Cook*[1]. This case concerned **8.30** the question of whether the provisions of the 1847 Act, in relation to plying for hire, extended to hackney carriage stands provided by the then British Railways Board on railway property outside railway stations. Byelaw 22(2) of the British Railways Board Byelaws required a hackney carriage proprietor to apply for permission from the British Railways Board, before the hackney carriage could be used on a British Rail stand, this being in addition to the requirement to hold a licence under section 38 of the 1847 Act. In this case no such permission had been obtained and the prosecution was brought against both the proprietor and the driver of the hackney carriage in question. They contended that section 76 of the Public Health Act 1925 meant that, because the general provisions of the hackney carriage licensing regime were extended to stands at railway stations, they did not need the permission of the British Railways Board. That view was accepted by the magistrate, who acquitted the driver and proprietor. The prosecution appealed by way of case stated. Widgery LCJ gave the judgment of the court. He noted that section 76 of the 1925 Act had been passed because cases prior to that supported the view that a licence was not required if the person was plying for hire on private property. He concluded (at 349L):

'It is contended however that under section 76 some new right to ply for hire was thereby conferred, but, in my judgment, that is not so. The position after the passing of the Act of 1925 was that the licensing system under the Act of 1847 was extended to a new area. It was extended to the area of the railways and to railway premises, and anyone wishing to ply for hire on railway premises thereafter required a licence under the Act of 1847, despite the fact that the property was private property, but nothing in the way of a further right was thereby conferred.

Once the Act of 1925 was passed, the position in Cardiff, and for all I know in other places as well, was simply this. The typical taxi driver who wished to serve customers in the area, whether they came from airport, railway stations, bus stations or elsewhere, would need the ordinary 1847 Act licence in order to carry on his trade in Cardiff at all. In addition to that, if he wanted to serve passengers in Cardiff General Station he would have to make his peace with the Railways Board in as much as he would require their consent under their byelaws before he could ply for hire within the confines of the railway property. That, in my understanding of the position, is how the law now stands, and it follows from that that the magistrate was in error when he considered, as he evidently did from the form of his case, that the effect of section 76 was to give a new right which had not previously existed in that it licensed taxi drivers to ply for hire in Cardiff.'

1 [1977] RTR 345.

Khan v Evans

8.31   A different question, although it initially concerned a railway station stand, was answered in *Khan v Evans*[1]. The question was when did a contract between driver and passenger come into existence? *Khan v Evans* concerned a prosecution of a licensed hackney carriage driver for plying for reward on railway premises without authority to do so, contrary to the British Railways Board Byelaws 1965, byelaw 22(2). His defence was that, as he had been hailed before he was on railway premises, when he actually entered the railway premises, he was already under contract to the persons who had hailed him to take them anywhere they wished to go and, consequently, he was not plying. That defence failed before the magistrates and Mr Khan appealed by way of case stated to the High Court. Judgment was given by Robert Goff LJ, who stated (at 37C):

'Three questions are posed for our consideration by the justices. They ask whether they were correct in law in holding that:

"(1) the process of plying for reward continues until a contract was made between the driver of a hackney carriage and a prospective passenger to convey that passenger for reward;

(2) no such contract could be made merely by the prospective passengers hailing the driver of the hackney carriage and his responding to the hail by driving from the public road on to railway premises; and

(3) such a contract did not come into existence until the driver of the hackney carriage has spoken to the prospective passenger and agreed to convey him or her."

For the defendant [the driver], Mr Irvine addressed no argument to us on the first question. He therefore accepted that the first question should be answered in the affirmative.

I turn then to the second and third questions. On these questions, Mr Irvine [for the defendant, the driver] made the following submissions. He submitted that when the defendant was driving his taxi along the public road with his "For Hire" sign displayed, his conduct amounted to an invitation to treat. Next he submitted that the action of the two women in hailing the defendant amounted to an offer to hire him. Then, when the defendant decided to accept that offer and changed course, turning towards the two women, his conduct in so doing amounted to an acceptance of that offer, whereupon a contract came into existence. It follows that on those submissions the contract was made before the defendant's hackney carriage entered upon the railway premises. So, says Mr Irvine, no offence was committed on the facts of the present case.

I am perfectly content to view the action of a cab driver such as the defendant in driving along a road with the "For Hire" sign exhibited on his cab as constituting an invitation to treat in the sense of an invitation to enter into negotiations for a contract, which does not bind anybody and is simply a preliminary to a contract possibly coming into existence.

I then come to Mr Irvine's second submission, which was that when the two women hailed the cab they were making an offer to hire the cab, by which he must have meant an offer which if accepted would result in a binding contract. The difficulty with this proposition as I see it is that the terms of any such offer are not known; and in particular it is not known to what destination the person hailing the cab wishes to be taken, or what fare would be charged for conveying him to that destination.

An example was put to Mr Irvine in the course of argument. Let it be supposed that somebody standing at Brighton station sees a cab coming along the road with its "For Hire" sign displayed. He hails it, intending to ask to be taken to John O'Groats. If Mr Irvine's submission is right, as soon as that cab driver seeing the passenger on the side of the road turns his cab towards that person with the intention of accepting him as a fare a binding contract comes into existence. It must follow, if this submission is right, that that passenger is bound to go in that cab to John O'Groats and that the cab driver is bound to take him there. It also follows that the only way in which the fare could be ascertained for that journey would be on the basis that a reasonable fare would be charged and paid. It only needs an example such as that to reveal the difficulties which Mr Irvine faces in putting his argument.

Another example put to Mr Irvine in the course of argument was this. Let it be supposed that a prospective passenger standing on the side of the road wants to be taken home. He sees a cab coming along displaying a "For Hire" sign. He hails it and it turns towards him but gets stuck for a moment in the traffic. Thereupon another cab driver passing by sees him standing at the side of the road and drives up to him, and he gets into that second cab. On Mr Irvine's example the passenger would at that point of time be guilty of a breach of contract vis-à-vis the first driver and it is possible that the second driver would be guilty of the wrong of inducing a breach of contract between the passenger and the first driver. Again the example, in my judgment, reveals the problems underlying Mr Irvine's argument.

In my judgment, as a matter of sheer common sense, when a prospective passenger sees a cab coming along the public highway showing a "For Hire" sign and hails it, all he is doing is indicating to the cab driver a wish or intention to hire his cab. He is doing no more than indicating a desire to negotiate with the cab driver for the purpose of making a contract of carriage. The material terms have not been agreed at that point in time. When the cab driver drives up in answer to that hail, his action is still part and parcel of the process of negotiation which may lead to a binding contract. When the driver comes to the side of the road and lowers his window and the passenger says, "Will you please take me to –" whatever the address may be and the driver says "Yes", there may be at that point in time a contract, but certainly not before that point of time. If the destination is within the area to be served it may be that the cab driver is bound to accept the passenger. If it is outside a certain area it may be that he is at liberty to refuse to take the passenger, but a bargain can be struck as to the fare to be paid for carrying the passenger to that place. But of course none of the facts giving rise to problems of that kind are made known by the simple act of the person standing on the pavement and hailing the cab, or by the cab driver answering the hail.

All of this demonstrates, in my judgment, that at that point of time the parties are still in the stage of what is called invitation to treat or negotiation, but that no offer capable of being accepted and so creating a binding contract has yet been made.

For those reasons I am unable to accept Mr Irvine's submissions.

It is right that I should record that Mr Irvine referred us to section 53 of the Town Police Clauses Act 1847, but I do not think it is necessary to go into that section which in my judgment has no bearing upon the question in this case.

Addressing myself to the second and third questions posed by the justices, I for my part would answer both those questions in the affirmative.'

Whilst this judgment obviously applies to the question of when a hiring is made on railway premises, the concept of contract in relation to hackney carriage hiring is a useful point.

1 [1985] RTR 33.

HACKNEY CARRIAGE ZONES

8.32 Most local authorities license hackney carriages to ply throughout the area of their district. However, there are some districts where there are zones for hackney carriages. This means that the district is subdivided and hackney carriages are licensed in that zone, rather than within the whole district.

8.33 The existence of hackney carriage zones stems from local government reorganisation in 1974 under the terms of the Local Government Act 1972 ('the 1972 Act')[1].

1 For a concise overview of the history of zoning please see the explanatory notes issued by the Department of the Environment, Transport and the Regions (in May 1997) in relation to England, and February 1998, in relation to Wales) reproduced in Appendix II.

Local government reorganisation

8.34 Briefly, hackney carriages are licensed by local authorities under the provisions of the Town Police Clauses Act 1847 and 1889. Although the 1847 Act was originally adoptive, it was applied to all urban sanitary districts by section 171 of the Public Health Act 1875. These became either urban districts or boroughs under the Local Government Act 1894. By virtue of the Local Government Act 1933, hackney carriage licensing was an urban district council, borough council and county borough council function, although there were a few rural district councils which also undertook hackney carriage licensing until the application of the 1972 Act on 1 April 1974.

The Local Government Act 1972

The 1972 Act created two tiers of local government within England and **8.35**
Wales, and amalgamated many of the former smaller areas of local government that had been responsible for hackney carriage licensing. Under the
1972 Act, urban district councils, rural district councils, borough councils and
county borough councils were abolished and were replaced with district councils and metropolitan district councils. The areas of the new districts were,
sometimes, the area of a previous authority, but, in many cases, were amal-
gamations of a number of previous authorities and parts of other previous
authorities.

Section 180 of, and Schedule 14, Part II to, the 1972 Act had the effect of **8.36**
applying section 171(4) of the Public Health Act 1875 (which applied hackney carriage licensing to urban districts and specified that the prescribed
distance was within the area of any urban district) to the areas which it had
applied to immediately before the establishment of the new authorities on 1
April 1974. This meant that hackney carriage licensing could only take place
in those parts of the country where it had taken place prior to 31 March 1974.

The consequences of this were that there were districts (both metropolitan **8.37**
and non-metropolitan) in England and Wales where hackney carriage licensing did not apply throughout the area of the entire district. It would apply
only where it had applied before 1 April 1974.

It was possible for the new district council to pass a resolution under para- **8.38**
graph 25 of Part II of Schedule 14 to the 1972 Act. By that resolution, the
council could abolish hackney carriage licensing within their district by stating that section 171(4) of the Public Health Act 1875 should not apply
throughout the district. However, such a resolution had to be passed before
1 April 1975 (within one year of the creation of the new authority).

Alternatively, the new authority could pass a resolution, under paragraph **8.39**
25(3) of Part II of Schedule 14 to the 1972 Act, applying the provisions of
hackney carriage licensing to its entire district. That would have the effect of
extending the licensing regime from the areas where it had applied before
reorganisation, to the entire post-reorganisation district, as one area with no
zones.

A third possibility was that the new local authority did nothing and continue **8.40**
to have zones, and also the possibility of areas where there was no licensing
of hackney carriages in the district.

As a result, a number of authorities have, in fact, had hackney carriage **8.41**
zones since 1974 and, as there was no mandatory requirement to extend
hackney carriage licensing under the 1972 Act, there was also a number of
areas where there was no licensing of hackney carriages.

The Transport Act 1985

8.42   That situation changed with the introduction of section 15 of the Transport Act 1985.

> **'Extension of taxi licensing in England and Wales**
>
> 15–(1) Where, immediately before the commencement of this section, the provisions of the Town Police Clauses Act 1847 with respect to hackney carriages and of the Town Police Clauses Act 1889 (as incorporated in each case in the Public Health Act 1875) were not in force throughout the whole of the area of a district council in England and Wales whose area lies outside the area to which the Metropolitan Public Carriage Act 1869 applies, those provisions (as so incorporated) shall—
>
> (*a*) if not then in force in any part of the council's area, apply throughout that area; and
>
> (*b*) if in force in part only of its area, apply also in the remainder of that area.
>
> (2) Where part only of a district council's area lies outside the area to which the Act of 1869 applies, that part shall, for the purposes of subsection (1) above, be treated as being the area of the council.
>
> (3) So much of any local Act as enables a district council to bring to an end the application of the provisions mentioned in subsection (1) above to the whole or any part of their area shall cease to have effect.'

It can be seen that section 15(1)(*a*) provides that, if there had been no hackney carriage licensing in any part of the council's area, then the provisions of the Town Police Clauses Acts 1847 and 1889 would apply throughout its area; and, if the hackney carriage licensing provisions of those two Acts only applied in part of the local authority area, then they would also apply in the remainder of the local authority's area.

8.43   The Department of the Environment, Transport and the Regions (and the Department of Transport before it[1]) takes the view that the effect of section 15 of the Transport Act 1985, in areas where hackney zoning existed, was not to abolish zones, but rather to create an extra zone in the part of the local authority's district where hackney carriage licensing had not applied up until the introduction of section 15.

1 Circular 8/86: see Appendix II.

8.44   Again, at any time after 1985, a local authority could pass an extension resolution under paragraph 25 of Part II of Schedule 14 to the 1972 Act to abolish zones within its district and to have one area for hackney carriage licensing which would cover the entire area of the district.

8.45   It seems that, if hackney carriage zones did exist, then byelaws could only be passed by the post-1974 district council in relation to those zones within its district where hackney carriage licensing applied. If the new authority inherited byelaws from a previous constituent authority, then those byelaws would only be enforceable in the zone to which they now applied.

If an authority had zones, then each zone was effectively a district and any **8.46** licence which was granted would only be effective within the zone. In addition, any question over numbers would relate to the zone and each zone could have its own limit on hackney carriages (provided that there was no significant demand for hackney carriage services which remained unmet within the zone).

That, then, was the situation after the introduction of the Transport Act 1985.

The 1990s reorganisation

The situation was then further complicated by the new local government **8.47** reorganisation which took place in the 1990s. For the first time, England and Wales were treated differently and, although the rationale behind the reorganisations in both countries was the same, the consequences were slightly different[1].

1 See the Department of the Environment, Transport and the Regions guidance notes: Appendix II.

The effects of the 1990s reorganisation are, in many ways, much the same as **8.48** the effects of the reorganisation of 1974. If a new authority comprises parts of two or more post-1974 districts, then each of those constituent parts will constitute a zone for the purposes of hackney carriage licensing. Licences which cover an old district (a new zone within a new authority) will be valid only within the area of the old district. This will be so irrespective of new authority boundaries, so, if an old district has been bisected and split between two new authorities, a hackney carriage licence for the old district will be effective in the area of the old authority (which now lies in two new local authority areas) but will be ineffective in any areas of either of the new authorities which lie outside the area of the former council. The same will apply to byelaws inherited by new authorities from constituent authorities: they will remain enforceable within the area of the previous district, possibly by two or more new authorities, depending upon the geography of the situation.

Passing an extension resolution

The only way to overcome this is for the new authority to pass an extension **8.49** resolution under paragraph 25 of Part II of Schedule 14 to the 1972 Act, abolishing zones and applying hackney carriage licensing throughout the area of the new authority. This route is also open to any local authority which has zones as a result of the 1974 reorganisation, and wishes to remove these so as to have a single hackney carriage licensing regime throughout the area of the district. Paragraph 25(1) of Schedule 14 requires that notice of the proposed resolution be given in accordance with paragraph 25(5) and the resolution then has to be approved by the Secretary of State (paragraph 25(4)) However, the experience of some authorities has shown that the Secretary of State imposes a considerable number of requirements upon an authority that has passed such a resolution and seeks the authority of the Secretary of State to implement it. These include:

• maps of the area showing the existing zones and the proposed district-wide area (the local authority area);
• statements as to:

- the reasons behind the proposal;
- the effect on the public;
- any responses or objections received as a result of the statutory notices;
- the number of hackney carriages in the existing zones;
- a copy of the fare table to apply in the new area;
- details of the size and nature of the new area; and
- the numbers policy (if any) to apply in the new area.

8.50 The Secretary of State is required to approve the resolution, but Schedule 14 does not give any grounds for disapproval. It therefore appears that all the Secretary of State can do is satisfy himself that the requirements laid down in the Schedule have been complied with. The only reason for not approving the resolution would be some procedural irregularity or non-compliance. Any other reasons for refusal would appear to be ultra vires the powers of the Secretary of State.

8.51 Unless, and until, such a resolution is passed in any authority which has zones, irrespective of whether these are post-1974 authorities or authorities that have been created as a result of the latest reorganisation in both England and Wales, zones will continue to apply. The effect of this is that the authority is unable to treat its area as one hackney carriage licensing district and must continue to treat each area separately.

8.52 Although there is nothing to prevent the local authority granting what are, in effect, multiple licences to a hackney carriage to enable it to ply for hire within all the zones within its district, the local authority cannot pass district-wide byelaws or impose a district-wide fare structure. This does not mean that different fares need to apply in different zones, although they could do so if that was the desire of the authority, but it does mean that each zone will require its own fare structure and any fare increases must be treated on a zone basis. This means that although the same fares can apply, they will have to be implemented by means of two or more fare increases.

8.53 In relation to fees for hackney carriage proprietors' licences and drivers' licences, again, these can only be levied on a zoned basis.

8.54 It can be seen that zones can and do exist, but the only action that a local authority can take is to remove all zones or accept the situation as it is. There is no power available to a local authority to either merge some zones to create a smaller number or, alternatively, to create new zones, thereby further subdividing its district.

HACKNEY CARRIAGE PROPRIETOR'S LICENCE

The granting of the licence

8.55 A hackney carriage needs a licence granted by the district council under section 37 of the 1847 Act. Such a licence is referred to in the legislation as a hackney carriage proprietor's licence, but is often referred to in day-to-day usage as a hackney carriage vehicle licence.

'Commissioners may licence hackney carriages

37 A district council may from time to time licence to ply for hire within the prescribed distance, or if no distance is prescribed, within five miles from the General Post Office of the city, town, or place to which the special Act refers (which in that case shall be deemed the prescribed distance), hackney coaches or carriages of any kind or description adapted to the carriage of persons.'

The local authority can limit the numbers of hackney carriage proprietors' licences that it is prepared to grant but only if it is "satisfied that there is no significant demand for the services of hackney carriages (within the area to which the licence would apply) which is unmet'[1].   **8.56**

1 This is considered in more detail at paras 8.99–8.133.

Section 40 of the 1847 Act, in addition to laying down the requirement to apply for a licence, also places a requirement upon the proprietor or proprietors to sign 'a requisition' for a licence. This details the information that should be contained within that requisition, including the full name and address of the applicant, together with anyone else who is involved in the keeping, employ or letting for hire of the hackney carriage in question. In the case of there being more than one proprietor, eg a partnership, each person with an interest in the vehicle has to complete a requisition.   **8.57**

The case of *Challoner v Evans*[1] makes it clear that the plate belongs to the local authority and cannot be disposed of separately from the vehicle. In this case, the defendant sold the vehicle, but attempted to retain the plate and 'rent' the plate to the purchaser of the vehicle. When he applied for renewal of the licence, he committed an offence under section 40, as he declared that he was the proprietor of the hackney carriage when he had, in fact, sold the vehicle. In that case, Croom-Johnson LJ concluded: **8.58**

> 'In my view, on the facts as the Justices found them, Mr Evans [who applied for the renewal] was not concerned in the employment for hire of any Hackney carriage by Mr Holledge [the owner of the vehicle]. It was Mr Holledge who was employing the Vauxhall Cavalier for hire. The same position would have continued had the licence been granted in accordance with the application which was made on the 29th November 1984. It is quite clear on the facts found by the justices that it was Mr Holledge and nobody else who was the proprietor of the Hackney carriage. In those circumstances, in filling in his own name as the sole proprietor of the vehicle Mr Evans did commit the offence with which he was charged.'

Most local authorities have standard forms for this application, or requisition, for a hackney carriage proprietor's licence and a specimen form is to be found in Appendix IV.

1 (1986) Times, 22 November.

One of the standard requirements in a hackney carriage proprietor's licence application (and, indeed, in a private hire vehicle application) is a requirement that the application must be accompanied by a registration document for the vehicle and a valid insurance certificate for the vehicle. In the case of *Cannock Chase District Council v Alldritt*[1] (a case which   **8.59** primarily concerns the granting of hackney carriage proprietors' licences), a second question arose. It was considered in the judgment of Mann LJ as follows:

> 'A second point raised by the Crown Court, and which arose out of a consideration of the applications made by Mr. Alldritt [the applicant for a number of hackney carriage proprietors' licences] was this:
>
>> "Was the Crown Court correct in holding as unlawful the condition imposed by the District Council, that an applicant for a hackney carriage licence must present, with his application, a certificate of insurance in respect of the vehicle it is sought to licence that is valid at the time of making the application?"
>
> The district council has, as might be expected, a form of application for licence in respect of Hackney carriage vehicles, and it seeks information. Under the rubric "insurance" there are questions as to the name of the company, as to whether all third party and passenger risks are covered, as to the period of the policy and as to its date. Overleaf there is the admonition, "This application must be accompanied by the following: (i) Registration Document for the Vehicle (ii) Valid Insurance Certificate, (iii) Fee".
>
> The Crown Court seems to have proceeded upon the basis that an application would be treated as invalid by the district council unless accompanied by a valid insurance certificate. Mr. Stephens on behalf of the council disclaims, as I understand him, that position. He draws attention to section 57(1) of the Local Government (Miscellaneous Provisions) Act 1976 which provides:
>
>> "A district council may require any applicant for a licence under the Act of 1847 or under this Part of this Act to submit to them such information as they may reasonably consider necessary to enable them to determine whether the licence should be granted and whether conditions should be attached to any such licence."
>
> Mr. Stephens submits that the insurance requests are requests which are reasonable within the meaning of that power. I agree with that submission without hesitation. I also agree that where there is a certificate of insurance it would be reasonable to require its production for inspection. However, I could not agree that an application should not be considered unless it is accompanied by a certificate of insurance. That requirement is not one which in my view is authorised by section 57, or for that matter any other provision in relation to the licensing of vehicles, and accordingly a refusal to entertain on that ground would in any judgement be unlawful.
>
> As I understand it, the district council does not dissent from that and is content that its request for information might be answered "not yet arranged" or "to be arranged". Such an answer might well be one for a person who has not previously had a licence for his vehicle and who does not wish to incur expenditure on insuring it as a Hackney before he gets a plate for it. I think the difficulty would be removed if the form made it clear that there was a qualification " . . . if any".
>
> Thus, if the question posed by the Crown-Court which I have read is read in the sense in which I thik it is intended to be read the answer is that it is unlawful to refuse to consider an application unless a certificate of insurance is in force. However, a request for information is in my view perfectly appropriate.'

It therefore seems that an application can be made on the basis that, if it is successful, a policy of insurance will be provided, rather than it being a condition precedent to the consideration of the application. This certainly seems reasonable, although a local authority would be well advised not to part with the licence, once it has been granted, until they confirm the existence of the insurance policy. This principle would appear to be capable of being extended to the matter of the vehicle registration document as well. An applicant may be reluctant to invest in a vehicle until he is certain that he will be granted a licence. A similar approach would appear reasonable.

1 (28 January 1993, unreported), DC.

Procedure

There are specific points which need to be contained within the licence itself as issued by the local authority and those are laid down in section 41 of the 1847 Act. They include: **8.60**

- the name and address of everyone who is either a proprietor or who has an interest in the vehicle; and
- the number of the licence which corresponds to the number on the plate attached to the hackney carriage.

In addition, local authorities are given a wide discretion, by section 41, to include any other information that they think may be relevant.

The local authority must register the licence, after it has been completed, and that registration must be recorded in 'a book to be provided by the Clerk of the Commissioners' for that purpose. Section 42 of the 1847 Act goes on to state that there should be 'columns or places for entries to made of every offence committed by any proprietor or driver or person attending such carriage'. It is quite sensible that this information be recorded and that it should be recorded by the local authority. What is less clear is whether compliance with the law is achieved if the information is recorded in any form other than in a book. A number of local authorities use computer programs for recording this information and even those authorities that are not yet as advanced in the world of information technology tend to use card indexes or some other filing mechanism. The use of 'a book' is now extremely antiquated.   **8.61**

Whatever method is used, to fully comply with the requirements of section 42 of the 1847 Act, it must be open to inspection by anyone, not just someone either involved in the trade or from the local authority itself, at any reasonable time without payment. 'Reasonable time' is usually taken to mean during the normal office hours of the local authority concerned.   **8.62**

Conditions

8.63 Section 47 of the Local Government (Miscellaneous Provisions) Act 1976 ('the 1976 Act') gives the local authority discretionary powers in relation to hackney carriage proprietors' licences:

> **'Licensing of hackney carriages**
>
> 47–(1) A district council may attach to the grant of a licence of a hackney carriage under the Act of 1847 such conditions as the district council may consider reasonably necessary.
>
> (2) Without prejudice to the generality of the foregoing subsection, a district council may require any hackney carriage licensed by them under the Act of 1847 to be of such design or appearance or bear such distinguishing marks as shall clearly identify it as a hackney carriage.
>
> (3) Any person aggrieved by any conditions attached to such a licence may appeal to a magistrates' court.'

The power to attach conditions is extremely wide. There are a wide range of conditions imposed by local authorities. They include the appearance of the vehicle, including size, colour and age.

Size, colour and age

8.64 In the case of *R v Hyndburn Borough Council, ex p Rauf and Kasim*[1], the High Court held that it was possible, under section 47(1), to impose the condition on the grant of a licence that no licence would be granted to a vehicle that was over a specified age. Hyndburn Borough Council had introduced the following policy to improve the reliability, safety and overall standards of the vehicles licensed by the council:

> '(1) That private hire and hackney carriage vehicles must be no more than 3 years old when first registered [ie licensed as a private hire and hackney carriage vehicle];
>
> (2) That the maximum age of a private hire and hackney carriage vehicle must be no more than 7 years;
>
> (3) That the maximum age of an FX4 [purpose designed and built hackney carriage] must be no more than 11 years.'

This was challenged on the grounds that it was unlawful, going beyond the powers contained in either section 47(1) of the 1976 Act, in relation to hackney carriages, or section 48(2) of the same Act, in relation to private hire vehicles; that it fettered the discretion of the authority; and was *Wednesbury* unreasonable. Dismissing the application, Kennedy J stated:

> 'In the present case . . . this local authority did give such consideration as was appropriate to this application. It indicated in the letter which it wrote in reply to it that the application was refused in line with the policy and that did not indicate that it was shutting its ears to any application, either considered individually or an application which amounted to an application to change the policy as a whole.
>
> In those circumstances, it seems to me, the stance adopted by the local authority in relation to the application was a lawful one and therefore on the substantive ground . . . the application fails.'

1 (1992, unreported).

It is worth noting that the reason for the distinction made between the 'ordinary' vehicles and FX4s was because London-style cabs have a separate chassis and are designed for the hackney carriage trade, whereas saloon vehicles are of a unitary construction and are not purpose designed. **8.65**

Some authorities had imposed age policies, but allowed an 'exemption clause' to prevent an allegation that, by imposing such a policy, they were fettering their discretion[1]. These policies were usually worded to allow vehicles to be licensed by the local authority, if they were older than allowed by the age policy, but only if they were 'exceptionally well-maintained' or in 'exceptional condition'. Such wording led to appeals against refusals because of different interpretation of 'exceptional' etc. As there was no 'exemption clause' in the policy of Hyndburn Borough Council, the judgment in the case supports the view that exemption clauses are not necessary, provided the policy is just that, a policy, not an immutable rule. **8.66**

Reference is often made to the case of *Sharpe v Nottingham City Council*[1] in relation to age policies. This was a Crown Court decision where the court decided that a blanket policy did fetter the discretion of the local authority. However, as the *Hyndburn* case postdates the *Sharpe* case by some 11 years and is a High Court decision, it is the more reliable decision on this point. **8.67**

1   [1981] CLY 2537.

Section 47(2) of the 1976 Act allows the local authority to impose conditions specifically in relation to the design or appearance of the hackney carriages which they licence and this has been the subject of a number of court cases. **8.68**

Possibly the most important, is the case of *R v Wirral Metropolitan Borough Council, ex p the Wirral Licensed Hackney Carriage Owners Association*[1]. Wirral Metropolitan Borough Council resolved that from a certain date, all hackney carriages licensed by the council would have to be of a purpose-built type. Originally, the resolution specifically stated 'FX4', but it was suggested, and accepted, that this might conflict with Article 30 of the Treaty of Rome. The resolution was amended to become a specification, rather than a specific make or model of vehicle. One of the reasons for this policy was that it was important for the public to be able to distinguish between hackney carriages and private hire vehicles. Another reason concerned the general suitability of that type of vehicle for hackney carriage work. The Wirral Licensed Taxi Drivers Association challenged the decision. In dismissing the application, Glidewell J said (at 161, paragraph 39): **8.69**

> 'What are the Council's functions under this legislation in relation to the licensing of taxi cabs? As I see it they are to achieve, so far as they can, the safety, convenience and comfort of passengers in hackney carriages, the safety of other road users and to ensure that there is some way in which those who wish to use either hackney carriages or private hire vehicles can readily distinguish the one type of vehicle from another. That the last is a proper object is to my mind made clear by section 47(2) of the 1976 Act. I conclude, on the material before me, that the councils primary purpose was indeed . . . to introduce a requirement which served to distinguish hackney carriage vehicles from private hire vehicles. But I cannot find that it was the sole purpose, nor can I find that in arriving at its decision,

the Council did not take into account other factors. Putting it the other way round, I am satisfied on the material before me that the Council did take into account other factors: safety and convenience. It was not only entitled to do so, but was obliged to do so and it did so. What I think in effect the Council has done, through its relevant committee and the assistance of various reports it has had, is, it has said

"We want to ensure that hackney carriages are readily distinguishable from private hire vehicles. We are told that it could be done simply by ensuring that hackney carriages are all of one colour, or bearing distinguishing signs, or we could require that they are all of a particular description. If we adopt the latter requirement it will have the added advantage that we shall be ensuring that the vehicle does have the advantages of robustness, added safety, added convenience of passengers, and that is our view. Thus we take those matters into account in deciding that that is the best way of distinguishing."

I know I am interpreting what the Council has said. This is in effect what is to be read into the reports [placed before it]. I cannot say that in arriving at its decision the Council either took some irrelevant consideration into account, or came to a conclusion to which no reasonable authority could ever have come.'

1 [1983] CMLR 150.

8.70 This has been followed in the case of *R v Luton Borough Council, ex p Mirza (Riaz Ahmed)*[1].

Luton Borough Council had a policy that new or renewed hackney carriage proprietors' licences would only be granted to vehicles which were London-style cabs and which were wheelchair accessible or specifically manufactured hackney carriages or minibuses capable of carrying wheelchairs. Mr Mirza had an accident in his hackney carriage and could not afford to repair it, so asked Luton Borough Council if they would allow him to run a saloon vehicle as a hackney carriage in the intervening period. This was considered by the local authority and rejected. Mirza applied for a judicial review and leave was granted. This case was actually an application for leave to be set aside and that can only be done on the grounds that the substantive application will clearly fail. Accordingly, a full judgment was given by Brooke J. There were three grounds argued:

1. That there was an alternative statutory remedy,
2. That the policy conflicted with Article 30 of the Treaty of Rome, and
3. That the decision was *Wednesbury* unreasonable.

1 [1995] COD 231.

8.71 The first argument failed and the judgment concentrated on the question of alleged incompatibility between the policy and Article 30 of the Treaty of Rome. The decision in *R v Metropolitan Borough Council of Wirral, ex p The Wirral Licensed Taxi Owners Association*[1] was approved, as were some obiter remarks in the unreported case of *R v Doncaster Metropolitan Borough Council, ex p Kelly*[2], where Harrison J approved the *Wirral* approach. Although the European cases of *Keck*[3] and *Boermans*[4] were referred to, these did not detract from the principle in the *Wirral* case. Brooke J stated:

'I accept Mr Calver's [for the Council] submissions that the wide policy provided by the Council in this case does not offend against art 30 of the

Treaty of Rome. The provisions apply, so far as Mr Mirza is concerned, if he wishes to acquire a vehicle which would qualify for a licence under the Council's policy, to all relevant traders operating within the national territory as well as to the traders abroad within the other Member States. They affect in the same manner, in law and in fact, the marketing of the products in each country.

Although Mr Crystal valiantly sought to argue that the judgments of the English Courts, particularly, the judgment of Glidewell J, went on a misunderstanding of the principles of European Law, I am completely satisfied that the present jurisprudence of the court makes it quite clear that a provision, such as that laid down by the Luton Borough Council, does not offend art 30. Accordingly, I regard the art 30 point, as did Glidewell J eleven years ago and Harrison J on a provisional basis last July, as unarguable.'

Finally, he rejected the argument that the decision of the local authority was unreasonable in *Wednesbury* terms by saying:

'At all events, I have seen a great mass of evidence which shows that this was a policy which the Council, in the exercise of the discretion given to it by statute, could reasonably and lawfully enter into.'

This case usefully reinforces the fact that the *Wirral* decision was rightly decided.

1 [1983] CMLR 150. See para 8.69.
2 (20 October 1994, unreported).
3 Cases C-267 268/91 [1993] ECRI–6097, ECJ.
4 Cases C-401/92 402/92 [1994] ECRI–2199, ECJ.

The adoption by local authorities of a policy of only granting hackney car- **8.72** riage proprietors' licences to London-style cabs has become increasingly popular in urban areas and is often referred to as a 'mandatory order'. This has no legal meaning, but is generally accepted to refer to a situation where an all-London-style cab policy is in force.

As was outlined in the *Wirral* case, such policies must be worded extremely **8.73** carefully to avoid any charge of anti-competitive behaviour under European law. Policies that refer to specific makes of vehicle are unlikely to succeed should such a challenge be mounted. The most successful way of wording the policy is by measurement of internal and external features, door openings, turning circle etc, and the specification adopted by the Public Carriage Office in London appears to satisfy the most stringent criteria available.

Wheelchair-accessible

Some authorities have gone further, and have required not only an all- **8.74** London-style cab fleet, but that the fleet itself should be comprised of all wheelchair-accessible vehicles. This was pioneered in the late 1980s by Manchester City Council and was challenged in the case of *R v Manchester City Council, ex p Reid and McHugh*[1]. In the mid 1980s, Manchester City Council were concerned about the provision of transport services for disabled people who used wheelchairs and, when they decided to increase the size of the hackney carriage fleet in Manchester by 100 vehicles, they imposed a condition upon those licences requiring the successful applicant to provide a vehicle which was not only based on a London-style cab, but which was either already converted for wheelchair access or to convert it within a specified period of time at their own expense. This condition was challenged as being unreasonable. Simon Brown J heard the application for judicial review. He considered the judgment in *R v Wirral Metropolitan Borough Council*[2] and stated (at 185):

'The decision [in the *Wirral* case] is, of course, authority for saying that a council is obliged to have regard to safety and convenience, but not for the converse proposition that the safety, convenience and comfort of passengers are the *only* considerations (apart from section 47(2) of the Act of 1976 question of identification) open to an authority determining what conditions to impose. As it seems to me conditions imposed for the other considerations could well be legitimate, for instance those controlling the display of advertisements, such, indeed, as formed part of the city council's own standard conditions. Even, however, were this not so, I have no difficulty whatever in regarding a facility for transporting the wheelchair-bound disabled as directly relating to the "safe, comfortable and convenient functioning of the taxi" and thus squarely within Mr Frizgerald's [who appeared for the applicants] own formulation. Nor am I in the least attracted to the submission that the wheelchair-bound disabled (or rather that proportion of them who are particularly advantaged by being enabled to remain in their chairs) are too small a minority of the population to be properly regarded as an integral part of the general public. On the contrary, I prefer Mr Hugill's approach that the general public must be taken to comprise many physical minority groups, including for instance the obese, the unusually tall, young children and the disabled.

Ultimately, it must always be a question of fact and degree whether the minority is so small or the advantage to them is so slight or the cost of complying with the provision is so great that the imposition of such a condition cannot be justified.

Mr Fitzgerald further stresses the phrase "reasonably necessary" within the condition-making power. He contends that even putting the city council's case at its highest it was their conclusion only that the proposed facility was an ideal rather than a necessity, their evidence being couched in the explicit language of desirability, not need. This submission also I reject. It seems to me that desirability shades into necessity: what is clearly desirable in the interests of the safety and comfort can by the same token properly be regarded as reasonably necessary.

Nor do I accept Mr Fitzgerald's argument that the conversion condition can be impugned as not reasonably relating to the purpose of the condition-making power, but imposed rather for an ulterior object, that of solving the wider and more general problem of the disabled within Manchester's public transportation system. The contention here is that the council were exercising the power of compulsion over new taxi drivers to make good deficiencies elsewhere in the transport system. But I can see no objection to the council having regard to the existence or lack of alternative facilities for the disabled when deciding how to exercise this condition-making power.'

1 (1989) 88 LGR 180.
2 [1983] CMLR 150. See para 8.69.

In fact subsequent developments prior to this hearing took the policy of **8.75**
Manchester City Council even further because they then imposed a condition
requiring conversion of all vehicles holding existing licences or the replacement of the vehicle with a purpose-built wheelchair-accessible vehicle. The
costs for this were to be recovered through an increase in fares and, as a consequence, by the beginning of 1992 Manchester had the first English fleet of
hackney carriages which were all accessible for wheelchair-using travellers.

Livery

In addition to the actual mechanical specification of the vehicle, conditions **8.76**
can be attached in relation to its visual appearance and a number of authorities have liveries for their hackney carriages. In some cases, this is the
traditional black, especially in the case of purpose-built vehicles, but other
authorities are rather more imaginative and have contrasting bonnet and
boot lids or doors. Once again, the justification for this is to assist the travelling public in identifying a hackney carriage. Other conditions of a similar
type include the requirement for illuminated roof signs, possibly with or
without specified wording, badges affixed to the vehicles in prominent
places (eg on the doors, on the roof or wherever the council may think fit)
and the presence of specified wording on the vehicles' sides.

Some authorities allow 'sponsored' vehicles, whereby the vehicle is painted **8.77**
in a particular livery advertising a certain product or company. This is popular in large cities on purpose-built vehicles, but seems less common on
either saloon-type vehicles or in rural areas. Of those authorities that do
allow such sponsored vehicles, a number have within the conditions requirements that the design must be submitted to the council for prior approval,
and some stipulate that any sponsorship that endorses either alcohol or
tobacco products will not be accepted. It is not entirely clear the extent of
the powers a local authority has to limit the type of advertisement which it
will allow through sponsored vehicles, other than preventing advertisement
which in themselves would be unlawful.

Other conditions applied to hackney carriage proprietors' licences under **8.78**
section 47(1) of the 1976 Act include:

• carrying of first aid kits;
• cleanliness and tidiness of the vehicle;
• carrying of a fire extinguisher;
• advertising to be displayed on or in the vehicle only with the approval of
  the local authority;
• requirement to carry a passenger's guide or hearing dog.

Appeal against any conditions imposed

Section 47(3) of the 1976 Act gives a right to 'any person aggrieved by any **8.79**
conditions attached to such a [hackney carriage proprietor's] licence may
appeal to a magistrates' court'[1]. It should be noted that it is only when the
condition has been attached to such a licence that an appeal can be brought,
and that a proposal made by the council that a condition will be imposed is
not sufficient to trigger the appeal mechanism.

1 For the mechanics of this please see Chapter 3 on appeals.

8.80   It is worth making the point here that, whilst it is clear that there is a statutory appeal mechanism, in general, it should be exhausted before the question of judicial review arises[1]. However, in the situation outlined above, where the condition has yet to be applied to any licence, but the proposal has been adopted by the council in respect of future licences, it seems that there would then be a possibility of seeking a judicial review of that decision. Although this is possible, in practical terms, especially in relation to cost, it would probably be more effective for the aggrieved parties (which will undoubtedly be more than one member of the trade) to wait until the condition is actually applied to a licence and then back an appeal by that licence holder against the provision rather than seek a judicial review.

1   See, eg *R v Blackpool Borough Council, ex p Red Cab Taxis* [1994] RTR 402, QBD, Chapter 3, para 3.32.

THE LICENCE ITSELF

Procedure

8.81   Section 43 of the 1847 Act makes it a requirement that the licence should be sealed by the district council and should not last for more than a year. Where, however, the 1976 Act has been adopted, it is acceptable for the licence simply to be signed by an authorised officer rather than sealed.

8.82   The 1976 Act, however, makes no alteration to the prohibition on granting hackney carriage proprietors' licences for more than a year. Section 5 of the Town Police Clauses Act 1889 allows for licences to be granted for a shorter period and a number of district councils use this provision to take the licence up to a general renewal date that the council has. Some authorities have hackney carriage proprietors' licences which all expire on the same date, whereas others take the view that from whenever the licence is granted the licence will run for a year and, accordingly, their renewals are staggered throughout the year.

8.83   Section 44 of the 1847 Act requires a proprietor to inform the council within seven days of a change of address and imposes a penalty for failing to comply with this requirement of a fine not exceeding level one on summary conviction. It also requires the council 'by their clerk' to endorse the change on the licence and sign it. Again, many authorities issue a substitute licence in these circumstances and, whilst this may not be absolutely legally correct, will certainly make for greater clarity in situations where proprietors move more than once within the year. It does not take a great deal of imagination to realise how complex a licence could become if the proprietor moved two or three times throughout the life of the licence.

8.84   If the proprietor transfers his interest to another person he must, under section 49 of the 1976 Act, inform the council of this change within 14 days of the transfer. This must be notified in writing and he must specify the name and address of the person to whom his interest has been transferred. Once such a notice has been received by the district council, then, under section 42 of the 1847 Act, the council must register it. Provided that such notice is given to the council within the 14-day period, the council cannot refuse to register it.

R v Weymouth Borough Councils, ex p Teletax (Weymouth) Ltd

This was confirmed in the case of *R v Weymouth Borough Council, ex p* **8.85**
Teletax (Weymouth) Ltd[1], which addressed the question of whether a local
authority had to record a transfer of a hackney carriage proprietor's
licence on the sale of such a licence from one licensee to another. This
point is not specifically addressed in the legislation. In this case, Teletax
Ltd bought five hackney carriages from existing proprietors who had current licences and applied to Weymouth Borough Council for those
licenses to be transferred to them. The council was reluctant to do this,
apparently because it felt that by purchasing the licences Teletax had
acquired proprietors' licences ahead of people who had been in a waiting
list for some time.

Goddard LCJ stated (at 590):

> 'What then is the effect of these sections [of the Town Police Clauses Act
> 1847]? In my opinion, they clearly show that the licence is granted to the
> carriage, and that the licence remains in force for a year from the time
> when it is granted, or until the next annual licensing meeting of the com-
> missioners, if they appoint a date before the annual granting of these
> licences. What then is to happen if during that a year a change of propri-
> etorship takes place? There is the vehicle; it has a licence attached to it.
> There is nothing in this Act which says that the vehicle may not be sold,
> or may only be sold with the consent of the council. There is no provision
> here to say that if a person has obtained a licence for a cab and disposes of
> it, or dies, that he or his personal representatives must surrender the
> licence. What is necessary is that the register should be kept in order and
> kept up to date. Therefore, it seems to me that, by necessary implication,
> a person who buys a cab which has been licensed is under a duty to go to
> the local authority and say: "I am now the proprietor of this cab which you
> licensed for a year; please therefore enter me in the register as the propri-
> etor, and substitute my name on the licence granted in respect of the cab,
> in the place of the name of the earlier proprietor."'

His Lordship took the view that there was no power for the local authority not to register the transfer of these licences. Atkinson J concurred with
Lord Goddard and added (at 593):

> 'There is one consideration, however, which I think assists the applicants
> here, and that is the position of the proprietor who has sold his hackney
> carriage. He must be entitled to have his name removed from the register,
> and to have his name removed from the licence which has been granted.
> If he gave notice to the commissioners, similar to the notice required by
> section 44, I should have thought that if they refused to remove his name
> from the register, he could come here for mandamus to make them do so.
> This seems to indicate that the council must be bound to take notice of
> changes of ownership and to keep their register accurate in accordance
> with the true position. If the old proprietor has a right to his name
> removed, I should have thought it was equally clear that the new propri-
> etor has a right to have his name inserted in the place of that of the old
> proprietor.'

However, the council may then (provided the 1976 Act has been adopted)
refuse to renew the licence for the new proprietor under section 60(1) of the
1976 Act. It is arguable that this sanction could be imposed where the
council impose a total number of hackney carriage proprietors' licences

that they are prepared to issue, but it is difficult to sustain this argument if there are no objections to the new proprietor themselves.

1   [1947] KB 583.

8.86   It is interesting to note that in neither the 1847 Act nor the 1976 Act are there any qualification requirements for hackney carriage proprietors on first application. On renewal, section 60(1)(*b*) and (*c*) of the 1976 Act may have an effect if the council take the view that the proprietor has either committed an offence under either the 1847 or 1976 Act, in the case of 60(1)(*b*), or 'any other reasonable cause', in relation to section 60(1)(*c*). That wording does not have to be construed *ejusdem generis* with the wording contained in section 60(1)(*a*) or (*b*). That means that 'any other reasonable cause' does not have to be linked in any way with an offence committed under hackney carriage legislation and the council can take any other matter into account.

Norwich City Council v Thurtle and Watcham

8.87   This was the decision in the case of *Norwich City Council v Thurtle and Watcham*[1]. Mr Watcham had held eight private hire vehicle licences and was convicted for dishonestly handling goods. The goods were car seats which had been stolen and which he used as seats in one of his private hire cars. On conviction, Norwich City Council revoked his vehicle licences under the powers contained in section 60(1)(*c*) of the 1976 Act. Mr Thurtle, who held a private hire driver's licence, was convicted of being concerned with another in stealing a motor car. Again, on conviction Norwich City Council revoked his driver's licence under section 61(1)(*b*). Both appealed to the magistrates' court, who ruled that 'any other reasonable cause' had to be construed *ejusdem generis* with the grounds contained in either section 60(1)(*a*) and (*b*), in the case of a vehicle licence, or section 61(1)(*a*), in the case of a driver's licence. As a consequence, the magistrates upheld the appeals. Norwich City Council appealed by way of the case stated and the matter was considered by Comyn J. He dealt with the actual question very briefly:

> 'In my judgment the justices were not correct to construe the words in question as applicable only to matters *ejusdem generis* with those immediately before set out.'

The judge then spent some considerable time expanding on this statement and giving his reasons:

> 'In my judgment the words "any other reasonable cause" are at large and cover anything and everything which might be regarded as a reasonable reason for depriving a person of his vehicle licence. It is impossible to define in any general terms what circumstances might arise. Endless possibilities suggest themselves. The all-important word is "reasonable".'

He continued:

> 'I would only add at this stage that criminal convictions of any kind – in particular criminal convictions relating to motor vehicles, or motor vehicle parts or accessories – could, in my judgment, amount to "any other reasonable cause". Equally I wish to make it quite plain that, in my judgment, they do not automatically do so. Every case has got to be considered in its own context as to whether there is or is not a reasonable cause.'

Furthermore, it would not be a reasonable cause in my judgment that revocations had been made of drivers' licences under section 61 or operators' licensed under section 62. This matter of reasonable cause must be decided in every case on its own facts and in a common sense, down-to-earth way. It would not be right to seek to fetter a court in how it approaches the matter.'

This comment related to the argument which was advanced that, as a persons private hire driver's licence was being revoked, there was no point in not revoking his vehicle licences. This argument seems difficult to follow, as it would be possible for a vehicle proprietor to allow other licensed drivers to drive his cars. It found no favour with the judge, who said 'I do not agree. These are all separate matters'. He then concluded as follows:

'The Case Stated goes on to say that the justices were asked to construe the section, and in particular sub-section (1)(*c*). They say that it was argued on the respondent's behalf that handling stolen goods could not be a ground for revoking his vehicle licence. I have already indicated that I do not agree with that. It could be a ground. Whether it should have been a ground is another matter and is a matter for the justices now to decide.

The Case Stated goes on to say that the appellant (the council) argued that the Public Health Committee had an unfettered discretion within the normal meaning of the words. I agree with that statement and that contention, but only to this extent. They had the discretion within the wide meaning, as I find it, of those words; not a discretion so unfettered as to make them feel that they were compelled by reason of the conviction to suspend or revoke the licence.'

1 (21 May 1981, unreported, DC.)

Accordingly, 'any other reasonable cause' could relate to any other ground **8.88** on which the council felt the new proprietor was unsuitable. The most obvious grounds would be that he has a criminal record, possibly unrelated to taxis, which would cause the council concern if he was to be involved in the hackney carriage trade or that there was some other reason which makes him unsuitable. It is not necessary for the council to consider whether or not the new proprietor is a fit and proper person, but that is probably as good a test as any.

As the words 'any other reasonable cause' appear to be able to apply to any- **8.89** thing, then it is arguable that where there is a numbers policy in force a council could refuse a transfer to a new proprietor because there is a waiting list of people for hackney carriage proprietors' licences. However, this would not be reasonable, as it would effectively amount to a ban on transfer of a hackney carriage vehicle licence, which is not prohibited by the legislation. Indeed, the legislation in section 49 of the 1976 Act would appear to specifically envisage such transfers taking place naturally.

INSPECTION OF VEHICLES

Local authorities need to be satisfied that the hackney carriages operating **8.90** within their area are safe to do so. Section 50(1) of the 1976 Act allows the local authority to request the proprietor to present the vehicle for test at whatever place the council specify. It is interesting to note that the place of test must be 'within the area of the council' and, if the council use test facilities which are actually outside their council area, then a hackney carriage proprietor could legitimately refuse to attend at that location for a test.

8.91   If the hackney carriage is not being used (and this would appear to indicate that it is off the road for some considerable period rather than simply not working at that precise time), then the council can by notice ask the proprietor where it is. The proprietor must tell them its location and allow them to inspect and test. Again, it appears that the legislation specifically envisages that the vehicle will be tested wherever it is currently stored, which may well be in conditions which would not allow for a complete test. Obviously, if the vehicle is not insured, taxed, tested or roadworthy it would not be possible to require it to be moved to the council's test site, but if those considerations do not apply, then, to enable a test to be undertaken, it would need to be moved to the council's test site, although the legislation does not specifically allow this. It will probably be necessary to move the vehicle to an approved testing site to ensure that the provisions of the Health and Safety at Work etc Act 1974 are maintained in respect of the testers themselves.

8.92   Section 50(2) of the 1976 Act also applies in relation to vehicles which are the subject of an application for a hackney carriage proprietor's licence, but for which no licence has been in force previously and again, it is likely that they would need to be transported to the council's test site to enable a comprehensive and acceptable test to be undertaken.

8.93   Testing of vehicles is obviously important if the hackney carriage has been involved in any kind of accident. Section 50(3) of the 1976 Act requires the proprietor to inform the district council 'as soon as reasonably practicable' and, in any case, within 72 hours of any accident causing 'damage materially affecting the safety, performance or appearance of the hackney carriage . . . or the comfort or convenience or persons carried therein'. Once such a notice has been received the local authority will undoubtedly wish to inspect the vehicle and can use the provisions of section 50(1) to require the vehicle to be presented for testing, if it is still running, or if it is off the road, the provisions of section 50(2) can be used to require an inspection.

8.94   Section 50(4) of the 1976 Act allows an authorised officer of the council to inspect both the licence and the insurance policy in force for the vehicle.

8.95   Section 50(1) of the 1976 Act limits the number of times that an inspection can be made of a hackney carriage to three in any one year and most authorities use this for their regular inspections. Some inspect bi-annually, but very few appear to make full use of the provision for three inspections per year. However, if an accident notice under section 50(3) is received, then the vehicle can be inspected by an authorised officer of the council or a police constable, under section 68 of the 1976 Act:

> **'Fitness of hackney carriages and private hire vehicles**
>
> **68** Any authorised officer of the council in question or any constable shall have power at all reasonable times to inspect and test, for the purpose of

ascertaining its fitness, any hackney carriage or private hire vehicle licensed by a district council, or any taximeter affixed to such a vehicle, and if he is not satisfied as to the fitness of the hackney carriage or private hire vehicle or as to the accuracy of its taximeter he may by notice in writing require the proprietor of the hackney carriage or private hire vehicle to make it or its taximeter available for further inspection and testing at such reasonable time and place as may be specified in the notice and suspend the vehicle licence until such time as such authorised officer or constable is so satisfied:

Provided that, if the authorised officer or constable is not so satisfied before the expiration of a period of two months, the said licence shall, by virtue of this section, be deemed to have been revoked and subsections (2) and (3) of section 60 of this Act shall apply with any necessary modifications.'

This allows the authorised officer to inspect and test the vehicle. If it does not satisfy the council's requirements then a notice can be issued requiring the vehicle to be submitted for a re-test and the licence can be suspended until such time as the vehicle satisfactorily passes any subsequent test. This is an extremely useful provision and is essential for keeping the hackney carriage vehicles operating within the area of the council in a satisfactory and safe condition.

8.96 It is interesting to note that, if the vehicle is not presented in a fit condition within two months of the date of the original notice being issued, then the licence itself is deemed to be revoked. If the licence is deemed to be revoked after the expiry of the two-month period, then there is a right of appeal against that revocation by virtue of section 60(2) and (3) of the 1976 Act. However, it does not appear that there is a right of appeal against the suspension of the vehicle pending the improvements required in the notice. Although section 60 allows the council to suspend or revoke the proprietor's licence on the grounds that 'that the hackney carriage . . . is unfit for use as a hackney carriage' (section 60(1)(a)), if the suspension has been imposed under section 68 after an inspection then such right of appeal does not appear to exist.

8.97 This seems anomalous, as both sections refer to the fitness of the hackney carriage as being the reason for action being taken. It seems unsatisfactory that a local authority can avoid having its decision being challenged by means of appeal if it uses the section 68 procedure as opposed to the section 60 procedure. If a local authority were to specifically decide to use the section 68 procedure in such cases, then its decision would arguably be open to challenge as unreasonable if, and only if, it could be argued that the sole justification for that decision was to prevent hackney carriage proprietors from having a right of appeal against the suspension.

APPLICANTS FOR PROPRIETORS' LICENCES

8.98 On an application for a proprietor's licence, the district council does not appear to be able to refuse to issue the licence for any specified reasons, provided the applicant has signed the required requisition for the licence as laid down in section 40 of the 1847 Act. However, the power to issue a licence is discretionary, not mandatory. The only certain ground on which a licence cannot be refused is if there is a significant demand which remains unmet.

'No significant demand which is unmet'

8.99   Until the introduction of the Transport Act 1985, local authorities had an unrestricted discretion to limit the number of hackney carriages which they would licence. Section 16 of the Transport Act 1985 removed that discretion by amending the wording of section 37 of the 1847 Act. Section 16 stated:

> **'Taxi licensing: control of numbers**
>
> **16** The provisions of the Town Police Clauses Act 1847 with respect to hackney carriages, as incorporated in any enactment (whenever passed), shall have effect—
>
> (*a*)   as if in section 37, the words "such number of" and "as they think fit" were omitted; and
>
> (*b*)   as if they provided that the grant of a licence may be refused, for the purpose of limiting the number of hackney carriages in respect of which licences are granted, if, but only if, the person authorised to grant licences is satisfied that there is no significant demand for the services of hackney carriages (within the area to which the licence would apply) which is unmet.'

As a result of this, the local authority can only refuse to grant a hackney carriage proprietor's licence if they are satisfied that there is 'no significant demand for the services of hackney carriages (within the area to which the licence would apply) which is unmet'. This has led to two distinct situations: those authorities which do limit the number of hackney carriages and those which do not.

Deregulation of hackney carriages or delimitation of numbers?

8.100   The removal of the numerical limit is often (and misleadingly) referred to as 'deregulation of hackney carriages'. This is an unfortunate and emotive turn of phrase which suggests that if the number is not set, there is no regulation whatsoever of hackney carriages. This is, of course, not the case, as all quality controls remain on both the vehicle and the driver, and it is only the quantity control which is removed. A better expression is 'delimitation of numbers' which more accurately reflects the action that is taken.

8.101   The rationale behind the introduction of section 16 of the Transport Act 1985 was that local authorities would no longer be able to control the numbers of hackney carriages. However, it has not worked out like that in many parts of the country. Indeed, some people take the view that the only effect of section 16 has been to create an entirely new industry in the form of bodies who conduct surveys for local authorities to establish whether or not there is an unmet demand for hackney carriage services.

8.102   The litigation in this area has been considerable. This is understandable, as many persons' livelihoods are at stake. In areas where a limit on hackney carriage numbers is maintained, hackney carriage proprietors' licences have a value. As with any market, these values fluctuate according to demand and that demand varies between local authority areas and also in response to other factors. At the time of writing, reports indicate that market value for hackney carriage proprietors' licences ranges from around £2,000 to upwards of £30,000. Obviously, if somebody has invested considerable sums in such a licence, they will be loath to see that value wiped out by a decision by the local authority to delimit numbers. On the other hand, many local authorities take the view that limiting hackney carriage numbers is an unacceptable form of protectionism, which does not provide the travelling public with the best service.

As with any dispute, there are strong arguments on both sides. An unregu- **8.103** lated free-for-all in the provision of hackney carriage services would not be acceptable. However, as mentioned earlier, all quality control provisions remain in place, it is merely that the market will find the level for the number of hackney carriages which an area can sustain.

It is often argued that delimitation will lead to congestion and unacceptably **8.104** high numbers of hackney carriages plying and ranking within the local authority area. Such vast increases appear to be rare among those authorities which have delimited numbers, especially bearing in mind the capital outlay which is required to invest in a suitable vehicle on the part of a potential proprietor. When this is offset against the uncertainty of the rewards which a hackney carriage proprietor's licence is likely to return, it is understandable why the threatened exponential rise in hackney carriage numbers in many areas has not been experienced.

The arguments in relation to overcrowding and congestion are also difficult **8.105** to translate into reality. Even if a local authority experienced an increase in hackney carriage numbers of some two-or three-hundred vehicles, in terms of the actual traffic flow in most town centres, that would represent a very small percentage increase.

It is undoubtedly true that an increase in hackney carriage numbers can lead **8.106** to additional pressure on hackney carriage stands, but there does not appear to be any local authority in England or Wales which is able to provide stands for all its hackney carriages. This is notwithstanding the requirement contained in byelaw 7 of the model byelaws, which requires the driver of a hackney carriage, when plying for hire and not actually hired, to 'proceed with reasonable speed to one of the stands fixed by the byelaw' and to go to the next one, if full, and so on. Realistically, it must always be expected that some vehicles will be unable to rank at any given time and they will be either plying for hire, undertaking hire or simply not working at that given time.

Provided that the local authority maintains quality control, delimitation is **8.107** not a problem for hackney carriage services. A number of local authorities have combined delimitation with the introduction of age policies and liveries with a view to using the change as a method of increasing the quality of the hackney carriage fleet, as well as using the increase in outlay required for a person to enter the trade as a method of tempering significant increases, which may lead to the congestion difficulties and unacceptable losses for existing trade members.

Guidance for local authorities

8.108   In 1985, the Department of Transport issued a circular[1] giving guidance on the then new restriction on the power of local authorities to limit the number of hackney carriages that they would licence. Paragraphs 26–28 stated:

> '*Grant of taxi licences*
>
> **26.** Section 16 [Transport Act 1985] will also be brought into effect on 6 January [1986]. This section qualifies the power which district councils now have under the Town Police Clauses Act 1847 to refuse to grant taxi licences in support of a policy of limiting the number of taxis in their area. Under the section a district council may refuse an application for a licence in order to limit the number of taxis if, but only if, they are satisfied that there is no significant unmet demand for taxi services within the area to which the licence would apply. An applicant whose licence is refused by a district council has a right of appeal to the Crown Court. The section does not require district councils to limit the number of taxi licences they issue for this reason; it forbids them to restrict numbers for any other reason. The powers of district councils to refuse licences or put conditions on them, relating to the fitness of the applicant or his vehicle are undiminished. In view of the fact that these vehicles may now be authorised to carry passengers at separate fares, district councils may wish to review the conditions of fitness laid down for these vehicles and the enforcement of maintenance standards. The attention of district councils is drawn to the provisions of paragraph 1 of Schedule 7, which establishes that taxis may be licensed with up to eight passenger seats.
>
> *Advice on the grant of taxi licences*
>
> **27.** District councils may wish to review their policy on the control of hackney carriage numbers in the light of the section [16 of the Transport Act 1985]. Limitation of taxi numbers can have many undesirable effects – an insufficiency of taxis, either generally or at particular times or in particular places; insufficient competition between the providers of taxi services, to the detriment of their customers; and prices for the transfer of taxi licences from one person to another which imply an artificial restriction of supply. Under the section a district council may refuse a licence to restrict numbers only if *satisfied* that there is not significant unmet demand for taxis in the relevant area. If there is an appeal, it will be for the council to convince the court that they had reasonable grounds for being so satisfied. It will not, in general, be sufficient for a district council to rely on the assertion of existing taxi licence holders that the demand is already catered for. They have evidence only of the demand which they satisfy and it will be for the council themselves to seek for and examine the evidence of unmet demand. There may be those who have given up trying to use taxis because of the inadequacy of the service and there may be latent demand in parts of a district that have not been adequately served – where those who wish to use taxis may not have demonstrated their demand since there had been no opportunity of having it satisfied. Moreover, if the applicant for a new taxi licence proposed to use it to provide a new service – for instance under section 12 – and had reasonable grounds to believe that there would be a demand for his service if he provided it, a council which wished to refuse a licence would have to satisfy themselves that the demand would not be forthcoming. Overcrowding at taxi ranks is not of itself evidence that there is no unmet demand. It may be that the provision of ranks has hitherto been too limited and the council should look actively for sites for further ranks.

28. There are a number of district councils which already exercise no control on the number of taxis in their areas without causing problems of over supply. However, the Department [of Transport] accepts that in some areas the total abandonment of quantity control could lead to an initial over-supply of taxis before market forces could bring about an equilibrium between supply and demand. In order to avoid possible disruption, a district council faced with a large number of new applicants, could, in the Department's view, reasonably grant a proportion of the applications, deferring consideration of the remainder until the effects of granting the first tranche could be assessed.'

1 DoT circular 3/85, reproduced in Appendix II.

Increasing numbers of hackney carriages and surveys: case law

It is not surprising that there has been significant litigation on this area. Although some of the cases appear to conflict, it is possible to discern a line of reasoning. The cases are considered in chronological order.   **8.109**

Tudor v Ellesmere Port and Neston Borough Council

The first reported High Court decision was that in *Tudor v Ellesmere Port and Neston Borough Council*[1]. This case is authority for the view that the rules of natural justice must be followed in an appeal against refusal to grant a hackney carriage proprietor's licence. An assertion that the applicant was not a fit and proper person was introduced during the final speech made on behalf of the council and the appellant had no opportunity to rebut the allegations. In relation to unmet demand, it was decided that, although an application for two licences had been made and turned down by the council, by the time the appeal was heard by the Crown Court, the provisions of the Transport Act 1985 were in force and, in the absence of any evidence as to the demand, the council conceded that it could no longer refuse to grant the licences merely by reason of numbers.   **8.110**

1 (1987) Times, 8 May.

R v Reading Borough Council, ex p Egan

The next case to be considered was *R v Reading Borough Council, ex p Egan*[1]. The facts are that, on the introduction of section 16 of the Transport Act 1985, Reading Borough Council took the advice given in the Department of Transport circular 3/85. Until the introduction of the Transport Act 1985 the council had licensed 50 hackney carriages. It was then proposed to grant an additional 30 licences, then 'wait and see' and assess the impact of those additional licences on the demand for hackney carriages, in accordance with the circular. This was challenged, by means of judicial review. Judgment was handed down by Nolan J. His decision was as follows (at 404A):   **8.111**

'The question before me, however, is a different one, namely, whether a council which is unsure of the presence or absence of unmet demand, but which fears that immediate and total de-restriction may cause over-provision, is entitled to issue a limited number of further licences as a temporary measure, and as a means of obtaining the evidence by which the presence or absence of unmet demand can finally be established.

I wish that I could answer this question in the affirmative. The dangers of over-provision were clearly accepted by the law prior to 1985, as is shown by the judgment of Lord Goddard CJ in *Rex v Weymouth Borough Council, ex p Teletax (Weymouth) Ltd* [1947] KB 583 and are recognised in paragraph 28 of the circular as still existing. If there is an unnecessarily large number of taxis, there may be great and unnecessarily difficulties in supervising and controlling them. The fact that a policy of total de-restriction has worked without problems in other areas does not mean it will work without problems in Reading. But in my judgment the language of section 16 is too clear to allow these considerations to prevail. By its own admission the council was not satisfied on 28th January 1986 and for that matter is not satisfied now as to the absence of unmet demand. It is surprising, but clear, that the Act of 1985 made no provision for any interim period during which licensing authorities might have an opportunity to establish, by market research or otherwise, the presence or absence of unmet demand. It follows that from the time section 16 came into force on 6th January 1986 the council and any other council which is unable to feel satisfied that there is no significant unmet demand had been obliged to grant applications for licences in respect of suitably qualified vehicles without limit of number. Paragraph 28 of the circular appears to me to incorporate an erroneous view of the law.'

1 (1987)[1990] RTR 399n (the case dates from 1987, but it was not reported until 1990).

R v Great Yarmouth Borough Council, ex p Sawyer

8.112   The next case, *R v Great Yarmouth Borough Council, ex p Sawyer*[1], is important in relation to the making of the decision of whether or not to delimit the number of hackney carriages. When section 16 of the Transport Act 1985 was first proposed in the Transport Bill, Great Yarmouth Borough Council considered its position in relation to hackney carriage licensing. Until then the number had been limited, but, prior to the introduction of the Act, consideration of the position took place. At that time the council reconsidered. The Transportation Sub-Committee took the view that the number should be maintained as there was no significant unmet demand, but also asked the trade to look into methods of providing evidence to support that view. The sub-committee did not have delegated powers but was reporting to the full committee and at the full committee the decision was made to delimit the number of hackney carriages operating within the borough. That decision was approved by full council. Judicial review was sought of that decision on the basis that it was, firstly, unreasonable in *Wednesbury* terms and, secondly, that irrelevant matters had been taken into account. The irrelevant matters were alleged to be a consideration by Great Yarmouth Borough Council as to what actions were being taken in respect of the new legislative requirements by other authorities in Norfolk.

1 (1987) [1989] RTR 297n, CA.

8.113   In relation to the argument of irrationality, Woolf LJ stated (at 301L):

'. . . looking at the position, as this court does, on appeal from Hodgson J and as did the judge [in the Crown Court], on the basis of the material which was available to the committee when it came to its decision, the position is clear. There is not the beginning of a case to show that the decision of the transportation committee was irrational'.

Woolf LJ carried on and stated that the appeal was bound to fail (at 302K):

'In coming to that conclusion, I would emphasise two matters. First of all, the role of the judge was an extremely limited role, having regard to the provisions of the Act to which I have made reference. The judge, in coming to his conclusion, was not purporting to express any view as to the merit of the decision of the authority. The authority was given the responsibility, under the licensing legislation, as amended, of coming to a decision with regard to whether or not they were prepared to maintain their previous policy. They came to that decision, and the courts can only intervene if it is shown that the authority has gone about its task in a way which was unlawful.

The other matter which I would mention is that clearly, on the material put before this court, the individual taxi drivers may suffer material hardship as a result of the change of policy. With regard to their problems, the court has in mind the evidence, but because of the role of the courts to which I have already made reference, there is no basis for intervening on the grounds of the individual hardship of individual drivers.'

Bingham LJ considered the matter and came to the same conclusion. He stated (at 303G):

'In the council reaching that decision, a number of matters entered into the council's thinking. The members plainly knew of the council's own previous policy. They also clearly knew of the policy of the Act. They appreciated the difficulty of proving the lack of unmet demand, despite the strong representations of the local taxi proprietors. They appreciated the cost of defending proceedings unsuccessfully. Inquiries showed that most authorities in the area were adopting a policy of de-restriction. Accordingly, the council decided that it would adopt a policy of de-restriction.

I see nothing irrational or unlawful in that process of consideration. A council does not need a reason under the Act to adopt a policy of de-restriction. Therefore, a decision to de-restrict is very hard to challenge on the grounds of irrationality, although no doubt, that could be done if the decision was made for obviously unsustainable reasons.'

Finally, Dillon LJ gave a concurring judgment which led to a unanimous decision of the Court of Appeal. In a short judgment he stated (at 304B):

'On the facts, I see no indication that the council took into account matters that they should not have taken into account. In particular, I think they were entitled to be told what action other district councils in Norfolk would be taking in relation to the Act. Beyond that I see no basis on the facts for any conclusion that the council acted unreasonably in forming the view, as deposed to by Mr Emslie, that they could not be satisfied that there was no unmet demand for hackney carriages in the area, and in consequently deciding to de-restrict the number of hackney carriages operating in the borough. They could not decide to restrict the number unless they were satisfied that there was no significant unmet demand. They were not bound to make further inquires or have surveys conducted in order to see more clearly whether there was or was not unmet demand.'

8.114 This case is authority for the proposition that a local authority can at any time decide to delimit the number of hackney carriages for which it will grant licences, subject only to the proviso that that decision must not, of itself, be *Wednesbury* unreasonable. Provided that the council has taken into consideration the relevant matters and, conversely, has not considered anything irrelevant, it can decide to take that course of action.

8.115   As to what would be relevant matters will be a matter of fact in every case, but obvious ones would include:

- The financial impact on existing licence holders who may have invested in their licence.
- The potential reduced custom of existing licence holders.
- Congestion on hackney carriage stands.
- Congestion on the roads generally.
- Benefits to the travelling public of additional vehicles.
- The opportunity for others to become involved in the trade as a means of securing a livelihood.
- The costs of commissioning a survey.
- The costs of defending appeals against refusals to grant licences, either with or without a survey.

Stevenage Borough Council v Younas

8.116   The case of *Stevenage Borough Council v Younas*[1] is a High Court decision, which follows the view given by the Court of Appeal in the *Great Yarmouth* case[2], eg that the broad approach could be adopted. Stevenage Borough Council commissioned a survey and the Crown Court gave the following case for an appeal against a refusal to grant a licence to Mr Younas (at 406L):

> 'We were satisfied that it had been demonstrated that there was no significant demand for the services of hackney carriages within the area of the Stevenage Borough Council which was unmet subject to one proviso. This proviso is as follows. We heard certain evidence relating to the demand for the services of hackney carriages near a particular night-club in Stevenage after midnight. This evidence was to some extent conflicting and we did not find it necessary to resolve such conflicts in the evidence as there were although we were not prepared to reject the appellant's on this point.
>
> We concluded, however, that bearing in mind the evidence relating to the demand for the services of hackney carriages after midnight, the council could not be satisfied that there was no significant demand for the services of hackney carriages within the area of Stevenage Borough Council which was unmet.
>
> The question for the opinion of the court was stated as follows:
>
> . . . whether on the evidence before the court' – that is, before the Crown Court –
>
> "It was correct in law to hold that the council could not be satisfied that there was no significant demand for the services of hackney carriages within the area of the council which was unmet".'

Pill J concluded (at 408G) that the findings of the Crown Court did not:

> 'in my judgment prevent the council from being satisfied in the terms of the section. A broader approach is legitimate on the wording of the section. The Crown Court were wrong in law in reaching the conclusion which they did . . . I accept that the burden upon the council is a heavy one. The Crown Court found however that, subject to one point, that burden had been satisfied.'

This case supports the view that, even if a survey finds that there is some unmet demand at some place in the district at a particular time, this itself is not sufficient to demonstrate significant unmet demand, if the rest of the time demand is satisfied. It is a test of the degree of significance of the unmet demand, rather than simply the existence of it.

1 (1988)[1990] RTR 405n, QBD.
2 *R v Great Yarmouth Borough Council ex p Sawyer* (1987) [1989] RTR 297n, CA. See para 8.112.

R v Halton Borough Council, ex p Gunson

R v Halton Borough Council, ex p Gunson[1] concerned a decision by Halton Borough Council to re-impose a numerical limit on the number of hackney carriage proprietors' licences which it would grant. Before the introduction of the Transport Act 1985 there were 60 hackney carriage vehicles and 261 private hire vehicles. On 1 April 1986, the authority delimited the number of hackney carriage vehicle licences it would issue and, by December 1986, there were a 158 hackney carriages and only 66 private hire vehicles. Representations were received by the council from the trade to the effect that there were too many hackney carriages. As a result, the authority set up a 'taxi working party'. This enquired into all aspects of hackney carriage and private hire provision and reported that, although there were a lot of hackney carriages, there was a sparse service in some parts of the borough and recommended that no limit should be imposed. It warned that, if a limit was imposed, the present inadequate service would deteriorate even further. This was to be reported to a meeting of the taxi committee (the panel which considered the granting of hackney carriage vehicle licences and setting a number limit) and, two days before that meeting, a circular was published by the taxi driver association to all the members of the committee. It was argued that as a consequence of that circular, the committee departed from the recommendation in the taxi working party's report and imposed a limit which was the number of hackney carriage licences in existence on that date. Challenge was made by way of judicial review to the imposition of the numerical limit on the grounds that it was unreasonable and, on a second ground, that an assurance had been given by a councillor that no limit would be imposed.

8.117

1 (29 July 1988, unreported).

In allowing the application, Otton J stated:

8.118

'In approaching this case and in arriving at my conclusions. I start with the effect of section 16 of the 1985 Act. It is clear that the effect of the amendment to sub-paragraph (*b*) is to transform the permissive "may" from the earlier Act into a partial mandatory "must". Unless the authority is "satisfied there is no significant demand which is unmet it is obliged to issue a licence to an otherwise suitable applicant". It also has the effect that an authority can adopt a policy of no numerical restriction of licences. By the use of the double negative and the emphatic phrase "if but only if", the construction becomes clear in the way that I have adumbrated. It may be that the Committee did in fact carry out the necessary exercise under section 16 of the Town Police Clauses Act 1847. Unfortunately, there is no evidence, or insufficient evidence, that they did. There is no adequate minute of the meeting. There is no adequate record of what occurred at the meeting. This is surprising in view of the fact that it was of such importance and one would have expected a proper record to be kept by the officials to the borough council, including its Chief Executive, or affidavits to be sworn covering these proceedings. The affidavit of Mr Redican [a member of the Committee who proposed the introduction of the numerical limit] only speaks for himself and the affidavit falls short of showing that even he had section 16 clearly and accurately in his mind in proposing the motion that he did. There is no affidavit from the Chairman of the Committee. There is no affidavit from the Chief Executive. The affidavit from Miss Kenny does not take the matter further in this regard. There is no evidence that they even considered the Working Party report, apart from the record that I have read, leading up to the resolution and recommendation. If they did carry out an extensive debate on the implication of the Working Party report, they did not record any evidence of "no significant unmet demand". Indeed, the record of the Working Party suggested and recommended to the contrary. There is no evidence that the Committee correctly considered or complied with their statutory duty under section 16. It is true that the 8th July document from the taxi drivers was before them but there is no suggestion that this document was tested or evaluated. In any event, it did not directly address the question of unmet demand but only the hardship to existing taxi drivers which is not the same thing.

In the surprising absence of any evidence as to how the decision was arrived at, I am left with an overwhelming sense of unease that they were too readily persuaded to bring down the shutter at the behest of the taxi drivers lobby and in particular as a result of its circular letter of the 8th July two days before the meeting. Consequently, I am not prepared to draw the inference that they did reach their conclusion correctly or reach a lawful conclusion. In my judgment the burden of proof on this aspect is upon the council and in spite of Miss Hamilton's [for the council] tenacious argument I have come to the conclusion that the burden has not been discharged. Consequently, I have no option but to rule that the decision is unlawful.'

On the second ground he found that the statement which had been made by the Chairman of the Working Party, that there would be no change in policy without prior notice was not binding. He stated:

'. . . this statement is distinguishable from the statements made in *R v Liverpool Corpn, ex p Liverpool Taxi Fleet Operators Association* [1972] 2 QB 299. The statement which came from the Chairman of the Working Party was not binding and was not meant to be binding either upon the Committee or upon the Council.'

This case is, effectively, the antithesis of the *Great Yarmouth* decision where it was held that the authority could decide to deregulate unless that decision was in itself *Wednesbury* unreasonable. In the present case of *R v Halton Borough Council, ex p Gunson*, it was decided that as the decision to relimit was not based on any evidence at all, it was in itself irrational and, therefore, unlawful.

R v Brighton Borough Council, ex p Bunch

8.119 The next case, dating from 1989 is *R v Brighton Borough Council, ex p Bunch*[1]. Brighton Borough Council commissioned a survey in June 1986 which found that there was no significant unmet demand for hackney carriage services within the borough. As a result, they resolved not to issue any new hackney carriage licences, but decided to have a second survey in the following year. This was undertaken and the conclusions were reported to the licensing sub-committee of the council in November 1987. This showed that, generally, there was no change in the position from the previous year (that is, there was no significant unmet demand) but that there were times of poor service. The report stated:

> 'Poor service is not caused by a shortage of licensed taxis but is due to the reluctance of existing drivers to work anti social hours. . . . The council have undoubtedly licensed sufficient taxis for all reasonable needs and there would be no problems in meeting demand if better operating practices were adopted.'

The council accepted this view and resolved that no new hackney carriage licences would be granted, but that the council should review the working practices of the existing drivers with the trade itself. This was challenged by way of judicial review and the matter was considered by Kennedy J in the Divisional Court. He concluded that the approach of the Court of Appeal in the *Great Yarmouth* case[2] was correct and that a broad approach could be taken by looking at the area of the borough council as a whole. As a result, short periods of poor service did not mean that there was unmet demand.

1　[1989] COD 558.
2　*R v Great Yarmouth Borough Council, ex p Sawyer* (1987) [1989] RTR 297n, CA. See para 8.112.

It is interesting to note that it was recognised that the approach by the surveyors was correct. The report in the digest reads (at 560):　**8.120**

> 'It was abundantly clear that a competent person had been instructed to carry out an independent survey, that he had done so with skill and care, and that the respondents [the Borough Council] had then taken proper steps to circulate and to receive comments upon the survey which had been produced. No more could reasonably be required of them.'

The application for judicial review was dismissed and Kennedy J stated that the challenge should not have been made by way of judicial review, but rather should have been by way of an appeal to the Crown Court against the refusal to grant the licence applied for. This case once again supports the view that the broad approach can be taken, when considering the question of the significance of any unmet demand for hackney carriage services.

Ghafoor v Wakefield Metropolitan Borough Council

The approach in *R v Reading Borough Council, ex p Egan*[1] was not followed　**8.121** in the case of *Ghafoor v Wakefield Metropolitan Borough Council*[2]. Until the introduction of section 16 of the Transport Act 1985, Wakefield Metropolitan Borough Council had maintained a limit on the number of hackney carriages it would licence. The council commissioned a survey which stated that there was an unmet demand for hackney carriage services. As a consequence, the council decided to issue five licences. The unsatisfied applicants, who had not received a licence, appealed to the Crown Court, which dismissed the appeal. A further appeal was made to the High Court. Four specific questions were raised:

'What was the correct approach for the Crown Court to adopt in determining appeals from the local authority? Should the Crown Court seek to determine how a reasonable council would have acted if it had heard the evidence heard by the Crown Court or should it exercise its own judgment?

Did the Crown Court apply the law correctly in this case, in particular:

(*a*) did the Crown Court apply the correct burden of proof?
(*b*) did the Crown Court apply the correct standard of proof?
(*c*) was the Crown Court right in adopting a broad approach to the question of demand?

Was the Crown Court right in concluding that there was no significant unmet demand for taxi services in Wakefield?

In the light of the Crown Court's determination in September 1987 that the council had failed to establish that there was a significant unmet demand for hackney carriages in Wakefield and in the light of the Crown Court's present findings on the question of delay, would the applicants have a sense of grievance that could result in their having a genuine and reasonable feeling that justice had not been seen to be done?'

1   (1987) [1990] RTR 399n. See para 8.111.
2   [1990] RTR 389, QBD.

8.122   Webster J considered paragraph 28 of DoT circular 3/85. Although that approach had been ruled unlawful by Nolan J in *R v Reading Borough Council ex p Egan*[1], Webster J disagreed with that interpretation and stated (at 394J):

'With great respect to the judge, I cannot agree either with that view or his decision that section 16 obliged local authorities which were unable to feel satisfied that there was no significant unmet demand to issue new hackney carriage licences without limit of number. In my view the effect of section 16 is, as I have said, merely to deprive the licensing authority of the discretion, which it would otherwise have, to refuse a particular application by a fit and proper person for the purpose of limiting the number of taxis except when it is satisfied that there is no significant unmet demand within the area; but there is nothing, in my view, to prevent an authority from advising itself in one way or another about the number of taxis which would have to be licensed in order to meet all significant demand and, having granted licences up to that number, from refusing the next application or applications after that number had been reached unless, by that time, the circumstances have changed so that the authority could no longer be satisfied that there was, given the total number of licences then issued, no significant unmet demand.'

He continued (at 395E):

'I therefore conclude that the council in the present case were acting perfectly properly in assessing the number of licences needed to satisfy the significant unmet demand and, having done so, in issuing only that number of licences provided that, when any further application was made, they satisfied themselves afresh as to the absence of significant unmet demand before deciding to refuse that application.'

In relation to the specific questions, Webster J decided that the Crown Court did apply the correct burden of proof and were correct in their approach, that it is upon the local authority to show that there is no unmet demand. In relation to standard of proof, it is that which is applicable in civil proceedings (ie the balance of probabilities). Finally, he accepted the Court of Appeal's view that a broad approach in relation to demand could be taken, rather than a narrow approach on the basis that there was a specific delay at a specific rank at a specific time.

1   (1987) [1990] RTR 399n. See para 8.111.

R v Middlesbrough Council, ex p I J H Cameron (Holdings) Ltd

This approach, rather than the *Reading* approach, was followed in *R v*   **8.123**
Middlesbrough Council, ex p I J H Cameron (Holdings) Ltd[1]. The question in this case was whether a deferral of a decision as to whether or not to grant a hackney carriage proprietor's licence amounted to a refusal. In this case, an application was made for 25 hackney carriage proprietors' licences in January 1989. No response was received from the local authority, so, in March of the same year, the solicitors for the applicant wrote to the council asking for a decision. In April, the council committee deferred the issue of additional licences until a survey had been undertaken to ascertain whether or not there was significant unmet demand. The results of that survey were received by the council in June and, in July 1989, the applicant was notified that his applications had been refused. The applicant asserted that the delay amounted to a refusal and that if the council could not satisfy itself as to the extent of any unmet demand, following the ruling in *R v Reading Borough Council, ex p Egan*[2], they must grant the licences applied for. The High Court (in front of Popplewell J) held that a deferral for a comparatively short period of time, in order to conduct a survey as to unmet demand, did not amount to a refusal and, therefore, it did not follow the decision of Nolan J in the *Reading* case.

1   [1992] COD 247.
2   (1987) [1990] RTR 399. See para 8.111.

Cannock Chase District Council v Alldritt

Cannock Chase District Council v Alldritt[1] concerned an application for six   **8.124**
hackney carriage proprietors' licences. Cannock Chase District Council had a policy of limiting numbers, which was supported by a survey. Mr Alldritt applied for six hackney carriage licences with a view to operating in the town of Rugeley. The district of Cannock Chase comprises significant areas of rural countryside and three quite distinct towns: Cannock, Hednesford and Rugeley. The assertion made by Mr Alldritt was that there was unmet demand in Rugeley and that was where he proposed to use the vehicles, if successful in his application. The view of the council, based on their survey, was that, although there was greater demand in Rugeley than elsewhere in the district, taking the district as a whole, there was no significant unmet demand. They refused the applications. Mr Alldritt appealed to the Crown Court and the Crown Court upheld his appeal. The district council appealed by way of case stated and the High Court dismissed their appeal. The High Court does not appear to have been referred to any other cases. In the Crown Court, the view was quite clearly taken that the expression 'the area' could include a part of the area of the district council and did not have to relate to the entire area. The matter was considered by the High Court, and Man LJ gave the following judgment:

'The council is concerned at certain of the language employed by the Crown Court in its decision. In particular it is concerned that the Crown Court is indicating to the council that the phrase "the area" in section 16 means in effect any part of the area. I can understand that concern. However, although I understand the concern, it seems to me to be a point of no materiality in the instant proceedings. These proceedings were not review proceedings. Were they such, this court would have had to consider whether the council had properly directed itself, and if it had whether its conclusion was perverse. However, that did not arise because the appeal to the Crown Court involves a hearing de novo. It is the Crown Court which then becomes vested with the power of refusing by reference to the consideration in section 16 of the Act of 1985. I emphasise "power" because as a matter of statutory language there is no obligation to refuse upon that ground. It is quite plain that in this case the Crown Court considering the matter de novo decided not to exercise the power conferred by section 16. The observations about the council's entitlement to do so I, for my part, would regard as by the way. The court was not concerned with the council's entitlement. It was exercising the powers of licensing de novo. The Crown Court was perfectly entitled to proceed in the way in which it did. There is here no question on the construction of the Act of 1847, as enlarged by section 16 of the Act of 1985.'

This judgment seems at odds with the decision in *R v Brighton Borough Council, ex p Bunch*[2]. Whether the same result would have been obtained had the court had the benefit of reference to such cases as *Bunch* and *R v Great Yarmouth Borough Council, ex p Sawyer*[3] is a matter of some conjecture. However, the geography of the area appears to have been an overriding consideration in the minds of both the Crown Court and the High Court. It appears that this case should not be taken as indicating that the rulings in *Bunch* and *Sawyer* are wrong, but rather that the court will on occasion tailor their judgments to the reality of the situation.

1 (28 January 1993, unreported.)
2 [1989] COD 558.
3 (1987) [1989] RTR 297n, CA.

R v Leeds City Council, ex p Mellor

8.125 The approach that a deferral did not amount to a refusal was followed in *R v Leeds City Council, ex p Mellor*[1]. This case concerned two points. Firstly, there was an assertion that an application for a hackney carriage vehicle licence was effectively refused when the decision was deferred to obtain more information as to unmet demand. In this case, that argument was rejected by the High Court. Secondly, however, the case is more useful because it is the only High Court decision which concerns an approach by the local authority which involved a 'points system' to determine which applicants should be granted vehicle licences. It was argued that by using such a system, proper consideration could not be given to merits of individual applications and, as a consequence, the council was fettering its discretion, which was inconsistent with the general liberalising tenor introduced by the Transport Act 1985. The High Court decided (judgment given by Hutchison J) that it was not possible to argue that the points criteria system was *Wednesbury* unreasonable, although, in relation to the specific applicant (Mr Mellor), the council had not treated him fairly, as he had a long-standing application.

1 [1993] COD 352.

8.126 This judgment is extremely useful, as many authorities which limit the numbers of hackney carriages they will licence, conduct surveys to ascertain whether there is any significant unmet demand. If the survey finds that there is unmet demand, a recommendation is usually made as to how many extra vehicle licences should be granted to satisfy that demand. The local authority then has the difficulty of trying to determine which applicants should be granted licences. Many authorities have drawn up points systems based upon a number of criteria to determine the allocation. The *Leeds* case is extremely important and it supports the view that such a process is acceptable, provided the mechanism is not, in itself, *Wednesbury* unreasonable.

Kelly and Smith v Wirral Metropolitan Borough Council

More recently, the Court of Appeal case of *Kelly and Smith v Wirral* **8.127** *Metropolitan Borough Council*[1] has considered a number of points. These include the mechanism of allocation to be employed when it is found that there is significant unmet demand, whether that finding is by the council or the Crown Court, and the question of deferred decisions.

The case concerned two applications to Wirral Metropolitan Borough Council for hackney carriage proprietors' licences. Wirral Metropolitan Borough Council had a policy of limiting the number of hackney carriages that it would licence at the time. Mr Kelly applied for ten hackney carriage proprietors' licences which were refused on the grounds that there was no significant unmet demand. He appealed to the Crown Court which upheld his appeal and ordered the council to issue the ten licences to Mr Kelly. The council appealed against that to the High Court which upheld the appeal by deciding that the Crown Court should not have ordered the issuing of the licences to Mr Kelly but should have remitted the matter back to the council for consideration in the light of the Crown Court's conclusion on demand. Mr Kelly appealed against that decision to the Court of Appeal. The argument against the granting of the ten licences centred on the fact that there were other people on the waiting list who had applied for licences a great deal earlier than Mr Kelly and they would be prejudiced if he was granted ten licences and they received none.

1 (1996) Times, 13 May, CA.

Auld LJ noted the approach of Webster J in *Ghafoor v Wakefield Metropolitan* **8.128** *Borough Council*[1]. He went on to say:

> 'In my judgment, it is a necessary part of the licensing function that the licensing authority, whether a local authority or the Crown Court on appeal from it, or a combination of the two of them, apply in relation to each applicant a system which is fair to all current applicants. That can only be done in any particular application where a local authority maintains that there is no significant unmet demand, by a determination of its extent and how it is to be matched with all the current competing applications, including that of the particular applicant. Picking up Laws J's words in relation to Mr Kelly that I have already cited, "it follows, as night the day, that a further process of inquiry had to take place before a . . . decision could be made whether to grant the licences" to him. In my judgment also, there is nothing in Section 16 of the 1985 Act, in its requirement that a licensing authority must grant a licence if it is not satisfied that there is no significant unmet demand, to prevent the authority, whether council or court, from examining in the context of an individual application the general state of unmet demand by reference to all

outstanding applications. A court, like a local authority may be faced with a number of applications/appeals; in such a circumstance, the court cannot sensibly or properly consider each application in isolation.'

He concluded:

'Accordingly, I am of the view that Laws J correctly remitted Mr Kelly's applications to the Council for its consideration in the light of the Crown Court's unchallenged conclusion on demand.'

1 [1990] RTR 389, QBD. See para 8.121.

8.129 Mr Smith's appeal was similar, but concerned a particularly important point, which was whether a right of appeal arose when a local authority failed to grant a hackney carriage proprietor's licence within a reasonable period of time. No specific decision had been made to refuse, but there was delay. This delay could occur because the council wished to commission a survey, or simply through failure on the part of council to reach a decision. The argument raised by Mr Smith was that such a delay amounted a 'withholding' of a licence and, accordingly, gave rise to a right of appeal under section 7 of the Public Health Act (Amendment) Act 1907. Again, Auld LJ gave the judgment of the court and stated:

'In my judgment, the words and intention of section 7 are plain. In the context of licensing, section 7(1)(b) provides a right of appeal where a local authority has made a determination whether to grant or refuse a licence, and section 7(1)(b) provides the same right where a local authority, by its failure to make a determination, withholds a licence. Here, the Council withheld a licence from Mr Smith by not deciding on his application. As Laws J mentioned, this interpretation may pose difficulties in determining the date of withholding for the purpose of fixing the start of the three weeks' appeal period, for example, where the local authority has no established cycle of licensing meetings. But the Crown Court will need to consider the particular circumstances of each case, bearing in mind always that withholding is a form of continuing inaction and that it may not be appropriate to adopt an overly rigorous attitude to the time limit for appealing in such a case. That is not an issue that could cause any difficulty for Mr Smith. Shortly after his third and last application for a licence in January 1993, his solicitors wrote to the Council seeking a decision within 28 days, and he lodged his appeal within a day or two of the end of that period.'

8.130 It can be seen, therefore, that simply succeeding on appeal at the Crown Court by demonstrating that there is unmet demand for hackney carriage services which is significant is not, in itself, sufficient to guarantee the appellant a hackney carriage proprietors' licence, as the council will then have to consider the fact that there is unmet demand and decide upon its criteria for granting licences. This point was addressed by Staughton LJ in the *Kelly* case:

'I agree that these appeals should be dismissed for the reasons given by Auld LJ. The only point that has made me pause is the thought that Mr Kelly and Mr Smith, having borne the heat and burden of litigation while others have done nothing, may end up with no licences and see other profit by their efforts. It may be that Mr Smith is in no danger in that respect, as he has been an applicant since 1986. But is there a risk that Mr Kelly will receive nothing? I would hope that the Council can take into account, amongst other relevant circumstances, the fact that he has shown himself so keen to have a licence that he has even engaged in litigation for that purpose, while others have not. But it is for the Council, in the first instance, to decide whether any and if so what weight should be given to that factor.

If it were only a question of assessing the number of new licences required to meet demand, I would have thought that the question could have been remitted to the Crown Court. Unless they merely acted on the absence of evidence that there was no unmet demand, they must have had evidence of unmet demand. That evidence could well have established the extent of the shortfall. But as the claims of other subsisting applicants also fall to be considered, I agree that the application should be remitted to the Wirral Council for reconsideration.'

Conclusion to be drawn

What then is the net result of these cases?   **8.131**

- The laws of natural justice apply to the process (*Ellesmere Port and Neston*).
- If the authority cannot demonstrate there is no unmet demand, the licences must be granted (*Ellesmere Port and Neston, Wirral*).
- It is possible to delimit at any time, subject only to the requirement that such a decision must not be *Wednesbury* unreasonable (*Great Yarmouth*), or indeed re-limit subject to the same requirements (*Halton*).
- In assessing unmet demand, a broad approach should be taken and small areas or times of short supply may not indicate a need for more licences (*Great Yarmouth, Stevenage, Brighton*, but consider *Cannock Chase*).
- If a limit is in place and additional licences are to be granted to meet any unmet demand, they can be allocated in batches, allowing the impact of each tranche to be assessed (*Wakefield*, not following *Reading*).
- Additional licences can be allocated by means of a 'points system' provide it is not unreasonable (*Leeds*).
- A deferment in making a decision amounts to a refusal (*Wirral*, not following *Middlesbrough* and *Leeds*).
- If licences are to be granted following an appeal, it is for the local authority to allocate them, according to its criteria, not the court, according to the success of the appeal (*Wirral*).

Surveys

8.132

Finally, it is necessary to mention surveys. They are the only acceptable method of demonstrating whether demand for hackney carriage services is met or, if it is not, the extent of the shortfall. In *R v Brighton Borough Council, ex p Bunch*[1], an independent survey carried out by a competent person attracted judicial approval. Surveys conducted by the council's officers are likely to be seen as partial and, therefore, unlikely to be capable of being relied on in any appeal against a refusal to grant a hackney carriage proprietor's licence.

1 [1989] COD 558.

8.133   Independent surveys are expensive to commission, but essential if the local authority is going to successfully defend a refusal to grant additional licences. The costs of such a survey can be recovered from the hackney carriage trade via an increase in licence fees. In areas where the 1976 Act has been adopted, section 70(1)(*c*) allows the recovery of:

> 'any reasonable administrative or other costs in connection with the foregoing and with the control and supervision of hackney carriages and private hire vehicles.'

and, in areas where the 1976 Act is not in force, section 35(3)(*c*) of the Transport Act 1981 states:

> 'any reasonable administrative or other costs in connection with the foregoing and with the control and supervision of hackney carriages.'

This is an approach which can prove unpopular with the hackney carriage trade, as it will increase their fees, but as the maintenance of a limit on numbers is arguably in the interests of the existing licence holders, such complaints seem ill-founded.

Application for renewal

8.134   It is only on renewal that the provisions of section 60(1) of the 1976 Act come into play. On an application for a renewal, these provisions are extremely useful. They allow the council to refuse an application on the grounds either that the vehicle itself is unsuitable or that the applicant himself is unsuitable for some reason. This will often involve a consideration of the applicant's criminal record. However, a police check under the powers contained in section 47 of the Road Traffic Act 1991 (which inserted subsection (1A) into sections 51 (licensing of drivers of private hire vehicles) and 59 (qualifications of drivers of hackney carriages) of the 1976 Act) does not apply in relation to hackney carriage proprietors' licences. Accordingly, to enable a local authority to ascertain the character of an applicant for a hackney carriage proprietor's licence it will be necessary to require the applicant to reveal any convictions that he may have. This is most effectively undertaken by requiring the applicant to complete a statutory declaration listing his previous convictions. This statutory declaration[1], should make it clear that, following the *Waveney* case[2], spent convictions can be considered and that, therefore, all convictions, (whether spent or otherwise) should be included in the list. The council can then consider any convictions revealed in accordance with its policy, as it would do in relation to a driver's licence.

1   An example of which is contained in Appendix IV.
2   *Adams v Waveney District Council* [1997] 2 All ER 898. See Chapter 5, para 5.20ff.

8.135   Many authorities do require applicants for all licences, in relation to hackney carriage and private hire activities, to complete a statutory declaration in these terms and then take the precaution of keeping them in the applicant's file from year to year. On a number of occasions, comparison between a current application and a former one may reveal that some offences have been omitted. As the information is contained in a statutory declaration, such lack of information is prima facie perjury and a number of authorities have

passed such information to the police who in turn have successfully prosecuted for perjury. Such conviction is then, of course, an additional
conviction which must be revealed in future applications.

Chapter 9

The use of hackney carriages

INTRODUCTION

The practical aspects of hackney carriages, including consideration of taximeters and fares; disabled people; stands; non-motorised hackney carriages; hiring hackney carriages at separate fares; and the use of bus lanes will be addressed in this chapter. **9.1**

TAXIMETERS

Almost all hackney carriages have a taximeter fitted, but this is not a statutory requirement. There is nothing in either the Town Police Clauses Act 1847 ('the 1847 Act') or the Local Government (Miscellaneous Provisions) Act 1976 ('the 1976 Act') which requires hackney carriages to have meters, but most local authorities do make it a requirement, either by means of byelaws made under section 68 of the 1847 Act or as a condition attached to the hackney carriage proprietor's licence under section 47(1) of the 1976 Act. In each case, those provisions, whether byelaws or conditions, will require the meter to be calibrated and sealed. Section 68 of the 1976 allows inspection of the meter and subsequent suspension of the proprietor's licence if the accuracy of the taximeter is unsatisfactory. **9.2**

Most local authorities have a number of different types of meter which are acceptable to them and hackney carriage proprietors can use any from the approved list. Directive (EEC) 77/95 laid down pan-European requirements for hackney carriage meters. These were introduced into the UK by the Taximeters (EEC Requirements) Regulations 1979[1], together with the Measuring Instruments (EEC Pattern Approval Requirements) (Fees) Regulations 1981[2] and the Measuring Instruments (EEC Pattern Approval Requirements) (Fees) (No 2) Regulations 1981[3]. These govern the overall approval of taximeters and are not of a direct concern to local authorities, who will only approve taximeters which have already been shown to comply with the Regulations. **9.3**

1 SI 1979/1379, as amended by the Measuring Instruments (EEC Requirements) (Fees) (Amendment) Regulations 1980, SI 1980/168.
2 SI 1981/279.
3 SI 1981/1825.

THE POWER OF THE LOCAL AUTHORITY TO SET FARES

9.4 Local authorities have a power to set fares for hackney carriages and in reality most do. This can be done in one of three ways:

1. under a special (local) Act of Parliament;
2. under byelaws made under section 68 of the 1847 Act; or
3. under section 65 of the 1976 Act.

9.5 The first route, using a special Act, is a completely impractical method.

9.6 Some local authorities still use the byelaw method. If such byelaws are in place, it is often stated that the provisions of the Hackney Carriage Fares (Amendment of Byelaws) Order 1981[1] can be used to vary them. To a limited extent, this is true, but this mechanism is now obsolete.

1 SI 1981/400.

Section 65 of the Local Government (Miscellaneous Provisions) Act 1976

9.7 This leaves the use of section 65 of the 1976 Act. This is really the only practical method. It gives the local authority a degree of flexibility, together with the advantages of speed in relation to any changes to the fares that the local authority may decide to make.

'**Fixing of fares for hackney carriages**

65–(1) A district council may fix the rates or fares within the district as well for time as distance, and all other charges in connection with the hire of a vehicle or with the arrangements for the hire of a vehicle, to be paid in respect of the hire of hackney carriages by means of a table (hereafter in this section referred to as a "table of fares") made or varied in accordance with the provisions of this section.

(2) (*a*) When a district council make or vary a table of fares they shall publish in at least one local newspaper circulating in the district a notice setting out the table of fares or the variation thereof and specifying the period, which shall not be less than fourteen days from the date of the first publication of the notice, within which and the manner in which objections to the table of fares or variation can be made.

(*b*) A copy of the notice referred to in paragraph (*a*) of this subsection shall for the period of fourteen days from the date of the first publication thereof be deposited at the offices of the council which published the notice, and shall at all reasonable hours be open to public inspection without payment.

(3) If no objection to a table of fares or variation is duly made within the period specified in the notice referred to in subsection (2) of this section, or if all objections so made are withdrawn, the table of fares or variations shall come into operation on the date of the expiration of the period specified in the notice or the date of withdrawal of the objection or, if more than one, of the last objection, whichever date is the later.

(4) If objection is duly made as aforesaid and is not withdrawn, the district council shall set a further date, not later than two months after the first

specified date, on which the table of fares shall come into force with or without modifications as decided by them after consideration of the objections.

(5) A table of fares made or varied under this section shall have effect for the purposes of the Act of 1847 as if it were included in hackney carriage byelaws made thereunder.

(6) On the coming into operation of a table of fares made by a council under this section for the district, any hackney carriage byelaws fixing the rates and fares or any table of fares previously made under this section for the district, as the case may be, shall cease to have effect.

(7) Section 236(8) (except the words "when confirmed") and section 238 of the Local Government Act 1972 (except paragraphs (c) and (d) of that section) shall extend and apply to a table of fares made or varied under this section as they apply to byelaws made by a district council.'

At first sight, this seems a cumbersome procedure, but is in fact not particularly difficult. The method is laid out in the accompanying flow chart on pp 144–145.

The provisions of section 65(5) of the 1976 Act are worth noting in that if **9.8**
the district council has byelaws and has hitherto used byelaws as its fare setting method, then, once the provisions of section 65 have been used, the byelaws themselves cease to exist.

It is worth noting that if any post-1974 local Act of Parliament incorporated **9.9**
the provisions of the 1847 Act and itself set fares for hackney carriages, then it would appear that the local authority is unable to use the provisions of section 65 to vary those fares and must seek repeal of that section of the local Act before any fares set under section 65 would take effect. This is because, although section 65(5) specifically states that any fares made by byelaws are overridden, it does not apply to special Acts of Parliament.

Once the fares have been made, by whatever method, they then apply to **9.10**
hackney carriages which are licensed to ply for hire within the district.

THE FARE SHOWN ON THE METER

Offence to charge more than the fare shown

Within the district, it is an offence under section 58 of the 1847 Act to **9.11**
charge more than the fare shown on the meter, plus any legitimate extras and this is punishable by a fine not exceeding level 3 on the standard scale. This also applies to fares made under section 65 of the 1976 Act, notwithstanding the fact that section 58 refers to either byelaws or special Acts. This is because section 65(5) makes it clear that fares made under provisions of section 65 take effect as if they were contained in byelaws.

Agreements as to fares

Section 54 of the 1847 Act allows agreement to be made in advance of the **9.12**
hiring of a hackney carriage that a sum less than that shown at the end of the

FLOW CHART FOR SETTING HACKNEY CARRIAGE FARES

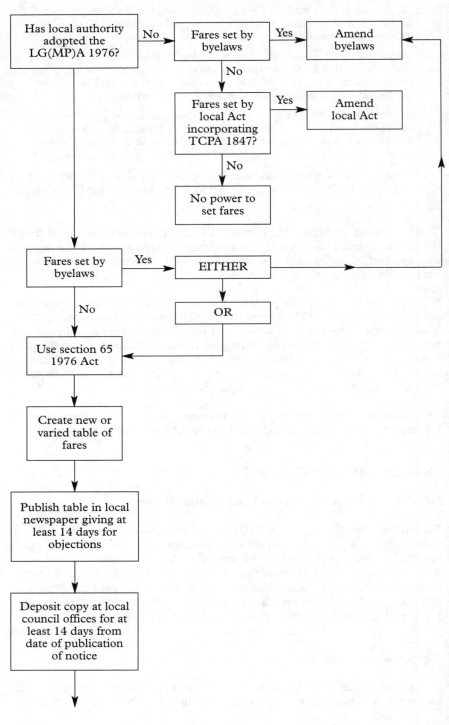

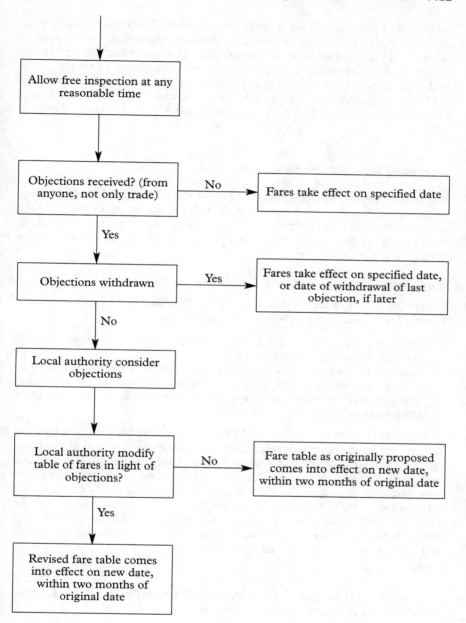

hiring will be paid, and once such an agreement has been made it is an offence for the proprietor or driver to demand more than was agreed in advance. This situation only covers specific occasions when the agreement is clearly made in advance, and does not cover the situation where, at the end of the hiring, the hirer either disputes the fare or does not have sufficient means of payment to cover the fare. In those cases, the fare itself is due under the contract entered into between the hirer and the driver or proprietor.

Accepting less than the fare shown

9.13   There has been some debate as to whether the driver is entitled to accept less than the fare shown on the meter. As this is a matter of contract and the only legislative controls concern the fare shown on the meter, it is difficult to see the basis for this argument, as a party to a contract is able to agree to variation of the terms at any point.

R v Liverpool City Council, ex p Curzon Ltd

9.14   The point has been clarified by the case of *R v Liverpool City Council, ex p Curzon Ltd*[1]. This case considered two questions:

1. whether it was lawful for a hackney carriage driver to charge less than the fare shown on the meter; and
2. whether the meter had to be calibrated to show the fares that the city council had set or whether, if the proprietor of the hackney carriage was prepared to offer a universal discount on those fares, it could be calibrated to reflect the lower fare.

In this particular case, Liverpool City Council had introduced a two-tier rate of fares, the difference being between a daytime rate and a nighttime rate. Curzon Ltd wished to continue to run simply at the daytime rate and not charge passengers the extra for hirings which took place when the nighttime rate was in force. The City Council suspended the licences of the vehicles that were not equipped with the new meter under section 68 of the 1847 Act and Curzon Ltd challenged the lawfulness of that suspension. The case was heard before McCullough J, who reviewed both the legislation and the Liverpool City Council's byelaws.

1 (1983) unreported.

9.15   In answer to the first question (whether the driver had to charge the fare that was shown on the meter) stated:

> '. . . I am persuaded that the statutes do not empower a district council to impose on drivers, whether by making bylaws or fixing a table of fares, a fare structure to which they must adhere. Such doubt as there is should be resolved in favour of the less restrictive construction. It is my view that the statutes prevent a driver from charging more than the fare prescribed, but not less, they do not empower a district council to prevent him from charging less.
>
> The great majority of drivers will, no doubt, want to charge the full prescribed fare. But if others do not, they may, at least *before* the commencement of the hiring, agree to take less. Whether a district council

may prevent a driver, at the end of or during the period of hire, from waiving part (or, indeed, the whole) of the charge which the law entitles him to demand is perhaps less clear, in that no section in either Act expressly contemplates such waiver. Mr. Braithwaite [for the City Council] said that, other than that such a driver would commit no criminal offence, he reserved he question.

I see nothing in the Acts which gives power to the council to prevent such waiver. There must have been, during the 146 years since 1847, many thousands of occasions when passengers have discovered that the fare exceeds the amount of money they are carrying and drivers have let them off the difference. Waiver in similar circumstances is commonplace in many areas of life. In my judgment, short of contractual restriction, there is nothing to prevent a driver from doing this if he wants'.

In relation to the second question of the calibration of the meter, he considered at length the meaning of the word 'accuracy' in section 68 of the 1976 Act. He stated:

'Mr Braithwaite's submission that an accurate meter is one which displays the fare prescribed in the table of fares assumed that the council was empowered to require a driver to charge according to the current table of fares, which is a proposition I have rejected. He concedes that if, as I have held, a driver is entitled to charge what he likes up to the prescribed maximum, his meter is accurate if it is set according to his own scale of charges. This effectively concludes the second question against the council.

I can see why he [Mr Braithwaite] made the concession. It fits well with clause 5 c of the bylaws. What the passenger wants to know is what he has to pay. The driver is only entitled to charge what is displayed on his meter. . . . If the driver is only going to charge, say, half the rate allowed in the table of fares, then half that rate is what the passenger will expect to see on the meter. Similarly, as with the drivers of Curzon Ltd's cabs, if they are only going to charge day rates at night, then what the meter should show is the fare according to the day rate. The concession makes it unnecessary for me to consider whether, even although a driver proposes to charge less than the fare allowed by the table of fares, his meter should nevertheless display the fare according to the table of fares, leaving it to him to tell the passenger that he will take less.'

It was held, therefore, that a one-tier meter which only charged the day rate was not unlawful for lacking accuracy, despite the fact that the City Council wished to impose two-tier charging for its hackney carriages.

Conditions to prevent the driver accepting less than the fare shown

This case appears to settle the matter. However, there is a view that it is possible to prevent a hackney carriage driver accepting less than the fare shown on the meter by means of a condition applied to the hackney carriage proprietor's licence. The question which would apply in this case is whether the condition was 'reasonably necessary' and this is debatable. The argument in favour of such a condition is to prevent squabbles on hackney carriage stands, when the second or third cab in line is known to offer discounts on the meter fare, when the first two do not. However, apart from the possible threat to public order that such a situation may present, it is difficult to see how such a condition is required to protect the public, as it must be beneficial to the public to be able to take advantage of reduced fares, if the drivers and proprietors are prepared to offer them.

9.16

No means to pay the fare

9.17   Where the hirer does not have the means to pay the fare at the end of the journey, section 66 of the 1847 Act states that in the case of refusal to pay the fare, the fare itself, together with any costs, can be recovered before 'one justice'. This would utilise the provisions of section 58 of the Magistrates' Court Act 1980 for recovery of a civil debt. It is not clear, in practice, how often this is undertaken, but, if it is, such action would be by way of complaint. This action was taken and was the subject of a High Court decision, in *R v Kingston-upon-Thames Justices, ex p Martin*[1]. The case turned on the question of whether an adjournment should have been allowed and that is not relevant here. What is of interest is the fact that a hackney carriage driver sought to recover the sum of £34.60 in this fashion. The passenger refused to pay the amount shown on the meter, as he said that an agreement in advance had been for a fare of £15.00. In the absence of the defendant, the matter was proved and the driver recovered the sum owing.

1   [1994] Imm AR 172.

The approach taken by the driver

9.18   In practice, the approach employed by hackney carriage drivers, when faced with the situation of passengers who cannot pay the fare, is to return them to the point at which they were picked up. Although this incurs additional costs for the driver, it ensures that the passenger has not actually benefited from their breach of contract. It is, of course, open to passengers to negotiate with the driver to accept a lesser fare or possibly to accept property as security for the fare to be paid in due course. As with any contractual dealings such agreements must not be arrived at by the use of threats, force or violence, as the parties must be able to bargain freely.

9.19   Another practice is for the driver to take the passengers to the nearest police station. As this is not a criminal matter, it is difficult to see what involvement the police might have, unless it can be shown after inquiry by the police, that there was never any intention to pay the fare. In such a case, the criminal law might become involved as the passenger obtained goods or services by deception contrary to section 1 of the Theft Act 1978.

9.20   Although it is possible to understand the provocation which might lead a taxi driver to use intimidatory methods to recover their fare, such action is, of course, completely unacceptable. In some areas, especially on late night hirings, some drivers ask for a deposit to be made against the fare before the hiring commences. Provided that the balance is returned where the final fare does not exceed the deposit, then this is an acceptable and, indeed, reasonable method of operation. Whilst the protection of the travelling public is the paramount aim of the licensing regime, it must always borne in mind that those involved in the trade are trying to earn a living and must be allowed to take all reasonable steps to achieve this.

Agreements to pay more than the fare shown

Section 55 of the 1847 Act outlaws any agreement to pay more than the **9.21** fare shown on the meter, irrespective of what may have been agreed beforehand. If any overpayment of this nature is made, it can be recovered through the magistrates' courts as a civil debt[1]. In addition, the driver who demanded the excess can not only be prosecuted and fined, but also, if the excess demanded has not been repaid, he can be imprisoned for up to one month, unless the excess is repaid during that time. This seems to be an extraordinary provision and one can only think that such agreements were a major problem in the middle of the last century. The fine is level three on the standard scale and no other legislative provision governing hackney carriages or private hire vehicles carries a risk of imprisonment for breach. No records of any imprisonment for such a transgression have been found and it is difficult to say what view modern magistrates would take of such a situation.

1 See para 9.17 above.

Tipping

This does not, however, prohibit the tipping of a hackney carriage driver at **9.22** the end of the hiring. This is one area of service where a tip is often given and, provided no agreement to tip was made in advance (in which case it would be outlawed by section 55 of the 1847 Act), the hirer is at liberty to tip whatever amount they may wish. As this is a gratuity and there is no contractual provision covering it, the driver should not expect this and, although he may feel aggrieved if a tip is not forthcoming, no action can be taken against the passenger.

POTENTIAL HIRER WITH INSUFFICIENT FUNDS

The situation where the potential hirer does not have sufficient funds to take **9.23** him the distance which he wishes to travel according to the fares set can be overcome in one of two ways: either by the driver discounting the fare at the end of the hiring or, alternatively, by an agreement to take the hirer a specified distance in exchange for a specified sum. This is governed by section 56 of the 1847 Act, which allows passengers (up to the maximum number that the hackney carriage is permitted to carry) to be carried a specified distance in return for a specified sum of money. This must not be less than the distance such a sum would have carried them according to the fares and, if that is the case, ie, the hirer was actually charged more under this agreement than they would have been for the same distance under the fares, then the driver commits an offence.

'WAITING TIME'

9.24 If the hire is to include a period during which the driver must wait, eg whilst a visit is made by the hirer before being returned to the original pick-up point, then section 57 of the 1847 Act allows a deposit to be made by the hirer to the driver to cover, not only his fare, but, any anticipated waiting time. Once that deposit has been made it is an offence for the driver to refuse to wait.

9.25 Most local authorities build 'waiting time' into their fare structure, but if they have not done so, section 57 of the 1847 Act provides a statutory fee of 7p per half hour of waiting time. It is not known whether there are any authorities who expect their drivers to wait for such rates of payment.

SECTIONS 66 AND 69 OF THE LOCAL GOVERNMENT (MISCELLANEOUS PROVISIONS) ACT 1976

9.26 There are two provisions in the 1976 Act in relation to fares other than the setting of them and these are to be found in sections 66 and 69.

Fare greater than that shown on meter

9.27 Section 66 of the 1976 Act prohibits any demand of a fare greater than that shown on the meter for hirings which end outside the area of the district council in which the hackney carriage is licensed, unless such agreement has been made in advance. In practice, when the hirer states the destination to the driver, the driver will probably realise if the destination is outside the district and should explain to the hirer that this will be for an agreed fee, as opposed to a meter fee, but if this is not the case, the driver is bound to charge not more than the meter. If this provision is not complied with an offence is committed under section 66(2).

Prolongation of journey

9.28 The other provision contained in section 69 concerns the prolongation of journeys, either by distance or time where it was not reasonably necessary. This covers the situation where a taxi driver literally and metaphorically takes a passenger 'for a ride', exploiting the fact that the passenger does not know the area, solely to increase the fare. It must be recognised that this has to be unreasonable prolongation and, therefore, legitimate deviation from the shortest route to avoid congestion, roadworks or other similar situations is not unlawful. Equally, if the passenger specifically requests to go via a certain point, then that is a request made by the hirer, to which the driver should acquiesce.

9.29 Enforcement of this particular section can be extremely difficult in situations where hirers feel that they have been taken further than was necessary, but do not know the area and are, not only unsure as to where they should have been taken, but are also in most cases unsure where they actually were taken. In addition, a great many hirers do not appreciate the significance of waiting times in most fare structures and that hirings at busy periods of time in congested cities can cost considerably more than a similar hiring at quiet off-peak times.

DISABLED PEOPLE AND HACKNEY CARRIAGES

'London-style' vehicles and other vehicles

Hackney carriages provide a valuable transport service for a great many disabled people, offering, as they do, a door-to-door service, in reasonable comfort, with personal service on a one-to-one basis from the driver. This has long been recognised both within local authorities and the trade itself and specially adapted or designed vehicles have been available for a number of years. These are often 'London-style' vehicles, which are now built to accommodate one wheelchair in the passenger compartment. Access is gained via ramps from the near-side of the vehicle and the passenger travels in their wheelchair facing backwards and secured by means of special seat-belts. The ramps are carried in the boot, when not being used, and this provides a good method of transport for wheelchair using disabled persons. It is important to recognise that not all disabled people use wheelchairs all the time. As disabilities take many forms, such vehicles are not always ideal for persons who are not wheelchair-dependent all the time. There are also other vehicles that have been adapted to carry wheelchair-using passengers, including some of the modern 'people carrier' vehicles from a variety of manufacturers. **9.30**

In addition, for non-purpose-built vehicles (ie ordinary saloon cars in areas where there are no 'mandatory orders'), swivel seats are available from a number of manufacturers. These replace the front passenger seat and actually swing either round, or round and out, to make it easier for people to get in. For the non-wheelchair user, these can be extremely satisfactory, but, as always, this is dependent upon the nature of the disability the person has. **9.31**

It was the availability of the London-style cabs, which were actually purpose-built to carry wheelchairs, which led Manchester City Council, in the mid-1980s, to consider the service of transport for disabled people, as outlined earlier[1]. Arguments have raged over the worth of such an approach: primarily over the question of how much use is actually made of these vehicles by people using wheelchairs and whether that use is justified in relation to the costs that were involved. As all new purpose built vehicles are built to carry wheelchairs, and as the number of older vehicles that would need converting to be able to be granted a licence in such circumstances reduces, this argument carries less weight. In addition, reports from disabled groups have emphasised the reassurance that people who use wheelchairs feel in any town or city where all the hackney carriages are wheelchair-accessible. They know that they are always able to get home by making their way to a hackney carriage stand and will be able to get the first hackney carriage in the rank rather than having to either wait on the off-chance that an accessible vehicle appears or have to phone and make booking arrangements. **9.32**

1 See Chapter 8, para 8.74.

Sections 32–38 of the Disability Discrimination Act 1995

9.33   This concept has been taken a stage further by the passing of the Disability Discrimination Act 1995 ('the 1995 Act') of which Part V (sections 32–38) applies to hackney carriages. This is one of the pieces of legislation that refers to hackney carriages as 'taxis', the definition in section 32(5) making it clear that 'taxi' means a hackney carriage but it does exclude hackney carriages drawn by horses or other animals.

'New licences conditional on compliance with taxi accessibility regulations

34–(1) No licensing authority shall grant a licence for a taxi to ply for hire unless the vehicle conforms with those provisions of the taxi accessibility regulations with which it will be required to conform if licensed.

(2) Subsection (1) does not apply if such a licence was in force with respect to the vehicle at any time during the period of 28 days immediately before the day on which the licence is granted.

(3) The Secretary of State may by order provide for subsection (2) to cease to have effect on such date as may be specified in the order.

(4) Separate orders may be made under subsection (3) with respect to different areas or localities.'

9.34   These provisions are not yet in force and, at the time of writing, there is no indication when they will be effective. Draft regulations have yet to be published for consultation and it remains to be seen when and, indeed, if they are.

Taxi accessibility regulations

9.35   Once Part V of the 1995 Act is in force, a district council will be unable to grant a licence for a hackney carriage, unless it conforms with the taxi accessibility regulations requirements (section 34(1)), unless it is a renewal for a vehicle which was previously licensed. That exemption is contained in section 34(2), but is unlikely to last forever, as the Secretary of State has the power under section 34(3) to make an order stating that the exemption no longer applies. This does not need to be a nationwide order, as section 34(4) allows for such orders to be made 'with respect to different areas or localities'. This suggests that such orders will be available in respect of local authority areas or possibly even parts of local authority areas. The justification for only applying such an order to a part of a local authority area would appear to only make sense where zoning is in force.

Exemption from taxi accessibility regulations

9.36   Section 35 of the 1995 Act contains powers which will allow the Secretary of State to make 'exemption regulations which would enable a local authority to apply for exemption from the requirements of section 34 that all hackney carriages licensed after a certain date must comply with the accessibility regulations'.

'Exemption from taxi accessibility regulations

35–(1) The Secretary of State may make regulations ("exemption regulations") for the purpose of enabling any relevant licensing authority to apply to him for an order (an "exemption order") exempting the authority from the requirements of section 34.

(2) Exemption regulations may, in particular, make provision requiring a licensing authority proposing to apply for an exemption order—
(*a*) to carry out such consultations as may be prescribed;
(*b*) to publish the proposal in the prescribed manner;
(*c*) to consider any representations made to it about the proposal, before applying for the order;
(*d*) to make its application in the prescribed form.
(3) A licensing authority may apply for an exemption order only if it is satisfied—
(*a*) that, having regard to the circumstances prevailing in its area, it would be inappropriate for the requirements of section 34 to apply; and
(*b*) that the application of section 34 would result in an unacceptable reduction in the number of taxis in its area.

(4) After considering any application for an exemption order and consulting the Disabled Persons Transport Advisory Committee and such other persons as he considers appropriate, the Secretary of State may—
(*a*) make an exemption order in the terms of the application;
(*b*) make an exemption order in such other terms as he considers appropriate; or
(*c*) refuse to make an exemption order.

(5) The Secretary of State may by regulations ("swivel seat regulations") make provision requiring any exempt taxi plying for hire in an area in respect of which an exemption order is in force to conform with provisions of the regulations as to the fitting and use of swivel seats.

(6) The Secretary of State may by regulations make provision with respect to swivel seat regulations similar to that made by section 34 with respect to taxi accessibility regulations.

(7) In this section—
"exempt taxi" means a taxi in relation to which section 34(1) would apply if the exemption order were not in force;
"relevant licensing authority" means a licensing authority responsible for licensing taxis in any area of England and Wales other than the area to which the Metropolitan Public Carriage Act 1869 applies; and
"swivel seats" has such meaning as may be prescribed.'

As yet, no regulations have been published under this section of the 1995 **9.37** Act, but section 35(3) contains the outline criteria for the basis of such an application. At present, it is impossible to say what these criteria will actually mean in practice, but it would seem sensible to assume that the nature of the local authority area will be of considerable significance. It is difficult to see what arguments can be used in predominantly urban areas to suggest that disabled accessible hackney carriages are not required. Such arguments may carry more weight in predominantly rural areas where the use of hackney carriages is predominantly on a pre-booked basis (ie acting effectively as private hire vehicles). In those situations, it may be possible to argue that a requirement to provide disabled-accessible vehicles will place a burden on proprietors which is too onerous to carry, taking into account the nature of the work they undertake and the number of disabled people within the locality. It may be necessary to undertake surveys to demonstrate the percentage of the population who are wheelchair-using disabled and would be able to make use of such facilities. It seems unlikely that there is a significant difference between the percentage of a population in a rural area who are wheelchair-using as against an urban area, but this will remain to be seen.

9.38 The Secretary of State cannot grant an exemption until consultation has taken place with the Disabled Persons Transport Advisory Committee (DiPTAC) and 'such other persons as he considers appropriate'. If the application is successful and the exemption is granted, the Secretary of State can then use his powers contained in section 35(5) of the 1995 Act to require swivel seats to be fitted to all hackney carriages within the exempted area, thereby providing some provision for disabled persons. Again, no regulations have been drafted under this section and it remains to be seen whether the Secretary of State uses this power.

9.39 As always, it is difficult to look into the future but as these provisions do not apply to private hire vehicles and as in a great many rural areas hackney carriages are largely used effectively as private hire vehicles, apart from some late night work at pub and club closing times, it may well be that proprietors feel that the costs involved in either adapting their existing hackney carriage or purchasing a new vehicle which would comply with the requirements is too great. They will simply cancel their hackney carriage proprietor's licence and seek a private hire vehicle licence for the same vehicle. This, of course, only applies where the vehicle is of a saloon or people-carrier type and not a London-style cab. This scenario has been foreseen to an extent by the wording of section 35(3)(*b*), but it remains to be seen what is considered an 'unacceptable reduction in the number of taxis in [the local authority] area'.

9.40 There would seem to be a good argument to say that if the vehicles are still available as private hire vehicles and if the predominant use pattern is for private hire type use, then a reduction in the number of hackney carriages may not, in fact, be unacceptable because transport provision will be maintained.

9.41 To overcome this and make genuine transport provision for disabled people, it will be necessary to extend the regime of the 1995 Act to private hire vehicles through the swivel seat approach. It remains to be seen whether this is, in fact, the outcome.

Provisions to ensure that a driver must carry a disabled passenger

9.42 Sections 36 and 37 of the 1995 Act make it clear that drivers of 'regulated taxis' (ie a hackney carriage which complies with the taxi accessibility regulations) must carry a wheelchair-using passenger. The driver must also provide him with such assistance as may be reasonably required at no extra charge. The same considerations and requirements apply to passengers with guide dogs and hearing dogs. Each section contains provisions to allow drivers to apply to the licensing authority for an exemption certificate. In relation to wheelchair-carrying under section 36, such an exemption can be sought (under subsection (8)) on either medical grounds or the driver's physical condition. In relation to dogs under section 37, the criteria are medical grounds (subsection (5)), but the licensing authority must take into account, 'the physical characteristics of the taxi which the applicant drives or those of any kind of taxi in relation to which he requires the certificate' (subsection (6)).

These provisions are intended to overcome the very real difficulties that **9.43** have been encountered by some disabled people. Although the hackney carriage is adapted to carry a wheelchair, many disabled people have not been able to take advantage of this due to a refusal by the driver to carry them. Whilst this is a breach of most local authorities' conditions enforcement is as always somewhat difficult and the usual attempted justification is that loading and unloading a wheelchair-using person takes a considerable amount of time, for which the driver is not remunerated.

In relation to guide dogs and hearing dogs, again, there have been a number **9.44** of reported problems where carriage of the dog has been refused on the grounds that it may make a mess of the vehicle. This breaches the conditions of many local authorities, but the enforcement considerations still apply.

It is, therefore, widely accepted that hackney carriages provide an extremely **9.45** useful and usable form of transport for disabled persons, but it remains to be seen how effective the provisions of the 1995 Act will be in providing a genuinely useful service countrywide for persons with varying types of disability.

HACKNEY CARRIAGE STANDS

One of the distinguishing features of hackney carriages is that it can 'rank **9.46** up'. Hackney carriages can wait at approved ranks, referred to as 'stands' in the legislation, and await the arrival of a hirer.

CREATION OF A STAND

There are, in fact, two methods of creating hackney carriage stands: **9.47**

1. byelaws made under section 68 of the 1847 Act; and
2. section 63 of the 1976 Act;

but, in practice, there is effectively only one.

The original method was for hackney carriage stands to be created by the byelaws made under section 68 of the 1847 Act and many authorities have stands which were created this way.

If an authority has not adopted the 1976 Act then the byelaws route remains **9.48** the only way of creating and changing hackney carriage stands. When the time delay of amending byelaws is taken into account can be a slow and unwieldy method of responding to the changes which occur in towns and cities across the country.

Section 63 of the Local Government (Miscellaneous Provisions) Act 1976

9.49   The second, and more usual, method of creating hackney carriage stands is contained in section 63 of the 1976 Act. This allows district councils to 'appoint stands for hackney carriages' either on public highways or private land and the stands can be for either continual or part-time use.

Private stands

9.50   If the land in question does not form part of the highway, then the consent of the owner of the land is required. 'Private' stands were considered in *R v Great Western Trains Ltd, ex p Frederick*[1]. This case concerned an application for leave to apply for judicial review of a decision of Great Western Trains Ltd to grant sole and exclusive rights to one company to ply for hire from the hackney carriage stand at Newport Central Station. This decision was challenged by hackney carriage drivers who were excluded from using the station rank by virtue of the new agreement.

1   [1998] COD 239.

9.51   Five points were considered by Popplewell J. Firstly, had there been sufficient consultation with the trade (represented by the applicants) by Great Western Trains Ltd to enable the trade to put forward arguments as to why the proposed arrangements should not have gone ahead? As a letter had been sent to each of the existing hackney carriage drivers, who had permission to use the station rank, explaining the situation and as it was made clear that their permissions to use the station stand were going to expire on a set date, Popplewell J found that there was sufficient consultation, even taking into account the ruling in *R v Liverpool Corpn, ex p Liverpool Taxi Fleet Operators' Association*[1].

1   [1972] 2 QB 299.

9.52   The second point was, if there had not been consultation, was the application for leave for judicial review out of time?, to which the judge found that it was.

9.53   The third question raised an argument that the agreement between Great Western Trains Ltd and between the taxi company was contrary to section 64 of the Town Police Clauses Act 1847 because it required the taxi company to supply Great Western Trains Ltd with, amongst other things, the names of responsible persons such as supervisors who would be responsible for policing the hackney carriage stand. Under the agreement there was an obligation on the proprietor to police the area of the stand. Popplewell J dismissed this argument, but gave some useful indications of what is meant by section 64:

> 'As I understand the argument, by giving exclusive use of the stand to Dragon Taxis, there is said to be a breach of section 64, because it will hinder or obstruct the driver of the applicant's vehicles contrary to that section. If, as I indicated in the course of argument, all that was required was for the proprietor, either himself or through the respondents, to take out an injunction against the applicants, that is also said to be something which would hinder the drivers like the applicants.

It seems to me that section 64, to put it in a very simple way, is there to prevent a punch-up between rival licence holders. The whole language of "obstruct", "hinder", "wrongfully", "in a forcible manner" and so on is not dealing with the situation in this case, when one lot of drivers have been given the right and the others have not. It is to deal with the situation on the ground when rival drivers may take the matter into their hands. I am wholly unpersuaded that section 64 has any bearing on the facts of the instant case.'

The final question was whether an agreement, in relation to the use of a **9.54** hackney carriage stand which was sited on private land, was susceptible to judicial review. Popplewell J concluded that the provision of a hackney carriage stand was not part of the statutory function of the railway company under the provisions of the Railways Act 1993 and that the provision of a hackney carriage stand was ancillary to its statutory function and, accordingly, not susceptible to judicial review, although, in relation to their statutory matters, he stated:

'. . . in my judgment, the Great Western Train Company are susceptible to judicial review, that susceptibility exists only in relation to those of the decisions which in some way are either statutorily underpinned or involve some other sufficient public law element.'

Finally, he concluded that the application itself was out of time.

This case is useful to the extent that it demonstrates (albeit that it is only an **9.55** application for leave and not a full judicial review of the situation) that a railway company can enter into an exclusive arrangement with one hackney carriage 'company' to use a hackney carriage stand at a railway station. In the case of a railway company, that decision itself is not subject to judicial review and any policing of the arrangements that are imposed upon the hackney carriage company are not in breach of section 64 of the 1847 Act. By extension, it would appear that such an arrangement could apply to an airport or, indeed, at any other large undertaking where there is private land upon which a hackney carriage stand could be created, eg out-of-town shopping centres or sports centres, entertainment complexes etc.

Public highway stands

If the stand is to be on a public highway, the consent of the highway author- **9.56** ity is required. In areas with county councils, the highway authority is the county council, but, in unitary and metropolitan areas, it is the same council discharging both highway and hackney carriage licensing functions. Whether this actually makes it any easier in practice to obtain the consent of the highway authority seems to be open to question, but, in theory, it should ease the process considerably.

Under section 63(1) of the 1976 Act, the district council can determine the **9.57** number of hackney carriages that can use the stand and they also have a power to vary that number.

Before a new stand is created or the maximum number of vehicles which can **9.58** use the stand is varied, notice must be given to the Chief Officer of Police. A public notice must also be provided in one local newspaper. Any objections which are received within 28 days of the first publication of the public notice must be taken into account, together with the comments of the Chief Officer of Police, before such a stand is appointed or the number is varied. There are limitations on the siting of hackney carriage stands and those are contained within section 63(3) of the 1976 Act. They are effectively to prevent obstructions or impediments caused by hackney carriage stands in relation to premises or any buses or other public service vehicles that may be using the road or any depots or bus stations nearby (see flow chart on p 160).

9.59　This is the modern and most satisfactory way of creating hackney carriage stands. Once this method has been used, section 63(4) of the 1976 Act makes it clear that any hackney carriage stands created under byelaws are now deemed to have been made under section 63 and the byelaws themselves cease to have effect.

9.60　Hackney carriage stands are an important feature of both the trade and urban life and their existence and use should be subject to frequent consideration. Towns and cities are developing places and the need for stands varies as time goes by. What may have been a busy area ten or twenty years ago, leading to the provision of viable well-used stands, may have altered significantly as a result of development. There are a great many stands around the country which have fallen into disuse but which still exist under the legislation. Equally, there are many areas of the country where hackney carriage stands would be extremely useful and heavily used, but where no provision has been made in recent years. This leads to the problem of hackney carriage drivers creating unofficial ranks in areas of high demand. The difficulties that these can give rise to are those of congestion, obstruction of access to premises and bus stops, parking offences and the fact that the stand itself is not protected solely for the use of hackney carriages.

THE USE OF THE STAND

9.61　Once the stand has been created under section 63, whether directly or deemed to be created under section 63 by virtue of appearing in former byelaws, then section 64 of the 1976 Act protects that stand during the hours of use for the benefit of hackney carriages.

Section 64 of the Local Government (Miscellaneous Provisions) Act 1976

9.62　Section 64(1) of the 1976 Act makes it an offence for any person to, 'cause or permit any vehicle other than a hackney carriage to wait on any stand for hackney carriages' and this is a comprehensive ban on all other vehicles. The only defence which is available is under section 64(5), in relation to a PSV, and that is only on the grounds of avoiding obstruction to traffic to enable passengers to be dropped off or 'other compelling reason[s]'. It is not actually clear what reason would be so compelling to afford a defence under this section, but it would seem reasonable that any action taken to avoid an accident or to protect life or health would be a good defence. Conversely, it is less likely to succeed if the justification is that the bus stop ahead was full.

Rodgers v Taylor[1] confirms that, if there is a parking restriction on a street and **9.63** there is also a hackney carriage stand on that street, hackney carriages can only wait on the stand whilst they are plying for hire or waiting for a fare. They cannot simply use it as a parking place. In this case, the defendant was a licensed hackney carriage driver who parked his hackney carriage on a hackney carriage stand on a street in which there was a waiting restriction. He locked his hackney carriage and left it unattended for about an hour. He was prosecuted under section 5(1) of the Road Traffic Regulation Act 1984 and article 5(1)(*c*) of the City of Gloucester (Eastgate Street) (Waiting Regulation) Order 1982. There was an exception within the traffic order whereby a vehicle could wait for 'so long as may be necessary' for a number of specified reasons, which included 'if the vehicle is a licensed hackney carriage, to wait at an authorised hackney carriage stand, during the period of time for which the stand is authorised to operate'. There was no time limit on the operation of the stand and it was argued that that exception allowed the defendant to use the stand as a parking place.

McNeill J gave the judgment of the court and concluded (at 766):

> 'I take the view that the only sensible construction of those words is "so long as may be necessary to enable it to wait as a licensed hackney carriage for the purposes of the licensed hackney carriage stand", that is to say, for the period during which the licensed driver is entitled to operate as such with his licensed carriage.'

1 [1987] 85 LGR 762.

These two sections provide a useful and workable framework for the provi- **9.64** sion of hackney carriage stands. Stands are vital if the hackney carriage trade is to be able to perform its functions and fully realise its potential of providing transport for individuals. It is especially important that ranks are provided at locations that are suitable for disabled persons and at other locations which are convenient for use by persons for whom other forms of transport are less accessible, such as parents with prams or pushchairs and those who are infirm, as opposed to disabled.

To enable these provisions to work effectively, vigilance is required on the **9.65** part of local authorities both in taking action against those who park on hackney carriage stands illegally and also in assessing whether the stands are in the right place, whether new ones should be created or whether obsolete ones should be removed.

TAXI HAILING POINTS

One local authority (Kirklees Metropolitan Borough Council) has intro- **9.66** duced what it refers to as 'taxi hailing points'. This is intended to provide an alternative to a stand, either where there is insufficient space for a stand or the location would not prove sufficiently popular with the public or the trade to justify the creation of a stand.

A hailing point is just that. It is a specific point where the public know that **9.67** they will be able to hail a hackney carriage. Although the public can hail a hackney carriage anywhere and no particular provision is required, the

159

FLOW CHART FOR GRANTING HACKNEY CARRIAGE STANDS

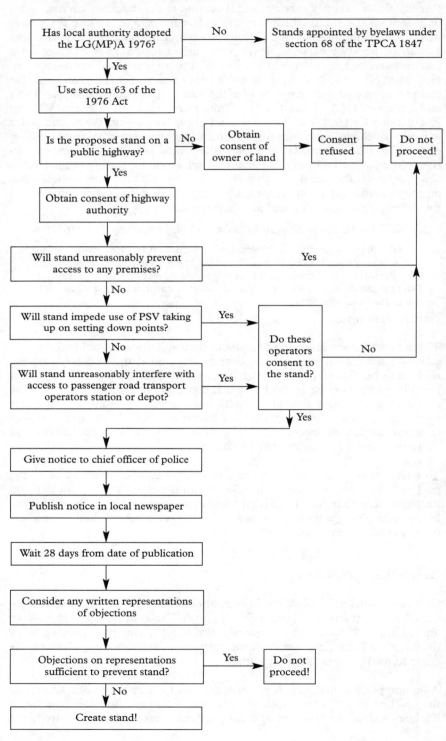

theory of hailing points are that the drivers will know where they are and will ensure that they pass them on a regular basis.

The pilot scheme of Kirklees Metropolitan Borough Council seems to have   **9.68**
been a success and more hailing points are likely to be created in the future. As there is no provision for the hackney carriage to wait, as there is on a stand, no lengthy procedures are required before a hailing point is created, as all that is required is the erection of a suitable sign.

It should be noted that a hailing point is not an 'authorised place' for the   **9.69**
purposes of hiring a taxi at separate fares under the provisions of sections 10–13 of the Transport Act 1985[1], it is simply somewhere to hail a hackney carriage for use at one fare.

1 See para 9.78ff.

BYELAWS

Byelaws can be made under section 68 of the 1847 Act and section 6 of the   **9.70**
1889 Act to regulate a large variety of matters relating to hackney carriage operation, both of the vehicles and the drivers, together with such matters as stands.

The entire scope of the powers are to be found in the specific sections[1], but   **9.71**
the main matters of concern today include:

- Conduct of proprietors and drivers (section 68 of the 1847 Act).
- Wearing of badges by drivers (section 68 of the 1847 Act).
- Display of the licence number (section 68 of the 1847 Act).
- Number of seats in the vehicle (section 68 of the 1847 Act).
- Safe keeping and return of lost property (section 68 of the 1847 Act).
- Notice of fares to be levied (section 6 of the 1889 Act).

1 See Appendix I.

Model byelaws are contained in the Annex to Department of Transport cir-   **9.72**
cular 8/86[1], and the procedure for making byelaws is contained in section 236 of the Local Government Act 1972[2].

1 See Appendix II.
2 For further information please see *Butterworths Local Government Law*, Division A, Chapter 3.

Penalties for breach of byelaws are to be found in section 183 of the Public   **9.73**
Health Act 1875, and offences are summary only.

NON-MOTORISED HACKNEY CARRIAGES

Same statutory provisions as motorised vehicles

It must be borne in mind that not all vehicles that carry the public are   **9.74**
motorised. Many seaside resorts have horse-drawn carriages which are

licensed as hackney carriages. If they are hackney carriages, then all the statutory provisions applicable to motorised vehicles apply to them. There are no exceptions contained within the legislation for vehicles which are not motorised (other than in relation to the 1995 Act[1]). Accordingly, it will be necessary for a driver of a horse-drawn hackney carriage to hold a hackney carriage driver's licence and the prerequisite to that is that he holds a DVLA licence. In addition, the local authority may impose such conditions as they think fit on the vehicle licence and also, arguably, on the driver's licence.

1 See para 9.33.

Whether a vehicle is a hackney carriage

9.75   In recent years another type of vehicle has also made its presence felt and that is the pedal powered rickshaw or 'trishaw'. This was defined in the case of *R v Cambridge City Council, ex p Lane*[1] by Sir Richard Scott VC (at 157) as:

> 'A trishaw is a cross between a rickshaw and a tricycle. Like a tricycle it has three wheels, a single front wheel and two rear wheels. Over the rear wheels a compartment in which passengers may sit is suspended. The vehicle is an adaptation of a rickshaw, replacing the individual running on the ground and pulling the vehicle with an individual using the cycle technique to provide the power for propelling the vehicle.'

The question arose in this case as to whether a trishaw was a hackney carriage or a stage coach. This distinction was important because if it was a hackney carriage, Cambridge City Council could impose conditions on both vehicle and driver licences. This matter was heard by the Court of Appeal in July 1998 and, in a lengthy judgment, Sir Richard Scott considered the legislation in detail. This included full consideration of the distinction between a hackney carriage and a stage coach. His determination was follows (at 167):

> 'I have come to the conclusion that Mr Lane's trishaws are within the definition of a hackney carriage in section 38 and are not excluded by the proviso. They are, therefore, licensable under section 37 and, if that is right, sections 47 and 59 of the 1976 Act apply to them.'

This view was supported by Peter Gibson J and Schiemann LJ who were also sitting.

1 [1999] EHLR 156, CA.

9.76   It is clear, therefore, that both horse-drawn and person-drawn vehicles are hackney carriages. This does, however, give rise to some difficulties. If a local authority has a numerical limit on the number of hackney carriage proprietors' licences that it will grant, that must include any horse-or person-drawn vehicles. There is no provision within the legislation for there to be a test for the demand for motorised hackney carriages as opposed to non-motorised hackney carriages. They are all treated the same and, accordingly, any non-motorised hackney carriages must be included in any surveys to assess demand and, likewise, licences granted to non-motorised hackney carriages must be included in the total number of licences that the authority will grant.

The second problem will arise when the provisions of the 1995 Act are finally introduced. This is because section 32(5) states: **9.77**

"'taxi" means a vehicle licensed under:

(*a*) section 37 of the Town Police Clauses Act 1847, or
(*b*) section 6 of the Metropolitan Public Carriage Act 1869

but does not include a taxi which is drawn by a horse or other animal.'

Although this will overcome any difficulty in relation to horse drawn vehicles, trishaws do not appear to be exempt from the 1995 Act and it is difficult to see how a trishaw can be made accessible for wheelchairs.

HIRING HACKNEY CARRIAGES AT SEPARATE FARES

The Transport Act 1985 introduced the concept of hackney carriages being used as part of a local transport service. With the deregulation of buses, which the Transport Act also introduced, an opportunity was seen for hackney carriages to be used effectively as small buses to enable groups of people to be transported at separate fares by hackney carriage, rather than by a public service vehicle[1]. **9.78**

1 These provisions are contained in the Transport Act 1985, ss 10–13. See Appendix I.

A scheme must be created by the local authority

Before hackney carriages can be used in this way a scheme has to be created by the local authority. Local authorities have a discretion as to whether or not to do this, but are placed under a duty to do it if a request is made in writing by least 10% of the current (at the time that the request is made) holders of hackney carriage proprietors' licences[1]. **9.79**

1 Transport Act 1985, s 10(4).

The scheme must specify where hackney carriages can be hired, which are referred to as 'authorised places', and must also 'specify the requirements to be met for purposes of the scheme in relation to the hiring of taxis at separate fares'. It is less than clear what this means but it would appear to include the frequency of hackney carriages visiting authorised places and other matters of that nature. **9.80**

Under section 10(6) of the Transport Act 1985, the local authority is given a discretion in relation to the scheme to include provisions relating to fares, any kind of indication on the vehicle that it is available for the hiring at separate fares, the type of arrangements that are in place for such use and any conditions that they may wish to apply. Once a scheme is in place, it can be varied by the local authority if they wish to modify it in any way[1]. **9.81**

1 Transport Act 1985, s 10(7).

Finally, the Secretary of State is also given a power to impose schemes by order should he think fit. **9.82**

9.83 It is not clear how many, if, indeed, any, schemes have been created since the introduction of this legislation and, if they do exist, how effective they are.

Advance bookings

9.84 Section 11 of the Transport Act 1985 allows advance booking of both hackney carriages and private hire vehicles at separate fares, provided that all the passengers book the journey in advance and each of them agree to the fact that other people would be present paying their own fare. No scheme is required to enable this to take place and the arrangement can be made at any time. Again, no data appears to exist as to how often this provision is used, but there are probably occasions when it might prove useful.

9.85 When a hackney carriage is being used under the terms of section 10 or 11, it is still subject to the same controls as it would be if it was used conventionally as a hackney carriage. Enforcement of the scheme will lie with the local authority.

A restricted PSV operator's licence

9.86 The final possibility introduced by the Transport Act 1985 is contained in section 12, which enables the hackney carriage proprietor to apply to the Traffic Commissioners for a restricted PSV operator's licence. This would enable him to then use his hackney carriage to provide 'a local service with one or more stopping places within the area of the authority which granted the taxi licence of the vehicle in question'. Section 12 is subject to the provisions contained in the Local Services (Operation by Taxis) Regulations 1986[1]. Again, it is not clear how many restricted PSV operators' licences have been granted to hackney carriage proprietors since the availability of this power[2].

1 SI 1986/587. See Appendix I.
2 See DoT circular 7/86 explaining these provisions, Appendix II.

9.87 The Transport Act 1985 was seen as a great liberalising piece of legislation which would open up transport services to competition. In relation to hackney carriages, its success has been limited. A number of local authorities still impose quantity restrictions on hackney carriages, thereby automatically reducing competition in that area of the local transport field, and the idea of hackney carriages becoming an integral part of a deregulated local bus service does not appear to have fulfilled the expectations of the government of the day.

BUS LANES AND DOUBLE WHITE LINES

9.88 In a number of parts of the country, hackney carriages are allowed to use bus lanes under the provisions of the Road Traffic Regulations Act 1984.

Those who support this take the view that hackney carriages are an integral part of public transport and therefore should be entitled to use bus lanes in the same way as buses.

The case of *R v Oxfordshire County Council, ex p Measor*[1] concerned a decision **9.89** by Oxfordshire County Council to prohibit the use of bus lanes in certain parts of Oxford City by hackney carriages. This was challenged by means of judicial review by the secretary of the City of Oxford Licensed Taxi Cab Association. The challenge was based on the grounds that; firstly, the county council was wrongly advised in law in that it was not possible to devise a sign which allowed the use by bus lanes of hackney carriages; secondly, that the decision to ban hackney carriages from the bus lanes was taken without any proper enquiry in to the effect that would be caused if hackney carriages were allowed to use the bus lanes; thirdly, that there should have been a public enquiry; and finally, that the decision was contrary to the county council's transport policy, which was to give priority to public transport. The matter was considered by Popplewell J, who dismissed the application. He took the view that the incorrect advice concerning the sign was 'a comparatively small part of the decision-making process' and he decided 'in my judgment, it played little or no part in the decision of the councillor's'.

In relation to the second point concerning the absence of proper enquiry he stated:

> 'The question arises, were the County Council entitled, through their members and all these various committees, to use their own observations and common sense to decide whether the presence of taxis in a bus lane was likely to be of advantage in the flow of traffic for the public generally? They concluded that the buses were more likely to travel more speedily and without interference if there were not taxis in the bus lane. It is very difficult to fault that conclusion. It is, to me, self-evident, the more traffic there is in the bus lanes, the less speedily buses will move. They were entitled to form the view which they had formed from their own observations that this was the risk. I do not put it any higher than that. There was a risk that if taxis went down the bus lane then private hire vehicles would follow. Again, it is self-evident, irrespective of taxis going in the bus lanes, that private citizens do use bus lanes. But anything that discourages private citizens from using the bus lane is to be encouraged. The whole purpose of this exercise was to ensure that the general public had the use of public service vehicles to the best advantage of the public.
>
> Accordingly, I am not persuaded that it was unreasonable for these bodies to form their own view, either from their own experience, or applying their own sense, and to come to a conclusion that the exclusion of taxis from bus lanes was likely to be conducive to the proper movement of public service vehicles in these particular roads.'

He concluded that the county council were quite within their rights to decide not to hold a public enquiry.

Finally, in relation to the argument that the county council had departed from their policy to give priority to public transport, he stated the following:

> 'Finally it is submitted that the respondent's policy was to give priority to public transport and public transport means, and it is accepted, taxis. The failure to allow taxis is therefore in breach of that policy. I take the view that the County Council were perfectly entitled, in relation to giving priority to public transport, to make a distinction between various forms

165

of public transport. They were not bound under the policy to give priority to taxis in addition to giving priority to buses. Giving priority to public transport is a general phrase which they have followed, namely, by providing bus lanes for public service vehicles.'

1 (4 July 1997, unreported).

9.90 This case demonstrated that it will ultimately be a matter for the local authority (being the highway authority) to decide whether or not to allow hackney carriages to use bus lanes. There will always be variation across the country as different local authorities will have different views. The same would apply to the use of bus lanes by private hire vehicles. Indeed, it is difficult to see much of an argument that would prohibit private hire vehicles from using bus lanes whilst allowing hackney carriages to do so, but that is the stance that is currently taken by many local authorities.

9.91 Finally, consideration has been given to hackney carriages parking on hackney carriage stands[1], but the case of *McKenzie v DPP*[2] concerned a hackney carriage picking up a fare where double white lines (no overtaking) were painted in the middle of the road. It was decided that the driver of a hackney carriage did not commit an offence if he stopped to pick up or drop off passengers at a point where double white lines were painted down the centre of the road. It is usually an offence for a vehicle to park on such a stretch of road as a result of regulation 26(2)(*a*) of the Traffic Sign Regulations 1994. There are some exceptions contained in paragraph (3) of regulation 26 and the High Court decided that the use of a hackney carriage when somebody is boarding or alighting fell within the exception contained in regulation 27(3)(*a*)(i) 'to enable a person to board or alight from the vehicle . . . the vehicle cannot be used for such a purpose without stopping on the length of road'.

1 Rodgers v Taylor (1986) 85 LGR 762. See para 9.63.
2 [1997] RTR 175.

Chapter 10

Hackney carriage drivers

INTRODUCTION

The role of the hackney carriage driver is important, as the cases of *Hawkins v Edwards*[1] and *Yates v Gates*[2] show[3]. A hackney carriage is always a hackney carriage and as a result can only be driven by a person who holds a valid hackney carriage driver's licence. This chapter examines how such a licence is obtained and to whom it can be granted.

10.1

1 [1901] 2 KB 169.
2 [1970] 1 All ER 754.
3 See Chapter 8, paras 8.3–8.5.

GRANTING THE LICENCE

In areas where the Local Government (Miscellaneous Provisions) Act 1976 has been adopted

The requirement to hold a hackney carriage driver's licence is contained in section 46 of the Town Police Clauses Act 1847 ('the 1847 Act').

10.2

> **'Drivers not to act without first obtaining a licence**
>
> **46** No person shall act as driver of any hackney carriage licensed in pursuance of this or the special Act to ply for hire within the prescribed distance without first obtaining a licence from the commissioners, which licence shall be registered by the clerk to the commissioners, and such fee as the commissioners may determine shall be paid for the same; and every such licence shall be in force until the same is revoked except during the time that the same may be suspended as after mentioned.'

It can be seen that this requires the district council to register the drivers' licences, which they issue, and allows the district council to charge 'such fee as [they] may determine shall be paid'.

Further provisions relating to the actual grant of a driver's licence are contained in the Local Government (Miscellaneous Provisions) Act 1976 ('the 1976 Act'), especially section 53(1)(*b*), which allows the district council to grant licences to hackney carriage drivers for up to three years. Some authorities do grant three-year licences, but the majority grant licences for

10.3

a year. This is felt to give the district council more control over hackney carriage drivers, as there is a more frequent assessment of the qualifications of the driver in relation to his abilities, both medical and personal.

10.4 Section 47 of the 1847 Act makes it an offence for anyone to drive a hackney carriage, unless they hold a current hackney carriage driver's licence. This section also makes it clear that, even if a driver's licence is held, but has been suspended, then in fact the person does not hold a licence and would commit an offence under section 47.

10.5 A hackney carriage proprietor will breach section 47 by allowing an unlicensed hackney carriage driver to drive the vehicle. In the case of *Darlington Borough Council v Thain*[1], the view that a hackney carriage could only be driven by a person who held a hackney carriage driver's licence was restated. The argument that a hackney carriage could be driven by anyone when it was not working as a hackney carriage was rejected.

1 [1995] COD 360.

10.6 In addition, the lending or parting with a hackney carriage driver's licence is also an offence. The only occasion in which a hackney carriage driver's licence can be parted with is to comply with section 48 of the 1847 Act which requires the proprietor of a hackney carriage to retain the licences of those he employs as drivers.

10.7 A fee can be charged for the grant of a hackney carriage driver's licence[1].

1 See Chapter 4.

Criteria for the grant of a licence

10.8 It is now necessary to consider what criteria must be met before a person can be granted a hackney carriage driver's licence.

Section 59 of the Local Government (Miscellaneous Provisions) Act 1976

10.9 The 1847 Act is silent as to any qualification that the driver must hold or any criteria that must be met before a hackney carriage driver's licence can be granted. Such requirements are, however, contained in section 59(1) of the 1976 Act.

> **'Qualifications for drivers of hackney carriages**
>
> **59**–(1) Notwithstanding anything in the Act of 1847, a district council shall not grant a licence to drive a hackney carriage—
>
> (*a*) unless they are satisfied that the applicant is a fit and proper person to hold a driver's licence; or
>
> [(*b*) to any person who has not for at least twelve months been authorised to drive a motor car, or is not at the date of the application for a driver's licence so authorised].'

Section 59 places two obstacles in the way of the potential hackney carriage driver.

1. That the 'applicant is a fit and proper person to hold a [hackney carriage] driver's licence'.

2.   That the person must have 'been authorised to drive a motor car' for at least 12 months before the date of application, not the date of grant.

With regard to the second obstacle, 'authorised to drive a motor car' is defined in section 59(1A)[1]. This states: **10.10**

'**59**–(1A) For the purposes of subsection (1) of this section a person is authorised to drive a motor car if—

(a)   he holds a licence granted under Part III of the Road Traffic Act 1988 (not being a provisional licence) authorising him to drive a motor car, or

(b)   he is authorised by virtue of section 99A(1) of that Act to drive in Great Britain a motor car.'

In reality, this may lead to a situation where a full driving licence has been held for considerably longer than 12 months by the time the grant of the licence is made, due to delays in the administrative process.

1   There are now two subsection (1A)s to section 59 and this one should be subsection (1B). This appears to be due to a mistake in the Queen's Printer's copy of SI 1996/1974.

The case of *Crawley Borough Council v Crabb*[1] deals with the situation where   **10.11**
a person has been disqualified from driving. This can be as a result of too many points being added to a licence as a result of road traffic offences[2] or for any other reason with, eg drink-driving the mandatory minimum one-year ban[3]. In *Crabb*, a private hire driver had held a DVLA licence since 1974. On 16 August 1993, he was disqualified from driving for six months. That disqualification ended on 24 February 1994 and, on 2 March 1994, he applied to Crawley Borough Council for a private hire driver's licence. The council refused the application on the grounds that he had not held a licence for a 12-month period prior to the date of application. The driver (Mr Crabb) appealed and the magistrates granted him a licence. The council appealed, by way of case stated, and judgment was given by Carnwath J. He stated (at 206D):

'As a matter of ordinary language, it seems to me that a person who has held a licence for 12 months in the past, and does in fact hold a licence at the date of application, is entitled to qualify, notwithstanding that there is no continuity between the two periods.

If that interpretation leads to unworkability, or to an absurdity, then no doubt one would seek to adjust the reading accordingly. However, I do not think that can be said here. One could understand a policy that a period of 12 months following a disqualification should be required, but equally one can see, if someone has served his disqualification period and is considered to be a fit and proper person to hold a licence (under section 51(1)(a)) then he should be entitled to claim a new licence and should not be further penalised. I cannot say that the interpretation taken by the justices is so absurd or unjust as to justify changing or reinterpreting the words.

It is also necessary to bear in mind that the section is not specifically concerned with the consequences of the disqualification. It is concerned with the general position in relation to the grant of licences. It would not be right to interpret it by reference to some supposed purpose which is related to problems arising from disqualification.'

This confirms that a further period of one year does not have to elapse after the applicant has been allowed to drive again before he can seek a hackney carriage driver's licence. Provided that at least one year has elapsed since he passed his driving test and was originally authorised to drive, then the statutory test is satisfied.

1   [1996] RTR 201, QBD.
2   Road Traffic Offenders Act 1988, ss 28, 29 and 35, Sch 2, amended by the Road Traffic Act 1991.
3   Road Traffic Act 1988, s 4 and the Road Traffic Offenders Act 1988, ss 34 and 97, Sch 2.

10.12   However, at least one local authority has a policy of not granting a hackney carriage driver's licence until at least two years has elapsed following the return of the licence after any period of disqualification. This is one of its tests of fitness and propriety and, as such, is considered below.

The applicant must be a 'fit and proper person'

10.13   *Consideration of previous convictions*   It is the requirement that no licence should be granted to someone, unless they are a fit and proper person[1], that contains the biggest area of difficulty and causes decision-making committees or officers the most concern. As a result of the *Waveney* case[2], it is now clear that a local authority can consider all convictions, spent or not, which are relevant to an application for a licence[3]. The next step is to obtain details of those convictions.

1   Local Government (Miscellaneous Provisions) Act 1976, s 59(1)(*a*).
2   *Adamson v Waveney District Council* [1997] 2 All ER 898. See Chapter 5, para 5.20ff.
3   The question of previous criminal convictions and the effect of the Rehabilitation of Offenders Act 1974 were considered in Chapter 5.

10.14   It is possible to require the applicant to obtain a print out of the records held on the Police National Computer (PNC) under the powers contained in the Data Protection Act 1984. This should be delivered unopened by the applicant to the local authority. Since the repeal of section 59(1A) of the 1976 Act[1], this is the only way for the local authority to obtain a copy of the PNC print out.

1   See Chapter 5, para 5.28.

10.15   The guidance in Department of Transport circular 2/92[1] is still relevant in relation to the consideration of criminal convictions, but the parts of it relating to the police checks under sections 51(1A) and 59(1A) are now obsolete.

1   See Appendix II.

10.16   Since section 59(1A) of the 1976 Act was repealed, local authorities have to use other methods of ascertaining criminal records and the most usual and widely used is the statutory declaration.

10.17   The consideration of criminal convictions in relation to the holding of a licence is by no means an exact science. In 1992, the Department of Transport and Home Office circular contained (at Annex D) guidelines relating to the relevance of convictions. A number of local authorities have adopted these wholesale as their policy and used them to determine the fitness and propriety of an applicant.

10.18   The first case *R v Crewe and Nantwich Borough Council, ex p Barker*[1] concerned a decision by Crewe and Nantwich Borough Council to revoke a private hire driver's licence which had been granted to Mr Barker. There had been some history of complaints and concerns about Mr Barker and he had been warned in the past about his behaviour in relation to his licence. He applied for renewal of his licence on September and on that application form he referred to a conviction for 'handling'. In giving judgment, MacPherson J stated:

> 'That was totally inaccurate. The offences were fourfold offences which took place on various dates in 1993 to which I have already referred. He was arrested in July 1994, I was told today. He may have appeared before the court in August 1994, on the way to his eventual conviction and sentence, but to say that he was convicted of an offence and to indicate "August 1994 – handling in Crewe" was not correct. What took place was that on 7 September 1994 he did appear in the magistrates' court and pleaded guilty to four serious offences. The Memorandum of Conviction . . . records convictions on 5 October 1994 and thus includes the sentence to which I have referred, namely 80 hours of community service, and reveals that he was convicted, on his own plea at summary trial, of using an MOT certificate which he believed to be false with the intention of inducing the Sun Alliance Insurance Company to accept it as genuine. He also admitted dishonestly receiving a stolen MOT certificate. There were two further offences which were parallel, but separate, one of using an MOT certificate with the intention of inducing the Highways Motor Policies of Lloyds to accept it as genuine and another of receiving stolen goods, namely, that MOT certificate.'

There was a meeting between an officer of the local authority and Mr Barker, during which time Mr Barker informed the local authority that the conviction was still pending and the case needed to go back to court. The local authority conducted the police check, but that did not reveal any offences because sentence was not passed until about a week after the search was conducted. The judge stated:

> 'The long and the short of it is, however, that it is palpable, in my judgment, and certainly probable, that on 15 September this man, Mr Barker, did not inform the Council that he had pleaded guilty to four serious offences.'

He continued:

> 'Why he did not do that and indicated that the matter was still pending is, perhaps, obvious. If he had disclosed the full situation then and there he would never have been granted a licence. It seems to me to be absurd to think that somebody who has been convicted of offences in relation to MOT certificate, and handling of stolen goods, and inducing insurance companies to think that the certificate is genuine, would or could or should ever be granted a driver's licence to drive a taxi or a hire car. That man is palpably dishonest. I cannot believe that it can be tolerated that people who have been dishonest in connection with motor vehicle documentation of that kind would be granted a licence. However, that is, to some extent, irrelevant.

> My views on that matter are strong and I express them.'

1 [1996] CLY 3969.

The question was then raised as to whether these were offences which had **10.19** been committed since the grant of the licence, in which case, the local authority could take action under section 61(1)(*a*) of the 1976 Act, or whether they were offences that had been committed prior to the grant of the licence, in which case, the local authority would have to take action under section 61(1)(*b*) of the same Act. Reference was made by MacPherson J to the case of *R v Recorder of Manchester*[1] as to whether a conviction is a conviction on the entering of a guilty plea or only on sentencing. The judge concluded:

> 'It seems to me, in the circumstances of this case, that the dual nature of the conviction referred to in the authority, to which both counsel have referred in their skeletons, means that in this case and for the purposes of a licence and proceedings of this kind the conviction was not complete until sentence.'

However, that argument seems to be unresolved in this case because the local authority revoked the licence under section 61(1)(*b*) – any other reasonable cause – the judge concluded:

> 'Looking at the whole picture, as they were entitled to do, in my judgment, they were able, under 61(1)(*b*), with the information which they then had in full, including the evidence from Mr Lee [from the council] and Mr Barker as to what happened on 15 September, to say that this man's licence should be revoked. That is what they did. It seems to me unlikely that any other body, looking at the same information, would have reached any different decision.'

There was an argument raised that the decision to revoke was *Wednesbury* unreasonable, but that was not pursued with any great vigour. MacPherson J concluded by saying:

> 'I conclude simply by saying this. If, in strictly legal terms, there had been something in Mr Wood's argument about s 61(1)(*b*) and if, therefore, there had been some legal flaw in the consideration of this case I would undoubtedly not have exercised my discretion to grant relief in the circumstances of this case. I have to look at the whole picture. Here is a man with previous history, with serious convictions in MOT certificates and insurance fraud, and giving misleading history. Here was a man who did not give full information to the person to whom he applied for the renewal of his licence. It seems to me that he has absolutely no merit whatsoever and he would not be entitled to the relief which is or may have been granted at the discretion of this court. On all hands, therefore, or on all sides, or in all directions, this application fails and it is dismissed.'

1 Unreported.

10.20   This case is useful as, firstly, it gives a graphic illustration of judicial displeasure in relation to a person with serious convictions seeking a private hire driver's licence. It has been followed in terms of judicial displeasure, rather than on any particular principles by the case of *Nottingham City Council v Farooq (Mohammed)*[1]. This case concerned a licensed private hire driver who did not inform Nottingham City Council of his conviction for theft and obtaining property by deception. That was in breach of the conditions applied to his licence. Subsequently, he applied to renew his licence and he failed to mention the convictions. As a consequence of a police check, the convictions came to light and the local authority decided not to renew his licence on the grounds that he was not a fit and proper person, as evidenced by the fact that he had not informed the authority of his convictions at the time and had then subsequently failed to declare them on his application form. He appealed and the magistrates granted him a licence, as he maintained that he had not committed the offences, but he had accepted responsibility for them to assist a friend. He also claimed that he had overlooked the need to report the matter to the local authority as he had completed the form in haste. In the magistrates' court his licence was granted because the magistrates accepted his arguments and, despite the advice of their clerk, went behind the convictions, concluding that he was a person who had behaved foolishly, rather than a person who at any stage had been deliberately deceitful. Nottingham City Council appealed by way of case stated and the matter was heard by Tucker J.

The first question which had been raised by the justices in the case was:

> 'Were we, the Justices, acting as a civil appeal court, entitled to review the merits of the respondent's convictions for theft and deception?'

Tucker J stated:

> 'To that my answer is unhesitatingly "No". The reason for that is that the convictions were recorded on a plea of guilty, and if they had been con-tested would have had to be proved so as to make the Justices sure of their truth. In other words, the Justices would have had to be satisfied beyond reasonable doubt of the respondent's guilt, whereas in a civil case a very different standard of proof applies, that is to say the balance of probabili-ties.
>
> In my opinion it is not open to Justices on a civil appeal such as this to review convictions, and I am glad to see that my opinion coincides with that of the Justices' clerk.'

Tucker J then referred to the case of *Adamson v Waveney District Council*[2] and *Hunter v Chief Constable of the West Midlands Police*[3]. He continued:

> 'So, although I have already indicated my answer to the question, my complete answer to the first question is this: that Justices acting as a Civil Appeal Court are not entitled to review the merits of the respondent's convictions for theft and deception.'

1   (1998) Times, 28 October.
2   [1997] 2 All ER 898.
3   [1982] AC 529.

The second question concerned the possibility of an adjournment to enable   **10.21**
the council to deal with the assertion that the appellant was not guilty of the matters for which he was convicted. Tucker J dismissed that as irrelevant because the magistrates could not go behind the conviction.

Three further questions which were contained in the case stated are   **10.22**
extremely important and the views of Tucker J are useful in relation to establishing fitness and propriety of an applicant for a licence. As a conse-quence, the remainder of his judgment is reproduced below:

> 'Then I come to the third question which is:
>
> > "In concluding that the incorrect completion of the forms for renewal of the respondent's licence, by omitting reference to the convictions, was through foolishness and ignorance rather than deliberate deception, was the court entitled to hold that the respondent was nonetheless a fit and proper person within the meaning of section 61 of the Local Government (Miscellaneous Provisions) Act 1976 to hold a licence?"

My answer to that question is in these terms. The Magistrates' Court is not precluded from finding that they are not satisfied that a person is not a fit and proper person within s 61 of the 1976 Act to hold a licence merely because he has not been guilty of deliberate deception. Failing to comply with the requirements of the 1976 Act due to extreme foolishness rather than deliberate deception is not a basis for holding that they are satisfied that the person is a fit and proper person to hold a driver's licence.

The Justices' fourth question is:

"Where a local authority had decided that a person was not a fit and proper person within the meaning of section 61 of the Local Government (Miscellaneous Provisions) Act 1976 because he made a false statement for the purposes of obtaining a combined hackney carriage driver's licence and private hire vehicle driver's licence and where the Justices are satisfied as a fact that the statement was false, should the Justices, in considering an appeal against the decision, have regard to whether the statement was made knowingly or recklessly in determining whether the person was a fit and proper person?'"

Pausing there. It is, of course, material to consider the terms of the appropriate section of the 1976 Act, which is section 57, subsection (1) of which provides:

"A district council may require any applicant for a licence . . . to submit to them such information as they may reasonably consider necessary to enable them to determine whether the licence should be granted. . . ."

Subsection (3) of that section provided:

"If any person knowingly or recklessly makes a false statement or omits any material particular in giving information under this section, he shall be guilty of an offence."

So my answer to the fourth question is this. The magistrates ought to consider whether an applicant making a false statement to obtain a licence did so knowingly or recklessly in considering whether he is a fit and proper person to hold a licence.

The fifth and final question which the Justices ask is:

"Was the decision one which no reasonable court could reach in the light of the case law in *Stepney Borough Council v Joffe* [1949] 1KB 599, DC[1] and the guidance contained in DOT Circular 2/92, Annex D, 13/97[2]?"

I have already referred to the decision in the Case mentioned by the Justices. As to the circular, that contains guidelines relating to the relevance of convictions. The general policy is set out, including the fact that the overriding consideration should be the protection of the public.

So far as offences of dishonesty are concerned, they are referred to under para 3(*g*) of the document in these terms:

"Hackney carriage and PHV drivers are expected to be persons of trust. The widespread practice of delivering unaccompanied property is indicative of the trust that business people place in drivers. Moreover, it is comparatively easy for a dishonest driver to defraud the public by demanding more than the legal fare etc. Overseas visitors can be confused by the change in currency and become 'fair game' for an unscrupulous driver. For these reasons a serious view should be taken of any conviction involving dishonesty. In general, a period of three to five years free of convictions should be required before entering an application."

Therefore, in answer to the question which the Justices posed, I am obliged to say that the decision was not one that the Magistrates' Court could reasonably come to on the material before it.'

It is thus clear from the case that a conviction which has not been appealed is a conviction, irrespective of the motives which led to a plea of guilty being entered.

1　See Chapter 3, para 3.14.
2　See Appendix II.

Other information as is considered necessary However, criminal convictions are **10.23** not the only criteria and a number of authorities require further information before they will consider an application. Section 57(1) of the 1976 Act allows a district council to require an applicant,

'to submit to the local authority such information as they may reasonably consider necessary to enable them to determine whether the licence should be granted or whether conditions should be attached to any such licence.'

Section 57(2) specifically allows a local authority to require a medical cer- **10.24** tificate certifying that the applicant is physically fit to be the driver of a hackney carriage. It also allows examination of the driver by a doctor[1] to assess his physical fitness. Guidance concerning medical fitness of drivers of vehicles carrying the public is available[2]. Some caution, however, must be exercised before guidelines are adopted in their entirety. For example, a reference in the guidelines to a medical report accompanying each applica-tion for a licence, which in many authorities could mean annual medicals where licences are only granted for one year, may not be felt to be appro-priate for hackney carriage (or private hire) drivers.

1　The 1976 Act uses the term Registered Medical Practitioner.
2　'*Medical Aspects of Fitness to Drive – A Guide for Medical Practitioners* produced by the Medical Commission on Accident Prevention (available from The Medical Commission on Accident Prevention, 35–43 Lincoln's Inn Fields, London, WC2A 3PN Tel: 0171 242 3176). This is supplemented by a booklet *At a Glance Guide to the Current Medical Standards of Fitness to Drive* issued by DVLA. The guide recommends that 'taxi drivers' (meaning both hackney carriage and private hire drivers) should be subject to the same requirements as Group II drivers.

A number of authorities require applicants for hackney carriage drivers' **10.25** licences to undertake driving tests (over and above the DVLA driving test) and some require tests of knowledge of the locality and also the ability to speak English.

The knowledge tests take a number of forms. They generally require appli- **10.26** cants to answer a number of questions about the best routes to take between specified places. This can include variations to take account of the time of day and, eg to represent rush hour traffic. One authority has recently intro-duced an 'A-Z' test designed to ascertain whether applicants can use an A-Z Guide of the area.

The test of the applicant's ability to speak English is considered especially **10.27** important in areas with airports or seaports.

10.28   Other factors that can be considered when assessing the fitness and propriety of an applicant, include the applicant's demeanour, appearance and behaviour before either officers or members.

10.29   There is no judicially approved test of fitness and propriety and, accordingly, a number of local tests have developed. These tend to be based on a test similar to the following:

> 'Would you (as a member of the licensing sub-committee or other person charged with the ability to grant a hackney carriage driver's licence) allow your son or daughter, spouse or partner, mother or father, grandson or granddaughter or any other person for whom you care, to get into a vehicle with this person alone?'

If the answer to this question (or a similar test) is an unqualified 'yes', then the test is probably satisfied. If there are any doubts in the minds of those who make the decision, then further consideration should be given as to whether this person is a fit and proper person to hold a hackney carriage driver's licence.

10.30   If the decision is taken that the licence should not be granted, then section 59(2) of the 1976 Act gives the applicant a right of appeal[1] to a magistrates' court against such refusal if they are 'aggrieved' by that refusal.

> '(2) Any applicant aggrieved by the refusal of a district council to grant a driver's licence on the ground that he is not a fit and proper person to hold such licence may appeal to a magistrates' court.'

1   The requirements in relation to appeals are fully considered in Chapter 3.

In areas where the Local Government (Miscellaneous Provisions) Act 1976 has not been adopted

Criteria for the grant of a licence

10.31   Only the provisions of the 1847 Act will cover the granting of a licence. This means that there are no specified criteria to be applied before a driver's licence can be granted. In those circumstances, a local authority can require an applicant to make a statutory declaration as to his previous convictions, which the local authority can consider under the powers contained in section 111 of the Local Government Act 1972[1]. Under the ruling in *Adamson v Waveney District Council*[2], this can include consideration of both unspent and spent convictions.

1   See *Butterworths Local Government Law*.
2   [1997] 2 All ER 898. See Chapter 5, para 5.20.

10.32   The local authority can adopt a policy regarding previous convictions, and could use the guidelines in Department of Transport and Home Office circular 2/92. Although there is no statutory requirement not to grant a licence to someone who is neither a fit and proper person, nor has held a licence to drive for at least a year, these would appear to be reasonable minimum criteria for the local authority to consider. However, this is by no means certain and a local authority that refused to grant a licence on either of those grounds must be prepared to defend itself on a subsequent appeal.

There is a right of appeal to a person aggrieved by the failure to grant such **10.33** a licence and this lies directly to the Crown Court. In the absence of a statutory basis, the argument that the local authority would need to adduce would appear to be the safety of the travelling public. This would be based on the overall rationale of the hackney carriage licensing regime being to protect the public and that the local authority could not grant the applicant a licence and remain within that requirement.

If an application was refused on this basis, the local authority would appear **10.34** to have to give reasons for the refusal.

It can be seen that reliance on the 1847 Act provisions alone in relation to **10.35** the grant of a hackney carriage driver's licence seems unsatisfactory, but, if the 1976 Act has not been adopted, there is no alternative available to the local authority.

Conditions and byelaws

It is not clear whether a local authority can attach conditions to a hackney **10.36** carriage driver's licence. There is no statutory provision which gives an express power to attach conditions and a number of local authorities rely on byelaws to regulate the conduct of their hackney carriage drivers.

However, it is arguable that conditions can be imposed, for the following **10.37** reasons. Section 57(1) of the 1976 Act states:

> 'A district council may require any applicant for a licence under the Act of 1847 or under this Part of this Act to submit to them such information as they may reasonably consider necessary to enable them to determine whether the licence should be granted and whether conditions should be attached to any such licence.'

This indicates that conditions can be attached to any licence granted under the 1847 Act. In addition, section 52(2) of the 1976 Act allows a person aggrieved by any conditions attached to the grant of a driver's licence to appeal to a magistrates' court. It is silent as to whether this is in relation to a private hire or hackney carriage driver's licence. As section 47(1) of the 1847 Act specifically allows the attachment of conditions to a hackney carriage proprietor's licence, in the absence of a similar provision, it is debatable whether there is a power to do so. It could also be argued that section 52(2) only applies to private hire drivers' licences, following on from section 52(1). On balance, however, it is suggested that conditions can be attached to a hackney carriage driver's licence. Unfortunately, there is apparently no case law on this point.

Byelaws can be made under the powers contained in section 68 of the 1847 Act **10.38** and section 6 of the Town Police Clauses Act 1889, both of which contain provisions for byelaws to regulate the behaviour of hackney carriage drivers. Many local authorities use byelaws which were made by local authorities abolished in 1974, but whose area is now part of the 'new' authority. This is possible by virtue of article 9(3) of the Local Authorities etc (Miscellaneous Provisions) Order 1974 and section 238 of the Local Government Act 1972. Model byelaws were published by Department of Transport circular 3/85[1] and the mechanism for making byelaws is contained in section 235 of the 1972 Act.

1 See Appendix II.

A LICENSED HACKNEY CARRIAGE DRIVER

The Town Police Clauses Act 1847

10.39   There are a number of provisions, applying to hackney carriage drivers, which exist with a view to protecting the public.

The duty to take a fare

10.40   Under section 53 of the 1847 Act the hackney carriage driver is under a duty to take a fare. It states:

> **'Penalty on driver for refusing to drive**
>
> 53 A driver of a hackney carriage standing at any of the stands for hack-ney carriages appointed by the commissioners, or in any street, who refuses or neglects, without reasonable excuse, to drive such carriage to any place within the prescribed distance, or the distance to be appointed by any byelaw of the commissioners, not exceeding the prescribed dis-tance, to which he is directed to drive by the person hiring or wishing to hire such carriage, shall for every such offence be liable to a penalty not exceeding [level 2 on the standard scale].'

There are a number of matters to be considered in relation to this section. Firstly, it should be noticed that this is not a blanket requirement, as the driver can refuse if he has a 'reasonable excuse'. This has been considered by a number of local authorities and occasional prosecutions have taken place in the magistrates' court.

10.41   There seems to be no reported High Court decision relating to the question of what is a 'reasonable excuse'. In the absence of such a decision, it will be a subjective matter for the magistrates to consider whether the refusal was reasonable. In certain areas of some large cities in England and Wales, hack-ney carriage drivers refuse to take fares after a certain time of night, due to their concerns about being attacked either by the passengers themselves or by persons in the area to which they have been asked to travel. It would appear to be difficult to argue against this, as the safety of the driver and, indeed, in certain circumstances, his passengers would appear to be a rea-sonable excuse for not taking the fare. This has serious implications for people who live in areas that are viewed in this light by the hackney carriage drivers, but a prosecution would appear unlikely to succeed.

10.42   The second point concerns the area within which a hackney carriage driver must take a fare. Section 53 refers to the 'prescribed distance, or the dis-tance to be appointed by the byelaw . . . not exceeding the prescribed distance'. The prescribed distance is now either the area of the district council (or unitary, metropolitan district, Welsh county or county borough council), unless the council has hackney carriage zones, in which case it will be the area of the zone in question. This is due to section 171 of the Public Health Act 1875, which incorporated the provisions of the 1847 Act and the

Town Police Clauses Act 1889 for all urban districts. The Local Government Acts 1894 and 1933 extended hackney carriage licensing to all urban districts, boroughs and county boroughs, and this continued under the Local Government Act 1972[1]. The Transport Act 1985 extended hackney carriage licensing to all districts in England and Wales.

1 Local Government Act 1972, s 180 and Sch 14, s 15, paragraphs 24 and 25.

10.43 Some local authorities may have byelaws which reduce the prescribed distance from the area of the local authority and there are some local Acts which extend it, eg the Greater Manchester Act 1981, which in relation to the ten metropolitan districts within Greater Manchester extend the prescribed distance to any hiring commencing within the district, and extending up to four miles from the district boundary, provided it is within the county of Greater Manchester.

Agreements as to fares

10.44 An agreement can be made in advance of the hire that a certain fare will be paid, which must be less than the fare which would be shown on the meter. Section 54 of the 1847 Act prohibits any increase in that agreed fare being made either during or at the conclusion of the hiring, and if a driver attempted to charge more than the agreed fare this would be an offence under that section. This does not, of course, prohibit charging less than the fare that is shown on the meter at the end of the journey if no agreement was made in advance[1].

1 See Chapter 9, para 9.14

Agreement to pay more than the legal fare

> '**Agreement to pay more than the legal fare**
>
> 55 No agreement whatever made with the driver, or with any person having or pretending to have the care of any such hackney carriage, for the payment of more than the fare allowed by any byelaw made under this or the special Act, shall be binding on the person making the same; and any such person may, notwithstanding such agreement, refuse, on discharging such hackney carriage, to pay any sum beyond the fare allowed as aforesaid; and if any person actually pay to the driver of any such hackney carriage, whether in pursuance of any such agreement or otherwise, any sum exceeding the fare to which such driver was entitled, the person paying the same shall be entitled, on complaint made against such driver before any justice of the peace, to recover back the sum paid beyond the proper fare, and moreover such driver shall be liable to a penalty for such exaction not exceeding [level 3 on the standard scale]; and in default of the repayment by such driver of such excess of fare, or of payment of the said penalty, such justice shall forthwith commit such driver to prison, there to remain for any time not exceeding one month, unless the said excess of fare and the said penalty be sooner paid.'

10.45 Section 55 of the 1847 Act makes it offence for a driver to demand more than the fare shown on the meter[1]. In such circumstances it is possible for the local authority to prosecute the driver and on conviction a fine not exceeding level 3 on the standard scale can be levied.

1 See Chapter 9, para 9.21.

10.46   Section 56 of the 1847 Act allows an agreement to be struck with the driver (or proprietor) of a hackney carriage that for a specified sum of money the passengers will be carried a fixed distance. This is provided that the actual charge does not work out as being more expensive than that which would be allowed by the meter[1].

1   See Chapter 9, para 9.23.

Penalty on proprietors, etc convicted of overcharging

'Penalty on proprietors, etc convicted of overcharging

10.47   **58** Every proprietor or driver of any such hackney carriage who is convicted of taking as a fare a greater sum than is authorised by any byelaw made under this or the special Act shall be liable to a penalty not exceeding [level 3 on the standard scale], and such penalty may be recovered before one justice; and in the conviction of such proprietor or driver an order may be included for payment of the sum so overcharged, over and above the penalty and costs; and such overcharge shall be returned to the party aggrieved.'

Section 58 of the 1847 Act prohibits a driver charging more than he should on the meter. This can be contrasted with section 55, which actually outlaws an agreement to pay more than the amount which would be displayed on the meter at the end of the journey.

House v Reynolds

10.48   This distinction is usefully illustrated by the case of *House v Reynolds*[1]. In this case, convictions had been secured against a number of hackney carriage drivers and hackney carriage proprietors for contravention of both sections 55 and 58 of the 1847 Act. A group of proprietors had arranged a centralised telephone booking service and prospective passengers who used this service were told that to book a hackney carriage by this method would incur a booking fee of 10p. That sum was collected at the end of the journey at the same time as the recorded fare was obtained from the passenger.

1   [1977] 1 WLR 88, QBD.

10.49   The first question was whether such a fee was contrary to the provisions of section 55 of the 1847 Act. Eveleigh J gave the leading judgment of the court. He quoted section 55 and then said (at 92C):

'In my view that section is striking at the payment by the passenger of something apart from, or over and above, the fare itself. It is aimed at a collateral agreement to the agreement to hire. Of course there has to be a connection between such agreement and the contract of hire. The words "No agreement whatever" are clearly to be read in the context of a hiring agreement but relate to something collateral thereto. In my view the booking agreement with which we are concerned in this case was an agreement collateral to the hiring agreement, but it did provide for the payment of such a sum more than the fare that was allowed. Consequently, there has been a breach of section 55.'

Slynn J agreed (as did Widgery LCJ). Slynn J stated (at 92H):

'Section 55, . . . is wide enough to cover a collateral agreement to pay money and covers the taking by a driver of a sum of over and above what is in the strict sense a fare. The agreement to pay a booking fee and the taking of a booking fee by the driver in the present case in my judgment fell within that section.'

It is interesting to note that it was argued that no offence had been committed by the 'driver, or with any person having or pretending to have the care of any such hackney carriage' because the arrangement to pay the 10p was made with the umbrella booking organisation. Eveleigh J defeated that argument with the following (at 92F):

'I should refer to one final argument addressed to the court by Mr Farquharson [for the defendants], who said that section 55 related to an agreement made with the driver or any person having or pretending to have the care of the hackney carriage, and he said that in the present case the agreement could not be said to have been made with the defendants, be it with the owner or be it with the driver, because the agreement was made with the organisation Streamline Taxis.

In my view that argument does not prevail. The telephonist was in my opinion acting as an agent on behalf of the defendants, be it the driver or be it the owner, or, to put it another way, the agreement was being made with the owner and the driver through the telephonist.'

It is quite clear, therefore, that this case outlaws a booking fee being levied for a telephone booking of a hackney carriage.

In relation to section 58 of the 1847 Act, Eveleigh J considered the matter (and it should be recognised that convictions had been obtained against in the case of *House* under both sections 55 and 58) and his judgment was as follows (at 92E):

'I turn now to section 58. It is important to emphasise the words in that section "taking as a fare". These are clearly to be contrasted with the words in section 55 which referred to the payment of "any sum exceeding the fare". Consequently, it seems to me that section 58 is dealing with the fare itself, with a sum of money paid and received as the fare. As I have already come to the conclusion that the 10p in this case was not paid as the fare but was something collateral thereto, it would follow that there is no offence under section 58.'

10.50

It would seem that the offence under section 58 of the 1847 Act is committed at the end of the journey when the demand is made for more than the fare that is shown on the meter (plus any allowable extras). This may affect in which magistrates' court the information should be laid, as it may be that the end of the hiring was in a different sessional division from that which covers the area of the local authority that licensed the hackney carriage and driver.

10.51

Ely v Godfrey

This point was considered in the case of *Ely v Godfrey*[1], which concerned a prosecution under section 309 of the Salford Improvement Act 1862. A hackney carriage driver had charged considerably more than the fare which was allowed by the byelaws for a journey which commenced within the borough of Salford but ended some eight-and-a-half miles beyond the borough boundary. The correct fare, as indicated by the byelaws, would have been 13 shillings but, in fact, the driver charged 25 shillings. Section 309 was

10.52

extremely similar in wording to section 55 of the 1847 Act and the driver was prosecuted in Salford Magistrates' Court. He appealed against conviction. One of the grounds for appeal was that the stipendiary magistrate sitting in Salford had no jurisdiction to try the case, as the alleged offence had taken place in another borough, some eight-and-a-half miles away from the Salford boundary. Salter J stated (at 84):

> 'I am of the opinion that this conviction cannot stand, on the ground that the learned magistrate who dealt with this matter had no jurisdiction to deal with it.
>
> In my opinion the offence of which this man was convicted was committed wholly on the arrival of the cab at Mile End Lane [in Stockport], at which time and place, as found in the case, the driver asked and received the sum of 25 shillings. If that was excess of the amount to which he was lawfully entitled, he committed the offence then and there; and that was a distance of seven or eight miles from the boundary of the jurisdiction of the stipendiary magistrate who dealt with this matter.'

1   (1922) 86 JP 82.

Carrying persons other than the hirer

10.53   Section 59 of the 1847 Act prohibits a driver (or proprietor) of a hackney carriage from carrying persons other than the hirer, unless the hirer has given his express consent. This was the principal point considered in *Yates v Gates*[1]. The situation was that two people (who were actually employees of the local authority) approached a hackney carriage. The driver was not present, but was in a nearby house. When he emerged from the house he was accompanied by a woman and a child. The two officers asked to hire the vehicle to take them to a destination, the driver stated that he would take the two officers first, then take the women and the child to their destination, and all five people got into the vehicle. The question which arose was whether the express consent which was required under section 59 could be obtained by acquiescence. Parker LCJ gave the judgment of the court (at 755J):

> 'The question . . . left to the court is: "Can consent be expressed by actions without words; if so, were Mr Smith's actions capable in law of amounting to express consent?" In my judgment express consent in this provision, whatever it may mean elsewhere, means positive consent, not an acquiescence in the form of an implied consent. It envisages that a driver of a taxi cab should ask the hirer whether he objects to somebody else being carried. Of course if he says "I have no objection", there is the express consent. It may be also, in answer to the first question raised by the justices, that the action might amount to consent, in that he might nod his head in answer to the question, but mere acquiescence, as I have said, would not in my judgment amount to express consent within the Act.'

1   [1970] 1 All ER 754.

Those who are prohibited from driving a hackney carriage

10.54   A person is prohibited from driving a hackney carriage without the consent of the proprietor under section 60 of the 1847 Act. Additionally, a hackney carriage driver who does have the consent of the proprietor to drive, but who allows another person who does not have such consent to drive, also commits an offence. In addition, any driver of a hackney carriage must hold a hackney carriage driver's licence[1].

1 See *Hawkins v Edwards* [1901] 2 KB 169 and *Yates v Gates* [1970] 1 All ER 754. See Chapter 8, paras 8.3–8.5 and Chapter 10, para 10.1.

In reality, although criminal offences exist, the resulting action is more likely   **10.55**
to be taken by the proprietor himself under contract, rather than to rely on
the local authority to take action under section 60.

The effect of other legislation on the Town Police Clauses Act 1847

Section 61 of the 1847 Act has effectively been rendered obsolete by the   **10.56**
provisions of the Road Traffic Act 1988. In 1847, there were no provisions
concerning drunken driving or 'wanton and furious driving', but there are
now and it is most unlikely that the local authority would take action under
section 61 in such circumstances. The police would undoubtedly be
involved and would wish to take action under the Road Traffic Act 1988 for
either dangerous driving, contrary to section 2 or careless and inconsiderate
driving, contrary to section 3.

Likewise, section 63 is effectively obsolete. This allows anyone, who is hurt   **10.57**
or has damage caused to themselves or property by the driver of a hackney
carriage, to seek compensation through the magistrates' court. However,
as this compensation cannot exceed £5, any claim for compensation would
appear to be best directed against the driver under the general civil law.

Section 62 still has some relevance. It is an offence for the driver of a hack-   **10.58**
ney carriage to 'leave it in any street or in any place of public resort or
entertainment, whether it be hired or not, without someone proper to take
care of it' and is punishable to a penalty on conviction not exceeding level 1
on the standard scale. In addition, a police constable can remove the hackney carriage to a place of safe custody. The section, in fact, refers to
removing the hackney carriage and any horses harnessed to it to a livery
stable, but in the age of motorised hackney carriages that is unlikely to be a
common occurrence, unless the area has horse-drawn hackney carriages,
which can still be found in many seaside towns.

It is interesting to note that, on the face of it, this section would apply to any   **10.59**
hackney carriage which is parked on a street or at any other public place,
irrespective of whether it is locked or not. This would appear to suggest, if
interpreted literally, that a hackney carriage can only be parked on private
land to which the public have no access (although it is less than clear
whether that access should be as of right or of fact). This seems most unreasonable in today's situation regarding motorised hackney carriages and it
would seem unlikely that any prosecution in relation to a hackney carriage
that was properly parked would succeed. However, in *Attridge v Attwood*[1] a
hackney carriage driver parked his vehicle with the handbrake on and the
engine switched off. He was prosecuted under section 62. He asserted that
the section only applied to horse-drawn vehicles, but that was rejected. The
High Court held that it would be a matter of fact and degree as to whether
a driver had taken sufficient precautions to satisfy the requirements of section 62. The case of *Rodgers v Taylor*[2] should also be noted.

1 [1964] Crim LR 45.
2 (1986) 85 LGR 762. See Chapter 9, para 9.63 in relation to a hackney carriage parking
on a stand.

10.60 If one driver attempts to prevent another hackney carriage from being hired in preference to his, he commits an offence under section 64 of the 1847 Act, as does someone who obstructs other hackney carriages. In relation to obstruction of other hackney carriages, this is more appropriately dealt with under other legislation, eg section 137 of the Highways Act 1980 (wilfully obstructing the passage of a highway) or regulation 103 of the Road Vehicles (Construction and Use) Regulations 1986 (causing or permitting a motor vehicle or trailer to stand on a road so as to cause unnecessary obstruction of the road). However, there may be situations where the drivers are in dispute as to whom should take the particular fare. In those circumstances section 64 may still be relevant[1].

1 This point was considered in *R v Great Western Trains Ltd, ex p Frederick* [1998] COD 239. See Chapter 9, para 9.50ff.

10.61 If a prosecution is brought against a driver for an offence under any provision of the 1847 Act and the driver is acquitted, section 65 allows him to claim 'such compensation for his loss of time in attending the said Justice touching or concerning such complaint or information as to the said Justice seems reasonable'. It is interesting to note that such compensation is to be paid, irrespective of whether or not the driver is legally represented, and it enables a person who is acquitted to claim compensation for his loss of time, and not just for costs involved in instructing a solicitor. It is unclear how often this section is used when a local authority either fails to secure a conviction or withdraws a summons before trial.

Provisions affecting drivers under the 1976 Act

10.62 Section 53(3) of the 1976 Act requires a hackney carriage driver to produce his driver's licence to either an authorised officer of the council or police constable, if so requested. It must be produced forthwith or within a five-day period[1] to either the council offices or the police station. 'Forthwith' has been defined as 'as soon as possible in all the circumstances, the nature of the act being done to be taken into account' in *Sameen v Abeyewickrema*[2]. It is unlikely that a hackney carriage driver would be able to produce his driver's licence immediately, as, by virtue of section 48 of the 1847 Act, the licence has to be retained by the proprietor of the hackney carriage. Unless the driver is also the proprietor, he is unlikely to have the licence with him.

1 Local Government (Miscellaneous Provisions) Act 1976, s 153(3)(*a*) and (*b*).
2 [1963] AC 597, PC.

Suspension and revocation of hackney carriage drivers' licences

The Town Police Clauses Act 1847

10.63 Section 50 of the 1847 Act states:

'**Revocation of licences of proprietors or drivers**

50 The commissioners may, upon the conviction for the second time of the proprietor or driver of any such hackney carriage for any offence under the provisions of this or the special Act with respect to hackney carriages, or any byelaw made in pursuance thereof, suspend or revoke, as they deem right, the licence of any such proprietor or driver.'

This is a reasonably restricted power as not only must two offences have been committed, but they must also be offences against the provisions of the 1847 Act, the 1889 Act or byelaws made under either of those statutory provisions. However, the case of *Bowers v Gloucester Corpn*[1] makes it clear that the two offences do not have to be identical, provided they are both contrary to the Acts of 1847 or 1889 or to byelaws. In this case, the licence holder had his licence revoked, as he had committed two different offences under the byelaws. He contended that section 50 could only be used if there were two identical offences committed. Parker LCJ, giving judgment, disagreed. He stated (at 210):

'In my judgment, the learned recorder came to a wrong conclusion in this case. It maybe, and I think that it is, a matter of first impression. When I first read the words in s. 50, it seemed to me that "any offence" meant what it said, "any offence", and that it was quite unnecessary before the power of revocation arises that there should be two convictions for two identical offences. It seems to me that that is so on general principles of construction. I think that this is a typical case where, in argument before the court, a confusion has arisen between a provision which is ambiguous and a provision which is difficult to interpret. It may well be that many sections of Acts are difficult to interpret, but can be interpreted by the proper canons of construction. A provision can only be said to be ambiguous in the sense that, if it be a penal section, it would be resolved in a manner most favourable to the citizen, where, having applied all the proper canons of interpretation, the matter is still left in doubt. In the present case, it seems to me, first, that, approaching this on ordinary canons of interpretation, "any" must be given the wide meaning which it undoubtedly bears. Secondly, the mischief aimed at by the Act of 1847 can also be taken into account, which is clearly that a strict control should be kept on taxicab drivers, and thirdly, or part and parcel of the second, the complete absurdity which arises, bearing in mind the mischief aimed at, if a man can show himself to be utterly unfitted to be a taxi-cab driver by committing thirty, forty or fifty offences, and yet not have his licence revoked because he had always committed a different offence.

In my judgment, "any" means what it says. There is clearly power here to revoke the licence and the matter should go back to the recorder with a direction that there was power to revoke, and that he should then consider the matter on its merits.'

The section itself is wide-ranging and no indication is given as to how long a suspension should be for. It would appear therefore to be limited to a 'reasonable' length of time.

1 (1963) 61 LGR 209.

The 1847 Act is as usual silent about rights of appeal, but an appeal would **10.64** be available to the Crown Court under the provision contained in section 7 of the Public Health Acts Amendment Act 1907[1].

1 See Chapter 3, para 3.9.

The Local Government (Miscellaneous Provisions) Act 1976

10.65 Section 61 of the 1976 Act states:

'Suspension and revocation of drivers' licences

61–(1) Notwithstanding anything in the Act of 1847 or in this Part of this Act, a district council may suspend or revoke or (on application therefor under section 46 of the Act of 1847 or section 51 of this Act, as the case may be) refuse to renew the licence of a driver of a hackney carriage or a private hire vehicle on any of the following grounds—

(a) that he has since the grant of the licence—
  (i) been convicted of an offence involving dishonesty, indecency or violence; or
  (ii) been convicted of an offence under or has failed to comply with the provisions of the Act of 1847 or of this Part of this Act; or
(b) any other reasonable cause.

(2)
(a) Where a district council suspend, revoke or refuse to renew any licence under this section they shall give to the driver notice of the grounds on which the licence has been suspended or revoked or on which they have refused to renew such licence within fourteen days of such suspension, revocation or refusal and the driver shall on demand return to the district council the driver's badge issued to him in accordance with section 54 of this Act.
(b) If any person without reasonable excuse contravenes the provisions of this section he shall be guilty of an offence and liable on summary conviction to a fine not exceeding [level 1 on the standard scale].
(3) Any driver aggrieved by a decision of a district council under this section may appeal to magistrates' court.'

10.66 Section 61 gives the local authority powers to suspend, revoke or (on an application for renewal) refuse to renew a hackney carriage driver's licence. The grounds are contained in section 61(1)(a) and (b) and are wide-ranging. It should be noted, however, that for action to be taken under section 61(1)(a), the offence has to have been committed since the grant of the licence. No consideration can be given under section 61 to any offence which took place before the grant of the licence, so in a situation where a licensing committee decides to tighten their criteria in relation to criminal offences, section 61 could not be used to refuse to renew a licence, if the offence was committed before the licence was originally granted.

10.67 Section 61(1)(a) includes offences of dishonesty, indecency or violence or offences under the 1847 Act or the 1976 Act. Section 61(1)(b) allows such action to be taken for 'any other reasonable cause'[1]. This would appear to include any action falling short of a criminal conviction and could arguably include a situation that led to a failed prosecution.

1 This can be for any matter, see *Norwich City Council v Watcham and Thurtle* (21 May 1981, unreported). See Chapter 8, para 8.87.

10.68 This can occur where the local authority or the Crown Prosecution Service has brought a prosecution and the driver was acquitted. It is still open to the local authority to consider the driver's position in relation to his driver's licence notwithstanding the acquittal. Depending on the circumstances, such action may constitute a reasonable cause for not renewing, suspending or revoking a driver's licence. On a subsequent appeal[1] the matter would be considered on the basis of the civil burden of proof (the balance of probabilities) as opposed to the criminal burden of proof (beyond all reasonable doubt).

1 Under the Local Government (Miscellaneous Provisions) Act 1976, s 61(3).

It is a fundamental rule of English law that a person cannot be tried twice for **10.69** the same crime. However, considering a person's previous convictions as evidence of his fitness and propriety to drive a hackney carriage does not amount to trying him twice. The rule that prevents double jeopardy is only applicable to criminal prosecutions and the consideration of a person's suitability to drive a hackney carriage is not a criminal matter. Such action is not unlawful as it does not amount to double jeopardy and no plea of *autrefois acquit* or *autrefois convict* can be made. Those pleas can only be made before a criminal court if it is alleged that a person is being tried for the same matter twice and that he has already been acquitted of the charge (*autrefois acquit*) or convicted of the charge (*autrefois convict*). Provided the consideration of non-convictions is taken in the interests of protecting the public, the local authority would appear to be able to take such action. It would remain to be seen if they were successful on a subsequent appeal, ie whether the court felt that the action taken was reasonable in the circumstances, but the line of action is open to them.

R v Maidstone Crown Court, ex p Olson

This view is supported by the case of *R v Maidstone Crown Court, ex p* **10.70** *Olson*[1]. In this case, Mr Olson was a hackney carriage driver and had been so for nine years. In June 1988, he was convicted of indecently assaulting a 15-year-old girl on her evidence that he had committed the assault in a country lane when she did not have enough money to pay her fare home. Upon conviction, Ashford Borough Council, who had granted him the hackney carriage licence, revoked it. However, in January 1989 the conviction was quashed on appeal on the grounds of misdirection of the jury. By virtue of the Criminal Appeal Act 1968, that counted as an acquittal. Accordingly, Mr Olson had never been convicted of the offence. He applied for another hackney carriage driver's licence, but the local authority was not satisfied that he was a fit and proper person and refused to grant the licence. Mr Olson appealed to the magistrates' court and the magistrate refused to allow the local authority to call the girl, who had been the complainant in the criminal case, to give evidence. As a consequence of this, there was effectively no evidence against Mr Olson and the magistrates allowed his appeal. Ashford Borough Council appealed to the Crown Court and argued that the magistrates had been wrong to exclude the complainant's evidence. As a preliminary point, the Crown Court judge was asked to rule on the admissibility or otherwise of the complainant's evidence. He ruled it admissible. The case was then adjourned so that Mr Olson could seek a judicial review of that decision.

1 [1992] COD 496.

10.71   The questions posed for the High Court were:

1. The jurisdiction of the High Court to consider the point.
2. The merits of the argument as to whether or not the evidence was admissible.
3. Where the burden of proof lay.
4. What the standard of proof was.
5. Whether there were grounds for estoppel or arguing an abuse of process.

The case was heard by Watkins LJ and May J. They decided (at 498) they did not have any jurisdiction to consider the matter. Notwithstanding that, on the application of both parties they were prepared to consider the merits:

> '*Burden of proof:* It was for the applicant to establish that he was a fit and proper person. It was accepted that he would discharge that burden if the local authority were not permitted to call the complainant to give evidence. It followed that the evidential burden shifted to the local authority. It should not, however, be overlooked that what they were seeking to do was to rebut the applicant's case that he was a fit and proper person. They were not seeking to prosecute him a second time.
>
> *Standard of proof:* It was necessary to the applicant's argument that the standard of proof in relation to the facts which the local authority sought to prove was the criminal standard. But these were not criminal proceedings. They were proceedings relating to the grant of a taxi licence. It was for the applicant to establish on the balance of probabilities that he was a fit and proper person. In seeking to rebut the applicant's contention that he was such a person, the local authority needed only to satisfy the civil standard of proof, even if the substance of what they sought to prove amounted to a criminal offence. Parliament did not intend that local authorities had to refuse licenses under this head only if they were *sure* that an applicant alleged to have committed a relevant offence had indeed committed it. The balance of public interest to see that those who drove taxis were fit and proper persons to do so did not argue for a criminal standard of proof here. The local authority had to establish what they sought to prove to a civil standard of proof commensurate with the occasion and the proportionate to the subject matter.
>
> *Estoppel and abuse:* There was no estoppel or abuse. The local authority were entitled to go behind the applicant's acquittal for the different purpose of seeking to rebut his contention that he was a fit and proper person to hold a taxi driver's licence. To that end, they were entitled to call the complainant to give evidence.'

McCool v Rushcliffe Borough Council

10.72   This approach was followed in *McCool v Rushcliffe Borough Council*[1], where the High Court not only agreed with the decision in *Olson*[2] and allowed hearsay evidence of an indecent assault which had not resulted in a conviction[3] but, in addition, confirmed that the standard of proof in licensing matters was a civil one (the balance of probabilities) rather than the tougher criminal test (beyond all reasonable doubt). Bingham LCJ, giving the judgment in *McCool* stated (at 896A):

> 'It is in my judgment very important to bear in mind the basis upon which that case [*R v Maidstone Crown Court ex parte Olson*] was proceeding

before this court, namely that the applicant was entitled to be regarded as a fit and proper person unless evidence of indecent assault could be adduced against him. It is also in my judgment very important to bear in mind the regulatory framework to which I have already made reference.

I return to section 51(1), from which it is plain that a district council has a mandatory obligation to grant a licence to an applicant for a licence to drive private hire vehicles, but that it is prohibited from granting a licence unless it is satisfied that the applicant is a fit and proper person to hold a driver's licence. It is no doubt right to regard an applicant as fit and proper if adequate evidence of good character and record is adduced and there is no rason to question or doubt it. But the local authority, or on complaint to them the justices, are not permitted to grant the licence unless they are satisfied that the applicant is fit and proper. They mail fail to be satisfied because adequate information of character and record is not forthcoming, as would be the case if an applicant failed to respond adequately to a request under section 57(1); or they might fail to be satisfied for any other good reason. It is in my view impossible to be prescriptive as to what might amount to a good reason. What will be (or may be) a good reason will vary from case to case and vary according to the context in which those words appear. The decision maker may take account of hearsay (as already indicated), provided it is hearsay which is not unreasonably thought to be worthy of credence, and such evidence need not be evidence which will withstand scrutiny according to the formal rules of a court of law. It is not a good reason if a local authority or justices rely on prejudice or assertions shown to be ill-founded or gossip or rumour or any other matter which a reasonable and fair-minded decision maker acting in good faith and with proper regard to the interests both of the public and the applicant would not think it right to rely on. But it is appropriate for the local authority or justices to regard as a good reason anything which a reasonable and fair-minded decision maker, acting in good faith and with proper regard to the interests both of the public and the applicant, could properly think it right to rely on. In my judgment the justices in this case did not exceed the bounds of appropriate evidence in reaching their decision.

I said earlier that the questions posed by the justices in my view called for reformulation. I would propose to reformulate the questions as follows:

"(1) Were we entitled to have regard to hearsay evidence of the indecent assault alleged against Mr McCool without direct evidence of it?"

To that question I would answer "Yes".

"(2) Did we apply a correct standard proof to the question for our determination?"

Again I would answer "Yes", save that the justices may well have applied a more rigorous standard than was called for in the circumstances.

"(3) Were we entitled on the findings made, if properly made, not to be satisfied that Mr McCool was a fit and proper person to be granted a private vehicle licence?"

To that question I would answer "Yes".'

1   [1998] 3 All ER 889, QBD.
2   *R v Maidstone Crown Court, ex p Olson* [1992] COD 496.
3   *Westminster City Council v Zestfair* (1989) 88 LGR 258 and *Kavanagh v Chief Constable of Devon and Cornwall* [1974] QB 624. See Chapter 2, paras 2.32 and 2.33.

10.73 Likewise, where a person is accused of a criminal offence, action can be taken before the hearing of the prosecution, provided that there is sufficient evidence to support the view that the suspension is on the basis of 'any other reasonable cause'. Local authorities must tread carefully in this area, for if there is insufficient evidence, the action may be unreasonable. It is necessary for local authorities to balance their duties to the public against their duties to the drivers that they licence and such decisions can be difficult.

10.74 One further area of difficulty concerns the suspension of a hackney carriage driver's licence. Refusal to renew or revocation is reasonably straightforward. Provided that the grounds laid down in section 61(1)(*a*) or (*b*) of the 1976 Act have been met, then the local authority can come to the conclusion that the person is no longer a fit and proper person to drive a hackney carriage. However, the use of a suspension is harder to justify. This is used by a great many authorities as a method of imposing a punishment upon a driver for transgressions of a nature which, although taken seriously by the local authority, are not sufficient to warrant a revocation. A suspension, however, can only be imposed because the person is no longer a fit and proper person to hold a hackney carriage driver's licence. The question that then arises is how they can become a fit and proper person simply through the passage of time. Obviously, in certain circumstances, if the person can demonstrate that they have not transgressed again, then the original misdemeanour becomes less important as time passes. As most local authorities grant a hackney carriage driving licence for only one year, it is, however, a little difficult to see how the impact of time within one year can justify a suspension.

10.75 The powers contained in section 61 are to protect the public. Although the protection of the public may directly result in the loss of livelihood of the driver, it is difficult to understand how the punishment of a driver by means of the use of the suspension provisions actually protects the public. If the matter is so serious that the public can only be protected by the driver not driving a hackney carriage, then it is arguable that revocation is the correct route, not suspension. Ultimately, it will be for local authorities to argue the justification of a suspension at any subsequent appeal to the magistrates' court under section 63(1).

10.76 A number of local authorities have introduced 'points systems' for hackney carriage drivers. This works on the basis that a transgression attracts a number of points and, once a specified number have been amassed on the driver's licence, then suspension for a period of time takes place. The system is analogous to the concept of points on a DVLA driving licence. These are introduced under conditions, but, again, the same concerns as outlined above regarding suspensions apply to these systems.

Chapter 11

Private hire vehicles: an introduction

Private hire vehicles represent a second category or type of vehicle that pro- **11.1**
vide services to the public by way of private independent transportation.

The rise in the numbers of 'mini-cabs' during the 1960s and early 1970s led **11.2**
to the passing and introduction of the Local Government (Miscellaneous
Provisions) Act 1976 ('the 1976 Act'), which introduced a regulatory framework for the control of private hire vehicles.

These provisions are adoptive and, as a consequence, there are a few areas **11.3**
of England and Wales where these provisions do not apply. In those areas no
licensing control exists over 'mini-cabs', their drivers or any other related
activity and that situation does pose a grave risk to the public. The situation
was similar within the metropolitan area of London, but the Private Hire
Vehicles (London) Act 1998 will impose a regime similar to that that which
exists under the 1976 Act outside the metropolitan area.

A private hire vehicle differs from a hackney carriage in a number of funda- **11.4**
mental ways:

1. The vehicle itself cannot resemble a hackney carriage. This is to enable
   it to be readily identified by the public as a private hire vehicle.
2. A private hire vehicle cannot ply for hire (that is, cruise the streets of
   the district until hailed by a prospective passenger[1]).
3. It cannot 'rank up', awaiting the approach of customers.
4. A private hire vehicle must be driven by a person who holds a private
   hire driver's licence issued by the same local authority that licences the
   vehicle (in this aspect, the situation is similar to the rules governing
   hackney carriages).
5. However, the similarity ends at this point because a private hire operator must control each and every private hire vehicle. The operator is
   the person who takes the bookings from the customer and arranges for
   the vehicle to go to wherever the customer requests. This is the only
   way in which private hire vehicles are able to collect their customers.

1 See Chapter 8, para 8.6ff.

It can therefore be seen that there are three players involved in the private **11.5**
hire function: the private hire driver; the private hire operator; and the

191

private hire vehicle. This can be contrasted with the situation that applies to hackney carriages, where all that is required is a licensed vehicle and licensed driver.

11.6   There are further variations between the two licensing regimes:

1. No limit can be placed upon the number of private hire vehicles that the district council will licence.
2. The district council has no power to prescribe fares for private hire vehicles.
3. The district council have no power to prescribe the type of vehicle, other than the requirement that the vehicle is satisfactory for its purpose, although the local authority can lay down minimum specifications for private hire vehicles. This can be contrasted with the 'mandatory orders' which enable local authorities to only license London-style taxis for hackney carriage work.
4. There are no private hire zones. The area for private hire operation is the total area of the local authority that has adopted the 1976 Act.

11.7   Although the private hire regime can be seen therefore as rather more relaxed than the hackney carriage regime, the overriding aims of providing the public with a safe and convenient method of transport remain the same and the differences in approach in no way undermine that fundamental consideration.

11.8   Almost all the legislative requirements concerning private hire vehicles are contained in the 1976 Act, but there are some provisions relevant to private hire vehicles in other Acts, notably the Transport Acts of 1980 and 1985.

11.9   One other area of considerable difference between the two regimes is that of byelaws. The use of byelaws, in relation to hackney carriages, is well-established and governed by the provisions of the Town Police Clauses Acts of 1847 and 1899. In relation to private hire vehicles, there is no overt power to make byelaws to regulate their conduct. It seems that such byelaws could be made by a local authority using the powers contained in section 235 of the Local Government Act 1972. This enables the local authority to make byelaws 'for the good rule and government' of its area. It is suggested that private hire byelaws could be made under this provision, if it could be demonstrated that the effect of such byelaws could be to improve the life of the citizens of the area. As yet, no authority has taken this route and it remains to be seen whether a council would feel that the benefits of doing so would be worthwhile, considering the time and costs involved. It also remains to be seen what a local authority would attempt to regulate by such byelaws, although the model byelaws for hackney carriages are probably a good basis.

Chapter 12

Private hire operators

INTRODUCTION

The term 'operate'

A private hire vehicle can only be despatched to a customer by a private hire
operator. This is a person who holds an operator's licence under section 55
of the Local Government (Miscellaneous Provisions) Act 1976 ('the 1976
Act'). This licence allows him to operate private hire vehicles. 'Operate' is
defined in section 80 of the 1976 Act as follows:

12.1

> '"operate" means in the course of business to make provision for the invi-
> tation or acceptance of bookings for a private hire vehicle;'

St Albans District Council v Taylor

It was decided in the case of *St Albans District Council v Taylor*[1] that there did
not have to be any payment for there to be a hiring and, therefore, if the
operator supplied vehicles at no charge, he was still operating. Taylor was a
private hire operator and was prosecuted for knowingly using an unlicensed
private hire vehicle and an unlicensed private hire driver. Short of both
vehicles and drivers to fulfil a booking, Taylor asked his wife to drive his customers to the destinations that they had asked to be taken to. He told her
not to be make any charge for the journey nor to accept a tip. He was
acquitted by the magistrates, who took the view that there was no hiring, as
no money had changed hands. On appeal by way of case stated, the matter
was heard by Russell LJ and Hodgson J. Russell LJ gave the leading judgment and concluded that there was no doubt that Mr Taylor was acting 'in
the course of business and therefore operating under the terms of section
80'. However, as the vehicles used were not licensed as private hire vehicles,
he continued:

12.2

> 'Much more difficult, however, is whether it is right to find, contrary to
> the findings of the justices, that the defendant was "operating" his wife's
> vehicles as private hire vehicles. I have come to the conclusion that he was
> because, in telling his wife to drive her own vehicle, he was making provi-
> sion for the acceptance of the bookings that had been made by his
> customers within the meaning of "operate" to be found in section 80.
> There was no cancellation of those bookings; on the contrary the defen-
> dant was fulfilling them. He was not engaging upon a purely domestic

arrangement such as would arise if Mrs Taylor was being asked to give a lift to friends of the defendant. The customers remained customers of the defendant despite what they were told by Mrs Taylor. whilst the wording of section 80 might have been more happily phrased I do not think that to say Mr Taylor was making "provision for the . . . acceptance of bookings" unduly strains the language when applied to the unusual circumstances of this case. This construction of the section certainly achieves the purpose of the legislation to which I have earlier referred.

There remains for consideration the words "private hire vehicle". Was the vehicle used by Mrs Taylor operated as a private hire vehicle? Private hire vehicle is also defined in section 80. It reads so far as material:

> ". . . 'private hire vehicle' means a motor vehicle . . . which is provided for hire with the services of a driver for the purpose of carrying passengers."

By paragraph 7 of the case the justices found

> "that there had been no hiring in respect of the informations relating to 7 and 13 July 1989 and that the vehicles were not operated as private hire vehicles . . ."

For my part I have to disagree with this finding. It is true that no payment in respect of the journeys was sought or paid. However, I am quite unable to accept that the journeys were undertaken without any consideration on a purely domestic or social, as opposed to a commercial, basis. Mr Taylor arranged for the carriage of his customers in order to fulfil what he regarded as his contractual obligation. Without that contractual obligation he would not have carried his customers on the journeys that they had booked with Mr Taylor's private hire vehicle business. No doubt in doing as he did Mr Taylor was protecting the good will of that business rather than let down his customers or transfer their custom to a competitor.

To constitute a hiring it is not necessary, in my judgment, that in all the circumstances there should be the payment of money. If the hirer can fairly be said to derive commercial benefit from the transaction then a hiring may take place, and in my view it did take place in the unusual circumstances of this case.

Accordingly, for the reasons I have endeavoured to outline, I have come to the conclusion that the justices fell into error by dismissing these informations.'

This view was supported by Hodgson J.

This is an important case as it makes very clear that money does not need to change hands for there to be a hiring in the course of business and also that, if the vehicle is used as a private hire vehicle, even if it is not a licensed private hire vehicle, it falls within the definition.

1   [1991] Crim LR 852.

The premises and fleet of an operator

12.3   The practical effect of this is that a private hire operator will have premises from which he controls a fleet of vehicles. There is no maximum limit to the size of this fleet, although the minimum would be one, as even a single private hire vehicle must be controlled by an operator to comply with the legislative requirements.

These premises, which are usually referred to as the private hire operator's 'base', will be equipped with telephone lines and may also be able to deal with personal callers. The customer either telephones or visits the operator's base and asks for a private hire vehicle to collect them from a certain point at a certain time. The operator will normally establish not only the collection point, but also the destination and will then arrange for a vehicle from his fleet to satisfy the booking. This is usually achieved by means of radio with transmission from the base to one or more of the vehicles, but could, alternatively, involve the use of mobile telephones. **12.4**

The operator will charge the driver or owner of the vehicle a fee for being part of that particular operator's fleet. **12.5**

The operations of private hire operators range from small concerns operating one or two vehicles up to sizeable undertakings in urban areas where an individual operator controls many hundreds of private hire vehicles. Notwithstanding the size of the fleet, the basic provisions remain the same and are considered in detail below. **12.6**

The starting point is section 46(1)(*d*) of the 1976 Act, which states: **12.7**

> '**46**–(1) Except as authorised by this Part of this Act—
>
> . . .
>
> (*d*) no person shall in a controlled district operate any vehicle as a private hire vehicle without having a current licence under section 55 of this Act;'

Contravention of this requirement is an offence by virtue of section 46(2), for which the maximum penalty is a fine not exceeding level 3 on the standard scale[1].

1 Local Government (Miscellaneous Provisions) Act 1976, s 76.

APPLICATION FOR AN OPERATOR'S LICENCE

The applicant must be a 'fit and proper person'

As outlined above[1], a private hire vehicle must be controlled by a private hire operator who holds a licence under section 55 of the 1976 Act. To comply with the legislation, a prospective operator must make an application to the district council under section 55(1) of the 1976 Act. This states: **12.8**

> '**55**–(1) Subject to the provisions of this Part of this Act, a district council shall, on receipt of an application from any person for the grant to that person of a licence to operate private hire vehicles grant to that person an operator's licence:
>
> Provided that a district council shall not grant a licence unless they are satisfied that the applicant is a fit and proper person to hold an operator's licence.'

Once an application has been received the council is then under a duty to grant an operator's licence to that person unless they are not satisfied that the applicant is 'a fit and proper person to hold an operator's licence'. This is the only ground on which an application can be refused[2].

1 See para 12.1.
2 These considerations are similar to those which apply to other licences and which have been considered in Chapter 5. See also Chapter 10, para 10.18ff.

12.9 Although the operator does not usually drive members of the public (unless he also holds a private hire driver's licence), he will be in possession of information about people's whereabouts and movements and will also be dealing with the public, either face to face or over the telephone. As a result, the need for him to be a fit and proper person is just as important.

Power to require applicants to submit information

12.10 Under section 57 of the 1976 Act, the local authority is given wide-ranging powers to seek information about a prospective private hire operator. Section 57(1) is a general power in relation to any licence, but section 57(2)(*b*) and (*c*) specifically relates to private hire operators.

'**Power to require applicants to submit information**

57–(1) A district council may require any applicant for a licence under the Act of 1847 or under this Part of this Act to submit to them such information as they may reasonably consider necessary to enable them to determine whether the licence should be granted and whether conditions should be attached to any such licence.

(2) Without prejudice to the generality of the foregoing subsection—

. . .

(*b*) a district council may require an applicant for an operator's licence to submit to them such information as to—
　(i)　the name and address of the applicant;
　(ii)　the addresses or address whether within the area of the council or not from which he intends to carry on business in connection with private hire vehicles licensed under this Part of this Act;
　(iii)　any trade or business activities he has carried on before making the application;
　(iv)　any previous application he has made for an operator's licence;
　(v)　the revocation or suspension of any operator's licence previously held by him;
　(vi)　any convictions recorded against the applicant;
as they may reasonably consider necessary to enable them to determine whether to grant such licence;

(*c*)　in addition to the information specified in paragraph (*b*) of this subsection, a district council may require an applicant for an operator's licence to submit to them—
　(i)　if the applicant is or has been a director or secretary of a company, information as to any convictions recorded against that company at any relevant time; any trade or business activities carried on by that company; any previous application made by that company for an operator's licence; and any revocation or suspension of an operator's licence previously held by that company;

     (ii) if the applicant is a company, information as to any convictions recorded against a director or secretary of that company; any trade or business activities carried on by any such director or secretary; any previous application made by any such director or secretary for an operator's licence; and any revocation or suspension of an operator's licence previously held by such director or secretary;

    (iii) if the applicant proposes to operate the vehicle in partnership with any other person, information as to any convictions recorded against that person; any trade or business activities carried on by that person; any previous application made by that person for an operator's licence; and any revocation or suspension of an operator's licence previously held by him.'

It can be seen that the questions that can be asked are wide-ranging and the questions contained in subsection 2(*b*) and (*c*) are not exclusive. Any information that is reasonably necessary can be sought from an applicant. It should be noted, however, that criminal convictions can only be established by a statutory declaration, Data Protection Act printout and DVLA checks[1].

1 See Chapter 5, para 5.30.

Section 57(3) of the 1976 Act is a wide-ranging offence provision: **12.11**

> '**57**–(3) If any person knowingly or recklessly makes a false statement or omits any material particular in giving information under this section, he shall be guilty of an offence.'

After this information has been obtained, the local authority must decide whether to grant a licence and, if so, whether it will be subject to conditions.

Section 55(4) allows an applicant aggrieved by either a failure to grant an   **12.12** operator's licence or by the conditions attached to that licence to appeal to the magistrates' court.

The licence itself can be granted for any period of up to five years[1]. It   **12.13** seems, however, that most authorities grant annual licences and the justification for that would appear to be that it is the most satisfactory way of keeping control over applicants who may be convicted of offences during the currency of a licence.

1 Local Government (Miscellaneous Provisions) Act 1976, s 55(2).

This situation is addressed by most local authorities who impose a condition   **12.14** on an operator's licence under section 55(3), requiring the holder of such a licence to inform the authority, within a specified period (either seven or fourteen days), of any conviction for any offence recorded against them during the currency of the licence.

CONDITIONS APPLIED TO PRIVATE HIRE OPERATORS' LICENCES

Section 55(3) of the 1976 Act allows the local authority to impose any con-   **12.15** ditions that they 'consider reasonably necessary' on a private hire operator's licence. The conditions that are imposed under this power vary widely from local authority to local authority but they include:

- ensure any vehicle hired attends punctually;
- if any rooms are provided for the public, for waiting or making bookings, they must be clean, adequately heated and ventilated and lit;
- no booking should be accepted unless the hirer knows the basis of the hire charge;
- not to permit people who are drunk to remain on the premises.

Address from which the operator may operate

12.16   In addition, the local authority will specify the address or addresses from which the operator may operate. It is important that these are correct and that, if the operator moves, he not only informs the local authority, but also ensures that a revised licence is issued. This point was made clear in the case of *Kingston-upon-Hull City Council v Wilson*[1]. This was an appeal by way of case stated against a decision by Kingston-upon-Hull City Magistrates to acquit Mr Wilson of three charges. Two involved the use of a private hire vehicle[2], but the remaining charge was operating a vehicle as a private hire vehicle in a controlled district without holding an operator's licence, contrary to section 46(1)(*d*). Mr Wilson did, in fact, hold a private hire operator's licence, but for a different address from that which was apparently being used by him to operate the vehicle from. It was argued that Mr Wilson had an operator's licence (which he did), but the operator's licence had a condition imposed on it that it was to operate vehicles from Francis Street in Hull and not Jipdane, another road in the city, and therefore he had operated without a licence. Buxton J stated:

> 'Mr Neish also argues that, nonetheless, Mr Wilson did have an operator's licence. Of course, he had a licence to operate private hire vehicles from Francis Street, in the city of Hull, as the Magistrates found. I do not accept, however, that that is an answer to this charge. First of all, it is clear that the condition imposed by the local authority was to operate vehicles from Francis Street and not from 4 Jipdane. I do not accept that operating a vehicle in breach of a condition of the licence is sufficient defence to a charge under section 46(*d*). Further, and this may be the same point, the section says:
>
>> "no person shall in a controlled district operate any vehicle as a private hire vehicle without having a current licence under section 55 of this Act;"
>
> That must, in common sense, mean without having a licence that currently applies to that operation, and clearly, on the findings of the Magistrates, Mr Wilson's Francis Street licence did not. Therefore the charge under section 46(1)(*b*) was made out.'

1   (1995) Times, 25 July.
2   See Chapter 13, para 13.38.

Parking at the operator's base

12.17   A number of authorities require a minimum number of parking places to be available at the premises used by the operator at their base. However, other authorities actually impose a condition that no private hire vehicles can park at the operator's base. The reasons for this difference seem to be based upon the concept of 'ranking'.

The local authorities that require operators to have parking places justify it **12.18** on the grounds of easing congestion. Private hire drivers do tend to return to their base between jobs and they park their cars nearby. If it is a sizeable operation, this can lead to serious congestion on adjoining roads, to the detriment of local residents and general passenger traffic. Accordingly, it is felt by many authorities that it is best that there are some car parking spaces which are available only for the private hire vehicles operated by that particular operator, as a way of easing this problem. This has the added advantage that, if a person wishes to take the services of a private hire vehicle by entering and making the booking at the premises, then there is the possibility that a vehicle will be immediately available.

Ranking

One argument that is used against a provision of car parking is that, where **12.19** two or more private hire vehicles have stopped together (as they would be outside their premises in a designated car park), this constitutes an unlawful rank. This is seen by some as an offence, as only hackney carriages can rank, and even then only at designated hackney carriage stands. This argument is not particularly attractive and is not in itself sufficient to warrant the policy of no parking places at private hire operators' premises. Even though a private hire vehicle has stopped, possibly in company with other private hire vehicles, this does not make it an unlawful rank. As a private hire vehicle cannot be booked from a rank (lawful or otherwise), it is difficult to see how the presence of such a vehicle stationary on the street, or any other area to which the public have access, such as a car park, can constitute a rank. It is simply a stationary private hire vehicle. This view is reinforced when it is considered that where an approach has been made to the driver of a stationary vehicle, assuming that he is sitting in it, by a prospective customer with a view to using the services of the vehicle, the driver would be duty-bound to refer the prospective customer to the operator to make the booking. This view is supported by the case of *Nottingham City Council v Woodings*[1], which makes it clear that a stationary private hire vehicle is only plying for hire if it is immediately available.

1 [1994] RTR 72. See Chapter 8, para 8.21.

Whilst it is accepted that, in reality, unlawful plying and, indeed, ranking **12.20** does take place, this is a matter which can and should be controlled by enforcement action, rather than by conditions against car parking spaces.

A better argument against the requirement to provide car parking spaces **12.21** concerns the nature of the premises in question. A great many private hire operators use small offices as their base and, when this is taken into account, together with the overall number of off-road car parking spaces available in many towns and cities, it is felt that it would not be reasonable to require an operator to be able to provide car parking spaces.

Parking within a specified distance of the base

12.22 Some authorities have attempted to impose a condition, which prohibits more than a specified number (usually very few, ie two or three) of private hire vehicles operated by that particular operator from parking within a specified distance of their base. Whilst the philosophy behind such a condition is understandable (to prevent congestion) it is difficult to see how such a condition can be enforced and, indeed, whether it is reasonable. Any vehicle which is insured, taxed and has (if necessary) a current MOT certificate can be parked at any legitimate parking place on the public highway at any time, subject only to parking restrictions. It is difficult to see how a local authority can erode those rights by a condition applied to the licence granted to a private hire operator.

Private hire vehicle must return to base

12.23 This can be contrasted with a condition, which is applied by at least one local authority, that, after each booking has been completed, the private hire vehicle must return to its operator's base before it can be despatched by the operator on another hiring. It is difficult to see what the justification is behind this condition. It would appear to be a recipe for considerable congestion in the vicinity of the private operator's base, a waste of time and fuel and a method of greatly increasing both environmental pollution and wear and tear on the vehicles involved. If the district in question is sizeable (and a great many districts are large geographic areas, both in England and Wales) and the operator is based near to a boundary with another district, the situation could arise that a vehicle is being despatched on a hiring across the district, returning across the district to the base, then being sent back from whence it came to pick up the next fare which was very close to the destination of the original fare. Such a condition would be manifestly absurd.

PLANNING PERMISSION

12.24 An important question is whether planning permission should be in place before an application for an operator's licence is considered or such licences granted, or whether planning permission can be sought subsequently.

12.25 Some local authorities take the view that planning permission is a condition precedent to the grant of an operator's licence. In those cases, no application for an operator's licence will be considered until permission for the use of the premises in question has been granted by the relevant local authority. It is important to bear in mind here that it is possible for the premises to be outside the area of the local authority granting the licence[1]. The justification for this approach appears to be that, once a private hire operator's licence has been granted, the licence holder may take the view that they can commence trading without the need for planning permission.

1 See the Local Government (Miscellaneous Provisions) Act 1976, s 57(2)(*b*)(ii).

The counter view is that licensing and planning, notwithstanding the fact **12.26** that both are considered by the same local authority, are separate and distinct matters. Provided it is made clear to the licence holder that the grant of an operator's licence does not allow the use of the premises as a private hire operator's base in the absence of planning permission, the difficulty should not arise.

This is not a point that has ever been challenged by the courts and it is a **12.27** matter for local authorities to consider. It is suggested, however, that the latter approach is the better, taking into account guidance in relation to planning. Paragraph C2 to Annex C of PPG1 states:

> 'Planning legislation should not normally be used to secure objectives achievable under other legislation. This principal of non-duplication should normally be maintained even though the powers and duties resulting from the other legislation may also be the concern of local authorities. But even where consent is needed under other legislation, the planning system may have an important part to play, for example in deciding whether the development is appropriate for the particular location. The grant of planning permission does not remove the need to obtain any other consents that may be necessary, nor does it imply that such consents will necessarily be forthcoming. Provided a consideration is material in planning terms, however, it must be taken into account in dealing with a planning application notwithstanding that other machinery may exist for its regulation.'

BOOKINGS

It is the operator with whom the public has direct initial contact, in order to **12.28** obtain the services of a private hire vehicle. Section 56 of the 1976 Act lays down the fundamental requirements that cover a provision of a private hire vehicle by an operator.

Contract is deemed to be made with the operator

Section 56(1) makes it clear that the contract which covers the journey **12.29** made in the vehicle is between the person booking the vehicle and the operator, even if the car is provided by an independent third party, who has himself, a contract with the operator. Section 56(1) states:

> '56–(1) For the purposes of this Part of this Act every contract for the hire of a private hire vehicle licensed under this Part of this Act shall be deemed to be made with the operator who accepted the booking for that vehicle whether or not he himself provided the vehicle.'

This has obvious implications in the event of any dispute over the service that is provided. It provides an easy method for the customer to take action against the operator, who is likely to be well known through advertisements and generally in the locality, whereas it may be difficult for a customer to identify which particular driver or vehicle he used, on the occasion in question.

If action is taken by an aggrieved customer against the operator under this **12.30** section, it will then be open to the operator to seek redress from the driver.

This will be on the basis that the driver failed to deliver the expected level of service under the contract which existed between the operator and driver-and-car combination, by which the use of the operator's services are obtained.

RECORDS KEPT BY OPERATORS

12.31   Sections 56(2) and (3) of the 1976 Act place a duty on a private hire operator to keep various records. However, it is left up to the council to decide what records are required both in relation to the journeys that are booked (section 56(2)) and the vehicles used (section 56(3)).

Journeys booked

12.32   Section 56(2) states:

> '56–(2) Every person to whom a licence in force under section 55 of this Act has been granted by a district council shall keep a record in such form as the council may, by condition attached to the grant of the licence, prescribe and shall enter therein, before the commencement of each journey, such particulars of every booking of a private hire vehicle invited or accepted by him, whether by accepting the same from the hirer or by undertaking it at the request of another operator, as the district council may by condition prescribe and shall produce such record on request to any authorised officer of the council or to any constable for inspection.'

It can be seen that this is a wide-ranging power that allows the local authority to impose a great many requirements as to record-keeping. This is implemented in different ways by various councils, but almost all insist on a bare minimum of records, including:

- The name of the hirer.
- The location of the pick-up point.
- The location of the destination.
- The time the private hire vehicle is required.
- The time that the booking was made.

Other details that some local authorities require include:

- Whether the booking was made by telephone or in person.
- The fare quoted for the journey.
- Other remarks, including details of whether the booking is a sub-contract from another operator or is to be sub-contracted by this operator.

12.33   These conditions enable the operator to:

1. Identify a particular booking.
2. Despatch a car at the right time to the right place.
3. To enable the local authority to ensure that a booking was made for a particular journey.
4. To provide a comprehensive record of bookings taken by the private hire operator.

From an enforcement perspective, it is the confirmation that a booking has been made before the journey was undertaken that is important. As mentioned above[1], it is an offence for a private hire vehicle to ply for hire; that is, to respond to anything other than a pre-booking, and this can frequently be evidenced by the fact that the operator has no record of the trip which was taking place when the vehicle was apprehended by enforcement officers.

1 This will be considered further in Chapter 13, which relates to private hire vehicles.

It is interesting to note that the legislation clearly envisages one private hire **12.34** operator passing a booking to another to enable it to be discharged, if the first operator, who was contacted, is unable to provide a vehicle at the given time. In that case, the operator who accepted the booking would need to record this and the second operator, who actually provided the vehicle, would need to maintain details in his records of both the booking and the vehicle provided. In these circumstances, again section 56(1) of the 1976 Act is extremely useful. This is because, in any dispute between the hirer and the operator, a contract is deemed to have been made with the first operator, who accepted the booking. They would then have to seek redress from the second operator, who, in turn, may look to the driver and vehicle that he provided for ultimate compensation.

Vehicles used

The second category of records that is required to be kept is outlined in **12.35** section 56(3) of the 1976 Act:

> '**56**–(3) Every person to whom a licence in force under section 55 of this Act has been granted by a district council shall keep such records as the council may, by condition attached to the grant of the licence, prescribe of the particulars of any private hire vehicle operated by him and shall produce the same on request to any authorised officer of the council or to any constable for inspection.'

Again, the onus is placed upon the council to state, by way of condition attached to the licence, precisely what records are required in relation to vehicle. The more usual ones include some method of identifying the vehicle that was used (registration number, plate number) and the driver who was driving at the time. In most cases, the records are maintained in a simple hand-written form in a notebook. Some of the large operations have computerised records and, indeed, sophisticated methods of tracking the vehicles that are providing private hire services to that particular operator, enabling the operator to despatch the most conveniently situated vehicle.

Inspection of records

Any authorised officer of the council or a police constable can, on request, **12.36** inspect the records maintained, by virtue of section 56(2) and (3) of the 1976 Act. Section 56(4) allows inspection of the licence granted to the operator by an authorised officer of the council or a police constable.

12.37 The local authority, through its officers, undertakes private hire enforcement. The powers in the Act are given to authorised officers. This is defined in section 80(1) as: 'any officer of a district council authorised in writing by the council for the purposes of this Part of this Act'.

12.38 This is the framework within which a private hire operator must work. The conditions imposed by local authorities are not especially onerous and most operators find it easy to comply with the requirements.

12.39 If it appears to an operator that any condition imposed is too onerous and, as a consequence, is unreasonable, there is a power of appeal contained in section 55(4) of the 1976 Act. This applies to an applicant who is aggrieved by 'any conditions attached to the grant of such a licence'. As is usual in the Act, the right of appeal lies to the magistrates' court and is by way of complaint[1].

1 See Chapter 3.

Operator must hold licences for vehicle and driver

12.40 One condition that is often imposed upon private hire operators, under section 56(3) of the 1976 Act, is the requirement that the operator holds both the private hire vehicle licence of any vehicle that he is operating and the private hire driver's licence of any driver who is driving in any such vehicle. This is a useful provision for both the local authority and the operator himself. From the local authority's perspective, it should enable them to satisfy themselves reasonably easily and quickly that the operator is indeed using licensed vehicles and drivers. From the operator's point of view, provided that he complies with the conditions and does indeed hold these licences, it should provide him with a complete defence to any charge under section 46(1)(e) of the 1976 Act.

> '**46**–(1) Except as authorised by this Part of this Act—
>
> . . .
>
> (e) no person licensed under the said section 55 shall in a controlled district operate any vehicle as a private hire vehicle—
>   (i) if for the vehicle a current licence under the said section 48 is not in force; or
>   (ii) if the driver does not have a current licence under the said section 51.
>
> (2) If any person knowingly contravenes the provisions of this section, he shall be guilty of an offence.'

It is an offence if a private hire operator 'knowingly contravenes the provisions of this section'.

To knowingly contravene

12.41 The use of the word 'knowingly' in this section requires the prosecution to prove knowledge or intent, and it is unfortunate that this is not a strict liability offence, which is the case with a great many other licensing offences in the area of local authority law.

The case of *Latif v Middlesbrough Borough Council*[1] relates to this 'knowledge'. A private hire operator was prosecuted under section 46 of the 1976 Act for two offences concerning the employment of an unlicensed private hire driver, in relation to his vehicle licence and also in relation to his operator's licence. He was convicted at the magistrates' court and his appeal to the Crown Court was dismissed. He then appealed to the High Court by way of case stated. **12.42**

Latif employed a Mr Din as a driver and, at the time the alleged offence was committed, Din did not have a private hire driver's licence. At some time prior to that, Latif had given Din the money to renew his private hire driver's licence, but Din had not done so. The question raised was whether Latif 'knowingly' used an unlicensed private hire driver. It was argued that Latif had done sufficient to overcome any suggestion that he had knowingly used an unlicensed driver, by providing Din with the money to renew his licence. The counter argument was that Latif should have done more to ensure that his driver was licensed.

Newman J stated:

> 'On the facts found the court concluded that being put on notice that Mr Din's licence was to expire on some date prior to 16 April and failing to make enquiries to ascertain the true position meant that the defendant had acted knowingly. In my judgment, there is no warrant for the word "knowingly" being construed so broadly as to encompass the facts as found. The facts went no further than establishing that the defendant was on notice that a situation might prevail on a particular day when it is alleged the offence was committed. Further, having given money to Mr Din to obtain a licence the defendant had good reason to believe he would have obtained one. Upon the facts as found and giving the word "knowingly" its normal meaning, which, in my judgment, in this statute it should have, the charges had not been made out.'

He reviewed a number of cases concerning knowledge which supported this view. Newman J came to the conclusion that, as the defendant had not deliberately shut his eyes as to whether Din had a licence or not, he could not be deemed to have been reckless as to whether or not he held a private hire driver's licence. Accordingly, on the facts, the appeal was allowed.

1 [1997] COD 486.

Knowledge is always extremely difficult to prove in any event, but it does not seem that this case makes it any more difficult. It is, to a large extent, confined to its own particular facts and if a condition is applied to both private hire vehicles and private hire operators' licences, requiring the proprietor or operator to hold a driving licence of any body they employ, it would then be more difficult to demonstrate a lack of knowledge. However, if the condition is imposed that the licences must be held by the operator, it makes it considerably more difficult for the operator to argue that he did not know that the vehicle or driver was not licensed. In addition, even if the local authority is unsuccessful in securing a conviction under section 46(1)(e), breach of a condition imposed under section 56 is itself an offence by virtue of section 56(5). Accordingly, a prosecution under that section may prove successful. Informations should be laid for both offences, and in fact, two convictions may be obtained. **12.43**

12.44   It can be seen that it is vital for private hire operators to comply with the requirements of the local authority, in relation to conditions, and also to comply with the legislative requirements that are placed upon them.

12.45   It is also important that the local authority carefully considers what conditions should be imposed on private hire operators and that those conditions are subsequently fully enforced. If there is any failure of compliance on the part of the operator, in addition to criminal sanctions, action can be taken by the local authority on renewal of the licence or, in serious situations, the licence can itself be suspended or revoked.

SUSPENSION, REVOCATION OR REFUSAL TO RENEW AN OPERATOR'S LICENCE

12.46   The provisions contained in section 62 of the 1976 Act gives the council significant powers to suspend or revoke an operator's licence or to refuse an application for renewal. Section 62 states:

> **'Suspension and revocation of operators' licences**
>
> **62**–(1) Notwithstanding anything in this Part of this Act a district council may suspend or revoke, or (on application therefor under section 55 of this Act) refuse to renew an operator's licence on any of the following grounds—
>
> (*a*)   any offence under, or non-compliance with, the provisions of this Part of this Act;
>
> (*b*)   any conduct on the part of the operator which appears to the district council to render him unfit to hold an operator's licence;
>
> (*c*)   any material change since the licence was granted in any of the circumstances of the operator on the basis of which the licence was granted; or
>
> (*d*)   any other reasonable cause.
>
> (2) Where a district council suspend, revoke or refuse to renew any licence under this section they shall give to the operator notice of the grounds on which the licence has been suspended or revoked or on which they have refused to renew such licence within fourteen days of such suspension, revocation or refusal.
>
> (3) Any operator aggrieved by a decision of a district council under this section may appeal to a magistrates' court.'

12.47   It can be seen that an offence (that is a conviction) for any matter under the 1976 Act is a ground for such action to be taken. Section 62(1)(*a*) goes considerably further than that because non-compliance with any provision of the 1976 Act is also a ground. Whilst such action would need to be reasonable, it does not have to be evidenced by a criminal conviction[1] and this gives the local authority considerable power, should they wish to exercise it.

1   See *R v Maidstone Crown Court, ex p Olson* [1992] COD 496 (Chapter 10, para 10.70); and *McCool v Rushcliffe Borough Council* (Chapter 10, para 10.72).

12.48   Section 62(1)(*b*) goes further still, by allowing the local authority to suspend, revoke or refuse to renew an operator's licence for 'any conduct on the part of the operator which appears to the district council to render him unfit to hold an operator's licence'. Again, no criminal conviction is necessary to support this and the test of whether such action is justified will be one of *Wednesbury* reasonableness.

Section 62(1)(*c*) is a general power which enables the local authority to **12.49** consider any changes that have taken place to the operator or other related matters since the licence was first granted and whether they are grounds for suspension, revocation or refusal to renew the operator's licence.

Section 62(1)(*d*) enables the local authority to take this action for 'any other **12.50** reasonable cause'. The decision in *Norwich City Council v Watcham and Thurtle*[1] was that 'any other reasonable cause' does not have to be construed *ejusdem generis* with the grounds set out in subsections (1)(*a*)–(*c*). This means that the 'any other reasonable cause' does not have to be similar to the matters listed in the other subsections.

1 (21 May 1981, unreported). See Chapter 8, para 8.87.

Thus, it can be seen that the powers of a local authority to take action, in **12.51** respect of an operator's licence, are extremely wide. Such actions should not be undertaken lightly by the local authority, as the operator's livelihood is at stake, but, if the circumstances require such action, they are useful powers.

There is a right of appeal given under section 62(3) to an operator who is **12.52** aggrieved by such an action. Section 62(2) requires the local authority to provide written notice of the grounds on which the action has been taken. In addition, they should provide reasons[1].

1 See Chapter 3 regarding appeals in general, and Chapter 2, para 2.54ff in relation to reasons.

PRIVATE HIRE OPERATORS: PROBLEM AREAS

There are a number of areas of activity in relation to private hire vehicles **12.53** that have caused difficulties in the past.

Cross-border hiring

All three licences must be issued by the same authority

This situation can arise where a booking is made with a private hire operator **12.54** which is not for a journey that commences and ends, and is throughout its course, wholly within the area of the local authority that has licensed the operator. A private hire operator can only operate a private hire vehicle which has been licensed by the same authority as that which granted his operator's licence. In addition, it must be driven by a private hire driver licensed by the same authority[1]. This is an interesting point, as an alternative interpretation of the provisions of section 46(1)(*d*) is that, provided a private hire vehicle is licensed, then the requirements of section 46(1)(*d*) are met, notwithstanding the fact that the vehicle has been licensed by a different district.

1 This was made clear in the case of *Dittah v Birmingham City Council* and *Choudry v Birmingham City Council* [1993] RTR 356.

12.55   The definition of a private hire vehicle is:

> 'a motor vehicle constructed or adapted to seat fewer than nine passengers, other than a hackney carriage or public service vehicle or a London cab, which is provided for hire with the services of driver for the purposes of carrying passengers'[1].

1   Local Government (Miscellaneous Provisions) Act 1976, s 80(1).

12.56   *Dittah v Birmingham City Council* and *Choudry v Birmingham City Council*[1] concerned private hire operators licensed by Birmingham City Council who were operating private hire vehicles licensed by Solihull Metropolitan Borough Council and driven by drivers also licensed by Solihull. Messrs Dittah and Choudhry (the operators) were prosecuted for knowingly operating a private hire vehicle which did not have a private hire drivers or vehicle licence contrary to section 46(1)(*e*)(i) and (ii) of the 1976 Act. The argument was that they were licensed, albeit not by Birmingham City Council, and, accordingly, no offence had been committed. The counter argument on behalf of the prosecution was that to satisfy section 46, the operator, vehicle and driver all had to be licensed by the same authority. The case was heard by Kennedy LJ and Clarke J, with Kennedy LJ giving the judgment. He referred to (at 363):

> '. . . a letter dated 25th June 1992 from the Department of Transport to the district secretary of the Bromsgrove District Council, paragraph 3 of which reads:
>
> > "In our view applying section 80(2) to sections 46(1)(*d*) and (*e*) has the effect that an operator requires a licence from the area in which he intends to operate and may operate only in that area vehicles and drivers licensed by the same district. This has the practical effect that an operator licensed in area A may only use vehicles and drivers licensed in area A but these vehicles and drivers will by virtue of section 75(2) exemption be able to go anywhere in the course of hiring."'

He continued (at 363):

> 'That in my judgment is an accurate statement of the law, whatever may have been said elsewhere in the past.'

As a consequence of that he concluded (at 363):

> 'Accordingly, in my judgment the answer to the question posed in each case must be that, as postulated, section 46(1)(*e*) of the Act of 1976 must be read subject to the provisions of section 80(2) of that Act, so as to require private hire operators licensed under section 55 of the Act to make use only of vehicles and drivers licensed by the council of the district by which the operators are licensed when operating in that controlled district. The alternative construction cannot be supported, and these appeals must be dismissed.'

1   [1993] RTR 356.

12.57   Further questions that arise concerning private hire operators are:

- Whether a private hire operator can take a booking for a journey which commences outside the area in which he is licensed.
- Whether a private hire operator can take a booking for a journey which terminates outside the area in which he was licensed.

- Whether a private hire operator can take a booking for a journey which goes outside the area in which he is licensed on the course of its journey.
- Whether a private hire operator can take a booking for a journey that never comes within the area in which he is licensed.

Section 75(1)(*a*) of the 1976 Act is of some assistance in this regard:

'75–(1) Nothing in this Part of this Act shall—

(*a*) apply to a vehicle used for bringing passengers or goods within a controlled district in pursuance of a contract for the hire of the vehicle made outside the district if the vehicle is not made available for hire within the district;'

Controlled district is defined in section 80(1):

'"controlled district" means any area for which this Part of this Act is in force by virtue of a resolution passed by a district council under section 45 of this Act;'

Section 75(2) also assists in relation to these points:

'75–(2) Paragraphs (*a*), (*b*) and (*c*) of section 46(1) of this Act shall not apply to the use or driving of a vehicle or to the employment of a driver of a vehicle while the vehicle is used as a private hire vehicle in a controlled district if a licence issued under section 48 of this Act by the council whose area consists of or includes another controlled district is then in force for the vehicle and a driver's licence issued by such a council is then in force for the driver of the vehicle.'

It is clear that, provided the three licences required in relation to a private **12.58** hire vehicle (operator, vehicle and driver) have all been issued by the same authority, that is to say they 'match', then the private hire vehicle can undertake journeys anywhere in England and Wales. That is irrespective of the local authority area where the journey commences, areas through which the journey passes and, ultimately, the area where the journey ends. In addition, advertisements for a private hire service can be placed anywhere and are not limited to the geographical area of the local authority which licenses the operator of the private hire service. These are the conclusions which can be drawn from the cases of *Adur District Council v Fry*[1] and *Windsor and Maidenhead Royal Borough Council v Khan*[2].

1 [1997] RTR 257.
2 [1994] RTR 87.

Private hire vehicle can undertake journeys anywhere in England and Wales

In *Adur District Council v Fry*[1], the situation concerned a booking for a **12.59** journey by a private hire vehicle which commenced, ended and throughout its length was within the district of Adur District Council. It was, however, undertaken by a private hire vehicle licensed by Hove Borough Council, driven by a driver who held a private hire driver's licence issued by Hove Borough Council and the booking was made with an operator based outside the area of Adur District Council, who also held an operator's licence issued by Hove Borough Council. It can be seen, therefore, that all three licences matched and the only question was whether it was lawful to undertake a journey in the area of another district council. The High Court decided that it was, judgment being given by Kay J. He concluded that no offence was committed in those circumstances due to the limited meaning of 'operate' contained in section 80(1). In coming to that conclusion, he relied upon the judgments in *Dittah and Choudhry v Birmingham City Council*[2], *Britain v ABC Cabs (Camberley) Ltd*[3] and *Windsor and Maidenhead Royal Borough Council v Khan*[4]. As a result the meaning of operate meant 'in the course of business to make provision for the invitation or acceptance of booking for a private hire vehicle' and could not be construed more widely. His conclusion was this (at 263A):

> 'The question posed in the case stated is:
>
> "Whether it was correct to say that the word 'operate' in section 46(1)(*e*) of the Local Government (Miscellaneous Provisions) Act 1976 only includes that part of the whole transaction taking place in the operator's premises."
>
> The question is, perhaps, too widely worded because it is possible to envisage activity taking place outside an operator's premises that might come within the definition provided by section 80(1). There was, however, no such activity in the circumstances of this case. I would, therefore, answer the question "Yes, in the circumstances of this case" and, accordingly, dismiss the appeal.'

1 [1997] RTR 257.
2 [1993] RTR 356.
3 [1981] RTR 395.
4 [1994] RTR 87.

Advertisements for a private hire service

12.60   Two questions were placed before the High Court for consideration in *Windsor and Maidenhead Royal Borough Council v Khan*[1]. The first was whether an offence of operating outside a controlled district was committed if an operator licensed in one district, with premises in that district, accepted a booking made by a telephone call from a person who was calling from outside that district. The second question was whether an offence was committed of operating without a licence, if advertisements were placed in telephone directories which circulated not only within, but outside the area of the local authority in which the person was to operate.

1 [1994] RTR 87.

12.61   In relation to the first question, considerable discussion took place in the magistrates' court in relation to contract and where the contract was made. The point, however, was not pursued at the subsequent appeal to the High Court and, accordingly, only one point was considered by McCullough J when giving judgment, and that concerned the question of advertisements in telephone directories. He observed that there was an exemption in relation to vehicle and drivers' licences when used outside the district in which they were licensed, by virtue of section 75(2), but then went on (at 91B):

> 'There is no corresponding provision for operator's licences. This is not necessary because of the restrictive meaning given to the word "operate" in the Act. Section 80(1) provides:

"'Operate' means in the course of business to make provision for the invitation or acceptance of bookings for a private hire vehicle . . ."

Thus, to take Maidenhead as an example, no operator's licence from the council is required merely because a private hire vehicle in the course of the business of its proprietor is driven through Maidenhead. An operator's licence issued by the council is only required by those who in the course of business make provision in Maidenhead for the invitation or acceptance of bookings for private hire vehicles.

The defendant operates a private hire business called Top Cars. Its offices are in Slough. Slough is adjacent to or very close to the borough but outside it. It is to be presumed that either Slough does not lie within a controlled district, or, if it is within a controlled district, that the defendant held a current operator's licence issued by the district council in whose area Slough lies. He did not, as is agreed, however, hold an operator's licence issued by the council. He had advertised Top Car's services in the local Yellow Pages and Thompson's classified directories. These publications covered several areas including Slough and Maidenhead.'

He concluded (at 92L):

'Before this court Mr Harrison's [for the council] sole submission is that the defendant "made provision for the invitation of bookings for a private hire vehicle" in Maidenhead by placing advertisements for his private hire business in directories which circulated in Maidenhead. The fact that they also circulated in Slough is, he submits, irrelevant.

I reject the submission. The considerations to which I have already referred make clear that, in its definition of the word "operate", Parliament was not referring to places which invitations might reach, but to places where provision is made for the invitation of bookings. Put an advertisement in a local newspaper in one part of England and it may be read in almost any other part of the country. The defendant made provision for the invitation of bookings at his office in Slough. What he did by advertising in the directories circulating in the area where he conducted his business, and in adjacent areas, was to inform the public that he had made such provision. His provision was nevertheless made in Slough, not in Maidenhead, nor in any of the other areas in which those directories circulate. That conclusion is not, in my judgment, affected by the fact that the directories circulated in a much wider area, or that the defendant named towns other than Slough, such as Maidenhead, in his advertisement. If Mr Harrison's submissions were right, it would mean that the defendant was operating not just the A576 KLT [the registration number of the vehicle in question in this case], which is named in this summons, but every one of his private hire vehicles 24 hours a day, seven days a week in Maidenhead, even on days when none of his vehicles ever went anywhere near Maidenhead. That would be nonsensical.'

The question of operating a private hire vehicle had been considered much earlier in the case of *Britain v ABC Cabs (Camberley) Ltd*[1]. This case concerned the despatch of a hackney carriage from Camberley to collect a passenger from a railway station in Farnborough. The hackney carriage was licensed by Surrey Heath Borough Council, in whose area Camberley lay, and Farnborough railway station was situated within the area of Rushmoor Borough Council. This raised two questions: firstly, whether it was an offence for a hackney carriage, licensed by a local authority which had not adopted Part II of the 1976 Act, to be used as a private hire vehicle in the

12.62

area of a neighbouring local authority which had adopted Part II of the 1976 Act; and, secondly, whether the collection of a passenger within a controlled district (Rushmoor) in pursuance of a contract of hire made outside the control district (Surrey Heath), 'was operating' for the purposes of Part II of the 1976 Act. Webster J decided that (at 403J):

> 'The question of law on which they seek the opinion of this court is whether, on a proper construction of section 46(1)(*d*) of the Act of 1976, the collection of a passenger within a controlled district in pursuance of a contract for hire made outside the controlled district was "operating" for the purposes of that subsection of the Act.
>
> I am satisfied that when the defendants' vehicle picked up the passenger at Farnborough Station, the only material act which the defendants did in the borough of Rushmoor controlled district, they were not "making provision for the invitation or acceptance of bookings" at all, whether for a private hire vehicle or for any other vehicle. In my judgment to conclude otherwise would be to strain the language of the definition far beyond breaking point. If they were making provision for the invitation or acceptance of bookings anywhere, they were doing that, it would seem to me, in their office at Camberley, which is not a controlled district. In my judgment therefore no offence was made out under section 46(1)(*d*) and the justices rightly dismissed that information.
>
> . . . it follows from the conclusion which I have reached about the second case, and the views I have already expressed, in my judgment for the purposes of section 46(1)(*a*) the vehicle at the time and place in question was to be regarded as what in fact it was, namely, a hackney carriage in respect of which a vehicle licence is in force. In my judgment therefore no offence was made out under section 46(1)(*a*) . . .'

1 [1981] RTR 395.

12.63   In some parts of the country, depending upon the geography of the locality, a great many private hire vehicles are used outside their own district. Bookings are regularly made with operators who are not licensed within the district in which the person making the booking resides.

12.64   The simplest way to establish whether or not an offence has been committed is to enquire whether all three licences have been issued by the same authority? If the answer to that is 'yes', then there is no restriction on the geographical area in which the journey can take place. Ultimately, this could lead to the somewhat absurd situation of a private hire vehicle undertaking a booking wholly within the area of eg Portsmouth City Council, but the vehicle, driver and operator being licensed by and the operator being based in Newcastle-upon-Tyne. Although this could lead to difficulties in enforcement (the practicalities of an officer wishing to inspect the records for a journey in Portsmouth that are held in Newcastle-upon-Tyne), it is not, in itself, unlawful. This is unlikely to occur, but the more commonly encountered scenario concerning neighbouring districts is a frequent occurrence.

12.65   The situation is different if the vehicle and driver are unlicensed. In the case of *Braintree District Council v Howard*[1], Mr Howard had not renewed his private hire vehicle and drivers' licences with Braintree District Council, so he operated from a caravan outside the district (it must be assumed that the district in which the caravan was situated was not a controlled district, that is to say, that authority had not adopted the provisions of the 1976 Act). Mr Howard's wife took telephone calls at an address within Braintree district, then called Mr Howard outside the district. He arrived, as booked, at an address within Braintree district, picked up his passengers and took them to another location within the district. The whole journey took place within the district. He was prosecuted for operating a vehicle as a private hire vehicle without a licence. He was acquitted and the council appealed. The High Court upheld the appeal. As he was completely unlicensed, section 56(1) did not apply, and as the journey took place wholly within a controlled district, the benefit of section 75(1)(a) did not apply. Mann LJ giving judgment stated (at 199C):

'The case then seeks the opinion of this court on two questions:

"(1) whether we were right in holding, as a point of law, that the provisions of either or both of sections 56 and 75 of the Local Government (Miscellaneous Provisions) Act 1976 were relevant to the facts so as to afford a defence to the offences alleged under section 46 of that Act; and (2) whether we were right in holding as a point of law that the contract between the prosecutor's witness Mr McCloud and the defendant was made when the defendant confirmed to his wife that he was willing to undertake that work."

Mr Singh on behalf of the prosecutor submits that the justices were in error in point of law in that neither section 56 nor section 75 have any materiality as to what occurred. I am bound to agree with him. Neither section has any arguable relevance to the charges against the defendant. Section 56(1) makes the provision in regard to operators of private hire vehicles. The defendant was not charged with any offence concerning operators. However, and importantly, the section applies only to contracts

"for the hire of a private hire vehicle licensed under this Part of this Act"

and this vehicle was not licensed under this Part of this Act and, accordingly, that section could have no application to the case.

Section 75(1)(a), likewise, has no application to the circumstances of this case so far as the journey from the Sugar Loaves along Swan Lane [wholly within Braintree District] is concerned. Section 75(1)(a) is dealing with the problem of the vehicle which brings passengers into a controlled district. That was not the case so far as the initial journey on 17 August is concerned.

Accordingly, neither section had any materiality to the problem which was before the justices and I can surmise that the justices were attracted by those sections as offering a way of escape from convicting in regard to circumstances which they found unattractive. However, that said, the justices were in error.

In my judgment, the question which they posed must, as to the first, be answered "no" while on that conclusion on the first, the second does not arise . . .'

1 [1993] RTR 193, DC.

Free-phones, advertisements adjacent to telephones and telephone diversions

Free-phones

12.66 One of the situations which is frequently encountered is the concept of the 'free-phone'. These are often located at supermarkets and shopping centres and are a dedicated phone line. The customer picks up the phone and is automatically connected to a specific private hire operator. There is no ability on the part of the customer to choose an operator; it is simply a telephone provided by that particular operator. The customer then states their location and destination and the operator despatches a vehicle to satisfy the booking.

12.67 The question becomes important if the free-phone is situated outside the area in which the operator is licensed (and, again, this is a matter of geography). If that is the case, is an offence being committed? The answer appears to be yes. The free-phone falls within the definition of operator contained in section 80(1) of the 1976 Act as it is provided in the course of business (the business of the private hire operator) and it is a provision for the invitation or acceptance of bookings for a private hire vehicle. The only reason for the existence of the free-phone is to book a private hire vehicle. If a person is operating within that definition and they are within a controlled district (that is to say the local authority in which the free-phone is situated has adopted the 1976 Act) then they need a licence issued by the authority in whose district the free-phone is situated. Unless such a licence is issued, it would appear to contravene the provisions.

Advertisements

12.68 This can be contrasted with the situation where private hire operators from outside the district in which a public telephone is situated place advertisements on and around the telephone. This often occurs in pubs and clubs, as well as supermarkets and other venues. In this case, it would appear that no offence is being committed, as the ruling in *Windsor and Maidenhead Royal Borough Council v Khan*[1] makes it clear that advertisements are not a provision for an invitation or acceptance of bookings.

1 [1994] RTR 87.

12.69 The distinction between the two situations is the element of choice. In the free-phone case there is no choice: the moment the telephone is connected only one operator can be used. However, in the case of advertisements, the customer is free to choose any private hire operator, whether they have an advertisement or not, irrespective of the operator's geographical location, to provide the service they require.

Telephone diversion

12.70 A situation, although not concerning free-phones, but a telephone diversion, arose in the case of *East Staffordshire Borough Council v Rendell*[1]. In this case, Mr Rendell was licensed as a private hire operator by Derbyshire Dales District Council. His base was near the border with East Staffordshire. He diverted his telephone from his base in Derbyshire Dales to a telephone situated in East Staffordshire. This meant that, when a person called the number in Derbyshire Dales to book a private hire vehicle, the telephone call was actually answered in East Staffordshire, and the vehicle (licensed by Derbyshire Dales as a private hire vehicle and driven by a person holding a Derbyshire Dales private hire driver's licence) was dispatched by a person who, although he held a Derbyshire Dales operator's licence, was physically located in East Staffordshire. The matter was considered by the High Court by way of case stated, the magistrates' court having decided no offence was committed. Simon Brown LJ stated:

'The ultimate question undoubtedly reduces to this: whether the respondent [Mr Rendell] by switching the telephone to Uttoxeter [in East Staffordshire] had thereby made a provision for bookings in Uttoxeter.'

He concluded his judgment:

'It seems to me quite impossible on a common sense approach to the provisions here in question to regard the respondent as having done other than to make provision for the acceptance of bookings in Uttoxeter, ie, in the East Staffordshire control (sic) district where he had no licence.

Certainly, on the day in question, and it appears to have been by no means an isolated day, he had made the clearest possible arrangements to ensure that those who sought to make bookings would be put through to Uttoxeter for such bookings to be accepted. In this case . . . there was in my judgment, substantial provision made, a clear and effective arrangement whereby bookings could be accepted in East Staffordshire.'

Sedley J supported that view:

'In my view, by publicising his Derbyshire Dales telephone number and then switching calls from there to East Staffordshire, where he had arranged for them to be answered, the respondent did two things: he made provision in Derbyshire Dales for the invitation of bookings and he also made provision in East Staffordshire for the invitation of bookings. To conclude that this was so requires no strained or expanded meaning of the statutory language, and it respects its somewhat mysterious syntax.'

1· (1995) Independent, 27 November, QBD.

The only way in which it would appear that either a free-phone or a telephone diversion to premises located outside the district in which the operator is licensed could be legitimate, is if the operator argued that this was, in fact, a second operator's base and, as such, was run under the licence granted by the authority with whom he was licensed. Such an argument appears to be possible due to the provisions of section 57(2)(b)(ii) of the 1976 Act which makes it clear that the Act foresees operators as not only having more than one address, but also those addresses do not necessarily have to be within the area of the council. **12.71**

No reference was made in the *East Staffordshire*[1] judgment to this apparent ability and, in fact, it seems to be at odds with the *East Staffordshire* decision. If it is possible to have an operator's base located outside the district, it would appear that once permission has been granted by the authority that licensed the operator to have a base outside their area, that permission by the authority would prevent the authority in whose area the base is situated from taking action under section 46(1)(d). In the context of the *East Staffordshire* case, this would mean that, had Derbyshire Dales granted Mr **12.72**

Rendell a licence to operate from premises in Uttoxeter, East Staffordshire could not prosecute him for making a provision for bookings in their area without a licence, as his Derbyshire Dales licence would cover that activity.

1 *East Staffordshire Borough Council v Rendell* (1995) Independent, 27 November, QBD.

12.73 Whether such an argument could succeed remains to be seen, but if there is any chance of it being successful, the operator must have both informed the local authority that licenses him that he is using a second base and obtained their permission to do so. In addition, he must have paid whatever licence fee may be levied by the local authority for such a second base. If this does succeed, local authorities may wish to place a condition on their operator's licences limiting the distance from their boundaries that they will allow an 'outside area' base. This would seem a reasonable condition, provided it is not too short, to enable effective and reasonable enforcement to take place. A distance of not more than five or ten miles would seem acceptable.

Exempted hiring

12.74 Section 75 of the 1976 Act provides for a number of exemptions from the requirements of private hire licensing. Some of these have implications for operators.

12.75 The largest area of dispute concerns the exemption contained in section 75(1)(*b*). This states:

> '75–(1) Nothing in this Part of this Act shall—
>
> (*b*) apply to a vehicle used only for carrying passengers for hire or reward under a contract for the hire of the vehicle for a period of not less than seven days;'

It therefore appears that any long-term contract would be able to be discharged by the provision of an unlicensed vehicle.

A specified vehicle, a defined length of contract and agreed period of notice

12.76 A number of cases have attempted to interpret the actual impact of this section. In *Pitts v Lewis*[1], there had been in existence for a number of years a contract between a night-club and a private hire operator for the supply of vehicle services for use by staff and customers of the club, if required, 24 hours a day, seven days a week, 365 days a year. An unlicensed vehicle (ie not a hackney carriage or private hire vehicle) was carrying passengers who were in fact paying for their fares although the private hire operator believed that the vehicle was being used under this contract. The question was whether the exemption applied. The magistrates found that the existence of the contract did provide a defence and acquitted the operator. The local authority (Coventry City Council) appealed by way of case stated. Parker LJ stated (at 74A):

> 'For a defence under section 75 to be made out it must in my view be a contract for hire for a minimum period of seven days and it must relate to a particular identified vehicle. If it does so relate it does not appear to me that the defence under section 75 is defeated merely because the vehicle is

not left in the possession or the control of the hirer for the whole of the period. I see no objection to the vehicle when not being used returning to the proprietor's premises. Nor do I see that section 75 requires the payment which is to be made, and which constitutes the vehicle as being a vehicle used for carrying passengers for hire or reward, to be a fixed fee. It is common in many parts of the vehicle hire business for vehicles to be hired on the basis that there shall be some fixed charge, but that in addition there should be charges related to either the mileage or the number of hours during which the vehicle is actually used. But it is imperative, if a defence under section 75 is to be made out, that the vehicle should be identified, and in such circumstances it would be a breach of contract for the proprietor to supply another vehicle.

Having said that, I ought perhaps to indicate that the contract might be one which in certain circumstances enables the proprietor to supply another vehicle if, for example, the designated vehicle suffered an accident or other mishap which rendered it impossible to supply it. In those circumstances different considerations might arise. The initial vehicle, as it seems to me, would fall within section 75, but whether the substitute vehicle would fall within section 75 would depend upon the balance of the period under the contract yet remaining. If it was for less than seven days then section 75 would not apply. If it were for more than seven days section 75 might apply, and that would depend in its turn on whether the substitute vehicle then became the contractual vehicle or whether it was intended that there should be a return to the original vehicle, in which case it might be clear that the substitute was not a vehicle which came within the provisions of section 75.'

1 [1989] RTR 71n.

In *Leeds City Council v Azam*[1], the facts were that a contract had been in existence for some 15 or 16 months between the defendant and a night-club for transporting their staff. 'The period of hire under the . . . contract would be determined by the customers' wishes and was not set at any minimum period of time.' The operator was prosecuted for operating an unlicensed vehicle. Mann LJ, giving judgment stated (at 70E):   **12.77**

'I have no doubt that the establishment of the inapplicability of Part II of the Act [of 1976], by reason of section 75(1)(*b*), is a task falling to the defendant. It is, in my view, plainly an exemption provision, and thus within section 101 of the Magistrates' Courts Act 1980. The burden of establishing the exemption is, of course, a burden discharged on the balance of probabilities.

I find it quite impossible to say that the burden has been discharged in this case because the contract, as found by the justices, simply does not respond to the words of section 75(1)(*b*).'

1 [1989] RTR 66.

The case of *Crawley Borough Council v Ovenden*[1] concerned an unlicensed vehicle, operator and driver, who was providing a service to the local education authority for school runs and who claimed not to need an operator's driver or vehicle licence because of the exception contained in section 75(1)(*b*).   **12.78**

The defendant was self-employed. There was no written contract between the local education authority and the driver, however, there was an implied contract from a course of dealing, as Mr Ovenden had provided this service for a number of years. He had been vetted by the education authority and was paid monthly by invoice raised by him. There was never an agreed maximum or minimum length of the term of contract, nor any notice provision. Finally, the vehicle that was currently being used was not the vehicle that was originally used to discharge the contract and, indeed, was the second replacement vehicle to have been provided by Mr Ovenden. The case was considered by way of case stated in the Queen's Bench Division. Mann LJ gave the judgment of the court.

1   [1992] RTR 60.

12.79   Firstly he noted with approval the decision in *Pitts v Lewis*[1] and also found that the decision in *Leeds City Council v Azam*[2] also applied. He then concluded (at 65B):

> 'Looking at the facts as found in this case it would be easy to conclude in conformity with *Pitts v Lewis (Note)* and *Leeds City Council v Azam* that here there was not a contract in relation to a particular vehicle and that the contract was, in truth, one for the provision of a service. Resting there, that would in my judgment be decisive of the matter. However, the matter cannot rest there because, despite the findings of fact which would inevitably lead to that conclusion, the justices in that part of the case in which they expressed their opinion said, at paragraph 5(2):
>
>> "We were further of the opinion that, although a substitute vehicle was now being used, the vehicle had been substituted due to depreciation on two occasions and that vehicle then became the contractual vehicle; the education authority was aware of the changes of vehicle and had noted the vehicle type to be the same, albeit an updated version."
>
> That opinion gives rise to a suspicion that the justices had in mind that there was a "contractual vehicle" despite the absence of any finding that there was.
>
> Mr Stephenson [for the local authority] accepts that here is disclosed the possibility that there may have been the allocation of a vehicle. However he says and in my judgment rightly says that, even if there was an allocation of a vehicle, the findings of fact which have been made are decisively against the application of the saving in section 75, that is to say, the findings that there was never an agreed minimum period or any minimum period of notice. Accordingly, on those findings the saving in section 75 could not in any event apply regardless of allocation.'

1   [1989] RTR 71n.
2   [1989] RTR 66.

12.80   These three cases (*Pitts v Lewis*[1], *Leeds City Council v Azam*[2] and *Crawley Borough Council v Ovenden*[3]) make it clear that to avail oneself of the exception contained in section 75(1)(*b*), it is necessary for there to be a specified vehicle, a defined length of contract (which must, obviously, be for more than seven days) and a specified notice period for termination of the contract. Unless those elements are in place, an offence will be committed by anyone who provides transport in the nature of private hire, unless all of the three licensed elements are present. In addition, it is clear that the burden is upon the defence to show that the exemption applies and not on the prosecution to show that it does not.

1   [1989] RTR 71n.

2 [1989] RTR 66.
3 [1992] RTR 60.

Finally, funeral directors and others providing vehicles in connection with   **12.81**
funerals are exempted from the private hire provisions by section 75(1)(*c*).
A similar allowance is made for wedding cars in section 75(1)(*cc*).

Chapter 13

Private hire vehicles

INTRODUCTION

13.1 Any vehicle used as a private hire vehicle must either be licensed as a private hire vehicle under the provisions of section 48 of the Local Government (Miscellaneous Provisions) Act 1976 ('the 1976 Act') or must be a hackney carriage[1]. Section 46(1)(a) makes it clear that unless a vehicle is licensed under section 48 it is an offence to be used within a controlled district as a private hire vehicle.

1 This exception will be considered at para 13.46ff.

POWERS RELATING TO LICENSING

13.2 The powers relating to the licensing of the vehicle are contained in section 48:

'**Licensing of private hire vehicles**

48–(1) Subject to the provisions of this Part of this Act, a district council may on the receipt of an application from the proprietor of any vehicle for the grant in respect of such vehicle of a licence to use the vehicle as a private hire vehicle, grant in respect thereof a vehicle licence:

Provided that a district council shall not grant such a licence unless they are satisfied—
(a) that the vehicle is—
  (i) suitable in type, size and design for use as a private hire vehicle;
  (ii) not of such design and appearance as to lead any person to believe that the vehicle is a hackney carriage;
  (iii) in a suitable mechanical condition;
  (iv) safe; and
  (v) comfortable;
(b) that there is in force in relation to the use of the vehicle a policy of insurance or such security as complies with the requirements of [Part VI of the Road Traffic Act 1988], and shall not refuse such a licence for the purpose of limiting the number of vehicles in respect of which such licences are granted by the council.

(2) A district council may attach to the grant of a licence under this section such conditions as they may consider reasonably necessary including, without prejudice to the generality of the foregoing provisions of this subsection, conditions requiring or prohibiting the display of signs on or from the vehicle to which the licence relates.'

As can be seen, this is a lengthy provision and there are a number of important points that arise from it.

13.3 It is worth noting that the district council are not placed under a duty to issue a licence once an application has been made, they have a discretion. This can be contrasted with the requirement to issue a licence to an operator under section 55(1) of the 1976 Act, unless, on the grounds of fitness and propriety, they have reason not to do so.

13.4 Section 48(1) of the 1976 Act does include provisos for situations where the council must not grant a licence in paragraphs (*a*) and (*b*). Section 48(1) also expressly prohibits any refusal to grant the proprietor's licence if that refusal is with a view to limiting the number of private hire vehicles licensed within the district. The consequence of this is that even if the vehicle is suitable and satisfactory, provided the refusal is not to limit numbers, the district council can refuse.

13.5 It is difficult to see what reasons for refusal other than to limit the numbers, the district council could put forward. However, it is possible to foresee the following situation if the provisions of the Disability Discrimination Act 1995 come into force. If significant numbers of hackney carriages stop seeking renewal of their licences as hackney carriages and instead seek the grant of licences as private hire vehicles, an argument could be put forward that the refusal to grant a private hire licence is not to limit the numbers of private hire vehicles, but to prevent a diminishing number of hackney carriage vehicles within the locality. Other than this, the point is probably academic.

THE TYPE OF VEHICLE

13.6 There is no such thing as a purpose-designed or purpose-built private hire vehicle, unlike a hackney carriage where 'London style' vehicles are available. Private hire vehicles come in all shapes and sizes and there is no normal or average vehicle. Section 48(1)(*a*) of the 1976 Act lays down certain criteria that have to be satisfied before the district council can license a vehicle as a private hire vehicle.

Criteria as to the vehicle

13.7 The first consideration is whether it is 'suitable in type, size and design for use as a private hire vehicle'. Most local authorities impose additional conditions under section 48(2) relating to the size and other specifications of the vehicle. These include requirements that the vehicle has four doors for driver and passenger access, together with minimum sizes for internal dimensions, such as seats and legroom, to ensure a reasonable standard of comfort for the passengers.

13.8 One area of interest concerns vehicles that are designed to carry more than four passengers apart from the driver. These used to be represented by estate cars, which had an additional row of seats fitted in the area which would normally be the boot area (traditionally models produced by Peugeot and Citröen), but tend now to have been superseded by so-called 'people carriers'. In relation to estate car vehicles, there was always concern about access to and egress from the rear row of seats. A great many authorities refused to license such vehicles for more than four passengers, as the only way to emerge from the rearmost row of seats was with the middle row tipped up and through the rear doors. This situation was, therefore, analogous to the use of a two-door car with passengers in the back seat, as one of the front seat passengers would have to get out to allow the rear seat passengers out and this was felt to be unsatisfactory. However, a number of authorities did license such vehicles as seven-seat private hire vehicles (or in some cases, as hackney carriages).

Similar considerations can arise with the modern people carrier-type cars, depending on the configuration of seats and doors. These vary from manufacturer to manufacturer, but it is an important consideration.   **13.9**

The primary concern raised in relation to the problem is the method of escape from the vehicle in the case of accident or emergency. It is felt by many people that immediate access to a door is necessary for all passengers and the driver, except the passenger sitting in the middle of the rear seat, who will hopefully be able to escape once the passengers sitting to either side have done so. The problem is that, if a seat has to be tipped up to enable this escape to be facilitated, then it is possible that, for whatever reason (injury, death etc), this may not be possible if the seat is occupied.   **13.10**

Other than that, there are no real restrictions on the type of vehicles that can be used as a private hire vehicle, other than that contained in section 48(1)(*a*)(ii): that it is 'not of such design and appearance as to lead any person to believe that the vehicle is a hackney carriage'.   **13.11**

This is an interesting question and the answer as to whether a certain vehicle could appear to be a hackney carriage will to a large extent depend upon the location in which it is to be licensed. Some local authorities have adopted 'mandatory orders', which means that only purpose-built vehicles (currently either FX4, Metro-cabs or TX1 vehicles) will be licensed as hackney carriages[1]. This leaves the field of saloons, estate cars and people carriers open for private hire work. In other areas, hackney carriages are themselves generally saloons, estate cars and people carriers, and distinctions between private hire and hackney carriage vehicles can become blurred.   **13.12**

1 See Chapter 8, para 8.64.

R v Bournemouth Borough Council, ex p Thompson

This point was considered in the case *R v Bournemouth Borough Council, ex p Thompson*[1], which concerned a judicial review of a decision by Bournemouth Borough Council to grant a private hire licence to an applicant for an Austin FL2 vehicle. It was similar in appearance to the vehicle that was then being produced as a purpose-built hackney carriage, which was an Austin FX4R. That was the 'classic' London-type cab at the time, and apparently the principal distinction between a FX4R and a FL2 was the absence of a 'For Hire' raised sign on the leading edge of the roof.   **13.13**

1 (1985) 83 LGR 662.

13.14   The challenge was launched on the grounds that the decision to grant a private hire vehicle licence to such a vehicle was flawed. The application was heard by Mann J, who gave judgment. He considered the facts and then said (at 667):

> 'The only way in which the decision upon his application could be flawed is by an appeal to the principle of irrationality: that is to say the principal adumbrated in *Associated Provincial Picture Houses Ltd v Wednesbury Corporation,* to the effect that a decision can be flawed if it is one which no reasonable local authority properly instructed could have reached. Neither the grounds on which relief is sought nor the affidavit in support of the application contain an appeal to that principle.'

He continued:

> 'It suffices for me to say that in regard to the limited function of this court, there is no material before me which would enable me to say that no committee properly instructed could reasonably have reached the conclusion which this committee did in regard to Mr Purkiss's application [the applicant]. They saw the vehicle. They knew all the local conditions. That on a later occasion – 1 November – they took a different view of the matter is, so far as I am concerned, neither here nor there.'

That dealt with the substance of the judicial review, and the finding that the decision to grant the licence was not *Wednesbury* unreasonable. In relation to the question of granting an Austin FL2 a private hire vehicle licence, Mann J said (at 667):

> 'What the committee had to ask itself was this: are we satisfied that the FL2 is not of such a design and appearance as to lead to any person to believe that the vehicle is a hackney carriage? I have read the definition of "hackney carriage" incorporated from the Act of 1847. Having regard to that definition, it seems to me that what the committee had to ask itself was this: is the FL2 of such design and appearance as to lead any person to believe that the vehicle is a vehicle plying for hire?
>
> It seems to me that the question has to be asked in relation to the local circumstances. That which may give rise to a belief in London is not necessarily the same as that which might give rise to a belief in Inverness. The likelihood of the belief occurring must depend upon local conditions and upon factors such as – and I would have supposed importantly – the composition of the local hackney carriage fleet. There is, in my judgment, no such thing as a vehicle which, as a matter of law, is in all places to be regarded inexorably as a hackney carriage.'

13.15   Although the references to Inverness and London are unfortunate (as both are outside the area in which the 1976 Act can take effect), the judgment is sound. It will be a matter of local consideration for the local authority to decide upon the type of vehicles it will grant private hire licences to. Obviously, if the hackney carriage fleet in the district is predominately made up of London-style cabs, then it would seem foolish to grant a private hire licence to a vehicle which bore a remarkable similarity to what would be well-known as a hackney carriage in the district. However, if the local hackney fleet is made up more of saloon-and people carrier-type vehicles, then the distinguishing factors may well be the question of whether or not roof signs are allowed, whether there is a hackney carriage livery, which must not be replicated on private hire vehicles, and so on. It would be for the local authority to balance these factors and come to its own conclusion in every case.

Other factors that come into play are the question of whether there is a livery imposed upon hackney carriages. If there is, then the distinction between a hackney carriage that will be liveried and undoubtedly carry a roof sign, and the private hire vehicle that will not carry a livery (or at least not the same livery) will be marked. **13.16**

It is open to a local authority to impose a livery upon private hire vehicles under section 48(2), but this is not a popular option. Indeed, it is not clear whether any authority has actually imposed this. **13.17**

The remaining factors contained in section 48(1)(*a*)(iii)–(v) of the 1976 Act concern the suitability of the mechanical condition of the vehicle and the safety and comfort of the vehicle. Local authorities have a power to test vehicles that are licensed as private hire vehicles under section 50(1), but no overt power to conduct tests on a vehicle that is the subject of an application. However, to satisfy themselves that the vehicle does indeed comply with the requirements laid down in section 48(1), it will be essential for a similar test to take place. However, this does not have to take place within the area of the local authority, unlike a test ordered under section 50[1]. **13.18**

1 See Chapter 8 paras 8.90ff in relation to the testing of hackney carriages.

Conditions as to the vehicle

Once the local authority are satisfied that the provisions of section 48(1) are satisfied, they can then consider whether to impose any conditions under section 48(2). There are a number of conditions which appear to be of almost universal application under this provision and they include: **13.19**

- The vehicle must be safe, clean and tidy.
- The plate must be securely attached.
- Provision of a first aid kit.
- Provision of a fire extinguisher.

As section 48(2) makes specific reference to signs displayed on the vehicle (either allowing or prohibiting such signs), the question of roof signs can usefully be considered here. **13.20**

Roof signs

A number of authorities either allow or, in some cases, require signs to be affixed to the doors, bonnets, boots and wings of private hire vehicles, stating the company name, telephone number etc and this is clearly allowable as a condition under section 48(2). Some authorities go further and require signs stating 'Pre booked only' or similar words to reinforce the fact that a private hire vehicle cannot ply for hire. There has for some years been less certainty over the question of roof signs on private hire vehicles. **13.21**

13.22   Hackney carriages have traditionally had roof signs. Some of these illumi-nate only when the vehicle is for hire (as on purpose-built vehicles) and others remain illuminated all the time. There is a widespread belief that the use of such signs on private hire vehicles is unlawful under the provi-sions of the Transport Act 1980, but that is not the case. Section 64(1) states:

> **'Roof-signs on vehicles other than taxis**
>
> **64**–(1)   There shall not, in any part of England and Wales outside the met-ropolitan police district and the City of London, be displayed on or above the roof of any vehicle which is used for carrying passengers for hire or reward but which is not a taxi—
>
> (*a*)   any sign which consists of or includes the word "taxi" or "cab", whether in the singular or plural, or "hire", or any word of similar meaning or appearance to any of those words, whether alone or as part of another word; or
>
> (*b*)   any sign, notice, mark, illumination or other feature which may sug-gest that the vehicle is a taxi.
>
> (2)   Any person who knowingly—
>
> (*a*)   drives a vehicle in respect of which subsection (1) is contra-vened; or
>
> (*b*)   causes or permits that subsection to be contravened in respect of any vehicle, shall be liable on summary conviction to a fine not exceeding £200.
>
> (3)   In this section "taxi" means a vehicle licensed under section 37 of the Town Police Clauses Act 1847, section 6 of the Metropolitan Carriage Act 1869, [section 10 of the Civic Government (Scotland) Act 1982] or any similar local enactment.'

It can be seen quite clearly from that wording that roof signs per se are not themselves illegal on private hire vehicles, but certain words are outlawed.

13.23   This matter was considered in *Yakhya v Tee*[1]. This case concerned a prose-cution brought by Reading Borough Council against a driver of a private hire vehicle which was displaying a roof sign. On the roof sign was a tele-phone number. He was prosecuted under section 64 of the Transport Act 1980 and convicted. He appealed by way of case stated. The appeal was heard by Robert Goff LJ and Mann J. Judgment was given by Mann J. In relation to the sign itself, he stated (at 124C):

> 'All that was stated about the sign on the roof is that it bore black numer-als on a light background, the last four digits of which were 8888. However, it was agreed before the court that the whole sign was a tele-phone number.'

Reference was made to the case of *Breame v Anderson*[2] which concerned a similar provision of the London Cab Act 1968 (section 4). In his judgment in this case, Mann J quoted from the judgment in Breame:

> 'Lord Parker CJ said, at p 39C, that the test for determining whether or not there had been a contravention of that provision [section 4 of the London Cab Act 1968] was:
>
> > "In my judgment one just looks at the vehicle with the sign on it, and asks as a matter of common sense: does it suggest that the vehicle is immediately for hire?"

Ashworth J said, at p 39E:

> "one looks at the sign on the vehicle and asks: does it suggest that which is forbidden?"'

Mann J then continued (at 125C):

> 'In our judgment, a court has to look at the vehicle of itself and in no particular context but with the sign on it and then ask, as a matter of common sense: does the sign suggest that the vehicle is a taxi?

> Applying that test, we ask: did the sign suggest that the vehicle was a taxi? The sign suggests a number of things. Amongst others it suggests that the vehicle was available for hire on a telephone call or it suggests a means of identifying the vehicle that a caller had ordered. Accordingly, and applying the test in *Breame v Anderson* we are of the opinion that the conclusion reached by the justices [to convict] was such that no properly instructed and reasonable bench of justices could have reached. In fairness to the justices we record that *Breame v Anderson* was not drawn to their attention.

> We now respond to the question which the justices ask. The first is:

> > "Whether the justices were correct in deciding that the sign displayed on the roof contravened the subsection in that it may have suggested that the vehicle was a taxi."

> The answer is no. The second is:

> > "whether the justices were correct in inferring that any sign displayed on the roof of a private hire vehicle, and in particular a sign containing a telephone number, would be in contravention of the subsection."

> The answer is no.'

1 [1984] RTR 122.
2 [1971] RTR 31.

As a consequence, a number of local authorities either allow or insist upon **13.24** roof signs on private hire vehicles. These include Manchester, where the roof sign carries the telephone number and name of the firm, and Newcastle-upon-Tyne, where the sign contains the telephone number and the words 'Advance Booking Only'. Luton Borough Council has also recently introduced roof signs for private hire vehicles as an experiment. The rationale behind such requirements is to aid the identification of private hire vehicles for the public. This is a matter that is seen as especially important in large urban areas, where a major problem concerns the use of unlicensed 'pirate' vehicles (that is, unlicensed vehicles driven by unlicensed drivers and not operated by a licensed operator).

The argument against roof signs is usually that they will lead to confusion in **13.25** the minds of the public between private hire vehicles and hackney carriages, but, in certain areas, this argument is weakened. In Manchester, for example, all hackney carriages have to be purpose-built, whereas private hire vehicles will include saloon cars, estate cars and people carriers, so the distinction is already reasonably obvious. It is acknowledged that this argument about confusion would be much more apparent in an area where saloon-type vehicles were licensed as hackney carriages.

13.26 Another consideration is the age of the vehicle in question. A number of authorities have age policies. It is arguable that these are even more important in relation to private hire vehicles than they are in relation to hackney carriages, as no private hire vehicles are purpose-built, whereas in most districts there are at least a few purpose-built hackney carriages[1].

1 For discussion of age policies and the requirements that enable them to be adopted and used successfully in relation to hackney carriages see Chapter 8, para 8.64.

THE PRIVATE HIRE VEHICLE LICENCE ITSELF

13.27 Section 48(3) and (4) of the 1976 Act outlines the requirements of the actual licence.

'**48**–(3) In every vehicle licence granted under this section there shall be specified—
(*a*) the name and address of—
  (i) the applicant; and
  (ii) every other person who is a proprietor of the private hire vehicle in respect of which the licence is granted, or who is concerned, either solely or in partnership with any other person, in the keeping, employing or letting on hire of the private hire vehicle;
(*b*) the number of the licence which shall correspond with the number to be painted or marked on the plate or disc to be exhibited on the private hire vehicle in accordance with subsection (6) of this section;
(*c*) the conditions attached to the grant of the licence; and
(*d*) such other particulars as the district council consider reasonably necessary.

(4) Every licence granted under this section shall—
(*a*) be signed by an authorised officer of the council which granted it;
(*b*) relate to not more than one private hire vehicle; and
(*c*) remain in force for such period not being longer than one year as the district council may specify in the licence.'

13.28 The licence must include:

• The name and address of the applicant;
• the name and address of anyone else with an interest in the vehicle;
• the number of the licence;
• any conditions attached to the licence; and
• such other particulars as the district council consider reasonably necessary.

Some authorities use this to include the make, colour and appearance of the vehicle, together with the number of seats for passengers that it is licensed to carry.

13.29 The licence itself can be granted for up to a year and must be signed by an authorised officer of the council.

Private hire plates

13.30 Section 48(5) of the 1976 Act requires that the council issue a plate. That plate must be 'exhibited on the vehicle' in such a way as the council requires, such requirements being specified by a condition attached to the licence.

There is a wide variation in private hire plates, with no recognisable standard in relation to size, information printed upon the plate, colour or any other aspect of design.

The case of *Solihull Metropolitan Borough Council v Silverline Cars*[1] makes it **13.31** clear that the design and content of the plate is entirely up to the local authority. In this case, Solihull Metropolitan Borough Council introduced a new and larger plate, by way of condition imposed upon the private hire vehicle licence granted under section 48, the condition being imposed under section 48(2). The new plate measured 4½ by 12¾ inches and replaced an earlier plate of 2¾ inches by 3¾ inches. The earlier plate was described in the judgment given by Mann LJ as being 'a modest mark'. Silverline Cars were aggrieved by the introduction of the new plate because their business was up-market executive hire where the appearance of the plate 4½ inches by 12¾ inches would, it was alleged, adversely effect the appearance of their vehicles and, therefore, their overall business profitability. They appealed against the imposition of the condition at the magistrates' court and lost and further appealed to the Crown Court. The Crown Court decided that the new plate was 'a vulgar sign' and allowed the appeal. The local authority appealed by way of case stated. In giving the judgment of the court, Mann LJ stated (at 146L):

'In times past, the district council's disc was a sticker, having overall dimensions of 2¾ inches by 3¾ inches; a modest mark. However, in 1987, for reasons which I need not entertain, a larger disc came into use. Its overall dimensions were some 4½ inches by 12¾ inches.

The proprietors operate a business of quality in which discretion is of the utmost importance. Whilst the proprietors were content with the smaller and earlier disc, they do not take to the larger disc which they regard as being not consonant with the nature of their undertaking. Hence the appeal to justices. Hence the appeal to the Crown Court.

I have some sympathy with the proprietors in their dislike of exhibiting the larger disc. I can well understand why they regard such an exhibition as not consonant with their business. However, sympathy is not enough. As I read the statute, the design and form of the plate or disc is wholly a matter for the district council. Their decision as to a particular form of plate or disc is no doubt subject to judicial review, in the event that the plate or disc is achieved as a result of perversity in accordance with *Associated Provincial Picture Houses Ltd v Wednesbury Corpn* [1948] KB 223. The design is not, however, a matter for the court. The court is concerned, and concerned only, with the condition as to exhibition. The matter of exhibition can be the subject of appeal, the form of the plate or disc is not the subject of appeal.'

1   [1989] RTR 142.

There were four questions raised in this case, concerning the type and exhi-   **13.32** bition of a private hire plate and they were dealt with comprehensively by the court. As they are useful and important points, the relevant questions and the answers given by Mann LJ (at 147F) are reproduced below in full:

'Turning to the questions posed in this case, I recite them and answer them as follows:

"(*a*) Whether the size and design of an identification disc can be considered in an appeal against a condition prescribing the matter in which it is to be displayed," the answer is, no.

"(*b*) Whether on the true construction of section 48(6) of the Act there is a requirement for a plate or disc to be exhibited on all licensed private hire vehicles subject to the exemptions under section 75 of the Act," the answer is, yes.

"(*c*) Whether the nature of the business conducted by the proprietors is relevant when considering an appeal against the condition concerning the manner of display of an identification disc," the answer is, no.

"(*d*) Whether it is within the court's powers to delete a condition as to display without replacing it with another condition when determining an appeal against a condition imposed under section 48(6) of the Act," the answer is, no. The court can of course vary [a condition].'

It is worth noting, and does not appear to have been made clear in the *Solihull* case[1], that under section 75(3)[2] it is open to the local authority to waive both the requirement to display plates on the vehicle and for the driver to wear a badge if it sees fit.

1 *Solihull Metropolitan Borough Council v Silverline Cars* [1989] RTR 142.
2 Local Government (Miscellaneous Provision) Act 1976. See para 13.36.

13.33   Some authorities have plates that simply state the name of the licensing authority, the licence number of the vehicle and the number of passengers it can carry. Others also include registration number, make and colour of the vehicle and expiry date of the vehicle licence.

13.34   There is no doubt that the more information that can be contained on the plate, the more use it is to members of the public, the authority itself and the police. A number of authorities, who issue new plates on renewal, have a system of colour-coding so that at any given time there are only two colours in existence. This provides an easy visual method of establishing whether the plate has expired, but necessitates the production of a new plate each year. Other authorities are able to make their plates last for many years, as the information on them does not change. It is entirely a matter for the local authorities concerned.

13.35   Some authorities impose a condition that there should be a front as well as a rear plate, again to enable members of the public to identify private hire vehicles more readily.

13.36   The requirement to display the plate can be lifted in one of two ways. Firstly, under section 75(1)(*d*) of the 1976 Act, if there is a contract for the hire of that specific vehicle for a period exceeding 24 hours. Secondly, under section 75(3), which allows the local authority to specify either certain occasions when the plate need not be displayed or, alternatively, that the district council can issue a notice which can be carried effectively in lieu of the plate being displayed. This is often used in relation to vehicles that provide chauffeur services and 'executive hire', as opposed to regular private hire short-haul bookings. In those cases under section 75(3), the requirement that the driver has to wear a badge is also waived.

ALWAYS A PRIVATE HIRE VEHICLE?

Once a vehicle has been licensed as a private hire vehicle, does that mean it **13.37**
is always a private hire vehicle? There are two cases of importance here,
Kingston-upon-Hull City Council v Wilson[1] and *Benson v Boyce*[2].

1   (1995) Times, 25 July.
2   [1997] RTR 226.

Kingston-upon-Hull City Council v Wilson

The first case concerned an appeal by way of case stated to the Divisional **13.38**
Court by Kingston-upon-Hull City Council against a decision by Kingston-
upon-Hull City Magistrates to acquit Mr Wilson of three charges which
were:

1.   Using a private vehicle as a private hire vehicle in the controlled district
     without having a licence (contrary to section 46(1)(*a*) of the 1976 Act.
2.   Driving a private hire vehicle in a controlled district without holding a
     private driver's licence (contrary to section 46(1)(*b*)). (There was a
     third charge relating to an operators' licence[1]).

1   This has been considered in Chapter 12, para 12.16.

The vehicle which Mr Wilson was driving was, in fact, licensed as a hackney **13.39**
carriage in a neighbouring district. Mr Wilson does not appear to have held
a hackney carriage or private hire driver's licence issued by Hull City council, although he did, in fact, hold a private hire operator's licence, but for a
different address from that which was apparently being used by him to
operate the vehicle from. Judgment in the case was given by Buxton J, who
stated:

> 'The only ground upon which it could be argued that, nonetheless, the
> vehicle that Mr Wilson drove was not a private hire vehicle, is that it was
> a hackney carriage. Mr Neish [for Mr Wilson] argues that this vehicle was
> a hackney carriage because it had been licensed as a hackney carriage in
> the Borough of Beverley, as I have indicated previously. That amounts to
> saying that once the vehicle is licensed anywhere as a hackney carriage,
> that precludes the application, in respect of that vehicle, of any part of sec-
> tion 46 of this Act anywhere else in the country. Thus, if Mr Wilson had
> driven his vehicle in other respects not in conformity with section 46 in
> Truro or Newcastle upon Tyne, the fact that it had been licensed in
> Beverley as a hackney carriage would preclude the application, by any
> local authority, of section 46(2).
>
> Mr Neish fairly conceded that this point was not taken in the *ABC Cabs*
> case. The court in that case was concerned with the construction of the
> more composite phrase "being a hackney carriage" in respect of which a
> vehicle is in force, and indeed in the *ABC Cabs* case there was a further
> charge under section 46(1)(*b*) of the Act which was disposed of under
> quite different grounds from those which I have already indicated that the
> court dealt with under section 46(1)(*a*). That step would not have been
> necessary if Mr Neish was right in saying that the possession of a hackney
> carriage licence makes a vehicle a hackney carriage for all purposes and for
> all time. It is true, as Mr Neish argued, that the court in the *ABC Cabs*
> case may have assumed or might have assumed that "hackney carriage" is,

as it were, a condition that applies to any vehicle wheresoever it is and in whatsoever circumstances. But the court in that case was not addressing that point and, for my part, I cannot accept that this Act intends it to be the case that in every case where a hackney carriage vehicle licence exists it follows thereafter that the vehicle so licensed cannot be susceptible to the rules applying to private hire vehicles.

First of all, as my Lord pointed out in argument, section 46(1)(*a*) speaks of a vehicle "not being a hackney carriage in respect of which a vehicle licence was in force" and goes on to prohibit the use of such a vehicle as a private hire vehicle. If it is right that such a licence automatically prevents the vehicle being a private hire vehicle that provision would make no sense. Secondly, and more generally, if one looks at the definition of "hackney carriage" in the Town Police Clauses Act 1847, which I have already read, it seems to me clear that that definition at least starts by looking at the function that the vehicle is performing and not at its nature, construction or inherent identity. If that is so it cannot, in my view, be the case that simply to licence a vehicle as a hackney carriage thereby makes that vehicle a hackney carriage for all time, even if it is functioning as a private hire vehicle. In my judgment, therefore, it is not enough that a hackney carriage licence exists to establish that this vehicle was a hackney carriage so that term is used in the definition of a "private hire vehicle" in section 80 of the 1976 Act.'

13.40   At no time was any reference made in *Kingston-upon-Hull City Council v Wilson*[1] to the decisions in *Hawkins v Edwards*[2] or *Yates v Gates*[3], which quite clearly state that a hackney carriage is always a hackney carriage. In conflict with this, Buxton J concluded that a vehicle could indeed be a hackney carriage in one district and a private hire vehicle in a second district.

1   (1995) Times, 25 July.
2   [1901] 2 KB 169. See Chapter 8, para 8.3.
3   [1970] 1 All ER 754, QBD. See Chapter 8, para 8.4.

Benson v Boyce

13.41   The situation appears to have been clarified by the case of *Benson v Boyce*[1]. This concerned a vehicle which was licensed as a private hire vehicle, but which was being driven by a person who did not hold a private hire driver's licence. The question raised was whether a private hire vehicle is only a private hire vehicle (and, therefore, only needs to be driven by a person with a private hire driver's licence) when it is working as a private hire vehicle or is it, following the approach taken in *Yates v Gates*[2] in relation to hackney carriages, always a private hire vehicle, irrespective of whether or not it is working? Mance J delivered a lengthy judgment on behalf of the Divisional Court. In the course of this he referred to both *Yates v Gates* and *Kingston-upon-Hull City Council v Wilson*[3]. He observed that there was no reference to *Yates v Gates* in the *Kingston-upon-Hull* case. Although he did not appear to regard the *Kingston-upon-Hull* case as conflicting with his conclusion (or indeed *Yates v Gates*), he concluded (at 236G):

'I consider that the correct interpretation of section 46(1)(*b*) is that it applies to all driving in a controlled district of a vehicle characterised under section 80(1) as a private hire vehicle, whatever the specific activity in connection with which the vehicle is in fact being driven. The two questions raised by the case stated are:

(1) Whether it is correct that the wording "provided for hire" in section 80 of the Local Government (Miscellaneous Provisions) Act 1976 relates to the nature of the vehicle rather than to the nature of the activity?

(2) Whether, on the correct interpretation of Part II of the Local Government (Miscellaneous Provisions) Act 1976, the Prosecution must prove an actual hiring of the vehicle in question at the material time in order to obtain a conviction for an offence under section 46(1)(*b*) of that Act?

In the context of this case, I would answer the first question in the affirmative and the second in the negative. I would therefore uphold the Justices' conviction of the appellant and dismiss the appeal.'

1   [1997] RTR 226.
2   [1970] 1 All ER 754, QBD. See Chapter 8, para 8.4.
3   (1995) Times, 25 July.

It seems that in the light of *Yates v Gates*[1] and *Benson v Boyce*[2], this element of   **13.42** the *Kingston-upon-Hull* case[3] is wrongly decided. It is difficult to see how a vehicle can be a hackney carriage at some time and a private hire vehicle at another time (all being in different districts), if the characteristics of either vehicle are that they are, at all times, a hackney carriage or a private hire vehicle.

1   [1970] 1 All ER 754, QBD. See Chapter 8, para 8.4.
2   [1997] RTR 226.
3   *Kingston-upon-Hull City Council v Wilson* (1995) Times, 25 July. See para 13.38.

METERS AND FARES

There is no power in any Act allowing a local authority to set the fares   **13.43** charged by private hire vehicles. It is entirely a matter for negotiation between the hirer and the operator as to the fare that will be charged. However, that provision can be limited if a meter is fitted to the vehicle.

Again, there is no power that enables a local authority to require a meter to   **13.44** be fitted, but if one is fitted, section 71 of the 1976 Act comes into play. This states:

'Taximeters

71–(1) Nothing in this Act shall require any private hire vehicle to be equipped with any form of taximeter but no private hire vehicle so equipped shall be used for hire in a controlled district unless such taximeter has been tested and approved by or on behalf of the district council for the district or any other district council by which a vehicle licence in force for the vehicle was issued.

(2) Any person who—
(*a*)   tampers with any seal on any taximeter without lawful excuse; or
(*b*)   alters any taximeter with intent to mislead; or
(*c*)   knowingly causes or permits a vehicle of which he is the proprietor to be used in contravention of subsection (1) of this section.

shall be guilty of an offence.'

13.45   It should be noted, however, that whilst the taximeter has to be tested and approved, there is still no power for the local authority to set a fare. The only time in which there is any form of control over the fare charged for private hire vehicles is when a hackney carriage is used for private hire services. In such a case, section 67 makes it clear that the fare charged cannot exceed that which would be charged under the table of fares applicable to hackney carriages and which would be entered into the meter of the vehicle. This only applies when the vehicle is booked other than by hailing in the street or being approached at a rank, that is, when it is booked through the telephone or is actually working for a private hire operator.

HACKNEY CARRIAGES USED AS PRIVATE HIRE VEHICLES

13.46   A question which often arises concerns the use of hackney carriages as private hire vehicles. This can occur in one of two ways. Firstly, the hackney carriage can be used effectively as a private hire vehicle because a booking is made with a person, either by telephone or in person, and a vehicle, which is a hackney carriage, is dispatched to fulfil the booking. Secondly, a private hire operator can operate a vehicle as a private hire vehicle, but the vehicle is licensed as a hackney carriage.

13.47   In the first situation, it is clear that the person who takes the booking and arranges the dispatch of the hackney carriage to fulfil the booking is making 'a provision for the invitation or acceptance of bookings[1]' and would need a private hire operator's licence. This view was supported in the Crown Court at Worcester in the case of *R v Franklyn and Carter*[2]. Although this is a Crown Court decision and only of persuasive value, it appears to correctly state the law. However, the vehicles would not need to be licensed as private hire vehicles because they are hackney carriages and, therefore, can be used as a private hire vehicle under section 46(1)(*a*) of the 1976 Act.

1   Local Government (Miscellaneous Provisions) Act 1976, s 80(1).
2   (27 June 1991, unreported.)

13.48   In relation to the second situation, again, the exemption contained in section 46(1)(*a*) of the 1976 Act enables a hackney carriage to be used as a private hire vehicle. In all cases, the driver must hold a hackney carriage driver's licence as a hackney carriage is always a hackney carriage[1].

1   *Hawkins v Edwards* [1901] 2 KB 169: see Chapter 8, para 8.3; and *Yates v Gates* [1970] 1 All ER 754, QBD: see Chapter 8, para 8.4.

13.49   If a hackney carriage is being used a private hire vehicle, the provisions of section 67 of the 1976 Act apply.

'Hackney carriages used for private hire

67–(1) No hackney carriage shall be used in the district under contract or purported contract for private hire except at a rate of fares or charges not greater than that fixed by the byelaws or table mentioned in section 66 of this Act, and, when any such hackney carriage is so used, the fare or charge shall be calculated from the point in the district at which the hirer commences his journey.

(2) Any person who knowingly contravenes this section shall be guilty of an offence.

(3) In subsection (1) of this section "contract" means—
(*a*) a contract made otherwise than while the relevant hackney carriage is plying for hire in the district or waiting at a place in the district which, when the contract is made, is a stand for hackney carriages appointed by the district council under section 63 of this Act; and
(*b*) a contract made, otherwise than with or through the driver of the relevant hackney carriage, while it is so plying or waiting.'

This makes it clear that the fare charged must not exceed the fare shown on the meter (if fitted) or the fares set by the local authority if no meter is fitted. In addition, the fare can only apply from the point of pick up, and no charge can be made for travelling to the pick-up point.

INSURANCE

The question of insurance is a source of considerable concern for all involved in private hire matters. Private hire insurance is usually specifically for the use of the vehicle as a private hire vehicle: that is for hire and reward providing a pre-booked service. The question that arises is whether such insurance is invalidated if the vehicle acts unlawfully and is used to ply for hire in contravention of section 45 of the Town Police Clauses Act 1847 ('the 1847 Act'). It is less than clear what the answer to this question is, as the insurance companies tend to have different underlying policies. Some take the view that, notwithstanding the fact that the vehicle is used in contravention of its licence, they will still cover third party losses. Ultimately, it will be a matter of fact in any subsequent prosecution as to whether the vehicle was insured or not. It is, however, quite clear that a 'policy of insurance' must be in place for the vehicle for private hire purposes before a private hire vehicle licence can be granted as a consequence of section 48(1)(*b*). **13.50**

Some authorities have taken the view that, if the driver of a private hire vehicle is prosecuted for unlawfully plying for hire contrary to section 45 of the 1847 Act, they will automatically bring criminal proceedings against the driver of the vehicle for driving without insurance. A number of authorities have been successful in these prosecutions. Many other local authorities take the view that driving without insurance is a matter for the police to investigate and then for the Crown Prosecution Service to bring proceedings, as it is an offence contrary to the Road Traffic Act 1988. **13.51**

This is not a point on which an easy answer can be given. A prosecution for driving without insurance can be brought under the Road Traffic Offenders Act 1988. Section 4 of that Act refers to a limited number of offences under the Road Traffic Act 1988, for which local authorities may prosecute. As driving without insurance is not one of those specified offences, it is arguable that a local authority has no power to bring such a prosecution. **13.52**

However, the alternative argument is that local authorities can use the power contained in section 222 of the Local Government Act 1972 to bring a prosecution for driving a private hire vehicle without insurance, as such a **13.53** prosecution is 'expedient for the promotion or protection of the interests of the inhabitants of their area'. Certainly, this seems to be the justification used by those authorities who do undertake prosecutions for driving without insurance and there is no record of that approach being challenged.

13.54 Local authorities which do undertake prosecutions for no insurance must be certain as to their powers to commence such an action, and be able to demonstrate those powers to the satisfaction of the court.

TRANSFER OF PRIVATE HIRE VEHICLES

13.55 Section 49 of the 1976 Act applies to private hire vehicles as it does to hackney carriages. This requires the proprietor who transfers his interest in a private hire vehicle to another person to give written notice to the district council detailing the name and address of the person to whom the private hire vehicle has been transferred. This requirement is waived if that person is already registered on the licence as a person having an interest in the vehicle. Likewise, section 50, in relation to testing, has identical implications in relation to proprietors of private hire vehicles as it does to hackney carriages[1].

1 See Chapter 8, paras 8.84ff and 8.95ff.

13.56 When the vehicle licence expires or is revoked, the local authority can require the return of the plate under the provisions of section 58(1) of the 1976 Act. It should be noted that the return of the plate is not automatic on expiry or revocation. Such action has to be instigated by the local authority serving notice on the proprietor requiring the return of the plate within seven days of the date of service of the notice. Failure to comply, on the part of the proprietor, with such notice is an offence by virtue of section 58(2). In this case, the plate can then be removed from the private hire vehicle by an authorised officer or police constable and the proprietor can be prosecuted. The maximum fine is level 3 on the standard scale and a continuing daily fine of £10 can be levied until the plate is surrendered.

SUSPENSION AND REVOCATION

13.57 Section 60 of the 1976 Act allows the local authority to suspend, revoke or refuse to renew a vehicle licence for one of the following reasons.

> '**60**–(1) Notwithstanding anything in the Act of 1847 or in this Part of this Act, a district council may suspend or revoke, or (on application therefor under section 40 of the Act of 1847 or section 48 of this Act, as the case may be) refuse to renew a vehicle licence on any of the following grounds—
> (*a*) that the hackney carriage or private hire vehicle is unfit for use as a hackney carriage or private hire vehicle;
> (*b*) any offence under, or non-compliance with, the provisions of the Act of 1847 or of this Part of this Act by the operator or driver; or
> (*c*) any other reasonable cause.'

13.58 The question of the unfitness of the vehicle will be a matter of fact in relation to its mechanical condition, safety and comfort. Alternatively, or if it is a vehicle which is newly presented, then it will be subject to any of the other matters contained in section 48(1).

Section 60(1)(*b*)[1] allows suspension, revocation or non-renewal of a licence for any offence under either the 1976 Act or the 1847 Act on the part of the operator or driver for any non-compliance with those provisions. Obviously, to prove an offence, a conviction will have to have been recorded, but non-compliance could be demonstrated in a way that falls short of a criminal conviction. **13.59**

1 See also Chapter 8, para 8.134.

Suspension, revocation or non-renewal can also be for 'any other reasonable cause'. Any other reasonable cause does not have be construed *ejusdem generis* with the preceding grounds, as demonstrated by the case of *Norwich City Council v Thurtle and Watcham*[1], which concerned the theft of car seats which were subsequently used in private hire vehicles. **13.60**

1 (21 May 1981, unreported.) See Chapter 8, para 8.87.

There is some difficulty here, in relation to the suspension, revocation or refusal to renew a vehicle licence. It is obvious that, if the vehicle is unsatisfactory for use as a private hire vehicle, suspension of the licence would make sense, as the period of suspension could be used to remedy the defects in the vehicle. Likewise, if the condition of the vehicle is so severe that no amount of work will bring it up to the required standard, then the licence should be revoked or not renewed. **13.61**

It is in relation to criminal convictions that the difficulties arise. Convictions are caused by people, not by the vehicle itself. To revoke the vehicle licence because of someone's convictions does seem unjust. Provided that the vehicle is safe and satisfactory, it can quite readily be driven by another person who holds a private hire driver's licence and, indeed, operated by another operator. Action can be taken against the people who committed the offence (assuming they hold either an operator's or driver's licence) by way of action against those respective licences. The only time where it would seem at all reasonable to take action against a vehicle licence because of somebody's convictions is when the proprietor of the vehicle does not hold either an operator's or driver's licence and simply makes money from the vehicle by renting it out. In those circumstances, the provisos, in relation to suspension, outlined above, in relation to operators' licences apply[1]. **13.62**

1 See Chapter 12, para 12.46ff.

Notice of any decision to suspend, revoke or refuse to renew a vehicle licence must be given to the proprietor in writing, stating the grounds on which the licence has been suspended, together with the reasons for that decision. This must be within 14 days of the decision. If the proprietor is aggrieved by that decision, he has a right of appeal to the magistrates' court under section 60(3) of the 1976 Act. **13.63**

TESTING OF VEHICLES

13.64   Section 68 of the 1976 Act allows any authorised officer of the council which licenses the vehicle or any police constable to inspect and test the vehicle[1].

1   See Chapter 8, para 8.95ff.

EXEMPT VEHICLES

13.65   Section 75 makes it clear that certain vehicles are exempt from the requirements of Part II of the 1976 Act. These are principally vehicles to be used in connection with a funeral or used wholly or mainly for the purpose of funerals by a person who is a funeral director[1]; and vehicles that are being used in connection with a wedding[2].

1   Local Government (Miscellaneous Provisions) Act 1976, s 75(1)(*c*).
2   Local Government (Miscellaneous Provisions) Act 1976, s 75(1)(*cc*).

13.66   In relation to the exemption applicable to vehicles used under a contract for hire for more than seven days[1] see Chapter 12, para 12.74ff.

1   Local Government (Miscellaneous Provisions) Act 1976, s 75(1)(*b*).

Chapter 14

Private hire drivers

INTRODUCTION

The role of the private hire driver is very similar to the role of the hackney **14.1**
carriage driver. Each is required to hold a licence, and to drive members of
the public in a licensed vehicle. Indeed, the similarities are so great that
some local authorities grant dual licences that serve as a licence to drive both
hackney carriages and private hire vehicles.

The case of *Benson v Boyce*[1] makes it clear that a private hire vehicle is **14.2**
always a private hire vehicle, and this makes it imperative that anyone who
drives a private hire vehicle holds a private hire driver's licence.

1 [1997] RTR 226. See Chapter 13, para 13.41.

The actual considerations that apply to private hire drivers' licences are to **14.3**
all intents and purposes identical to those that apply to hackney carriage
drivers.

LICENSING OF DRIVERS OF PRIVATE HIRE VEHICLES

The requirement to hold a licence is contained in section 46(1)(*b*) of the **14.4**
Local Government (Miscellaneous Provisions) Act 1976 ('the 1976 Act'):

'Vehicle, driver's and operators' licences

46–(1) Except as authorised by this Part of this Act—

(*a*) . . .

(*b*) no person shall in a controlled district act as driver of any private
hire vehicle without having a current licence under section 51 of this
Act;'

The licence itself is granted under section 51 of the 1976 Act:

'Licensing of drivers of private hire vehicles

51–(1) Subject to the provisions of this Part of this Act, a district council
shall, on the receipt of an application from any person for the grant to that
person of a licence to drive private hire vehicles, grant to that person a
driver's licence:

Provided that a district council shall not grant a licence—
(a) unless they are satisfied that the applicant is a fit and proper person to hold a driver's licence; or
[(b) to any person who has not for at least twelve months been authorised to drive a motor car, or is not at the date of the application for a driver's licence so authorised].

[(1B) For the purposes of subsection (1) of this section a person is authorised to drive a motor car if—
(a) he holds a licence granted under Part III of the Road Traffic Act 1988 (not being a provisional licence) authorising him to drive a motor car, or
(b) he is authorised by virtue of section 99A(1) of that Act to drive in Great Britain a motor car.]

(3) It shall be the duty of a council by which licences are granted in pursuance of this section to enter, in a register maintained by the council for the purpose, the following particulars of each such licence, namely—
(a) the name of the person to whom it is granted;
(b) the date on which and the period for which it is granted; and
(c) if the licence has a serial number, that number,

and to keep the register available at its principal offices for inspection by members of the public during office hours free of charge.'

A comparison with the provisions governing the licensing of hackney carriage drivers

14.5 These provisions are similar to those contained in section 59 of the 1976 Act, which govern the licensing of a hackney carriage driver in areas where the 1976 Act has been adopted.

14.6 However, there are slight differences which should be noted. It is not possible to simply treat the provisions as totally interchangeable.

14.7 Once an application has been made to the local authority for a licence to drive a private hire vehicle under section 51 of the 1976 Act, the local authority is under a duty to grant that licence[1], unless they are prevented from doing so under section 51(1)(a) or (b). This duty to grant a licence can be contrasted with the provisions for hackney carriage drivers' licences, where there is no requirement to grant a licence[2].

1 Local Government (Miscellaneous Provisions) Act 1976, s 51(1).
2 Town Police Clauses Act 1847, s 46: see Chapter 10, para 10.2.

14.8 The criteria and qualifications for a private hire driver are the same as those for hackney carriage drivers: the person must be a fit and proper person to hold a private hire driver's licence, and must have been authorised to drive a motor vehicle for a period of a least one year before the date of the application[1].

1 These are considered fully in Chapter 10, para 10.9.

14.9 The only methods available to assess the fitness and propriety of the applicant include the requirement that the applicant obain a print out of the records held against his name on the Police National Computer, to complete a statuary declaration and for the local authority to undertake a DVLA check. Again those provisions are identical to those relating to hackney carriage drivers[1].

1 See Chapter 10, para 10.13ff.

However, after that, the provisions of section 51 differ from section 59.   **14.10**
Section 51(2) gives an overt power to impose conditions on a private hire driver's licence, and this can be any condition which the local authority 'consider reasonably necessary'.

> '**51**–(2) A district council may attach to the grant of a licence under this section such conditions as they may consider reasonably necessary.'

Most local authorities do impose conditions on their private hire drivers' licences. As there is no specific power to make byelaws for private hire drivers, the ability to impose conditions is extremely useful.

In addition, the local authority has to maintain a register of private hire drivers' licences[1], including the following details: **14.11**

• the name of the person to whom it is granted;
• the date on which and the period for which it is granted; and
• if the licence has a serial number, that number.

The register has to be 'available at its principal offices for inspection by members of the public during office hours free of charge'. There is no statutory requirement as to the form the register should take[2]. Accordingly, computer records can be used, provided that there is some mechanism by which the register can be inspected.

1 Local Government (Miscellaneous Provisions) Act 1976, s 51(3).
2 This can be contrasted with the requirement in relation to hackney carriage proprietors' licences under the Town Police Clauses Act 1847, s 42, where the register has to be maintained in a 'book'.

If a person is aggrieved by either a refusal to grant a licence under section 51   **14.12**
of the 1976 Act or any conditions that are attached to that licence under section 51(2), he can appeal to the magistrates' court under section 52:

> '**Appeals in respect of drivers' licences**
>
> **52** Any person aggrieved by—
> (1) the refusal of the district council to grant a driver's licence under section 51 of this Act; or
> (2) any conditions attached to the grant of a driver's licence;
> may appeal to a magistrates' court.'[1]

1 The requirements in relation to appeals are considered in Chapter 3.

In relation to the application, and to enable the local authority to fully consider the applicant, section 57 of the 1976 Act allows the local authority to seek information. This specifically refers to a medical test. Some authorities also require 'knowledge' tests of the locality, and spoken English tests[1].   **14.13**

1 For full details see Chapter 10, paras 10.23–10.30.

Section 53(1)(*a*) of the 1976 Act allows a private hire driver's licence to be   **14.14**
granted for up to three years. However, as with hackney carriage drivers' licences, most authorities grant licences for one year, thereby requiring annual

renewals. This is felt to give a greater element of control over drivers. Although there is often imposed on drivers' licences a condition which requires the driver to notify the local authority of any convictions recorded against the driver during the currency of the licence, annual renewals are felt to provide an opportunity to ensure that drivers do comply with that requirement[1].

1 It should be noted that circular 2/92 (see Appendix II) only envisages a police check to be made every three years: for further details see Chapter 10, paras 10.8–10.22.

14.15   A fee can be charged for private hire drivers' licences under section 53(2) of the 1976 Act:

> '53–(2) Notwithstanding the provisions of the Act of 1847, a district council may demand and recover for the grant to any person of a licence to drive a hackney carriage, or a private hire vehicle, as the case may be, such a fee as they consider reasonable with a view to recovering the costs of issue and administration and may remit the whole or part of the fee in respect of a private hire vehicle in any case in which they think it appropriate to do so.'

It should be noted that this power is limited. It only allows for the recovery of the 'costs of issue and administration' and therefore no costs in relation to the enforcement of private hire drivers' licences can be built into the licence fee.

14.16   Section 54 of the 1976 Act places a duty on the local authority to issue drivers' badges when a licence is granted under section 51 to a private hire driver and section 54(2)(*a*) requires the driver to wear it at all times when acting as a private hire driver. Failure on the part of a licensed private hire driver to wear the badge is an offence.

14.17   It is worth noting that, as a private hire vehicle is always a private hire vehicle, at all times, when the vehicle is being driven, the driver must wear his badge under section 54(2)(*a*), irrespective of whether the vehicle is 'working' at the time.

14.18   A number of authorities, by condition attached to the driver's licence, require a second badge (which they issue free of charge) to be displayed in such a way within the vehicle so that the passenger can see the badge. The need for this second badge arose as it became apparent that the badge worn on the driver's chest may not easily be seen by the passenger, especially those seated behind the driver.

SUSPENSION OF A PRIVATE HIRE DRIVER'S LICENCE

14.19   **'Suspension and revocation of drivers' licences**

> **61**–(1) Notwithstanding anything in the Act of 1847 or in this Part of this Act, a district council may suspend or revoke or (on application therefor under section 46 of the Act of 1847 or section 51 of this Act, as the case may be) refuse to renew the licence of a driver of a hackney carriage or a private hire vehicle on any of the following grounds—
>
> (*a*) that he has since the grant of the licence—
>   (i) been convicted of an offence involving dishonesty, indecency or violence; or

(ii) been convicted of an offence under or has failed to comply with the provisions of the Act of 1847 or of this Part of this Act; or

(*b*) any other reasonable cause.

(2)

(*a*) Where a district council suspend, revoke or refuse to renew any licence under this section they shall give to the driver notice of the grounds on which the licence has been suspended or revoked or on which they have refused to renew such licence within fourteen days of such suspension, revocation or refusal and the driver shall on demand return to the district council the driver's badge issued to him in accordance with section 54 of this Act.

(*b*) If any person without reasonable excuse contravenes the provisions of this section he shall be guilty of an offence and liable on summary conviction to a fine not exceeding [level 1 on the standard scale].

(3) Any driver aggrieved by a decision of a district council under this section may appeal to a magistrates' court.'

Section 61 of the 1976 Act gives the local authority powers to suspend, revoke (or on an application for renewal, refuse to renew) a private hire driver's licence. This is exactly the same as the power available for hackney carriage drivers' licences under the same section[1]. **14.20**

1 Chapter 10, para 10.65.

It is an offence under section 69 of the 1976 Act for the driver of a private hire vehicle to unnecessarily prolong, either in distance or in time, the journey without reasonable cause[1]. **14.21**

1 This provision applies equally to hackney carriages and reference should be made to Chapter 9, paras 9.28–9.29 for a detailed study of this point.

PROBLEMS ARISING FROM THE RULING IN *BENSON v BOYCE*

As a private hire vehicle is always a private hire vehicle, it must be driven by a person who is a licensed private hire driver. This has led to two areas of difficulty. **14.22**

Firstly, in relation to the testing of a vehicle, either for the MOT test or by the local authority. If there is a test conducted on the public highway, then the driver of the vehicle must be a licensed private hire driver. In areas where the local authority have their own testers, it would be possible to license them as private hire drivers, but, in areas where that is not the case, it would be impossible to license all possible testers of such vehicles. This can be compared to the situation pertaining to hackney carriages. A hackney carriage is always a hackney carriage[1] and must always be driven by a licensed hackney carriage driver. There is, however, one exception, introduced into section 46 of the Town Police Clauses Act 1847 ('the 1847 Act') by section 139(2) and paragraph 3 of Schedule 7 to the Transport Act 1985, which allows a hackney carriage to be driven by a person not holding a hackney carriage driver's licence, if the vehicle or the driver is being tested. This was introduced for hackney carriages to overcome this difficulty and a similar provision is required for private hire vehicles. However, *Hawkins v Edwards* was decided in 1901 and *Yates v Gates* dates back to 1970, and this **14.23** exception was not enacted until 1985. It is hoped that Parliament will act to rectify this situation for private hire vehicles and drivers before a similar length of time elapses. The Home Office has consulted on this issue, but at the time of writing there is no indication as to the outcome of their activity.

1 *Hawkins v Edwards* [1901] 2 KB 169; *Yates v Gates* [1970] 1 All ER 754, QBD.

14.24 In the meantime, what are the options open to overcome the difficulty? If it is accepted that licensing the testers is impossible or, at best, not practicable, then the alternative is to consider the vehicle licence itself. It would be possible to suspend the vehicle licence under section 60(1)(c) of the 1976 Act for the duration of the test, thereby allowing a non-licensed driver to drive the vehicle without contravening section 46(1)(b) of the 1847 Act.

14.25 The second area of difficulty concerns the spouses or partners of licensed private hire drivers. As private hire vehicles are often used as a family vehicle when they are not working, it is necessary to consider the position of persons who may drive the vehicle during times that it is not working. Some authorities have decided to issue 'restricted' private hire drivers' licences. These do not allow the holder to drive a private hire vehicle when it is working, but do permit such a vehicle to be driven at other times. These authorities charge a lower fee for these licences. However, this does not seem possible as under section 53(2) of the 1976 Act, the local authority can only 'remit the whole or part of the fee in respect of a private hire vehicle' licence, not a driver's licence. Anyway, it is difficult to see why the local authority should wish to do so. Before such a 'restricted' licence can be granted, the same checks must be undertaken as for a full licence, as the local authority cannot grant a licence to anyone who does not fulfil the criteria in section 51(a) or (b) and, therefore, the cost to the local authority will be the same as for a full licence. It is suggested that it would be difficult to justify a complaint being made concerning the subsidy of these licences by either the other licence holders or the council itself. There seems to be no reason why such people should not apply for a 'normal' or 'full' private hire driver's licence. It will then be up to them to decide whether or not to use it to work the vehicle or simply to enable them to drive it when it is not working.

Appendices

Appendix I

Legislation

Town Police Clauses Act 1847

Hackney carriages

37. Commissioners may licence hackney carriages   And with respect to hackney carriages, be it enacted as follows:

The commissioners may from time to time licence to ply for hire within the prescribed distance, or if no distance prescribed, within five miles from the General Post Office of the city, town, or place to which the special Act refers, (which in that case shall be deemed the prescribed distance,) such number of hackney coaches or carriages of any kind or description adapted to the carriage of persons as they think fit.

Notes

Modification
Modified, in relation to hackney carriages, by the Transport Act 1985, s 16.

See Further
See further, in relation to a licensed taxi, licensed under this section, providing a local service under a special licence: the Local Services (Operation by Taxis) Regulations 1986, SI 1986/567.

38. What vehicles to be deemed hackney carriages   Every wheeled carriage, whatever may be its form or construction, used in standing or plying for hire in any street within the prescribed distance, and every carriage standing upon any street within the prescribed distance, having thereon any numbered plate required by this or the special Act to be fixed upon a hackney carriage, or having thereon any plate resembling or intended to resemble any such plate as aforesaid, shall be deemed to be a hackney carriage within the meaning of this Act; and in all proceedings at law or otherwise the term 'hackney carriage' shall be sufficient to describe any such carriage: Provided always, that no stage coach used for the purpose of standing or plying for passengers to be carried for hire at separate fares, and duly licensed for that purpose, and having thereon the proper numbered plates required by law to be placed on such stage coaches, shall be deemed to be a hackney carriage within the meaning of this Act.

40. Persons applying for licence to sign a requisition   Before any such licence is granted a requisition for the same, in such form as the commissioners from time to time provide for that purpose, shall be made and signed by the proprietor or one of the proprietors of the hackney carriage in respect of which such licence is applied for; and in every such requisition shall be truly stated the name and surname and place of abode of the person applying for such licence, and of every proprietor or part proprietor of such carriage, or person concerned, either solely or in partnership with any other person, in the keeping, employing, or letting to hire of such carriage; and any person who, on applying for such licence, states in such requisition the name of any person who is not a proprietor or part proprietor of such carriage, or who is not concerned as aforesaid in the keeping, employing, or letting to hire of such carriage, and also any person who wilfully omits to specify truly in such requisition as aforesaid the name of any person who is a proprietor or part proprietor of such carriage, or who is concerned as aforesaid in the keeping, employing, or letting to hire of such carriage, shall be liable to a penalty not exceeding [level 1 on the standard scale].

Notes

Amendment
Maximum penalty increased by the Criminal Justice Act 1967, s 92(1), Sch 3, Part I, and converted to a level on the standard scale by the Criminal Justice Act 1982, ss 37, 38, 46.

41. What shall be specified in the licences   In every such licence shall be specified the name and surname and place of abode of every person who is a proprietor or part proprietor of the hackney carriage in respect of which such licence is granted, or who is concerned, either solely or in partnership with any other person, in the keeping, employing, or letting to hire of any such carriage, and also the number of such licence which shall correspond with the number to be painted or marked on the plates to be fixed on such carriage, together with such other particulars as the commissioners think fit.

42. Licences to be registered   Every licence shall be made out by the clerk of the commissioners, and duly entered in a book to be provided by him for that purpose; and in such book shall be contained columns or places for entries to be made of every offence committed by any proprietor or driver or person attending such carriage; and any person may at any reasonable time inspect such book, without fee or reward.

43. Licence to be in force for one year only   Every licence so to be granted shall be under the common seal of the commissioners, if incorporated, or, if not incorporated, shall be signed by two or more of the commissioners, and shall not include more than one carriage so licensed, and shall be in force for one year only from the day of the date of such licence or until the next general licensing meeting, in case any general licensing day be appointed by the commissioners.

44. Notice to be given by proprietors of hackney carriages of any change of abode   So often as any person named in any such licence as the proprietor or one of the proprietors, or as being concerned, either solely or in partnership with any person, in the keeping, employing, or letting to hire of any such carriage, changes his place of abode, he shall, within seven days next after such change, give notice thereof in writing, signed by him, to the commissioners, specifying in such notice his new place of abode; and he shall at the same time produce such licence at the office of the commissioners, who shall by their clerk, or some other officer, endorse thereon and sign a memorandum specifying the particulars of such change; and any person named in any such licence as aforesaid as the proprietor, or one of the proprietors, of any hackney carriage, or as being concerned as aforesaid, who changes his place of abode and neglects or wilfully omits to give notice of such change, or to produce such licence in order that such memorandum as aforesaid may be endorsed thereon, within the time and in the manner limited and directed by this or the special Act, shall be liable to a penalty not exceeding [level 1 on the standard scale].

Notes

Amendment
Maximum penalty increased by the Criminal Law Act 1977, s 31(6), and converted to a level on the standard scale by the Criminal Justice Act 1982, ss 37, 46.

45. Penalty for plying for hire without a licence   If the proprietor or part proprietor of any carriage, or any person so concerned as aforesaid, permits the same to be used as a hackney carriage plying for hire within the prescribed distance without having obtained a licence as aforesaid for such carriage, or during the time that such licence is suspended as hereinafter provided, or if any person be found driving, standing, or plying for hire with any carriage within the prescribed distance for which such licence as aforesaid has not been previously obtained, or without having the number of such carriage corresponding with the number of the licence openly displayed on such carriage, every such person so offending shall for every such offence be liable to a penalty not exceeding [level 4 on the standard scale].

Notes

Amendment
Maximum penalty on any conviction increased and converted to a level on the standard scale by the Criminal Justice Act 1982, ss 37, 39, 46, Sch 3.

46. Drivers not to act without first obtaining a licence No person shall act as driver of any hackney carriage licensed in pursuance of this or the special Act to ply for hire within the prescribed distance without first obtaining a licence from the commissioners, which licence shall be registered by the clerk to the commissioners, [and such fee as the commissioners may determine shall be paid] for the same; and every such licence shall be in force until the same is revoked except during the time that the same may be suspended as after mentioned.

Notes

Amendment
Words in square brackets substituted by the Local Government, Planning and Land Act 1980, s 1(6), Sch 6.

47. Penalty on drivers acting without licence, or proprietors employing unlicensed drivers If any person acts as such driver as aforesaid without having obtained such licence, or during the time that his licence is suspended, or if he lend or part with his licence, except to the proprietor of the hackney carriage, or if the proprietor of any such hackney carriage employ any person as the driver thereof who has not obtained such licence, or during the time that his licence is suspended, as herein-after provided, every such driver and every such proprietor shall for every such offence respectively be liable to a penalty not exceeding [level 3 on the standard scale].

Notes

Amendment
Enhanced penalty on a subsequent conviction abolished, maximum penalty on any conviction increased and converted to a level on the standard scale by the Criminal Justice Act 1982, ss 35, 37, 38, 46.

48. Proprietor to retain licences of drivers, and to produce the same before justices on complaint In every case in which the proprietor of any such hackney carriage permits or employs any licensed person to act as the driver thereof, such proprietor shall cause to be delivered to him, and shall retain in his possession, the licence of such driver, while such driver remains in his employ; and in all cases of complaint, where the proprietor of a hackney carriage is summoned to attend before a justice, or to produce the driver, the proprietor so summoned shall also produce the licence of such driver, if he be then in his employ; and if any driver complained of be adjudged guilty of the offence alleged against him, such justice shall make an endorsement upon the licence of such driver, stating the nature of the offence and amount of the penalty inflicted; and if any such proprietor neglect to have delivered to him and to retain in his possession the licence of any driver while such driver remains in his employ, or if he refuse or neglect to produce such licence as aforesaid, such proprietor shall for every such offence be liable to a penalty not exceeding [level 1 on the standard scale].

Amendment
Maximum penalty increased by the Criminal Law Act 1977, s 31(6), and converted to a level
on the standard scale by the Criminal Justice Act 1982, ss 37, 46.

49. Proprietor to return licence to drivers except in case of misconduct
When any driver leaves the service of the proprietor by whom he is employed without having been guilty of any misconduct, such proprietor shall forthwith return to
such driver the licence belonging to him; but if such driver have been guilty of any
misconduct, the proprietor shall not return his licence, but shall give him notice of
the complaint which he intends to prefer against him, and shall forthwith summon
such driver to appear before any justice to answer the said complaint; and such justice, having the necessary parties before him, shall inquire into and determine the
matter of complaint, and if upon inquiry it appear that the licence of such driver has
been improperly withheld, such justice shall direct the immediate re-delivery of such
licence, and award such sum of money as he thinks proper to be paid by such proprietor to such driver by way of compensation.

50. Revocation of licences of proprietors or drivers   The commissioners may,
upon the conviction for the second time of the proprietor or driver of any such
hackney carriage for any offence under the provisions of this or the special Act with
respect to hackney carriages, or any byelaw made in pursuance thereof, suspend or
revoke, as they deem right, the licence of any such proprietor or driver.

**51. Number of persons to be carried in a hackney carriage to be painted
thereon**   *No hackney carriage shall be used or employed or let to hire, or shall stand or
ply for hire, within the prescribed distance, unless the number of persons to be carried by
such hackney carriage, in words at length, and in form following, (that is to say,) "To
carry .... persons," be painted on a plate placed on some conspicuous place on the outside of such carriage, and in legible letters, so as to be clearly distinguishable from the
colour of the ground whereon the same are painted, one inch in length, and of a proportionate breadth; and the driver of any such hackney carriage shall not be required to carry
in or by such hackney carriage a greater number of persons than the number painted
thereon.*

Notes

Amendment
Repealed, in relation to tramcars and trolley vehicles, by the Transport Charges &c
(Miscellaneous Provisions) Act 1954, ss 14(1), 15(2), Sch 2, Part IV.

**52. Penalty for neglect to exhibit the number, or for refusal to carry the pre-
scribed number**   *If the proprietor of any hackney carriage permit the same to be used,
employed, or let to hire, or if any person stand or ply for hire with such carriage, without
having the number of persons to be carried thereby painted and exhibited in manner aforesaid, or if the driver of any such hackney carriage refuse, when required by the hirer thereof,
to carry in or by such hackney carriage the number of persons painted thereon, or any less
number, every proprietor or driver so offending shall be liable to a penalty not exceeding
[level 1 on the standard scale].*

Notes

Amendment
Repealed, in relation to tramcars and trolley vehicles, by the Transport Charges &c
(Miscellaneous Provisions) Act 1954, ss 14(1), 15(2), Sch 2, Part IV.
Maximum penalty increased by the Criminal Law Act 1977, s 31(6), and converted to a level
on the standard scale by the Criminal Justice Act 1982, ss 37, 46.

Modification

Modified, in relation to the taxi code, by the Licensed Taxis (Hiring at Separate Fares) Order 1986, SI 1986/1386, art 4.

53. Penalty on driver for refusing to drive A driver of a hackney carriage standing at any of the stands for hackney carriages appointed by the commissioners, or in any street, who refuses or neglects, without reasonable excuse, to drive such carriage to any place within the prescribed distance, or the distance to be appointed by any byelaw of the commissioners, not exceeding the prescribed distance, to which he is directed to drive by the person hiring or wishing to hire such carriage, shall for every such offence be liable to a penalty not exceeding [level 2 on the standard scale].

Notes

Amendment

Maximum penalty increased and converted to a level on the standard scale by the Criminal Justice Act 1982, ss 37, 39, 46, Sch 3.

Modification

Modified, in relation to the taxi code, by the Licensed Taxis (Hiring at Separate Fares) Order 1986, SI 1986/1386, art 4.

54. Penalty for demanding more than the sum agreed for If the proprietor or driver of any such hackney carriage, or if any other person on his behalf, agree beforehand with any person hiring such hackney carriage to take for any job a sum less than the fare allowed by this or the special Act, or any byelaw made thereunder, such proprietor or driver shall be liable to a penalty not exceeding [level 1 on the standard scale] if he exact or demand for such job more than the fare so agreed upon.

Notes

Amendment

Maximum penalty increased by the Criminal Law Act 1977, s 31(6), and converted to a level on the standard scale by the Criminal Justice Act 1982, ss 37, 46.

Modification

Modified, in relation to the taxi code, by the Licensed Taxis (Hiring at Separate Fares) Order 1986, SI 1986/1386, art 4.

55. Agreement to pay more than the legal fare No agreement whatever made with the driver, or with any person having or pretending to have the care of any such hackney carriage, for the payment of more than the fare allowed by any byelaw made under this or the special Act, shall be binding on the person making the same; and any such person may, notwithstanding such agreement, refuse, on discharging such hackney carriage, to pay any sum beyond the fare allowed as aforesaid; and if any person actually pay to the driver of any such hackney carriage, whether in pursuance of any such agreement or otherwise, any sum exceeding the fare to which such driver was entitled, the person paying the same shall be entitled, on complaint made against such driver before any justice of the peace, to recover back the sum paid beyond the proper fare, and moreover such driver shall be liable to a penalty for such exaction not exceeding [level 3 on the standard scale]; and in default of the repayment by such driver of such excess of fare, or of payment of the said penalty, such justice shall forthwith commit such driver to prison, there to remain for any time not exceeding one month, unless the said excess of fare and the said penalty be sooner paid.

Notes

Amendment
Maximum penalty increased and converted to a level on the standard scale by the Criminal Justice Act 1982, ss 37, 39, 46, Sch 3.

Modification
Modified, in relation to the taxi code, by the Licensed Taxis (Hiring at Separate Fares) Order 1986, SI 1986/1386, art 4.

56. Agreements to carry passengers a discretionary distance for a fixed sum
If the proprietor or driver of any such hackney carriage, or if any other person on his behalf, agree with any person to carry in or by such hackney carriage persons not exceeding in number the number so painted on such carriage as aforesaid, for a distance to be in the discretion of such proprietor or driver, and for a sum agreed upon, such proprietor or driver shall be liable to a penalty not exceeding [level 1 on the standard scale] if the distance which he carries such persons be under that to which they were entitled to be carried for the sum so agreed upon, according to the fare allowed by this or the special Act, or any byelaw made in pursuance thereof.

Notes

Amendment
Maximum penalty increased by the Criminal Law Act 1977, s 31(6), and converted to a level on the standard scale by the Criminal Justice Act 1982, ss 37, 46.

Modification
Modified, in relation to the taxi code, by the Licensed Taxis (Hiring at Separate Fares) Order 1986, SI 1986/1386, art 4.

57. Deposit to be made for carriages required to wait   When any hackney carriage is hired and taken to any place, and the driver thereof is required by the hirer there to wait with such hackney carriage, such driver may demand and receive from such hirer his fare for driving to such place, and also a sum equal to the fare of such carriage for the period, as a deposit over and above such fare, during which he is required to wait as aforesaid, or if no fare for time be fixed by the byelaws, then the sum of [7p] for every half hour during which he is so required to wait, which deposit shall be accounted for by such driver when such hackney carriage is finally discharged by such hirer; and if any such driver who has received any such deposit as aforesaid refuses to wait as aforesaid, or goes away or permits such hackney carriage to be driven or taken away without the consent of such hirer, before the expiration of the time for which such deposit was made, or if such driver on the final discharge of such hackney carriage refuse duly to account for such deposit, every such driver so offending shall be liable to a penalty not exceeding [level 1 on the standard scale].

Notes

Amendment
First sum in square brackets substituted by the Decimal Currency Act 1969, s 10, rounded down to 7p in consequence of the abolition of the halfpenny, by Proclamation dated 31 December 1984; maximum penalty increased by the Criminal Law Act 1977, s 31(6), and converted to a level on the standard scale by the Criminal Justice Act 1982, ss 37, 46.

Modification
Modified, in relation to the taxi code, by the Licensed Taxis (Hiring at Separate Fares) Order 1986, SI 1986/1386, art 4.

58. Penalty on proprietors, etc convicted of overcharging   Every proprietor or driver of any such hackney carriage who is convicted of taking as a fare a greater sum than is authorized by any byelaw made under this or the special Act shall be liable to a penalty not exceeding [level 3 on the standard scale], and such penalty may be recovered before one justice; and in the conviction of such proprietor or driver an order may be included for payment of the sum so overcharged, over and above the penalty and costs; and such overcharge shall be returned to the party aggrieved . . .

Notes

Amendment
Maximum penalty increased and converted to a level on the standard scale by the Criminal Justice Act 1982, ss 37, 39, 46, Sch 3; words omitted repealed by the Statute Law Revision Act 1894.

Modification
Modified, in relation to the taxi code, by the Licensed Taxis (Hiring at Separate Fares) Order 1986, SI 1986/1386, art 4.

59. Penalty for permitting persons to ride without consent of hirer Any proprietor or driver of any such hackney carriage which is hired who permits or suffers any person to be carried in or upon or about such hackney carriage during such hire, without the express consent of the person hiring the same, shall be liable to a penalty not exceeding [level 1 on the standard scale].

Notes

Amendment
Maximum penalty increased by the Criminal Law Act 1977, s 31(6), and converted to a level on the standard scale by the Criminal Justice Act 1982, ss 37, 46.

Modification
Modified, in relation to the taxi code, by the Licensed Taxis (Hiring at Separate Fares) Order 1986, SI 1986/1386, art 4.

60. No unauthorized person to act as driver No person authorized by the proprietor of any hackney carriage to act as driver of such carriage shall suffer any other person to act as driver of such carriage without the consent of the proprietor thereof; and no person, whether licensed or not, shall act as driver of any such carriage without the consent of the proprietor; and any person so suffering another person to act as driver, and any person so acting as driver without such consent as aforesaid, shall be liable to a penalty not exceeding [level 1 on the standard scale] for every such offence.

Notes

Amendment
Maximum penalty increased by the Criminal Law Act 1977, s 31(6), and converted to a level on the standard scale by the Criminal Justice Act 1982, ss 37, 46.

61. Penalty on drivers for drunkenness, furious driving, etc If the driver or any other person having or pretending to have the care of any such hackney carriage be intoxicated while driving, or if any such driver or other person by wanton and furious driving, or by any other wilful misconduct, injure or endanger any person in his life, limbs, or property, he shall be liable to a penalty not exceeding [level 1 on the standard scale]; . . .

Notes

Amendment
Maximum penalty increased by the Criminal Law Act 1977, s 31(6), and converted to a level on the standard scale by the Criminal Justice Act 1982, ss 37, 46; words omitted repealed by the Statute Law (Repeals) Act 1989.

62. Penalties in case of carriages being unattended at places of public resort
If the driver of any such hackney carriage leave it in any street or at any place of
public resort or entertainment, whether it be hired or not, without some one proper
to take care of it, any constable may drive away such hackney carriage and deposit it,
and the horse or horses harnessed thereto, at some neighbouring livery stable or
other place of safe custody; and such driver shall be liable to a penalty not exceeding [level 1 on the standard scale] for such offence; and in default of payment of the
said penalty upon conviction, and of the expences of taking and keeping the said
hackney carriage and horse or horses, the same, together with the harness belonging
thereto, or any of them, shall be sold by order of the justice before whom such conviction is made, and after deducting from the produce of such sale the amount of the
said penalty, and of all costs and expences, as well of the proceedings before such justice as of the taking, keeping, and sale of the said hackney carriage, and of the said
horse or horses and harness, the surplus (if any) of the said produce shall be paid to
the proprietor of such hackney carriage.

Notes

Amendment
Maximum penalty increased by the Criminal Law Act 1977, s 31(6), and converted to a level
on the standard scale by the Criminal Justice Act 1982, ss 37, 46.

63. Compensation for damage done by driver   In every case in which any hurt
or damage has been caused to any person or property as aforesaid by the driver of
any carriage let to hire, the justice before whom such driver has been convicted may
direct that the proprietor of such carriage shall pay such a sum, not exceeding five
pounds, as appears to the justice a reasonable compensation for such hurt or
damage; and every proprietor who pays any such compensation as aforesaid may
recover the same from the driver, and such compensation shall be recoverable from
such proprietor, and by him from such driver, as damages.

64. Penalty on drivers obstructing other drivers   Any driver of any hackney
carriage who suffers the same to stand for hire across any street or alongside of any
other hackney carriage, or who refuses to give way, if he conveniently can, to any
other carriage, or who obstructs or hinders the driver of any other carriage in taking
up or setting down any person into or from such other carriage, or who wrongfully
in a forcible manner prevents or endeavours to prevent the driver of any other hackney carriage from being hired, shall be liable to a penalty not exceeding [level 1 on
the standard scale].

Notes

Amendment
Maximum penalty increased by the Criminal Law Act 1977, s 31(6), and converted to a level
on the standard scale by the Criminal Justice Act 1982, ss 37, 46.

65. Compensation to drivers attending to answer complaints not substantiated
If the driver of any such hackney carriage be summoned or brought before any justice to answer any complaint or information touching or concerning any offence
alleged to have been committed by such driver against the provisions of this or the
special Act, or any byelaw made thereunder, and such complaint or information be
afterwards withdrawn or quashed or dismissed, or if such driver be acquitted of the
offence charged against him, the said justice, if he think fit, may order the complainant or informant to pay to the said driver such compensation for his loss of time
in attending the said justice touching or concerning such complaint or information
as to the said justice seems reasonable; . . .

Notes

Amendment
Words omitted repealed by the Statute Law (Repeals) Act 1989.

66. Fare unpaid may be recovered as a penalty   If any person refuse to pay on demand to any proprietor or driver of any hackney carriage the fare allowed by this or the special Act, or any byelaw made thereunder, such fare may, together with costs, be recovered before one justice as a penalty.

67. *(Repealed by the Criminal Damage Act 1971, s 11(8), Schedule, Part I.)*

68. Byelaws for regulating hackney carriages   The commissioners may from time to time (subject to the restrictions of this and the special Act) make byelaws for all or any of the purposes following; (that is to say,)

For regulating the conduct of the proprietors and drivers of hackney carriages plying within the prescribed distance in their several employments, and determining whether such drivers shall wear any and what badges, and for regulating the hours within which they may exercise their calling:

For regulating the manner in which the number of each carriage, corresponding with the number of its licence, shall be displayed:

For regulating *the number of persons to be carried by such hackney carriages, and in what manner such number is to be shown on such carriage, and* what number of horses or other animals is to draw the same, and the placing of check strings to the carriages, and the holding of the same by the driver, and how such hackney carriages are to be furnished or provided:

For fixing the stands of such hackney carriages, and the distance to which they may be compelled to take passengers, not exceeding the prescribed distance:

For fixing the rates or fares, as well for time as distance, to be paid for such hackney carriages within the prescribed distance, and for securing the due publication of such fares:

For securing the safe custody and re-delivery of any property accidentally left in hackney carriages, and fixing the charges to be made in respect thereof.

Notes

Amendment
Words from 'the number' to 'such carriage, and' repealed, in relation to tramcars or trolley vehicles, by the Transport Charges &c (Miscellaneous Provisions) Act 1954, ss 14(1), 15(2), Sch 2, Part IV.

Modification
Modified, in relation to the taxi code, by the Licensed Taxis (Hiring at Separate Fares) Order 1986, SI 1986/1386, art 4.

Public Health Act 1875

Part IV
Local Government Provisions

Police Regulations

171. Incorporation of certain provisions of 10 & 11 Vict c 89 The provisions of the Town Police Clauses Act 1847, with respect to the following matters, (namely,)

(1) With respect to obstructions and nuisances in the streets; and
(2) With respect to fires; and
(3) With respect to places of public resort; and
(4) With respect to hackney carriages; . . .

shall, for the purpose of regulating such matters in urban districts, be incorporated with this Act,

The expression in the provisions so incorporated 'the superintendent constable,' and the expression 'any constable or other officer appointed by virtue of this or the special Act', shall, for the purposes of this Act, respectively include any superintendent of police, and any constable or officer of police acting for or in the district of any urban authority; and the expression 'within the prescribed distance' shall for the purposes of this Act mean within any urban district.

Notwithstanding anything in the provisions so incorporated, a license granted to the driver of any hackney carriage in pursuance thereof shall be in force for one year only from the date of the license, or until the next general licensing meeting where a day for such meeting is appointed.

Notes

Amendment
Words omitted repealed by the Public Health Act 1936, s 346, Sch 3, Part I.

Extent
This Act does not extend to Scotland.

Town Police Clauses Act 1889

3. Defining 'omnibus'

The term 'omnibus,' where used in this Act, shall include:

Every omnibus, char-à-banc, wagonette, brake, stage coach, and other carriage plying or standing for hire by or used to carry passengers at separate fares, to, from, or in any part of the prescribed distance;

but shall not include:

Any tramcar or tram carriage . . .:

Any carriage starting from and previously hired for the particular passengers thereby carried at any livery stable yard (within the prescribed distance) whereat horses are stabled and carriages let for hire, the said carriage starting from the said stable yard and being bonâ fide the property of the occupier thereof, and not standing or plying for hire within the prescribed distance:

Any omnibus belonging to or hired or used by any railway company for conveying passengers and their luggage to or from any railway station of that company, and not standing or plying for hire within the prescribed distance:

Any omnibus starting from outside the prescribed distance, and bringing passengers within the prescribed distance, and not standing or plying for hire within the prescribed distance.

Notes

Amendment
Words omitted repealed by the Transport and Works Act 1992, s 68(1), Sch 4, Pt I.
Date in force: 26 February 1998: see SI 1998/274, art 2.

4. Extending certain provisions of principal Act to omnibuses (1) The several terms 'hackney carriages', 'hackney coach', 'carriages', and 'carriage', whenever used in sections thirty-seven, forty to fifty-two (both inclusive), fifty-four, fifty-eight, and sixty to sixty-seven (both inclusive) of the principal Act shall, notwithstanding anything contained in section thirty-eight of that Act, be deemed to include every omnibus.

(2) The word 'driver' or 'drivers' when used in any of the said sections of the principal Act shall be deemed to include every conductor of any omnibus.

(3) For the purposes of sections fifty-four, fifty-eight, and sixty-six of the principal Act, the fare, according to the statement of fares exhibited on any omnibus, shall be deemed to be the fare allowed by the principal Act or authorised by any byelaw under that Act.

5. Licences may be granted for short periods Any licence may be granted under the principal Act to continue in force for such less period than one year as the Commissioners may think fit, and shall specify in the licence.

6. Byelaws The Commissioners may from time to time make byelaws for all or any of the following purposes, that is to say—

For regulating the conduct of the proprietors, drivers, and conductors of omnibuses plying within the prescribed distance in their several employments, and determining whether such drivers and conductors shall wear any and what badges:

For regulating the manner in which the number of each omnibus corresponding with the number of its licence shall be displayed:

. . .

For regulating the number and securing the fitness of the animals to be allowed to draw an omnibus, and for the removal therefrom of unfit animals:

For securing the fitness of the omnibus and the harness of the animals drawing the same:

For fixing the stands for omnibuses and the points at which they may stop a longer time than is necessary for the taking up and setting down of passengers desirous of entering or leaving the same:

For securing the safe custody and re-delivery of any property accidentally left in any omnibus, and fixing the charge to be made in respect thereof;

To provide for the carrying and the lighting of proper lamps for denoting the direction in which the omnibus is proceeding, and promoting the safety and convenience of the passengers carried thereby:

To provide for the exhibition on some conspicuous part of every omnibus of a statement in legible letters and figures of the fares to be demanded and received from the persons using or carried for hire in such omnibus:

To prevent within the prescribed distance—

(*a*) the owner, driver, or conductor of any omnibus, or any other person on their or his behalf, by touting, calling out, or otherwise, from importuning any person to use or to be carried for hire in such omnibus, to the annoyance of such person or of any other person;

(*b*) the blowing of or playing upon horns or other musical instruments, or the ringing of bells, by the driver or conductor of any omnibus, or by any person travelling on or using any such omnibus.

Provided that nothing in this Act contained shall empower the Commissioners to fix the site of the stand of any omnibus in any railway station, or in any yard adjoining or connecting therewith, except with the consent of the railway company owning such site.

Notes

Amendment
Words omitted repealed by the Transport Charges, etc (Miscellaneous Provisions) Act 1954, s 14(1), Sch 2, Part IV.

Public Health Act 1936

Appeals and other applications to courts of summary jurisdiction, and appeals to the [Crown Court]

Notes

Amendment
Words in square brackets substituted by virtue of the Courts Act 1971, s 56(2), Sch 9, Part I.

300. Appeals and applications to courts of summary jurisdiction (1) Where any enactment in this Act provides—

- (*a*) for an appeal to a court of summary jurisdiction against a requirement, refusal or other decision of a council; or
- (*b*) for any matter to be determined by, or an application in respect of any matter to be made to, a court of summary jurisdiction,

the procedure shall be by way of complaint for an order, and the Summary Jurisdiction Acts shall apply to the proceedings.

(2) The time within which any such appeal may be brought shall be twenty-one days from the date on which notice of the council's requirement, refusal or other decision was served upon the person desiring to appeal, and for the purposes of this subsection the making of the complaint shall be deemed to be the bringing of the appeal.

(3) In any case where such an appeal lies, the document notifying to the person concerned the decision of the council in the matter shall state the right of appeal to a court of summary jurisdiction and the time within which such an appeal may be brought.

Notes

Extent
This Act does not extend to Scotland.

301. Appeals to [Crown Court] against decisions of justices   Subject as hereinafter provided, where a person aggrieved by any order, determination or other decision of a court of summary jurisdiction under this Act is not by any other enactment authorised to appeal to [the Crown Court], he may appeal to such a court:

Provided that nothing in this section shall be construed as conferring a right of appeal from the decision of a court of summary jurisdiction in any case if each of the parties concerned might under this Act have required that the dispute should be determined by arbitration instead of by such a court.

Notes

Amendment
Section heading: words in square brackets substituted by virtue of the Courts Act 1971, s 56(2), Sch 9, Part I.
Words in square brackets substituted by the Courts Act 1971, s 56(2), Sch 9, Part I.

Extent

This Act does not extend to Scotland.

302. Effect of decision of court upon an appeal   Where upon an appeal under this Act a court varies or reverses any decision of a council, it shall be the duty of the council to give effect to the order of the court and, in particular, to grant or issue any necessary consent, certificate or other document, and to make any necessary entry in any register.

Notes

Extent

This Act does not extend to Scotland.

Local Government Act 1972

SCHEDULE 14
Amendment and Modification of Public Health Acts, Etc

Section 180

Part I
The Public Health Act 1936

1. . . .

2. Any reference to an urban authority or rural authority shall be construed as a reference to a local authority.

3. . . .

4. Without prejudice to paragraph 2 above, the following provisions, that is to say, sections . . . *79, 80,* . . . 263 and 264 shall apply throughout the district of every local authority.

5–17. . . .

18. The powers conferred by Part VIII on local authorities within the meaning of the Public Health Act 1936 shall be exercisable not only by such authorities but also by all local authorities within the meaning of this Act, whether or not they are local authorities within the meaning of that Act, and references in that Part to a local authority shall be construed accordingly.

19. All directions in force under section 267(1)(c) immediately before 1st April 1974 shall cease to have effect.

20. Any reference in section 278 to a local authority shall include a reference to a county council . . .

21, 22. . . .

Notes

Amendment
Paras 1, 3, 9, 21, 22,: amend the Public Health Act 1936.
Para 4: first words omitted repealed by the Building Act 1984, s 133(2), Sch 7; words in italics prospectively repealed by the Control of Pollution Act 1974, s 108, Sch 4, as from a day to be appointed; second words omitted repealed by the Environmental Protection Act 1990, s 162, Sch 16, Part III.
Paras 5–8: repealed by the Control of Pollution Act 1974, s 108, Sch 4.
Para 10: repealed by the Building Act 1984, s 133(2), Sch 7.
Paras 11, 12: repealed by the Environmental Protection Act 1990, s 162, Sch 16, Part III.
Paras 13–16: repealed by the Public Health (Control of Disease) Act 1984, s 78, Sch 3.
Para 17: repealed by the National Health Service Reorganisation Act 1973, s 57, Sch 5.
Para 20: words omitted repealed by the Local Government Act 1985, s 102, Sch 17.

Modification
Modified by the Waste Regulation and Disposal (Authorities) Order 1985, SI 1985/1884, art 5, Sch 2.

Extent
This Schedule does not extend to Scotland.

Part II
Other Enactments

Public Health Acts 1875 to 1925

23. Subject to the following provisions of this Schedule and the provisions of Schedule 26 to this Act, all the provisions of the Public Health Acts 1875 to 1925 shall extend throughout England and Wales, whether or not they so extended immediately before 1st April 1974.

24. Paragraph 23 above shall not apply to the following enactments, that is to say—

(a) so much of section 160 of the Public Health Act 1875 as incorporates the provisions of the Towns Improvement Clauses Act 1847 with respect to the naming of streets (hereafter in this Schedule referred to as 'the original street-naming enactment');

(b) section 171(4) of the said Act of 1875;

(c) . . .

(d) sections 21, 82, 83, and 85 of the Public Health Acts Amendment Act 1907; and

(e) sections 17 to 19 and 76 of the Public Health Act 1925;

and those enactments shall, subject to paragraph 25 below, apply to those areas, and only those, to which they applied immediately before 1st April 1974.

25. (1) Subject to sub-paragraphs (2) and (4) below, a local authority may after giving the requisite notice resolve that any of the enactments mentioned in paragraph 24 above shall apply throughout their area or shall cease to apply throughout their area (whether or not, in either case, the enactment applies only to part of their area).

(2) A resolution under this paragraph disapplying—

(a) section 171(4) of the Public Health Act 1875;

(b) . . .

(c) section 82, 83 or 85 of the Public Health Acts Amendment Act 1907; or

(d) section 76 of the Public Health Act 1925;

must be passed before 1st April 1975, but any other resolution under this paragraph may be passed at any time.

(3) A resolution under this paragraph applying either of the following provisions, that is to say, section 21 of the said Act of 1907 or section 18 of the said Act of 1925, throughout an area shall have effect as a resolution disapplying the other provision throughout that area and a resolution under this paragraph applying either of the following provisions, that is to say, the original street-naming enactment or section 19 of the said Act of 1925, throughout an area shall have effect as a resolution disapplying the other provision throughout that area.

(4) A resolution under this paragraph applying or disapplying section 171(4) of the Public Health Act 1875 throughout an area shall not have effect unless approved by the Secretary of State.

(5) The notice which is requisite for a resolution given under sub-paragraph (1) above is a notice:

(a) given by the local authority in question of their intention to pass the resolution given by advertisement in two consecutive weeks in a local newspaper circulating in their area; and

(b) served, not later than the date on which the advertisement is first published, on the council of every parish or community whose area, or part of whose area, is affected by the resolution or, in the case of a parish so affected but not having a parish council (whether separate or common), on the chairman of the parish meeting.

(6) The date on which a resolution under this paragraph is to take effect shall—

(a) except in the case of a resolution applying or disapplying section 171(4) of the Public Health Act 1875 throughout any area, be a date specified therein, being not earlier than one month after the date of the resolution; and

(b) in the said excepted case, be a date specified in the Secretary of State's approval of the resolution.

(7) A copy of a resolution of a local authority under this paragraph, certified in writing to be a true copy by the proper officer of the authority, shall in all legal proceedings be received as evidence of the resolution having been passed by the authority.

26. The following enactments shall not extend to Greater London, that is to say—

(a) sections 160 and 171 of the Public Health Act 1875;

(b) . . .

(c) sections 21 and 80 of the Public Health Acts Amendment Act 1907 and so much of section 81 of that Act as relates to the Town Police Clauses Act 1847;

(d) sections 17 to 19, 75 and 76 of the Public Health Act 1925.

27. (1) The powers conferred on certain authorities by the enactments to which this paragraph applies shall be exercisable not only by those authorities, but also by all local authorities within the meaning of this Act, whether or not they are local authorities for the purposes of the Public Health Acts 1875 to 1925, and references in those enactments to an urban authority or a local authority shall be construed accordingly.

(2) This paragraph applies to the following enactments, that is to say—

(a) section 164 of the Public Health Act 1875;

(b) section 44 of the Public Health Acts Amendment Act 1890;

(c) Part VI of the Public Health Acts Amendment Act 1907, as amended by Part VI of the Public Health Act 1925.

28. A district council [or, where they are not the highway authority, the council of a Welsh principal area] shall not without the consent of the highway authority—

(a) provide a clock under section 165 of the Public Health Act 1875 in a case where it overhangs a highway; or

(b) exercise any power under section 40 or 42 of the Public Health Acts Amendment Act 1890 or section 14 or 75 of the Public Health Act 1925 in relation to a highway.

29. A highway authority who are not a local authority within the meaning of the Public Health Acts 1875 to 1925 may exercise concurrently with the local authority powers conferred on the latter by section 153 of the Public Health Act 1875.

30. Any reference in section 161 of the said Act of 1875 to an urban authority shall, in relation to a metropolitan road within the meaning of the London Government Act 1963, be construed as a reference to the Greater London Council alone.

31. A local authority within the meaning of the Public Health Acts 1875 to 1925 may exercise the powers conferred by section 31 of the Public Health Acts Amendment Act 1907 without being empowered by an order made by the Secretary of State.

32. So much of section 76 of the said Act of 1907 as enables the Secretary of State to make rules governing the exercise by local authorities of their powers under that section shall cease to have effect.

33, 34. . . .

The Public Health Act 1961

35, 36. . . .

37. The powers conferred on a local authority by section 34 of that Act shall as respects England be exercisable also by a county council and references in that section to a local authority shall be construed accordingly.

38, 39. . . .

40. The powers conferred on a local authority by sections 44 and 46 of that Act shall, in the case of a street outside Greater London which is a highway, be exercisable by the highway authority as well as by the local authority.

41. . . .

42. The powers conferred by sections 52 to 54 of that Act on local authorities shall be exercisable not only by such authorities, but also by all local authorities within the meaning of this Act, whether or not they are local authorities within the meaning of that Act, and references in those sections to a local authority shall be construed accordingly.

43–49. . . .

Notes

Amendment
Paras 24–26: words omitted repealed by the Local Government (Miscellaneous Provisions) Act 1982, s 47, Sch 7, Part I.
Para 28: words in square brackets inserted by the Local Government (Wales) Act 1994, s 66(5), Sch 15, para 63.
Para 33: amends the Public Health Act 1925, s 16(1).
Para 34: amends the Parish Councils Act 1957, s 3(1).
Paras 35, 36: amend the Public Health Act 1961.
Paras 38, 39, 46, 47: repealed by the Public Health (Control of Disease) Act 1984, s 78, Sch 3.
Para 41: repealed by the Litter Act 1983, s 12(3), Sch 2.
Para 43: repealed by the Local Government Act 1985, s 102, Sch 17.
Para 44: amends the Local Government Act 1966, s 10.
Para 45: repealed by the Refuse Disposal (Amenity) Act 1978, s 12(2), Sch 2.
Para 48: repealed by the National Health Service Reorganisation Act 1973, s 57, Sch 5.
Para 49: amends the Deposit of Poisonous Waste Act 1972, s 5; prospectively repealed by the Control of Pollution Act 1974, s 108, Sch 4, as from a day to be appointed.

Extent
This Schedule does not extend to Scotland.

Rehabilitation of Offenders Act 1974

1. Rehabilitated persons and spent convictions   (1)   Subject to subsection (2) below, where an individual has been convicted, whether before or after the commencement of this Act, of any offence or offences, and the following conditions are satisfied, that is to say—

(a)   he did not have imposed on him in respect of that conviction a sentence which is excluded from rehabilitation under this Act; and

(b)   he has not had imposed on him in respect of a subsequent conviction during the rehabilitation period applicable to the first-mentioned conviction in accordance with section 6 below a sentence which is excluded from rehabilitation under this Act;

then, after the end of the rehabilitation period so applicable (including, where appropriate, any extension under section 6(4) below of the period originally applicable to the first-mentioned conviction) or, where that rehabilitation period ended before the commencement of this Act, after the commencement of this Act, that individual shall for the purposes of this Act be treated as a rehabilitated person in respect of the first-mentioned conviction and that conviction shall for those purposes be treated as spent.

(2)   A person shall not become a rehabilitated person for the purposes of this Act in respect of a conviction unless he has served or otherwise undergone or complied with any sentence imposed on him in respect of that conviction; but the following shall not, by virtue of this subsection, prevent a person from becoming a rehabilitated person for those purposes—

(a)   failure to pay a fine or other sum adjudged to be paid by or imposed on a conviction, or breach of a condition of a recognisance or of a bond of caution to keep the peace or be of good behaviour;

(b)   breach of any condition or requirement applicable in relation to a sentence which renders the person to whom it applies liable to be dealt with for the offence for which the sentence was imposed, or, where the sentence was a suspended sentence of imprisonment, liable to be dealt with in respect of that sentence (whether or not, in any case, he is in fact so dealt with);

(c)   failure to comply with any requirement of a suspended sentence supervision order.

[(d)   breach of any condition of a release supervision order made under section 16 of the Crime (Sentences) Act 1997.]

[(2A)   Where in respect of a conviction a person has been sentenced to imprisonment with an order under section 47(1) of the Criminal Law Act 1977, he is to be treated for the purposes of subsection (2) above as having served the sentence as soon as he completes service of so much of the sentence as was by that order required to be served in prison.]

(3)   In this Act 'sentence' includes any order made by a court in dealing with a person in respect of his conviction of any offence or offences, other than—

(a)   an order for committal or any other order made in default of payment of any fine or other sum adjudged to be paid by or imposed on a conviction, or for want of sufficient distress to satisfy any such fine or other sum;

(b)   an order dealing with a person in respect of a suspended sentence of imprisonment.

(4)   In this Act, references to a conviction, however expressed, include references—

(*a*)   to a conviction by or before a court outside Great Britain; and

(*b*)   to any finding (other than a finding linked with a finding of insanity) in any criminal proceedings . . . that a person has committed an offence or done the act or made the omission charged;

and notwithstanding anything in section 9 of the Criminal Justice (Scotland) Act 1949 or [section 1C] of the Powers of Criminal Courts Act 1973 (conviction of a person . . . discharged to be deemed not to be a conviction) a conviction in respect of which an order is made [discharging the person concerned] absolutely or conditionally shall be treated as a conviction for the purposes of this Act and the person in question may become a rehabilitated person in respect of that conviction and the conviction a spent conviction for those purposes accordingly.

Notes

Amendment
Sub-s (2): para (*d*) prospectively inserted by the Crime (Sentences) Act 1997, s 55, Sch 4, para 9(1), as from a day to be appointed.
Sub-s (2A): inserted by the Criminal Law Act 1977, s 47, Sch 9, para 11.
Sub-s (4): first words omitted repealed by the Children Act 1989, s 108(7), Sch 15; first and final words in square brackets substituted and second words omitted repealed, by the Criminal Justice Act 1991, ss 100, 101(2), Sch 11, para 20, Sch 13.

Modification
Modified by the Criminal Justice (Scotland) Act 1987, s 45(2), and the Criminal Justice Act 1988, s 170(1), Sch 15, para 47.

See Further
See further, in relation to the exclusion of confiscation orders made under the Drug Trafficking Act 1994 from the ambit of sub-s (2)(*a*) above: the Drug Trafficking Act 1994, s 65(2).
See further, in relation to the exclusion of confiscation orders made under the Proceeds of Crime (Scotland) Act 1995 from the ambit of sub-s (2)(*a*) above: the Proceeds of Crime (Scotland) Act 1995, s 47(2).

2. Rehabilitation of persons dealt with in service disciplinary proceedings
(1) . . . , for the purposes of this Act any finding that a person is guilty of an offence in respect of any act or omission which was the subject of service disciplinary proceedings shall be treated as a conviction and any punishment awarded [or order made by virtue of Schedule 5A to the Army Act 1955 or the Air Force Act 1955 or Schedule 4A to the Naval Discipline Act 1957] in respect of any such finding shall be treated as a sentence.

(2)–(4)   . . .

(5)   In this Act, 'service disciplinary proceedings' means any of the following—

(*a*)   any proceedings under the Army Act 1955, the Air Force Act 1955, or the Naval Discipline Act 1957 (whether before a court-martial or before any other court or person authorised thereunder to award a punishment in respect of any offence);

(*b*)   any proceedings under any Act previously in force corresponding to any of the Acts mentioned in paragraph (*a*) above;

[(*bb*) any proceedings before a Standing Civilian Court established under the Armed Forces Act 1976;]

(*c*)   any proceedings under any corresponding enactment or law applying to a force, other than a home force, to which section 4 of the Visiting Forces (British Commonwealth) Act 1933 applies or applied at the time of the proceedings, being proceedings in respect of a member of a home force who is or was at that time attached to the first-mentioned force under that section; whether in any event those proceedings take place in Great Britain or elsewhere.

Notes

Amendment
Sub-s (1): words omitted repealed by the Armed Forces Act 1996, s 35(2), Sch 7, Part III; words in square brackets inserted by the Armed Forces Act 1976, s 22(5), Sch 9, para 20(1).
Sub-ss (2)–(4): repealed, in relation to convictions to which sub-s (1) above applied before 1 October 1996, and repealed with retrospective effect for remaining purposes, by the Armed Forces Act 1996, ss 13(2), (6), 35(2), Sch 7, Part III.
Sub-s (5): para (*bb*) inserted by the Armed Forces Act 1976, s 22(5), Sch 9, para 20(3).

3. Special provision with respect to certain disposals by children's hearings under the Social Work (Scotland) Act 1968   Where a ground for the referral of a child's case to a children's hearing under the *Social Work (Scotland) Act 1968 is that mentioned in section 32(2)(g)* [Children (Scotland) Act 1995 is that mentioned in section 52(2)(i)] of that Act (commission by the child of an offence) and that ground has either been accepted by the child and, where necessary, by his parent or been established *to the satisfaction of the sheriff under section 42 of that Act, the acceptance or establishment* [(or deemed established) to the satisfaction of the sheriff under section 68 or 85 of that Act, the acceptance, establishment (or deemed establishment)] of that ground shall be treated for the purposes of this Act (but not otherwise) as a conviction, and any disposal of the case thereafter by a children's hearing shall be treated for those purposes as a sentence; and references in this Act to a person's being charged with or prosecuted for an offence shall be construed accordingly.

Notes

Amendment
Words in italics repealed and subsequent words in square brackets substituted, in relation to Scotland only, by the Children (Scotland) Act 1995, s 105(4), Sch 4, para 23(2).

4. Effect of rehabilitation   (1)   Subject to sections 7 and 8 below, a person who has become a rehabilitated person for the purposes of this Act in respect of a conviction shall be treated for all purposes in law as a person who has not committed or been charged with or prosecuted for or convicted of or sentenced for the offence or offences which were the subject of that conviction; and, notwithstanding the provisions of any other enactment or rule of law to the contrary, but subject as aforesaid—

> (*a*)   no evidence shall be admissible in any proceedings before a judicial authority exercising its jurisdiction or functions in Great Britain to prove that any such person has committed or been charged with or prosecuted for or convicted of or sentenced for any offence which was the subject of a spent conviction; and
>
> (*b*)   a person shall not, in any such proceedings, be asked, and, if asked, shall not be required to answer, any question relating to his past which cannot be answered without acknowledging or referring to a spent conviction or spent convictions or any circumstances ancillary thereto.

(2)   Subject to the provisions of any order made under subsection (4) below, where a question seeking information with respect to a person's previous convictions, offences, conduct or circumstances is put to him or to any other person otherwise than in proceedings before a judicial authority—

> (*a*)   the question shall be treated as not relating to spent convictions or to any circumstances ancillary to spent convictions, and the answer thereto may be framed accordingly; and
>
> (*b*)   the person questioned shall not be subjected to any liability or otherwise prejudiced in law by reason of any failure to acknowledge or disclose a spent conviction or any circumstances ancillary to a spent conviction in his answer to the question.

267

(3) Subject to the provisions of any order made under subsection (4) below,—

(a) any obligation imposed on any person by any rule of law or by the provisions of any agreement or arrangement to disclose any matters to any other person shall not extend to requiring him to disclose a spent conviction or any circumstances ancillary to a spent conviction (whether the conviction is his own or another's); and

(b) a conviction which has become spent or any circumstances ancillary thereto, or any failure to disclose a spent conviction or any such circumstances, shall not be a proper ground for dismissing or excluding a person from any office, profession, occupation or employment, or for prejudicing him in any way in any occupation or employment.

(4) The Secretary of State may by order—

(a) make such provisions as seems to him appropriate for excluding or modifying the application of either or both of paragraphs (a) and (b) of subsection (2) above in relation to questions put in such circumstances as may be specified in the order;

(b) provide for such exceptions from the provisions of subsection (3) above as seem to him appropriate, in such cases or classes of case, and in relation to convictions of such a description, as may be specified in the order.

(5) For the purposes of this section and section 7 below any of the following are circumstances ancillary to a conviction, that is to say—

(a) the offence or offences which were the subject of that conviction;

(b) the conduct constituting that offence or those offences; and

(c) any process or proceedings preliminary to that conviction, any sentence imposed in respect of that conviction, any proceedings (whether by way of appeal or otherwise) for reviewing that conviction or any such sentence, and anything done in pursuance of or undergone in compliance with any such sentence.

(6) For the purposes of this section and section 7 below 'proceedings before a judicial authority' includes, in addition to proceedings before any of the ordinary courts of law, proceedings before any tribunal, body or person having power—

(a) by virtue of any enactment, law, custom or practice;

(b) under the rules governing any association, institution, profession, occupation or employment; or

(c) under any provision of an agreement providing for arbitration with respect to questions arising thereunder;

to determine any question affecting the rights, privileges, obligations or liabilities of any person, or to receive evidence affecting the determination of any such question.

Notes

Modification
Modified by the Banking Act 1987, s 95.

5. Rehabilitation periods for particular sentences (1) The sentences excluded from rehabilitation under this Act are—

(a) a sentence of imprisonment for life;

(b) a sentence of imprisonment[, youth custody] [detention in a young offender institution] or corrective training for a term exceeding thirty months;

(c) a sentence of preventive detention;

    (*d*)   a sentence of detention during Her Majesty's pleasure or for life, [or under section 205(2) or (3) of the Criminal Procedure (Scotland) Act 1975,] or for a term exceeding thirty months, passed under section 53 of the Children and Young Persons Act 1933 [(young offenders convicted of grave crimes) or under section 206 of the said Act of 1975 (detention of children convicted on indictment)] [or a corresponding court-martial punishment];

    [(*e*)   a sentence of custody for life]

and any other sentence is a sentence subject to rehabilitation under this Act.

[(1A)   In subsection (1)(*d*) above 'corresponding court-martial punishment' means a punishment awarded under section 71A(3) or (4) of the Army Act 1955, section 71A(3) or (4) of the Air Force Act 1955 or section 43A(3) or (4) of the Naval Discipline Act 1957.]

(2)   For the purposes of this Act—

    (*a*)   the rehabilitation period applicable to a sentence specified in the first column of Table A below is the period specified in the second column of that Table in relation to that sentence, or, where the sentence was imposed on a person who was under [eighteen years of age] at the date of his conviction, half that period; and

    (*b*)   the rehabilitation period applicable to a sentence specified in the first column of Table B below is the period specified in the second column of that Table in relation to that sentence;

reckoned in either case from the date of the conviction in respect of which the sentence was imposed.

TABLE A

Rehabilitation periods subject to reduction by half for persons [under 18]

Sentence	Rehabilitation period
A sentence of imprisonment [detention in a young offender institution] [or youth custody] or corrective training for a term exceeding six months but not exceeding thirty months.	Ten years.
A sentence of cashiering, discharge with ignomiy or dismissal with disgrace from Her Majesty's service.	Ten years.
A sentence of imprisonment [detention in a young offenders institution] [or youth custody] for a term not exceeding six months.	Seven years.
A sentence of dismissal from Her Majesty's service.	Seven years.
Any sentence of detention in respect of a conviction in service disciplinary proceedings.	Five years.
A fine or any other sentence subject to rehabilitation under this Act, not being a sentence to which Table B below or any of subsections (3)[, (4A)] to (8) below applies.	Five years.

TABLE B

Rehabilitation periods for certain sentences confined to young offenders

Sentence	Rehabilitation period
A sentence of Borstal training.	Seven years.
[A custodial order under Schedule 5A to the Army Act 1955 or the Air Force Act 1955, or under Schedule 4A to the Naval Discipline Act 1957, where the maximum period of detention specified in the order is more than six months.	Seven years.]
[A custodial order under section 71AA of the Army Act 1955 or the Air Force Act 1955, or under section 43AA of the Naval Discipline Act 1957, where the maximum period of detention specified in the order is more than six months.	Seven years.]
A sentence of detention for a term exceeding six months but not exceeding thirty months passed under section 53 of the said Act of 1933 or under section [206 of the Criminal Procedure (Scotland) Act 1975.]	Five years.
A sentence of detention for a term not exceeding six months passed under either of those provisions.	Three years.
An order for detention in a detention centre made under [section 4 of the Criminal Justice Act 1982,] section 4 of the Criminal Justice Act 1961.	Three years.
[A custodial order under any of the Schedules to the said Acts of 1955 and 1957 mentioned above, where the maximum period of detention specified in the order is six months or less.	Three years.]
[A custodial order under section 71AA of the said Acts of 1955, or section 43AA of the said Act of 1957, where the maximum period of detention specified in the order is six months or less.	Three years.]

(3) The rehabilitation period applicable—

- (*a*)   to an order discharging a person absolutely for an offence; and
- (*b*)   to the discharge by a children's hearing under [69(1)(*b*) and (12) of the Children (Scotland) Act 1995] of the referral of a child's case;

shall be six months from the date of conviction.

(4) Where in respect of a conviction a person was conditionally discharged, bound over to keep the peace or be of good behaviour, . . . the rehabilitation period applicable to the sentence shall be one year from the date of conviction or a period beginning with that date and ending when the order for conditional discharge . . . or (as the case may be) the recognisance or bond of caution to keep the peace or be of good behaviour ceases or ceased to have effect, whichever is the longer.

[(4A) Where in respect of a conviction a person was placed on probation, the rehabilitation period applicable to the sentence shall be—

(*a*)   in the case of a person aged eighteen years or over at the date of his conviction, five years from the date of conviction;

(*b*)   in the case of a person aged under the age of eighteen years at the date of his conviction, two and a half years from the date of conviction or a period beginning with the date of conviction and ending when the probation order ceases or ceased to have effect, whichever is the longer.]

(5)   Where in respect of a conviction any of the following sentences was imposed, that is to say—

(*a*)   an order under section 57 of the Children and Young Persons Act 1933 or section 61 of the Children and Young Persons (Scotland) Act 1937 committing the person convicted to the care of a fit person;

(*b*)   a supervision order under any provision of either of those Acts or of the Children and Young Persons Act 1963;

[(*c*)   an order under section 413 of the Criminal Procedure (Scotland) Act 1975 committing a child for the purpose of his undergoing residential training;]

(*d*)   an approved school order under section 61 of the said Act of 1937;

(*e*)   . . . a supervision order under any provision of the Children and Young Persons Act 1969; or

(*f*)   a supervision requirement under any provision of the [Children (Scotland) Act 1995];

[(*g*)   a community supervision order under Schedule 5A to the Army Act 1955 or the Air Force Act 1955, or under Schedule 4A to the Naval Discipline Act 1957;

(*h*)   . . .]

the rehabilitation period applicable to the sentence shall be one year from the date of conviction or a period beginning with that date and ending when the order or requirement ceases or ceased to have effect, whichever is the longer.

(6)   Where in respect of a conviction any of the following orders was made, that is to say—

(*a*)   an order under section 54 of the said Act of 1933 committing the person convicted to custody in a remand home;

(*b*)   an approved school order under section 57 of the said Act of 1933; or

(*c*)   an attendance centre order under section 19 of the Criminal Justice Act 1948; [or

(*d*)   a secure training order under section 1 of the Criminal Justice and Public Order Act 1994;]

the rehabilitation period applicable to the sentence shall be a period beginning with the date of conviction and ending one year after the date on which the order ceases or ceased to have effect.

[(6A)   Where in respect of a conviction a detention and training order was made under section 73 of the Crime and Disorder Act 1998, the rehabilitation period applicable to the sentence shall be—

(*a*)   in the case of a person aged fifteen years or over at the date of his conviction, five years if the order was, and three and a half years if the order was not, for a term exceeding six months;

(*b*)   in the case of a person aged under fifteen years at the date of his conviction, a period beginning with that date and ending one year after the date on which the order ceases to have effect.]

(7)   Where in respect of a conviction a hospital order under [Part III of the Mental Health Act 1983] or under Part V of the Mental Health (Scotland) Act 1960 (with

or without [a restriction order] was made, the rehabilitation period applicable to the sentence shall be the period of five years from the date of conviction or a period beginning with that date and ending two years after the date on which the hospital order ceases or ceased to have effect, whichever is the longer.

(8) Where in respect of a conviction an order was made imposing on the person convicted any disqualification, disability, prohibition or other penalty, the rehabilitation period applicable to the sentence shall be a period beginning with the date of conviction and ending on the date on which the disqualification, disability, prohibition or penalty (as the case may be) ceases or ceased to have effect.

(9) For the purposes of this section—

    (a)   'sentence of imprisonment' includes a sentence of detention [under section 207 or 415 of the Criminal Procedure (Scotland) Act 1975] and a sentence of penal servitude, and 'term of imprisonment' shall be construed accordingly;

    (b)   consecutive terms of imprisonment or of detention under section 53 of the said Act of 1933 or [section 206 of the said Act of 1975] and terms which are wholly or partly concurrent (being terms of imprisonment or detention imposed in respect of offences of which a person was convicted in the same proceedings) shall be treated as a single term;

    (c)   no account shall be taken of any subsequent variation, made by a court in dealing with a person in respect of a suspended sentence of imprisonment, of the term originally imposed; and

    (d)   a sentence imposed by a court outside Great Britain shall be treated as a sentence of that one of the descriptions mentioned in this section which most nearly corresponds to the sentence imposed.

(10) References in this section to the period during which a probation order, or a . . . supervision order under the Children and Young Persons Act 1969, or a supervision requirement under the [Children (Scotland) Act 1995], is or was in force include references to any period during which any order or requirement to which this subsection applies, being an order or requirement made or imposed directly or indirectly in substitution for the first-mentioned order or requirement, is or was in force.

This subsection applies—

    (a)   to any such order or requirement as is mentioned above in this subsection;

    (b)   to any order having effect under section 25(2) of the said Act of 1969 as if it were a training school order in Northern Ireland; and

    (c)   to any supervision order made under section 72(2) of the said Act of 1968 and having effect as a supervision order under the Children and Young Persons Act (Northern Ireland) 1950.

[(10A)   The reference in subsection (5) above to the period during which a reception order has effect includes a reference to any subsequent period during which by virtue of the order having been made the Social Work (Scotland) Act 1968 or the Children and Young Persons Act (Northern Ireland) 1968 has effect in relation to the person in respect of whom the order was made and subsection (10) above shall accordingly have effect in relation to any such subsequent period.]

(11) The Secretary of State may by order—

    (a)   substitute different periods or terms for any of the periods or terms mentioned in subsections (1) to (8) above; and

    (b)   substitute a different age for the age mentioned in subsection (2)(a) above.

Notes

Amendment

Sub-s (1): in para (*b*) first words in square brackets inserted by the Criminal Justice Act 1982, ss 77, 78, Sch 14, para 36, second words in square brackets inserted by the Criminal Justice Act 1988, s 123(6), Sch 8, para 9(*a*); in para (*c*) word omitted repealed and in para (*e*) words in square brackets inserted, by the Criminal Justice Act 1982, ss 77, 78, Sch 14, para 36, Sch 16; in para (*d*), first words in square brackets inserted and second words in square brackets substituted, by the Criminal Justice (Scotland) Act 1980, s 83(2), Sch 7, para 24, final words in square brackets inserted by the Armed Forces Act 1976, s 22, Sch 9, para 20(4).

Sub-s (1A): inserted by the Armed Forces Act 1976, s 22, Sch 9, para 20(5).

Sub-s (2): in para (*a*) and heading to Table A, words in square brackets substituted (with insertional effect in relation to any sentence imposed on any person who was convicted before 1 October 1992 and was aged 17 at the date of his conviction) by the Criminal Justice Act 1991, ss 68, 101(1), Sch 8, para 5, Sch 12, para 22; in Table A first and third words in square brackets inserted by the Criminal Justice Act 1988, s 123(6), Sch 8, para 9(*b*), second and fourth words in square brackets inserted by the Criminal Justice Act 1982, s 77, Sch 14, para 37, final figure in square brackets inserted by the Criminal Justice and Public Order Act 1994, s 168(1), Sch 9, para 11(1)(*a*), (2); in Table B, words omitted repealed and third words in square brackets substituted by the Criminal Justice (Scotland) Act 1980, s 83(2), Sch 7, para 24, first and fifth words in square brackets inserted by the Armed Forces Act 1976, s 22, Sch 9, para 21(1), second and sixth words in square brackets inserted by the Armed Forces Act 1981, s 28, Sch 4, para 2, fourth words in square brackets inserted by the Criminal Justice Act 1982, s 77, Sch 14, para 37.

Sub-s (3): words in square brackets substituted by the Children (Scotland) Act 1995, s 105(4), Sch 4, para 23(3).

Sub-s (4): words omitted repealed by the Criminal Justice and Public Order Act 1994, s 168(1), (3), Sch 9, para 11(1)(*b*), (2), Sch 11.

Sub-s (4A): inserted by the Criminal Justice and Public Order Act 1994, s 168(1), Sch 9, para 11(1)(*c*), (2).

Sub-s (5): para (*c*) substituted by the Criminal Justice (Scotland) Act 1980, s 83(2), Sch 7, para 24; in para (*e*) words omitted repealed by the Children Act 1989, s 108(7), Sch 15; in para (*f*) words in square brackets substituted by the Children (Scotland) Act 1995, s 105(4), Sch 4, para 23(3); para (*g*) inserted by the Armed Forces Act 1976, s 22, Sch 9, para 21(2); para (*h*) inserted by the Armed Forces Act 1976, s 22, Sch 9, para 21(2), repealed by the Armed Forces Act 1991, s 26, Sch 3.

Sub-s (6): para (*d*) inserted by the Criminal Justice and Public Order Act 1994, s 168(2), Sch 10, para 30.

Date in force: 1 March 1998: see SI 1998/277, art 3(2).

Sub-s (6A): inserted by the Crime and Disorder Act 1998, s 119, Sch 8, para 35.

Date in force: to be appointed: see the Crime and Disorder Act 1998, s 121(2).

Sub-s (7): first words in square brackets substituted by the Mental Health Act 1983, s 148, Sch 4, para 39; second words in square brackets substituted by the Mental Health (Amendment) Act 1982, s 65(1), Sch 3, para 49.

Sub-s (9): words in square brackets substituted by the Criminal Justice (Scotland) Act 1980, s 83(2), Sch 7, para 24.

Sub-s (10): words omitted repealed by the Children Act 1989, s 108(7), Sch 15; words in square brackets substituted by the Children (Scotland) Act 1995, s 105(4), Sch 4, para 23(3).

Sub-s (10A): inserted by the Armed Forces Act 1976, s 22, Sch 9, para 21(3): repealed, in relation to Scotland only, by the Children (Scotland) Act 1995, s 105(4), (5), Sch 4, para 23(3), Sch 5.

6. The rehabilitation period applicable to a conviction (1) Where only one sentence is imposed in respect of a conviction (not being a sentence excluded from rehabilitation under this Act) the rehabilitation period applicable to the conviction is, subject to the following provisions of this section, the period applicable to the sentence in accordance with section 5 above.

(2) Where more than one sentence is imposed in respect of a conviction (whether or not in the same proceedings) and none of the sentences imposed is excluded from rehabilitation under this Act, then, subject to the following provisions of this section, if the periods applicable to those sentences in accordance with section 5 above differ,

the rehabilitation period applicable to the conviction shall be the longer or the longest (as the case may be) of those periods.

(3) Without prejudice to subsection (2) above, where in respect of a conviction a person was conditionally discharged or placed on probation and after the end of the rehabilitation period applicable to the conviction in accordance with subsection (1) or (2) above he is dealt with, in consequence of a breach of conditional discharge or probation, for the offence for which the order for conditional discharge or probation order was made, then, if the rehabilitation period applicable to the conviction in accordance with subsection (2) above (taking into account any sentence imposed when he is so dealt with) ends later than the rehabilitation period previously applicable to the conviction, he shall be treated for the purposes of this Act as not having become a rehabilitated person in respect of that conviction, and the conviction shall for those purposes be treated as not having become spent, in relation to any period falling before the end of the new rehabilitation period.

(4) Subject to subsection (5) below, where during the rehabilitation period applicable to a conviction—

(*a*) the person convicted is convicted of a further offence; and
(*b*) no sentence excluded from rehabilitation under this Act is imposed on him in respect of the later conviction;

if the rehabilitation period applicable in accordance with this section to either of the convictions would end earlier than the period so applicable in relation to the other, the rehabilitation period which would (apart from this subsection) end the earlier shall be extended so as to end at the same time as the other rehabilitation period.

(5) Where the rehabilitation period applicable to a conviction is the rehabilitation period applicable in accordance with section 5(8) above to an order imposing on a person any disqualification, disability, prohibition or other penalty, the rehabilitation period applicable to another conviction shall not by virtue of subsection (4) above be extended by reference to that period; but if any other sentence is imposed in respect of the first-mentioned conviction for which a rehabilitation period is prescribed by any other provision of section 5 above, the rehabilitation period applicable to another conviction shall, where appropriate, be extended under subsection (4) above by reference to the rehabilitation period applicable in accordance with that section to that sentence or, where more than one such sentence is imposed, by reference to the longer or longest of the periods so applicable to those sentences, as if the period in question were the rehabilitation period applicable to the first-mentioned conviction.

(6) . . . , for the purposes of subsection (4)(*a*) above there shall be disregarded—

(*a*) any conviction in England and Wales of [a summary offence or of a scheduled offence (within the meaning of [section 22 of the Magistrates' Courts Act 1980] tried summarily in pursuance of subsection (2) of that section (summary trial where value involved is small)], [or of an offence under section 17 of the Crime (Sentences) Act 1997 (breach of conditions of release supervision order)];

(*b*) any conviction in Scotland of an offence which is not excluded from the jurisdiction of inferior courts of summary jurisdiction by virtue of section 4 of the Summary Jurisdiction (Scotland) Act 1954 (certain crimes not to be tried in inferior courts of summary jurisdiction); and

[(*bb*) any conviction in service disciplinary proceedings for an offence listed in the Schedule to this Act;]

(*c*) any conviction by or before a court outside Great Britain of an offence in respect of conduct which, if it had taken place in any part of Great Britain, would not have constituted an offence under the law in force in that part of Great Britain.

(7) ...

Notes

Amendment
Sub-s (6): words omitted repealed, and para (*bb*) inserted, in relation to convictions to which s 2(1) hereof applied before 1 October 1996, and repealed and inserted with retrospective effect for remaining purposes, by the Armed Forces Act 1996, ss 13(3), (6), 35(2), Sch 7, Part III; in para (*a*) first words in square brackets substituted by the Criminal Law Act 1977, s 65(4), Sch 12, words in square brackets therein substituted by the Magistrates' Courts Act 1980, s 154, Sch 7, para 134, final words in square brackets prospectively inserted by the Crime (Sentences) Act 1997, s 55, Sch 4, para 9(2), as from a day to be appointed.
Sub-s (7): repealed by the Armed Forces Act 1996, s 35(2), Sch 7, Part III.

7. Limitations on rehabilitation under this Act, etc (1) Nothing in section 4(1) above shall affect—

(*a*) any right of Her Majesty, by virtue of Her Royal prerogative or otherwise, to grant a free pardon, to quash any conviction or sentence, or to commute any sentence;

(*b*) the enforcement by any process or proceedings of any fine or other sum adjudged to be paid by or imposed on a spent conviction;

(*c*) the issue of any process for the purpose of proceedings in respect of any breach of a condition or requirement applicable to a sentence imposed in respect of a spent conviction; or

(*d*) the operation of any enactment by virtue of which, in consequence of any conviction, a person is subject, otherwise than by way of sentence, to any disqualification, disability, prohibition or other penalty the period of which extends beyond the rehabilitation period applicable in accordance with section 6 above to the conviction.

(2) Nothing in section 4(1) above shall affect the determination of any issue, or prevent the admission or requirement of any evidence, relating to a person's previous convictions or to circumstances ancillary thereto—

(*a*) in any criminal proceedings before a court in Great Britain (including any appeal or reference in a criminal matter);

(*b*) in any service disciplinary proceedings or in any proceedings on appeal from any service disciplinary proceedings;

[(*bb*) in any proceedings on an application for a sex offender order under section 2 or, as the case may be, 20 of the Crime and Disorder Act 1998 or in any appeal against the making of such an order;]

[(*c*) in any proceedings relating to adoption, the marriage of any minor, the exercise of the inherent jurisdiction of the High Court with respect to minors or the provision by any person of accommodation, care or schooling for minors;

(cc) in any proceedings brought under the Children Act 1989;]

[(*d*) in any proceedings relating to the variation or discharge of a supervision order under the Children and Young Persons Act 1969, or on appeal from any such proceedings;]

(*e*) ...

(*f*) in any proceedings in which he is a party or a witness, provided that, on the occasion when the issue or the admission or requirement of the evidence falls to be determined, he consents to the determination of the issue or, as the case may be, the admission or requirement of the evidence notwithstanding the provisions of section 4(1); [or,

(*g*) ...

. . .

(3) If at any stage in any proceedings before a judicial authority in Great Britain (not being proceedings to which, by virtue of any of paragraphs (*a*) to (*e*) of subsection (2) above or of any order for the time being in force under subsection (4) below, section 4(1) above has no application, or proceedings to which section 8 below applies) the authority is satisfied, in the light of any considerations which appear to it to be relevant (including any evidence which has been or may thereafter be put before it), that justice cannot be done in the case except by admitting or requiring evidence relating to a person's spent convictions or to circumstances ancillary thereto, that authority may admit or, as the case may be, require the evidence in question notwithstanding the provisions of subsection (1) of section 4 above, and may determine any issue to which the evidence relates in disregard, so far as necessary, of those provisions.

(4) The Secretary of State may by order exclude the application of section 4(1) above in relation to any proceedings specified in the order (other than proceedings to which section 8 below applies) to such extent and for such purposes as may be so specified.

(5) No order made by a court with respect to any person otherwise than on a conviction shall be included in any list or statement of that person's previous convictions given or made to any court which is considering how to deal with him in respect of any offence.

Notes
Amendment
Sub-s (2): para (*bb*) inserted by the Crime and Disorder Act 1998, s 119, Sch 8, para 36.
Date in force: 1 December 1998: see SI 1998/2327, art 4(1)(k).
Sub-s (2): paras (*c*), (cc), (*d*) substituted for paras (*c*), (*d*) as originally enacted, by the Children Act 1989, s 108(5), Sch 13, para 35, amended, in relation to Scotland only, by the Children (Scotland) Act 1995, s 105(4), Sch 4, para 23(4)(*a*).
Sub-s (2): para (*e*) repealed by the Children (Scotland) Act 1995, s 105(4), (5), Sch 4, para 23(4)(*b*), Sch 5.
Sub-s (2): para (*g*) repealed by the Banking Act 1987, s 108(2), Sch 7, Pt I.
Sub-s (2): final words omitted repealed by the Children (Scotland) Act 1995, s 105(4), (5), Sch 4, para 23(4)(*c*), Sch 5.

8. Defamation actions (1) This section applies to any action for libel or slander begun after the commencement of this Act by a rehabilitated person and founded upon the publication of any matter imputing that the plaintiff has committed or been charged with or prosecuted for or convicted of or sentenced for an offence which was the subject of a spent conviction.

(2) Nothing in section 4(1) above shall affect an action to which this section applies where the publication complained of took place before the conviction in question became spent, and the following provisions of this section shall not apply in any such case.

(3) Subject to subsections (5) and (6) below, nothing in section 4(1) above shall prevent the defendant in an action to which this section applies from relying on any defence of justification or fair comment or of absolute or qualified privilege which is available to him, or restrict the matters he may establish in support of any such defence.

(4) Without prejudice to the generality of subsection (3) above, where in any such action malice is alleged against a defendant who is relying on a defence of qualified

privilege, nothing in section 4(1) above shall restrict the matters he may establish in rebuttal of the allegation.

(5) A defendant in any such action shall not by virtue of subsection (3) above be entitled to rely upon the defence of justification if the publication is proved to have been made with malice.

(6) Subject to subsection (7) below a defendant in any such action shall not, by virtue of subsection (3) above, be entitled to rely on any matter or adduce or require any evidence for the purpose of establishing (whether under *section 3 of the Law of Libel Amendment Act 1888* [section 14 of the Defamation Act 1996] or otherwise) the defence that the matter published constituted a fair and accurate report of judicial proceedings if it is proved that the publication contained a reference to evidence which was ruled to be inadmissible in the proceedings by virtue of section 4(1) above.

(7) Subsection (3) above shall apply without the qualifications imposed by subsection (6) above in relation to—

(*a*) any report of judicial proceedings contained in any bona fide series of law reports which does not form part of any other publication and consists solely of reports of proceedings in courts of law; and

(*b*) any report or account of judicial proceedings published for bona fide educational, scientific or professional purposes, or given in the course of any lecture, class or discussion given or held for any of those purposes.

(8) . . .

Notes

Amendment
Sub-s (6): words in italics prospectively repealed and subsequent words in square brackets prospectively substituted, by the Defamation Act 1996, s 14(4), as from a day to be appointed.
Sub-s (8): applies to Scotland only.

9. Unauthorised disclosure of spent convictions (1) In this section—

'official record' means a record kept for the purposes of its functions by any court, police force, Government department, local or other public authority in Great Britain, or a record kept, in Great Britain or elsewhere, for the purposes of any of Her Majesty's forces, being in either case a record containing information about persons convicted of offences; and

'specified information' means information imputing that a named or otherwise identifiable rehabilitated living person has committed or been charged with or prosecuted for or convicted of or sentenced for any offence which is the subject of a spent conviction.

(2) Subject to the provisions of any order made under subsection (5) below, any person who, in the course of his official duties, has or at any time has had custody of or access to any official record or the information contained therein, shall be guilty of an offence if, knowing or having reasonable cause to suspect that any specified information he has obtained in the course of those duties is specified information, he discloses it, otherwise than in the course of those duties, to another person.

(3) In any proceedings for an offence under subsection (2) above it shall be a defence for the defendant (or, in Scotland, the accused person) to show that the disclosure was made—

(*a*)   to the rehabilitated person or to another person at the express request of the rehabilitated person; or

(*b*)   to a person whom he reasonably believed to be the rehabilitated person or to another person at the express request of a person whom he reasonably believed to be the rehabilitated person.

(4)   Any person who obtains any specified information from any official record by means of any fraud, dishonesty or bribe shall be guilty of an offence.

(5)   The Secretary of State may by order make such provision as appears to him to be appropriate for excepting the disclosure of specified information derived from an official record from the provisions of subsection (2) above in such cases or classes of case as may be specified in the order.

(6)   Any person guilty of an offence under subsection (2) above shall be liable on summary conviction to a fine not exceeding [level 4 on the standard scale].

(7)   Any person guilty of an offence under subsection (4) above shall be liable on summary conviction to a fine not exceeding [level 5 on the standard scale] or to imprisonment for a term not exceeding six months, or to both.

(8)   Proceedings for an offence under subsection (2) above shall not, in England and Wales, be instituted except by or on behalf of the Director of Public Prosecutions.

Notes

Amendment

Sub-ss (6), (7): maximum fines increased and converted to levels on the standard scale by the Criminal Justice Act 1982, ss 37, 38, 46.

10. Orders   (1)   Any power of the Secretary of State to make an order under any provision of this Act shall be exercisable by statutory instrument, and an order made under any provision of this Act except section 11 below may be varied or revoked by a subsequent order made under that provision.

(2)   No order shall be made by the Secretary of State under any provision of this Act other than section 11 below unless a draft of it has been laid before, and approved by resolution of, each House of Parliament.

11. Citation commencement and extent   (1)   This Act may be cited as the Rehabilitation of Offenders Act 1974.

(2)   This Act shall come into force on 1st July 1975 or such earlier day as the Secretary of State may by order appoint.

(3)   This Act shall not apply to Northern Ireland.

[SCHEDULE
Service Disciplinary Convictions]

Notes

Amendment

Inserted, in relation to convictions to which s 2(1) hereof applied before 1 October 1996, and inserted with retrospective effect for remaining purposes, by the Armed Forces Act 1996, s 13, Sch 4.

Section 6(4)

[1. Any conviction for an offence mentioned in this Schedule is a conviction referred to in section 6(6)(*bb*) of this Act (convictions to be disregarded for the purposes of extending a period of rehabilitation following subsequent conviction).

Provisions of the Army Act 1955 and the Air Force Act 1955

2. Any offence under any of the provisions of the Army Act 1955 or the Air Force Act 1955 listed in the first column of the following table::

Provision	Subject-matter
Section 29	Offences by or in relation to sentries, persons on watch etc.
Section 29A	Failure to attend for duty, neglect of duty etc.
Section 33	Insubordinate behaviour.
Section 34	Disobedience to lawful commands.
Section 34A	Failure to provide a sample for drug testing.
Section 35	Obstruction of provost officers.
Section 36	Disobedience to standing orders.
Section 38	Absence without leave.
Section 39	Failure to report or apprehend deserters or absentees.
Section 42	Malingering.
Section 43	Drunkenness.
Section 43A	Fighting, threatening words etc.
Section 44	Damage to, and loss of, public or service property etc.
Section 44A	Damage to, and loss of, Her Majesty's aircraft or aircraft material.
Section 44B	Interference etc with equipment, messages or signals.
Section 45	Misapplication and waste of public or service property.
Section 46	Offences relating to issues and decorations.
Section 47	Billeting offences.
Section 48	Offences in relation to requisitioning of vehicles.
Section 50	Inaccurate certification.
Section 51	Low flying.
Section 52	Annoyance by flying.
Section 54	Permitting escape, and unlawful release of prisoners.

Section 55	Resistance to arrest.
Section 56	Escape from confinement.
Section 57	Offences in relation to courts-martial.
Section 61	Making of false statements on enlistment.
Section 62	Making of false documents.
Section 63	Offences against civilian population.
Section 69	Conduct to prejudice of military discipline or air-force discipline.

3. Any offence under section 68 (attempt to commit military offence) or 68A (aiding and abetting etc, and inciting, military offence) of the Army Act 1955 in relation to an offence under any of the provisions of that Act listed in paragraph 2.

4. Any offence under section 68 (attempt to commit air-force offence) or 68A (aiding and abetting etc, and inciting, air-force offence) of the Air Force Act 1955 in relation to an offence under any of the provisions of that Act listed in paragraph 2.

Provisions of the Naval Discipline Act 1957

5. Any offence under any of the provisions of the Naval Discipline Act 1957 listed in the first column of the following table:

Provision	Subject-matter
Section 6	Offences by or in relation to sentries, persons on watch etc.
Section 7	Failure to attend for duty, neglect of duty etc.
Section 11	Insubordinate behaviour.
Section 12	Disobedience to lawful commands.
Section 12A	Failure to provide a sample for drug testing.
Section 13	Fighting, threatening words etc.
Section 14	Obstruction of provost officers.
Section 14A	Disobedience to standing orders.
Section 17	Absence without leave etc.
Section 18	Failure to report deserters and absentees.
Section 21	Low flying.
Section 22	Annoyance by flying.
Section 25	Inaccurate certification.
Section 27	Malingering.

Section 28	Drunkenness.
Section 29	Damage to, and loss of, public or service property etc.
Section 29A	Damage to, and loss of, Her Majesty's aircraft or aircraft material.
Section 29B	Interference etc with equipment, messages or signals.
Section 30	Misapplication and waste of public or service property.
Section 31	Offences relating to issues and decorations.
Section 32	Billeting offences.
Section 33	Offences in relation to the requisitioning of vehicles etc.
Section 33A	Permitting escape, and unlawful release of prisoners.
Section 33B	Resistance to arrest.
Section 33C	Escape from confinement.
Section 34A	False statements on entry.
Section 35	Falsification of documents.
Section 35A	Offences against civilian population.
Section 38	Offences in relation to courts-martial.
Section 39	Conduct to the prejudice of naval discipline.

6. Any offence under section 40 (attempt to commit naval offence) or 41 (aiding and abetting etc, and inciting, naval offence) of the Naval Discipline Act 1957 in relation to an offence under any of the provisions of that Act listed in paragraph 5.]

Notes

Amendment
Inserted, in relation to convictions to which s 2(1) hereof applied before 1 October 1996, and inserted with retrospective effect for remaining purposes, by the Armed Forces Act 1996, s 13, Sch 4.

Local Government (Miscellaneous Provisions) Act 1976

Part II
Hackney Carriages and Private Hire Vehicles

45. Application of Part II (1) The provisions of this Part of this Act, except this section, shall come into force in accordance with the following provisions of this section.

(2) If the Act of 1847 is in force in the area of a district council, the council may resolve that the provisions of this Part of this Act, other than this section, are to apply to the relevant area; and if the council do so resolve those provisions shall come into force in the relevant area on the day specified in that behalf in the resolution (which must not be before the expiration of the period of one month beginning with the day on which the resolution is passed).

In this subsection 'the relevant area', in relation to a council, means—

    (*a*)   if the Act of 1847 is in force throughout the area of the council, that area; and

    (*b*)   if the Act of 1847 is in force for part only of the area of the council, that part of that area.

(3) A council shall not pass a resolution in pursuance of the foregoing subsection unless they have—

    (*a*)   published in two consecutive weeks, in a local newspaper circulating in their area, notice of their intention to pass the resolution; and

    (*b*)   served a copy of the notice, not later than the date on which it is first published in pursuance of the foregoing paragraph, on the council of each parish or community which would be affected by the resolution or, in the case of such a parish which has no parish council, on the chairman of the parish meeting.

(4) If after a council has passed a resolution in pursuance of subsection (2) of this section the Act of 1847 comes into force for any part of the area of the council for which it was not in force when the council passed the resolution, the council may pass a resolution in accordance with the foregoing provisions of this section in respect of that part as if that part were included in the relevant area for the purposes of subsection (2) of this section.

Notes

Extent
This Act does not extend to Scotland.

46. Vehicle, drivers' and operators' licences (1) Except as authorised by this Part of this Act—

    (*a*)   no person being the proprietor of any vehicle, not being a hackney carriage [or London Cab] in respect of which a vehicle licence is in force, shall use or permit the same to be used in a controlled district as a private hire vehicle without having for such a vehicle a current licence under section 48 of this Act;

    (*b*)   no person shall in a controlled district act as driver of any private hire vehicle without having a current licence under section 51 of this Act;

(c)   no person being the proprietor of a private hire vehicle licensed under this Part of this Act shall employ as the driver thereof for the purpose of any hiring any person who does not have a current licence under the said section 51;

(d)   no person shall in a controlled district operate any vehicle as a private hire vehicle without having a current licence under section 55 of this Act;

(e)   no person licensed under the said section 55 shall in a controlled district operate any vehicle as a private hire vehicle:

(i)   if for the vehicle a current licence under the said section 48 is not in force; or

(ii)   if the driver does not have a current licence under the said section 51.

(2)   If any person knowingly contravenes the provisions of this section, he shall be guilty of an offence.

Notes

Amendment
Sub-s (1): words in square brackets inserted by the Transport Act 1985, s 139(2), Sch 7, para 17.

Extent
This Act does not extend to Scotland.

47. Licensing of hackney carriages   (1)   A district council may attach to the grant of a licence of a hackney carriage under the Act of 1847 such conditions as the district council may consider reasonably necessary.

(2)   Without prejudice to the generality of the foregoing subsection, a district council may require any hackney carriage licensed by them under the Act of 1847 to be of such design or appearance or bear such distinguishing marks as shall clearly identify it as a hackney carriage.

(3)   Any person aggrieved by any conditions attached to such a licence may appeal to a magistrates' court.

Notes

Modification
Modified for certain purposes by the Licensed Taxis (Hiring at Separate Fares) Order 1986, SI 1986/1386, reg 4.

Extent
This Act does not extend to Scotland.

48. Licensing of private hire vehicles   (1)   Subject to the provisions of this Part of this Act, a district council may on the receipt of an application from the proprietor of any vehicle for the grant in respect of such vehicle of a licence to use the vehicle as a private hire vehicle, grant in respect thereof a vehicle licence:

Provided that a district council shall not grant such a licence unless they are satisfied—

(a)   that the vehicle is:
(i)   suitable in type, size and design for use as a private hire vehicle;
(ii)   not of such design and appearance as to lead any person to believe that the vehicle is a hackney carriage;
(iii)   in a suitable mechanical condition;
(iv)   safe; and
(v)   comfortable;

(b)   that there is in force in relation to the use of the vehicle a policy of insurance or such security as complies with the requirements of [Part VI of the Road Traffic Act 1988], and shall not refuse such a licence for the purpose of limiting the number of vehicles in respect of which such licences are granted by the council.

(2) A district council may attach to the grant of a licence under this section such conditions as they may consider reasonably necessary including, without prejudice to the generality of the foregoing provisions of this subsection, conditions requiring or prohibiting the display of signs on or from the vehicle to which the licence relates.

(3) In every vehicle licence granted under this section there shall be specified—

    (*a*)   the name and address of:
        (i)   the applicant; and
        (ii)   every other person who is a proprietor of the private hire vehicle in respect of which the licence is granted, or who is concerned, either solely or in partnership with any other person, in the keeping, employing or letting on hire of the private hire vehicle;
    (*b*)   the number of the licence which shall correspond with the number to be painted or marked on the plate or disc to be exhibited on the private hire vehicle in accordance with subsection (6) of this section;
    (*c*)   the conditions attached to the grant of the licence; and
    (*d*)   such other particulars as the district council consider reasonably necessary.

(4) Every licence granted under this section shall—

    (*a*)   be signed by an authorised officer of the council which granted it;
    (*b*)   relate to not more than one private hire vehicle; and
    (*c*)   remain in force for such period not being longer than one year as the district council may specify in the licence.

(5) Where a district council grant under this section a vehicle licence in respect of a private hire vehicle they shall issue a plate or disc identifying that vehicle as a private hire vehicle in respect of which a vehicle licence has been granted.

(6)

    (*a*)   Subject to the provisions of this Part of this Act, no person shall use or permit to be used in a controlled district as a private hire vehicle a vehicle in respect of which a licence has been granted under this section unless the plate or disc issued in accordance with subsection (5) of this section is exhibited on the vehicle in such manner as the district council shall prescribe by condition attached to the grant of the licence.
    (*b*)   If any person without reasonable excuse contravenes the provisions of this subsection he shall be guilty of an offence.

(7) Any person aggrieved by the refusal of a district council to grant a vehicle licence under this section or by any conditions specified in such a licence, may appeal to a magistrates' court.

Notes

Amendment
Sub-s (1): words in square brackets in para (*b*) substituted by the Road Traffic (Consequential Provisions) Act 1988, s 4, Sch 3, para 16.

Extent
This Act does not extend to Scotland.

49. Transfer of hackney carriages and private hire vehicles (1) If the proprietor of a hackney carriage or a private hire vehicle in respect of which a vehicle licence has been granted by a district council transfers his interest in the hackney carriage or private hire vehicle to a person other than the proprietor whose name is specified in the licence, he shall within fourteen days after such transfer give notice in writing thereof to the district council specifying the name and address of the person to whom the hackney carriage or private hire vehicle has been transferred.

(2) If a proprietor without reasonable excuse fails to give notice to a district council as provided by subsection (1) of this section he shall be guilty of an offence.

Notes

Extent
This Act does not extend to Scotland.

50. Provisions as to proprietors (1) Without prejudice to the provisions of section 68 of this Act, the proprietor of any hackney carriage or of any private hire vehicle licensed by a district council shall present such hackney carriage or private hire vehicle for inspection and testing by or on behalf of the council within such period and at such place within the area of the council as they may by notice reasonably require:

Provided that a district council shall not under the provisions of this subsection require a proprietor to present the same hackney carriage or private hire vehicle for inspection and testing on more than three separate occasions during any one period of twelve months.

(2) The proprietor of any hackney carriage or private hire vehicle—

   (a) licensed by a district council under the Act of 1847 or under this Part of this Act; or
   (b) in respect of which an application for a licence has been made to a district council under the Act of 1847 or under this Part of this Act;

shall, within such period as the district council may by notice reasonably require, state in writing the address of every place where such hackney carriage or private hire vehicle is kept when not in use, and shall if the district council so require afford to them such facilities as may be reasonably necessary to enable them to cause such hackney carriage or private hire vehicle to be inspected and tested there.

(3) Without prejudice to the provisions of [section 170 of the Road Traffic Act 1988], the proprietor of a hackney carriage or of a private hire vehicle licensed by a district council shall report to them as soon as reasonably practicable, and in any case within seventy-two hours of the occurrence thereof, any accident to such hackney carriage or private hire vehicle causing damage materially affecting the safety, performance or appearance of the hackney carriage or private hire vehicle or the comfort or convenience of persons carried therein.

(4) The proprietor of any hackney carriage or of any private hire vehicle licensed by a district council shall at the request of any authorised officer of the council produce for inspection the vehicle licence for such hackney carriage or private hire vehicle and the certificate of the policy of insurance or security required by [Part VI of the Road Traffic Act 1988] in respect of such hackney carriage or private hire vehicle.

(5) If any person without reasonable excuse contravenes the provisions of this section, he shall be guilty of an offence.

Notes

Amendment
Sub-ss (3), (4): words in square brackets substituted by the Road Traffic (Consequential Provisions) Act 1988, s 4, Sch 3, para 16.

Extent
This Act does not extend to Scotland.

51. Licensing of drivers of private hire vehicles (1) Subject to the provisions of this Part of this Act, a district council shall, on the receipt of an application from any person for the grant to that person of a licence to drive private hire vehicles, grant to that person a driver's licence—

Provided that a district council shall not grant a licence—

(*a*) unless they are satisfied that the applicant is a fit and proper person to hold a driver's licence; or
[(*b*) to any person who has not for at least twelve months been authorised to drive a motor car, or is not at the date of the application for a driver's licence so authorised].

[(1A) . . . .. .]

[(1B) For the purposes of subsection (1) of this section a person is authorised to drive a motor car if—

(*a*) he holds a licence granted under Part III of the Road Traffic Act 1988 (not being a provisional licence) authorising him to drive a motor car, or
(*b*) he is authorised by virtue of section 99A(1) [or section 109(1)] of that Act to drive in Great Britain a motor car.]
(2) A district council may attach to the grant of a licence under this section such conditions as they may consider reasonably necessary.

(3) It shall be the duty of a council by which licences are granted in pursuance of this section to enter, in a register maintained by the council for the purpose, the following particulars of each such licence, namely—

(*a*) the name of the person to whom it is granted;
(*b*) the date on which and the period for which it is granted; and
(*c*) if the licence has a serial number, that number,

and to keep the register available at its principal offices for inspection by members of the public during office hours free of charge.

Notes

Amendment
Sub-s (1): para (*b*) substituted by SI 1996/1974, reg 5, Sch 4, para 2(2).
Sub-s (1A): inserted by the Road Traffic Act 1991, s 47(1).
Sub-s (1A): repealed by the Police Act 1997, s 134, Sch 9, para 34, Sch 10.
     Date in force: 1 April 1998: see SI 1998/354, art 2(2)(*bb*).
Sub-s (1B): inserted by SI 1996/1974, reg 5, Sch 4, para 2(3) (note that this subsection was inserted as sub-s (1) but it is believed that it should be numbered sub-s (1B)).
Sub-s (1B): in para (*b*) words 'or section 109(1)' in square brackets inserted by SI 1998/1946, art 2.
     Date in force: 5 September 1998: see SI 1998/1946, art 1.

Extent
This Act does not extend to Scotland.

52. Appeals in respect of drivers' licences   Any person aggrieved by:

(1) the refusal of the district council to grant a driver's licence under section 51 of this Act; or

(2) any conditions attached to the grant of a driver's licence;

may appeal to a magistrates' court.

Notes

Extent
This Act does not extend to Scotland.

53. Drivers' licences for hackney carriages and private hire vehicles   (1)

(*a*)   Every licence granted by a district council under the provisions of this Part of this Act to any person to drive a private hire vehicle shall remain in force for three years from the date of such licence or for such lesser period as the district council may specify in such licence.

(*b*)   Notwithstanding the provisions of the Public Health Act 1875 and the Town Police Clauses Act 1889, every licence granted by a district council under the provisions of the Act of 1847 to any person to drive a hackney carriage shall remain in force for three years from the date of such licence or for such lesser period as they may specify in such licence.

(2) Notwithstanding the provisions of the Act of 1847, a district council may demand and recover for the grant to any person of a licence to drive a hackney carriage, or a private hire vehicle, as the case may be, such a fee as they consider reasonable with a view to recovering the costs of issue and administration and may remit the whole or part of the fee in respect of a private hire vehicle in any case in which they think it appropriate to do so.

(3) The driver of any hackney carriage or of any private hire vehicle licensed by a district council shall at the request of any authorised officer of the council or of any constable produce for inspection his driver's licence either forthwith or—

(*a*)   in the case of a request by an authorised officer, at the principal offices of the council before the expiration of the period of five days beginning with the day following that on which the request is made;

(*b*)   in the case of a request by a constable, before the expiration of the period aforesaid at any police station which is within the area of the council and is nominated by the driver when the request is made.

(4) If any person without reasonable excuse contravenes the provisions of this section, he shall be guilty of an offence.

Notes

Extent
This Act does not extend to Scotland.

54. Issue of drivers' badges   (1)   When granting a driver's licence under section 51 of this Act a district council shall issue a driver's badge in such a form as may from time to time be prescribed by them.

(2)

    (*a*)   A driver shall at all times when acting in accordance with the driver's licence granted to him wear such badge in such position and manner as to be plainly and distinctly visible.

    (*b*)   If any person without reasonable excuse contravenes the provisions of this subsection, he shall be guilty of an offence.

Notes

Extent
This Act does not extend to Scotland.

55. Licensing of operators of private hire vehicles   (1) Subject to the provisions of this Part of this Act, a district council shall, on receipt of an application from any person for the grant to that person of a licence to operate private hire vehicles grant to that person an operator's licence:

   Provided that a district council shall not grant a licence unless they are satisfied that the applicant is a fit and proper person to hold an operator's licence.

(2) Every licence granted under this section shall remain in force for such period, not being longer than five years, as a district council may specify in the licence.

(3) A district council may attach to the grant of a licence under this section such conditions as they may consider reasonably necessary.

(4) Any applicant aggrieved by the refusal of a district council to grant an operator's licence under this section, or by any conditions attached to the grant of such a licence, may appeal to a magistrates' court.

Notes

Extent
This Act does not extend to Scotland.

56. Operators of private hire vehicles   (1) For the purposes of this Part of this Act every contract for the hire of a private hire vehicle licensed under this Part of this Act shall be deemed to be made with the operator who accepted the booking for that vehicle whether or not he himself provided the vehicle.

(2) Every person to whom a licence in force under section 55 of this Act has been granted by a district council shall keep a record in such form as the council may, by condition attached to the grant of the licence, prescribe and shall enter therein, before the commencement of each journey, such particulars of every booking of a private hire vehicle invited or accepted by him, whether by accepting the same from the hirer or by undertaking it at the request of another operator, as the district council may by condition prescribe and shall produce such record on request to any authorised officer of the council or to any constable for inspection.

(3) Every person to whom a licence in force under section 55 of this Act has been granted by a district council shall keep such records as the council may, by condition attached to the grant of the licence, prescribe of the particulars of any private hire vehicle operated by him and shall produce the same on request to any authorised officer of the council or to any constable for inspection.

(4) A person to whom a licence in force under section 55 of this Act has been granted by a district council shall produce the licence on request to any authorised officer of the council or any constable for inspection.

(5) If any person without reasonable excuse contravenes the provisions of this section, he shall be guilty of an offence.

Notes

Extent
This Act does not extend to Scotland.

57. Power to require applicants to submit information (1) A district council may require any applicant for a licence under the Act of 1847 or under this Part of this Act to submit to them such information as they may reasonably consider necessary to enable them to determine whether the licence should be granted and whether conditions should be attached to any such licence.

(2) Without prejudice to the generality of the foregoing subsection—

  (a) a district may require an applicant for a driver's licence in respect of a hackney carriage or a private hire vehicle:
    (i)   to produce a certificate signed by a registered medical practitioner to the effect that he is physically fit to be the driver of a hackney carriage or a private hire vehicle; and
    (ii) whether or not such a certificate has been produced, to submit to examination by a registered medical practitioner selected by the district council as to his physical fitness to be the driver of a hackney carriage or a private hire vehicle;

  (b) a district council may require an applicant for an operator's licence to submit to them such information as to:
    (i)   the name and address of the applicant;
    (ii) the addresses or address whether within the area of the council or not from which he intends to carry on business in connection with private hire vehicles licensed under this Part of this Act;
    (iii) any trade or business activities he has carried on before making the application;
    (iv) any previous application he has made for an operator's licence;
    (v) the revocation or suspension of any operator's licence previously held by him;
    (vi) any convictions recorded against the applicant;

    as they may reasonably consider necessary to enable them to determine whether to grant such licence;

  (c) in addition to the information specified in paragraph (b) of this subsection, a district council may require an applicant for an operator's licence to submit to them:
    (i)   if the applicant is or has been a director or secretary of a company, information as to any convictions recorded against that company at any relevant time; any trade or business activities carried on by that company; any previous application made by that company for an operator's licence; and any revocation or suspension of an operator's licence previously held by that company;
    (ii) if the applicant is a company, information as to any convictions recorded against a director or secretary of that company; any trade or business activities carried on by any such director or secretary; any previous application made by any such director or secretary for an operator's licence; and any revocation or suspension of an operator's licence previously held by such director or secretary;
    (iii) if the applicant proposes to operate the vehicle in partnership with any other person, information as to any convictions recorded against that

person; any trade or business activities carried on by that person; any previous application made by that person for an operator's licence; and any revocation or suspension of an operator's licence previously held by him.

(3) If any person knowingly or recklessly makes a false statement or omits any material particular in giving information under this section, he shall be guilty of an offence.

Notes

Extent
This Act does not extend to Scotland.

58. Return of identification plate or disc on revocation or expiry of licence etc (1) On—

(a) the revocation or expiry of a vehicle licence in relation to a hackney carriage or private hire vehicle; or

(b) the suspension of a licence under section 68 of this Act;

a district council may by notice require the proprietor of that hackney carriage or private hire vehicle licensed by them to return to them within seven days after the service on him of that notice the plate or disc which—

(a) in the case of a hackney carriage, is required to be affixed to the carriage as mentioned in section 38 of the Act of 1847; and

(b) in the case of a private hire vehicle, was issued for the vehicle under section 48(5) of this Act.

(2) If any proprietor fails without reasonable excuse to comply with the terms of a notice under subsection (1) of this section—

(a) he shall be guilty of an offence and liable on summary conviction to a fine not exceeding [level 3 on the standard scale] and to a daily fine not exceeding ten pounds; and

(b) any authorised officer of the council or constable shall be entitled to remove and retain the said plate or disc from the said hackney carriage or private hire vehicle.

Notes

Amendment
Sub-s (2): first-mentioned maximum fine increased and converted to a level on the standard scale by virtue of the Criminal Justice Act 1982, ss 37, 38, 46.

Extent
This Act does not extend to Scotland.

59. Qualifications for drivers of hackney carriages (1) Notwithstanding anything in the Act of 1847, a district council shall not grant a licence to drive a hackney carriage—

(a) unless they are satisfied that the applicant is a fit and proper person to hold a driver's licence; or

[(b) to any person who has not for at least twelve months been authorised to drive a motor car, or is not at the date of the application for a driver's licence so authorised].

[(1A) . . . .]

[(1A) For the purposes of subsection (1) of this section a person is authorised to drive a motor car if—

(a) he holds a licence granted under Part III of the Road Traffic Act 1988 (not being a provisional licence) authorising him to drive a motor car, or

(b) he is authorised by virtue of section 99A(1) [or section 109(1)] of that Act to drive in Great Britain a motor car.]

(2) Any applicant aggrieved by the refusal of a district council to grant a driver's licence on the ground that he is not a fit and proper person to hold such licence may appeal to a magistrates' court.

Notes

Amendment
Sub-s (1): para (b) substituted by SI 1996/1974, reg 5, Sch 4, para 2(4).
First sub-s (1A): inserted by the Road Traffic Act 1991, s 47(1).
First sub-s (1A): repealed by the Police Act 1997, s 134, Sch 9, para 34, Sch 10.
    Date in force: 1 April 1998: see SI 1998/354, art 2(2)(bb).
Second sub-s (1A): inserted by SI 1996/1974, reg 5, Sch 4, para 2(5).
Second sub-s (1A): in para (b) words 'or section 109(1)' in square brackets inserted by SI 1998/1946, art 3.
    Date in force: 5 September 1998: see SI 1998/1946, art 1.

Extent
This Act does not extend to Scotland.

60. Suspension and revocation of vehicle licences (1) Notwithstanding anything in the Act of 1847 or in this Part of this Act, a district council may suspend or revoke, or (on application therefor under section 40 of the Act of 1847 or section 48 of this Act, as the case may be) refuse to renew a vehicle licence on any of the following grounds—

(a) that the hackney carriage or private hire vehicle is unfit for use as a hackney carriage or private hire vehicle;

(b) any offence under, or non-compliance with, the provisions of the Act of 1847 or of this Part of this Act by the operator or driver; or

(c) any other reasonable cause.

(2) Where a district council suspend, revoke or refuse to renew any licence under this section they shall give to the proprietor of the vehicle notice of the grounds on which the licence has been suspended or revoked or on which they have refused to renew the licence within fourteen days of such suspension, revocation or refusal.

(3) Any proprietor aggrieved by a decision of a district council under this section may appeal to a magistrates' court.

Notes

Extent
This Act does not extend to Scotland.

61. Suspension and revocation of drivers' licences (1) Notwithstanding anything in the Act of 1847 or in this Part of this Act, a district council may suspend or revoke or (on application therefor under section 46 of the Act of 1847 or section 51 of this Act, as the case may be) refuse to renew the licence of a driver of a hackney carriage or a private hire vehicle on any of the following grounds—

(a) that he has since the grant of the licence—

(i)   been convicted of an offence involving dishonesty, indecency or violence; or

(ii) been convicted of an offence under or has failed to comply with the provisions of the Act of 1847 or of this Part of this Act; or

(*b*)   any other reasonable cause.

(2)

(*a*)   Where a district council suspend, revoke or refuse to renew any licence under this section they shall give to the driver notice of the grounds on which the licence has been suspended or revoked or on which they have refused to renew such licence within fourteen days of such suspension, revocation or refusal and the driver shall on demand return to the district council the driver's badge issued to him in accordance with section 54 of this Act.

(*b*)   If any person without reasonable excuse contravenes the provisions of this section he shall be guilty of an offence and liable on summary conviction to a fine not exceeding [level 1 on the standard scale].

(3)   Any driver aggrieved by a decision of a district council under this section may appeal to a magistrates' court.

Notes

Amendment
Sub-s (2): maximum fine increased and converted to a level on the standard scale by virtue of the Criminal Justice Act 1982, ss 37, 38, 46.

Extent
This Act does not extend to Scotland.

62. Suspension and revocation of operators' licences   (1)   Notwithstanding anything in this Part of this Act a district council may suspend or revoke, or (on application therefor under section 55 of this Act) refuse to renew an operator's licence on any of the following grounds—

(*a*)   any offence under, or non-compliance with, the provisions of this Part of this Act;

(*b*)   any conduct on the part of the operator which appears to the district council to render him unfit to hold an operator's licence;

(*c*)   any material change since the licence was granted in any of the circumstances of the operator on the basis of which the licence was granted; or

(*d*)   any other reasonable cause.

(2)   Where a district council suspend, revoke or refuse to renew any licence under this section they shall give to the operator notice of the grounds on which the licence has been suspended or revoked or on which they have refused to renew such licence within fourteen days of such suspension, revocation or refusal.

(3)   Any operator aggrieved by a decision of a district council under this section may appeal to a magistrates' court.

Notes

Extent
This Act does not extend to Scotland.

63. Stands for hackney carriages   (1)   For the purposes of their functions under the Act of 1847, a district council may from time to time appoint stands for hackney carriages for the whole or any part of a day in any highway in the district which is maintainable at the public expense and, with the consent of the owner, on any land in the district which does not form part of a highway so maintainable and may from time to time vary the number of hackney carriages permitted to be at each stand.

(2) Before appointing any stand for hackney carriages or varying the number of hackney carriages to be at each stand in exercise of the powers of this section, a district council shall give notice to the chief officer of police for the police area in which the stand is situated and shall also give public notice of the proposal by advertisement in at least one local newspaper circulating in the district and shall take into consideration any objections or representations in respect of such proposal which may be made to them in writing within twenty-eight days of the first publication of such notice.

(3) Nothing in this section shall empower a district council to appoint any such stand—

(a) so as unreasonably to prevent access to any premises;

(b) so as to impede the use of any points authorised to be used in connection with a [local service within the meaning of the Transport Act 1985] [or PSV operator's licence granted under [the Public Passenger Vehicles Act 1981]], as points for the taking up or setting down of passengers, or in such a position as to interfere unreasonably with access to any station or depot of any passenger road transport operators, except with the consent of those operators;

(c) on any highway except with the consent of the highway authority;

and in deciding the position of stands a district council shall have regard to the position of any bus stops for the time being in use.

(4) Any hackney carriage byelaws for fixing stands for hackney carriages which were made by a district council before the date when this section comes into force in the area of the council and are in force immediately before that date shall cease to have effect, but any stands fixed by such byelaws shall be deemed to have been appointed under this section.

(5) The power to appoint stands for hackney carriages under subsection (1) of this section shall include power to revoke such appointment and to alter any stand so appointed and the expressions 'appointing' and 'appoint' in subsections (2) and (3) of this section shall be construed accordingly.

Notes

Amendment
Sub-s (3): first words in square brackets substituted by the Transport Act 1985, s 1, Sch 1, para 2; second words in square brackets substituted by the Transport Act 1980, s 43, Sch 5, Part II, words in square brackets therein substituted by the Public Passenger Vehicles Act 1981, s 88, Sch 7, para 19.

Extent
This Act does not extend to Scotland.

64. Prohibition of other vehicles on hackney carriage stands (1) No person shall cause or permit any vehicle other than a hackney carriage to wait on any stand for hackney carriages during any period for which that stand has been appointed, or is deemed to have been appointed, by a district council under the provisions of section 63 of this Act.

(2) Notice of the prohibition in this section shall be indicated by such traffic signs as may be prescribed or authorised for the purpose by the Secretary of State in pursuance of his powers under [section 64 of the Road Traffic Regulation Act 1984].

(3) If any person without reasonable excuse contravenes the provisions of this section, he shall be guilty of an offence.

(4) In any proceedings under this section against the driver of a public service vehicle it shall be a defence to show that, by reason of obstruction to traffic or for other compelling reason, he caused his vehicle to wait on a stand or part thereof and that he caused or permitted his vehicle so to wait only for so long as was reasonably necessary for the taking up or setting down of passengers.

Notes

Amendment
Sub-s (2): words in square brackets substituted by the Road Traffic Regulation Act 1984, s 146, Sch 13, para 36.

Extent
This Act does not extend to Scotland.

65. Fixing of fares for hackney carriages (1) A district council may fix the rates or fares within the district as well for a time as distance, and all other charges in connection with the hire of a vehicle or with the arrangements for the hire of a vehicle, to be paid in respect of the hire of hackney carriages by means of a table (hereafter in this section referred to as a 'table of fares') made or varied in accordance with the provisions of this section.

(2)

    (*a*) When a district council make or vary a table of fares they shall publish in at least one local newspaper circulating in the district a notice setting out the table of fares or the variation thereof and specifying the period, which shall not be less than fourteen days from the date of the first publication of the notice, within which and the manner in which objections to the table of fares or variation can be made.

    (*b*) A copy of the notice referred to in paragraph (*a*) of this subsection shall for the period of fourteen days from the date of the first publication thereof be deposited at the offices of the council which published the notice, and shall at all reasonable hours be open to public inspection without payment.

(3) If no objection to a table of fares or variation is duly made within the period specified in the notice referred to in subsection (2) of this section, or if all objections so made are withdrawn, the table of fares or variations shall come into operation on the date of the expiration of the period specified in the notice or the date of withdrawal of the objection or, if more than one, of the last objection, whichever date is the later.

(4) If objection is duly made as aforesaid and is not withdrawn, the district council shall set a further date, not later than two months after the first specified date, on which the table of fares shall come into force with or without modifications as decided by them after consideration of the objections.

(5) A table of fares made or varied under this section shall have effect for the purposes of the Act of 1847 as if it were included in hackney carriage byelaws made thereunder.

(6) On the coming into operation of a table of fares made by a council under this section for the district, any hackney carriage byelaws fixing the rates and fares or any table of fares previously made under this section for the district, as the case may be, shall cease to have effect.

(7) Section 236(8) (except the words 'when confirmed') and section 238 of the Local Government Act 1972 (except paragraphs (c) and (d) of that section) shall extend and apply to a table of fares made or varied under this section as they apply to byelaws made by a district council.

Notes

Modification
Modified for certain purposes by the Licensed Taxis (Hiring at Separate Fares) Order 1986, SI 1986/1386, art 4.

Extent
This Act does not extend to Scotland.

66. Fares for long journeys (1) No person, being the driver of a hackney carriage licensed by a district council, and undertaking for any hirer a journey ending outside the district and in respect of which no fare and no rate of fare was agreed before the hiring was effected, shall require for such journey a fare greater than that indicated on the taximeter with which the hackney carriage is equipped or, if it is not equipped with a taximeter, greater than that which, if the current byelaws fixing rates or fares and in force in the district in pursuance of section 68 of the Act of 1847 or, as the case may be, the current table of fares in force within the district in pursuance of section 65 of this Act had applied to the journey, would have been authorised for the journey by the byelaws or table.

(2) If any person knowingly contravenes the provisions of this section, he shall be guilty of an offence.

Notes

Modification
Modified for certain purposes by the Licensed Taxis (Hiring at Separate Fares) Order 1986, SI 1986/1386, art 4.

Extent
This Act does not extend to Scotland.

67. Hackney carriages used for private hire (1) No hackney carriage shall be used in the district under contract or purported contract for private hire except at a rate of fares or charges not greater than that fixed by the byelaws or table mentioned in section 66 of this Act, and, when any such hackney carriage is so used, the fare or charge shall be calculated from the point in the district at which the hirer commences his journey.

(2) Any person who knowingly contravenes this section shall be guilty of an offence.

(3) In subsection (1) of this section 'contract' means—

   (a) a contract made otherwise than while the relevant hackney carriage is plying for hire in the district or waiting at a place in the district which, when the contract is made, is a stand for hackney carriages appointed by the district council under section 63 of this Act; and

   (b) a contract made, otherwise than with or through the driver of the relevant hackney carriage, while it is so plying or waiting.

Notes

Modification
Modified for certain purposes by the Licensed Taxis (Hiring at Separate Fares) Order 1986, SI 1986/1386, art 4.

Extent
This Act does not extend to Scotland.

68. Fitness of hackney carriages and private hire vehicles Any authorised officer of the council in question or any constable shall have power at all reasonable times to inspect and test, for the purpose of ascertaining its fitness, any hackney carriage or private hire vehicle licensed by a district council, or any taximeter affixed to such a vehicle, and if he is not satisfied as to the fitness of the hackney carriage or private hire vehicle or as to the accuracy of its taximeter he may by notice in writing require the proprietor of the hackney carriage or private hire vehicle to make it or its taximeter available for further inspection and testing at such reasonable time and place as may be specified in the notice and suspend the vehicle licence until such time as such authorised officer or constable is so satisfied:

Provided that, if the authorised officer or constable is not so satisfied before the expiration of a period of two months, the said licence shall, by virtue of this section, be deemed to have been revoked and subsections (2) and (3) of section 60 of this Act shall apply with any necessary modifications.

Notes

Extent
This Act does not extend to Scotland.

69. Prolongation of journeys (1) No person being the driver of a hackney carriage or of a private hire vehicle licensed by a district council shall without reasonable cause unnecessarily prolong, in distance or in time, the journey for which the hackney carriage or private hire vehicle has been hired.

(2) If any person contravenes the provisions of this section, he shall be guilty of an offence.

Notes

Extent
This Act does not extend to Scotland.

70. Fees for vehicle and operators' licences (1) Subject to the provisions of subsection (2) of this section, a district council may charge such fees for the grant of vehicle and operators' licences as may be resolved by them from time to time and as may be sufficient in the aggregate to cover in whole or in part—

    (*a*)   the reasonable cost of the carrying out by or on behalf of the district council of inspections of hackney carriages and private hire vehicles for the purpose of determining whether any such licence should be granted or renewed;

    (*b*)   the reasonable cost of providing hackney carriage stands; and

    (*c*)   any reasonable administrative or other costs in connection with the foregoing and with the control and supervision of hackney carriages and private hire vehicles.

(2) The fees chargeable under this section shall not exceed—

    (*a*)   for the grant of a vehicle licence in respect of a hackney carriage, twenty-five pounds;

(*b*)   for the grant of a vehicle licence in respect of a private hire vehicle, twenty-five pounds; and

(*c*)   for the grant of an operator's licence, twenty-five pounds per annum;

or, in any such case, such other sums as a district council may, subject to the following provisions of this section, from time to time determine.

(3)

(*a*)   If a district council determine that the maximum fees specified in subsection (2) of this section should be varied they shall publish in at least one local newspaper circulating in the district a notice setting out the variation proposed, drawing attention to the provisions of paragraph (*b*) of this subsection and specifying the period, which shall not be less than twenty-eight days from the date of the first publication of the notice, within which and the manner in which objections to the variation can be made.

(*b*)   A copy of the notice referred to in paragraph (*a*) of this subsection shall for the period of twenty-eight days from the date of the first publication thereof be deposited at the offices of the council which published the notice and shall at all reasonable hours be open to public inspection without payment.

(4) If no objection to a variation is duly made within the period specified in the notice referred to in subsection (3) of this section, or if all objections so made are withdrawn, the variation shall come into operation on the date of the expiration of the period specified in the notice or the date of withdrawal of the objection or, if more than one, of the last objection, whichever date is the later.

(5) If objection is duly made as aforesaid and is not withdrawn, the district council shall set a further date, not later than two months after the first specified date, on which the variation shall come into force with or without modification as decided by the district council after consideration of the objections.

(6) A district council may remit the whole or part of any fee chargeable in pursuance of this section for the grant of a licence under section 48 or 55 of this Act in any case in which they think it appropriate to do so.

Notes

Extent
This Act does not extend to Scotland.

71. Taximeters   (1) Nothing in this Act shall require any private hire vehicle to be equipped with any form of taximeter but no private hire vehicle so equipped shall be used for hire in a controlled district unless such taximeter has been tested and approved by or on behalf of the district council for the district or any other district council by which a vehicle licence in force for the vehicle was issued.

(2) Any person who—

(*a*)   tampers with any seal on any taximeter without lawful excuse; or

(*b*)   alters any taximeter with intent to mislead; or

(*c*)   knowingly causes or permits a vehicle of which he is the proprietor to be used in contravention of subsection (1) of this section.

shall be guilty of an offence.

Notes

Extent
This Act does not extend to Scotland.

72. Offences due to fault of other person (1) Where an offence by any person under this Part of this Act is due to the act or default of another person, then, whether proceedings are taken against the first-mentioned person or not, that other person may be charged with and convicted of that offence, and shall be liable on conviction to the same punishment as might have been imposed on the first-mentioned person if he had been convicted of the offence.

(2) Section 44(3) of this Act shall apply to an offence under this Part of this Act as it applies to an offence under Part I of this Act.

Notes

Extent
This Act does not extend to Scotland.

73. Obstruction of authorised officers (1) Any person who—

(a) wilfully obstructs an authorised officer or constable acting in pursuance of this Part of this Act or the Act of 1847; or
(b) without reasonable excuse fails to comply with any requirement properly made to him by such officer or constable under this Part of this Act; or
(c) without reasonable cause fails to give such an officer or constable so acting any other assistance or information which he may reasonably require of such person for the purpose of the performance of his functions under this Part of this Act or the Act of 1847;

shall be guilty of an offence.

(2) If any person, in giving any such information as is mentioned in the preceding subsection, makes any statement which he knows to be false, he shall be guilty of an offence.

Notes

Extent
This Act does not extend to Scotland.

74. Saving for certain businesses Where any provision of this Part of this Act coming into operation on a day fixed by resolution under section 45 of this Act requires the licensing of a person carrying on any business, or of any vehicle used by a person in connection with any business, it shall be lawful for any person who—

(a) immediately before that day was carrying on that business; and
(b) had before that day duly applied for the licence required by that provision;

to continue to carry on that business until he is informed of the decision with regard to his application and, if the decision is adverse, during such further time as is provided under section 77 of this Act.

Notes

Extent
This Act does not extend to Scotland.

75. Saving for certain vehicles etc (1) Nothing in this Part of this Act shall—

(a) apply to a vehicle used for bringing passengers or goods within a controlled district in pursuance of a contract for the hire of the vehicle made outside the district if the vehicle is not made available for hire within the district;

(b) apply to a vehicle used only for carrying passengers for hire or reward under a contract for the hire of the vehicle for a period of not less than seven days;

(c) apply to a vehicle while it is being used in connection with a funeral or a vehicle used wholly or mainly, by a person carrying on the business of a funeral director, for the purpose of funerals;

[(cc) apply to a vehicle while it is being used in connection with a wedding;]

(d) require the display of any plate, disc or notice in or on any private hire vehicle licensed by a council under this Part of this Act during such period that such vehicle is used for carrying passengers for hire or reward—

(i) . . .

(ii) under a contract for the hire of the vehicle for a period of not less than 24 hours.

(2) Paragraphs (a), (b) and (c) of section 46(1) of this Act shall not apply to the use or driving of a vehicle or to the employment of a driver of a vehicle while the vehicle is used as a private hire vehicle in a controlled district if a licence issued under section 48 of this Act by the council whose area consists of or includes another controlled district is then in force for the vehicle and a driver's licence issued by such a council is then in force for the driver of the vehicle.

[(2A) Where a vehicle is being used as a taxi or private hire car, paragraphs (a), (b) and (c) of section 46(1) of this Act shall not apply to the use or driving of the vehicle or the employment of a person to drive it if—

(a) a licence issued under section 10 of the Civic Government (Scotland) Act 1982 for its use as a taxi or, as the case may be, private hire car is then in force, and

(b) the driver holds a licence issued under section 13 of that Act for the driving of taxis or, as the case may be, private hire cars.

In this subsection, 'private hire car' and 'taxi' have the same meaning as in sections 10 to 22 of the Civic Government (Scotland) Act 1982.]

[(2B) Paragraphs (a), (b) and (c) of section 46(1) of this Act shall not apply to the use or driving of a vehicle, or to the employment of a driver of a vehicle, if—

(a) a London PHV licence issued under section 7 of the Private Hire Vehicles (London) Act 1998 is in force in relation to that vehicle; and

(b) the driver of the vehicle holds a London PHV driver's licence issued under section 13 of that Act.]

(3) Where a licence under section 48 of this Act is in force for a vehicle, the council which issued the licence may, by a notice in writing given to the proprietor of the vehicle, provide that paragraph (a) of subsection (6) of that section shall not apply to the vehicle on any occasion specified in the notice or shall not so apply while the notice is carried in the vehicle; and on any occasion on which by virtue of this subsection that paragraph does not apply to a vehicle section 54(2)(a) of this Act shall not apply to the driver of the vehicle.

Notes

Amendment

Sub-s (1): para (cc) inserted and para (d)(i) repealed by the Transport Act 1985, s 139(2), Sch 7.

Sub-s (2A): inserted by the Civic Government (Scotland) Act 1982, s 16.
Sub-s (2B): inserted by the Private Hire Vehicles (London) Act 1998, s 39(1), Sch 1, para 1.
   Date in force: to be appointed: see the Private Hire Vehicles (London) Act 1998, s 40(2).

Extent
This Act does not extend to Scotland.

76. Penalties Any person who commits an offence against any of the provisions of this Part of this Act in respect of which no penalty is expressly provided shall be liable on summary conviction to a fine not exceeding [level 3 on the standard scale].

Notes

Amendment
Maximum fine increased and converted to a level on the standard scale by virtue of the Criminal Justice Act 1982, ss 37, 38, 46.

Extent
This Act does not extend to Scotland.

77. Appeals (1) Sections 300 to 302 of the Act of 1936, which relate to appeals, shall have effect as if this Part of this Act were part of that Act.

(2) If any requirement, refusal or other decision of a district council against which a right of appeal is conferred by this Act—

   (*a*) involves the execution of any work or the taking of any action; or
   (*b*) makes it unlawful for any person to carry on a business which he was lawfully carrying on up to the time of the requirement, refusal or decision;

then, until the time for appealing has expired, or, when an appeal is lodged, until the appeal is disposed of or withdrawn or fails for want of prosecution—

   (i) no proceedings shall be taken in respect of any failure to execute the work, or take the action; and
   (ii) that person may carry on that business.

Notes

Extent
This Act does not extend to Scotland.

78. Application of provisions of Act of 1936 Subsection (1) of section 283 and section 304 of the Act of 1936 shall have effect as if references therein to that Act included a reference to this Part of this Act.

Notes

Extent
This Act does not extend to Scotland.

79. Authentication of licences Notwithstanding anything in section 43 of the Act of 1847, any vehicle or driver's licence granted by a district council under that Act, or any licence granted by a district council under this Part of this Act, shall not be required to be under the common seal of the district council, but if not so sealed shall be signed by an authorised officer of the council.

Notes

Extent
This Act does not extend to Scotland.

80. Interpretation of Part II (1) In this Part of this Act, unless the subject or context otherwise requires—

'the Act of 1847' means the provisions of the Town Police Clauses Act 1847 with respect to hackney carriages;

'the Act of 1936' means the Public Health Act 1936;

. . .

'authorised officer' means any officer of a district council authorised in writing by the council for the purposes of this Part of this Act;

'contravene' includes fail to comply;

'controlled district' means any area for which this Part of this Act is in force by virtue of a resolution passed by a district council under section 45 of this Act;

'daily fine' means a fine for each day during which an offence continues after conviction thereof;

'the district', in relation to a district council in whose area the provisions of this Part of this Act are in force, means—

(*a*) if those provisions are in force throughout the area of the council, that area; and

(*b*) if those provisions are in force for part only of the area of the council, that part of that area;

'driver's badge' means, in relation to the driver of a hackney carriage, any badge issued by a district council under byelaws made under section 68 of the Act of 1847 and, in relation to the driver of a private hire vehicle, any badge issued by a district council under section 54 of this Act;

'driver's licence' means, in relation to the driver of a hackney carriage, a licence under section 46 of the Act of 1847 and, in relation to the driver of a private hire vehicle, a licence under section 51 of this Act;

'hackney carriage' has the same meaning as in the Act of 1847;

'hackney carriage byelaws' means the byelaws for the time being in force in the controlled district in question relating to hackney carriages;

['London cab' means a vehicle which is a hackney carriage within the meaning of the Metropolitan Public Carriage Act 1869;]

'operate' means in the course of business to make provision for the invitation or acceptance of bookings for a private hire vehicle;

'operator's licence' means a licence under section 55 of this Act;

'private hire vehicle' means a motor vehicle constructed or adapted to seat [fewer than nine passengers], other than a hackney carriage or public service vehicle [or a London cab] [or tramcar], which is provided for hire with the services of a driver for the purpose of carrying passengers;

'proprietor' includes a part-proprietor and, in relation to a vehicle which is the subject of a hiring agreement or hire-purchase agreement, means the person in possession of the vehicle under that agreement;

'public service vehicle' has the same meaning as in [the Public Passenger Vehicles Act 1981];

'taximeter' means any device for calculating the fare to be charged in respect of any journey in a hackney carriage or private hire vehicle by reference to the distance travelled or time elapsed since the start of the journey, or a combination of both; and 'vehicle licence' means in relation to a hackney carriage a licence under sections 37 to 45 of the Act of 1847 [in relation to a London cab a licence under section 6 of the Metropolitan Public Carriage Act 1869] and in relation to a private hire vehicle means a licence under section 48 of this Act.

(2) In this Part of this Act references to a licence, in connection with a controlled district, are references to a licence issued by the council whose area consists of or includes that district, and 'licensed' shall be construed accordingly.

(3) Except where the context otherwise requires, any reference in this Part of this Act to any enactment shall be construed as a reference to that enactment as applied, extended, amended or varied by, or by virtue of, any subsequent enactment including this Act.

[(4) In this Part of this Act, except where the context otherwise requires, references to a district council shall, in relation to Wales, be construed as references to a county council or county borough council.]

Notes

Amendment
Sub-s (1): definition omitted repealed by the Road Traffic (Consequential Provisions) Act 1988, s 3(1), Sch 1, Part I; definition 'London cab', second words in square brackets in definition 'private hire vehicle', and words in square brackets in definition 'vehicle licence', inserted by the Transport Act 1985, s 139(2), Sch 7, para 17(3); in definition 'private hire vehicle' first words in square brackets substituted by the Transport Act 1980, s 43, Sch 5, Part II, final words in square brackets inserted by the Transport and Works Act 1992, s 62(3); in definition 'public service vehicle' words in square brackets substituted by the Public Passenger Service Vehicles Act 1981, s 88, Sch 7, para 20.
Sub-s (4): inserted by SI 1996/3071, art 2, Schedule, para 1(8).

Extent
This Act does not extend to Scotland.

Transport Act 1980

Part IV
Miscellaneous and General

64. Roof-signs on vehicles other than taxis (1) There shall not, in any part of England and Wales outside the metropolitan police district and the City of London, be displayed on or above the roof of any vehicle which is used for carrying passengers for hire or reward but which is not a taxi—

(a) any sign which consists of or includes the word 'taxi' or 'cab', whether in the singular or plural, or 'hire', or any word of similar meaning or appearance to any of those words, whether alone or as part of another word; or

(b) any sign, notice, mark, illumination or other feature which may suggest that the vehicle is a taxi.

(2) Any person who knowingly—

(a) drives a vehicle in respect of which subsection (1) is contravened; or

(b) causes or permits that subsection to be contravened in respect of any vehicle,

shall be liable on summary conviction to a fine not exceeding £200.

(3) In this section 'taxi' means a vehicle licensed under section 37 of the Town Police Clauses Act 1847, section 6 of the Metropolitan Carriage Act 1869, [section 10 of the Civic Government (Scotland) Act 1982] or any similar local enactment.

Notes

Appointment
Commencement order: SI 1980/913.

Amendment
Sub-s (3): amended by the Transport Act 1985, s 139(2), Sch 7.

Transport Act 1981

Miscellaneous

35. Charges for licensing of cabs and cab drivers   (1), (2)   . . .

(3) Where section 70 of the Local Government (Miscellaneous Provisions) Act 1976 (fees for vehicle and operator's licences) is not in force in the area of a district council, the sums to be paid for a licence granted by the council under section 37 of the Town Police Clauses Act 1847 (licensing of cabs outside London) shall be such as the council may determine, and different sums may be so determined with respect to different descriptions of vehicle; and the sums so determined shall be such as appear to the council to be sufficient in the aggregate to cover in whole or in part—

    (*a*)   the reasonable cost of the carrying out by or on behalf of the district council of inspections of hackney carriages for the purpose of determining whether any such licence should be granted or renewed;

    (*b*)   the reasonable cost of providing hackney carriage stands; and

    (*c*)   any reasonable administrative or other costs in connection with the foregoing and with the control and supervision of hackney carriages.

[(3A) In subsection (3) above, references to a district council shall be read, in relation to Wales, as references to a county council or a county borough council.]

(4) This section does not extend to Scotland.

(5) This section comes into force on such day as the Secretary of State may by order made by statutory instrument, appoint, and different days may be so appointed for different purposes.

Notes

Appointment
Commencement orders: SI 1981/1331, SI 1982/310.

Amendment
Sub-ss (1), (2): amend the Metropolitan Public Carriage Act 1869, ss 6, 8.
Sub-s (3A): inserted by the Local Government (Wales) Act 1994, s 22(1), Sch 7, para 37.

Transport Act 1985

Taxis and hire cars

10. Immediate hiring of taxis at separate fares (1) In the circumstances mentioned in subsection (2) below, a licensed taxi may be hired for use for the carriage of passengers for hire or reward at separate fares without thereby—

(a) becoming a public service vehicle for the purposes of the 1981 Act or any related enactment; or

(b) ceasing (otherwise than by virtue of any provision made under section 13 of this Act) to be subject to the taxi code.

(2) The circumstances are that—

(a) the taxi is hired in an area where a scheme made under this section is in operation;

(b) the taxi is licensed by the licensing authority for that area; and

(c) the hiring falls within the terms of the scheme.

(3) In this section 'licensing authority' means—

(a) in relation to the London taxi area, the Secretary of State or the holder for the time being of any office designated by the Secretary of State for the purposes of this section; and

(b) in relation to any other area in England and Wales, the authority having responsibility for licensing taxis in that area.

(4) For the purposes of this section, a licensing authority may make a scheme for their area and shall make such a scheme if the holders of at least ten per cent. of the current taxi licences issued by the authority request the authority in writing to do so.

(5) Any scheme made under this section shall—

(a) designate the places in the area from which taxis may be hired under the scheme ('authorised places');

(b) specify the requirements to be met for the purposes of the scheme in relation to the hiring of taxis at separate fares; and

(c) if made otherwise than by the Secretary of State—

(i) include such provision, or provision of such description, as may be prescribed for the purposes of this sub-paragraph;

(ii) not include provision of any such description as may be prescribed for the purposes of this sub-paragraph.

(6) Subject to subsection (5) above, any scheme made under this section may, in particular, make provision with respect to:

(a) fares;

(b) the display of any document, plate, mark or sign for indicating an authorised place or that a taxi standing at an authorised place is available for the carriage of passengers at separate fares;

(*c*) the manner in which arrangements are to be made for the carriage of passengers on any such hiring as is mentioned in subsection (1) above; and

(*d*) the conditions to apply to the use of a taxi on any such hiring.

(7) A licensing authority may, subject to subsection (5) above, vary any scheme made by them under this section.

(8) Except in the case of a scheme made by the Secretary of State, any scheme under this section, and any variation of such a scheme, shall be made in accordance with the prescribed procedure.

(9) For the purposes of this section:

(*a*) the hiring of a taxi falls within the terms of a scheme if—
  (i)   it is hired from an authorised place; and
  (ii) the hiring meets the requirements specified by the licensing authority as those to be met for the purposes of the scheme; and

(*b*) a taxi is hired from an authorised place if it is standing at that place when it is hired and the persons hiring it are all present there.

(10) The power of the Secretary of State to make a scheme for the purpose of this section shall be exercisable by order.

Notes

Appointment
Commencement order: SI 1986/1088.

11. Advance booking of taxis and hire cars at separate fares   (1)   Where the conditions mentioned in subsection (2) below are met, a licensed taxi or licensed hire car may be used for the carriage of passengers for hire or reward at separate fares without thereby—

(*a*) becoming a public service vehicle for the purposes of the 1981 Act or any related enactment; or

(*b*) ceasing (otherwise than by virtue of any provision made under section 13 of this Act) to be subject to the taxi code or (as the case may be) the hire car code.

(2) The conditions are that—

(*a*) all the passengers carried on the occasion in question booked their journeys in advance; and

(*b*) each of them consented, when booking his journey, to sharing the use of the vehicle on that occasion with others on the basis that a separate fare would be payable by each passenger for his own journey on that occasion.

Notes

Appointment
Commencement order: SI 1986/1088.

12. Use of taxis in providing local services   (1)   Where the holder of a taxi licence—

(*a*) applies to the appropriate traffic commissioner for a restricted PSV operator's licence to be granted to him under Part II of the 1981 Act; and

(*b*) states in his application that he proposes to use one or more licensed taxis to provide a local service;

section 14 of the 1981 Act (conditions to be met before grant of PSV operator's licence) shall not apply and the commissioner shall grant the application.

(2) In this section 'special licence' means a restricted PSV operator's licence granted by virtue of this section.

(3) . . .

(4) Without prejudice to his powers to attach other conditions under section 16 of the 1981 Act, any traffic commissioner granting a special licence shall attach to it, under that section, the conditions mentioned in subsection (5) below.

(5) The conditions are—

(*a*) that every vehicle used under the licence shall be one for which the holder of the licence has a taxi licence; and
(*b*) that no vehicle shall be used under the licence otherwise than for the purpose of providing a local service with one or more stopping places within the area of the authority which granted the taxi licence of the vehicle in question.

(6) In subsection (5)(*b*) above 'local service' does not include an excursion or tour.

(7) The maximum number of vehicles which the holder of a special licence may at any one time use under the licence shall be the number of vehicles for which (for the time being) he holds taxi licences; and a condition to that effect shall be attached to every special licence under section 16(1) of the 1981 Act.

(8) Section 1(2) of the 1981 Act (vehicle used as public service vehicle to be treated as such until that use is permanently discontinued) shall not apply to any use of a licensed taxi for the provision of a local service under a special licence.

(9) At any time when a licensed taxi is being so used it shall carry such documents, plates and marks, in such manner, as may be prescribed.

(10) Such provisions in the taxi code as may be prescribed shall apply in relation to a licensed taxi at any time when it is being so used; and any such provision may be so applied subject to such modifications as may be prescribed.

(11) For the purposes of section 12(3) of the 1981 Act (which provides that where two or more PSV operators' licences are held they must be granted by traffic commissioners for different traffic areas), special licences shall be disregarded.

(12) A person may hold more than one special licence but shall not at the same time hold more than one such licence granted by the traffic commissioner for a particular traffic area.

(13) The following provisions shall not apply in relation to special licences or (as the case may be) the use of vehicles under such licences—

(*a*) sections 16(1A) and (2), 17(3)(*d*), 18 to 20 . . . and 26 of the 1981 Act; and
(*b*) section 26(5) and (6) of this Act;

and for the purposes of section 12 of that Act this section shall be treated as if it were in Part II of that Act.

Notes

Appointment
Commencement order: SI 1985/1887.

Amendment
Sub-s (3): repealed by the Deregulation and Contracting Out Act 1994, ss 68, 81, Sch 14, para 8, Sch 17.
Sub-s (13): figure omitted repealed by the Road Traffic (Driver Licensing and Information Systems) Act 1989, s 16, Sch 6. ˙

Modification
Sub-s (12) modified by the Operation of Public Service Vehicles (Partnership) Regulations 1986, SI 1986/1628, reg 5(1), Schedule, Part II.

13. Provisions supplementary to sections 10 to 12 (1) The Secretary of State may by order make such modifications of the taxi code and the hire car code as he sees fit for the purpose of supplementing the provision of sections 10 to 12 of this Act.

(2) Any order made under subsection (1) above may, in particular, modify any provision—

   (*a*) relating to fares payable by the hirer of a vehicle;
   (*b*) requiring the driver of any vehicle to accept any hiring, or to drive at the direction of a hirer, or (as the case may be) of a prospective hirer, to any place within or not exceeding any specified distance or for any period of time not exceeding a specified period from the time of hiring;
   (*c*) making the carriage of additional passengers in any vehicle which is currently subject to a hiring dependent on the consent of the hirer.

(3) In this section, and in sections 10 to 12 of this Act—

'licensed taxi' means—

   (*a*) in England and Wales, a vehicle licensed under—
      (i) section 37 of the Town Police Clauses Act 1847; or
      (ii) section 6 of the Metropolitan Public Carriage Act 1869;

or under any similar enactment; and

   (*b*) in Scotland, a taxi licensed under section 10 of the Civic Government (Scotland) Act 1982;

'London taxi area' means the area to which the Metropolitan Public Carriage Act 1869 applies;

'licensed hire car' means a vehicle which is licensed under section 48 of the Local Government (Miscellaneous Provisions) Act 1976 [or section 7 of the Private Hire Vehicles (London) Act 1998];

'hire car code', in relation to a licensed hire car used as mentioned in section 11 of this Act, means those provisions made by or under any enactment which would apply if it were hired by a single passenger for his exclusive use;

'related enactment', in relation to the 1981 Act, means any statutory provision (whenever passed or made) relating to public service vehicles in which 'public service vehicle' is defined directly or indirectly by reference to the provisions of the 1981 Act;

'taxi code', in relation to any licensed taxi used as mentioned in section 10, 11 or 12 of this Act, means—

   (*a*) in England and Wales, those provisions made by or under any enactment which would apply if the vehicle were plying for hire and were hired by a single passenger for his exclusive use; and (*b*)   in Scotland, the provisions of sections 10 to 23 of the Civic Government (Scotland) Act 1982, and Part I of that Act as it applies to these provisions; and

'taxi licence' means a licence under section 6 of the Metropolitan Public Carriage Act 1869, section 7 of the Town Police Clauses Act 1847 or any similar enactment, or a taxi licence under section 10 of the Civic Government (Scotland) Act 1982.

(4)   Any order made under subsection (1) above may contain such supplementary, incidental, consequential and transitional provisions (including provisions modifying any enactment contained in any Act other than this Act) as appear to the Secretary of State to be necessary or expedient in consequence of any modification of the taxi code or the private hire car code made by the order.

Notes

Appointment
Commencement orders: SI 1985/1887, SI 1986/1088.

Amendment
Sub-s (3): in definition 'licensed hire car' words 'or section 7 of the Private Hire Vehicles (London) Act 1998' in square brackets inserted by the Private Hire Vehicles (London) Act 1998, s 39(1), Sch 1, para 4.
    Date in force: to be appointed: see the Private Hire Vehicles (London) Act 1998, s 40(2).

14. Operation of taxis and private hire cars in Scotland for the carriage of passengers at separate fares   (1)   As respects Scotland, a taxi (other than a taxi which is for the time being operating a local service which is or requires to be registered under this Part of this Act, has been previously advertised and has a destination and route which are not entirely at the discretion of the passengers) or private hire car which is used for the carriage of passengers for hire or reward at separate fares shall not by reason of such use become a public service vehicle for the purposes of the 1981 Act or any related enactment.

(2)   In this section 'taxi' and private hire car' have the meanings given in section 23 of the Civic Government (Scotland) Act 1982 and 'related enactment' has the meaning given in section 13(3) of this Act.

Notes

Appointment
Commencement order: SI 1986/1794.

15. Extension of taxi licensing in England and Wales   (1)   Where, immediately before the commencement of this section, the provisions of the Town Police Clauses Act 1847 with respect to hackney carriages and of the Town Police Clauses Act 1889 (as incorporated in each case in the Public Health Act 1875) were not in force throughout the whole of the area of a district council in England and Wales whose area lies outside the area to which the Metropolitan Public Carriage Act 1869 applies, those provisions (as so incorporated) shall—

(*a*)   if not then in force in any part of the council's area, apply throughout that area; and

(*b*)   if in force in part only of its area, apply also in the remainder of that area.

(2)   Where part only of a district council's area lies outside the area to which the Act of 1869 applies, that part shall, for the purposes of subsection (1) above, be treated as being the area of the council.

(3) So much of any local Act as enables a district council to bring to an end the application of the provisions mentioned in subsection (1) above to the whole or any part of their area shall cease to have effect.

Notes

Appointment
Commencement order: SI 1986/1794.

See Further
See further: SI 1986/1794, art 8.

16. Taxi licensing: control of numbers   The provisions of the Town Police Clauses Act 1847 with respect to hackney carriages, as incorporated in any enactment (whenever passed), shall have effect—

(*a*)   as if in section 37, the words 'such number of' and 'as they think fit' were omitted; and

(*b*)   as if they provided that the grant of a licence may be refused, for the purpose of limiting the number of hackney carriages in respect of which licences are granted, if, but only if, the person authorised to grant licences is satisfied that there is no significant demand for the services of hackney carriages (within the area to which the licence would apply) which is unmet.

Notes

Appointment
Commencement order: SI 1985/1887.

Disability Discrimination Act 1995

Part V
Public Transport

Taxis

32. Taxi accessibility regulations (1)   The Secretary of State may make regulations ('taxi accessibility regulations') for the purpose of securing that it is possible—

(*a*)   for disabled persons—
  (i)   to get into and out of taxis in safety;
  (ii)   to be carried in taxis in safety and in reasonable comfort; and

(*b*)   for disabled persons in wheelchairs—
  (i)   to be conveyed in safety into and out of taxis while remaining in their wheelchairs; and
  (ii)   to be carried in taxis in safety and in reasonable comfort while remaining in their wheelchairs.

(2)   Taxi accessibility regulations may, in particular—

(*a*)   require any regulated taxi to conform with provisions of the regulations as to—
  (i)   the size of any door opening which is for the use of passengers;
  (ii)   the floor area of the passenger compartment;
  (iii) the amount of headroom in the passenger compartment;
  (iv)   the fitting of restraining devices designed to ensure the stability of a wheelchair while the taxi is moving;

(*b*)   require the driver of any regulated taxi which is plying for hire, or which has been hired, to comply with provisions of the regulations as to the carrying of ramps or other devices designed to facilitate the loading and unloading of wheelchairs;

(*c*)   require the driver of any regulated taxi in which a disabled person who is in a wheelchair is being carried (while remaining in his wheelchair) to comply with provisions of the regulations as to the position in which the wheelchair is to be secured.

(3)   The driver of a regulated taxi which is plying for hire, or which has been hired, is guilty of an offence if—

(*a*)   he fails to comply with any requirement imposed on him by the regulations; or

(*b*)   the taxi fails to conform with any provision of the regulations with which it is required to conform.

(4)   A person who is guilty of such an offence is liable, on summary conviction, to a fine not exceeding level 3 on the standard scale.

(5)   In this section—

'passenger compartment' has such meaning as may be prescribed;

'regulated taxi' means any taxi to which the regulations are expressed to apply;

'taxi' means a vehicle licensed under—

(a)   section 37 of the Town Police Clauses Act 1847, or
(b)   section 6 of the Metropolitan Public Carriage Act 1869,

but does not include a taxi which is drawn by a horse or other animal.

33. Designated transport facilities   (1)   In this section 'a franchise agreement' means a contract entered into by the operator of a designated transport facility for the provision by the other party to the contract of hire car services—

(a)   for members of the public using any part of the transport facility; and
(b)   which involve vehicles entering any part of that facility.

(2)   The Secretary of State may by regulations provide for the application of any taxi provision in relation to—

(a)   vehicles used for the provision of services under a franchise agreement; or
(b)   the drivers of such vehicles.

(3)   Any regulations under subsection (2) may apply any taxi provision with such modifications as the Secretary of State considers appropriate.

(4)   In this section—

'designated' means designated for the purposes of this section by an order made by the Secretary of State;

'hire car' has such meaning as may be prescribed;

'operator', in relation to a transport facility, means any person who is concerned with the management or operation of the facility;

'taxi provision' means any provision of—

(a)   this Act, or
(b)   regulations made in pursuance of section 20(2A) of the Civic Government (Scotland) Act 1982,

which applies in relation to taxis or the drivers of taxis; and

'transport facility' means any premises which form part of any port, airport, railway station or bus station.

34. New licences conditional on compliance with taxi accessibility regulations   (1)   No licensing authority shall grant a licence for a taxi to ply for hire unless the vehicle conforms with those provisions of the taxi accessibility regulations with which it will be required to conform if licensed.

(2)   Subsection (1) does not apply if such a licence was in force with respect to the vehicle at any time during the period of 28 days immediately before the day on which the licence is granted.

(3)   The Secretary of State may by order provide for subsection (2) to cease to have effect on such date as may be specified in the order.

(4)   Separate orders may be made under subsection (3) with respect to different areas or localities.

35. Exemption from taxi accessibility regulations   (1)   The Secretary of State may make regulations ('exemption regulations') for the purpose of enabling any relevant licensing authority to apply to him for an order (an 'exemption order') exempting the authority from the requirements of section 34.

(2) Exemption regulations may, in particular, make provision requiring a licensing authority proposing to apply for an exemption order—

    (*a*)   to carry out such consultations as may be prescribed;

    (*b*)   to publish the proposal in the prescribed manner;

    (*c*)   to consider any representations made to it about the proposal, before applying for the order;

    (*d*)   to make its application in the prescribed form.

(3) A licensing authority may apply for an exemption order only if it is satisfied—

    (*a*)   that, having regard to the circumstances prevailing in its area, it would be inappropriate for the requirements of section 34 to apply; and

    (*b*)   that the application of section 34 would result in an unacceptable reduction in the number of taxis in its area.

(4) After considering any application for an exemption order and consulting the Disabled Persons Transport Advisory Committee and such other persons as he considers appropriate, the Secretary of State may—

    (*a*)   make an exemption order in the terms of the application;

    (*b*)   make an exemption order in such other terms as he considers appropriate; or

    (*c*)   refuse to make an exemption order.

(5) The Secretary of State may by regulations ('swivel seat regulations') make provision requiring any exempt taxi plying for hire in an area in respect of which an exemption order is in force to conform with provisions of the regulations as to the fitting and use of swivel seats.

(6) The Secretary of State may by regulations make provision with respect to swivel seat regulations similar to that made by section 34 with respect to taxi accessibility regulations.

(7) In this section—

'exempt taxi' means a taxi in relation to which section 34(1) would apply if the exemption order were not in force;

'relevant licensing authority' means a licensing authority responsible for licensing taxis in any area of England and Wales other than the area to which the Metropolitan Public Carriage Act 1869 applies; and

'swivel seats' has such meaning as may be prescribed.

36. Carrying of passengers in wheelchairs (1) This section imposes duties on the driver of a regulated taxi which has been hired:

    (*a*)   by or for a disabled person who is in a wheelchair; or

    (*b*)   by a person who wishes such a disabled person to accompany him in the taxi.

(2) In this section—

'carry' means carry in the taxi concerned; and

'the passenger' means the disabled person concerned.

(3) The duties are—

    (*a*)   to carry the passenger while he remains in his wheelchair;

    (*b*)   not to make any additional charge for doing so;

    (*c*)   if the passenger chooses to sit in a passenger seat, to carry the wheelchair;

(*d*) to take such steps as are necessary to ensure that the passenger is carried in safety and in reasonable comfort;

(*e*) to give such assistance as may be reasonably required—

    (i) to enable the passenger to get into or out of the taxi;

    (ii) if the passenger wishes to remain in his wheelchair, to enable him to be conveyed into and out of the taxi while in his wheelchair;

    (iii) to load the passenger's luggage into or out of the taxi;

    (iv) if the passenger does not wish to remain in his wheelchair, to load the wheelchair into or out of the taxi.

(4) Nothing in this section is to be taken to require the driver of any taxi—

(*a*) except in the case of a taxi of a prescribed description, to carry more than one person in a wheelchair, or more than one wheelchair, on any one journey; or

(*b*) to carry any person in circumstances in which it would otherwise be lawful for him to refuse to carry that person.

(5) A driver of a regulated taxi who fails to comply with any duty imposed on him by this section is guilty of an offence and liable, on summary conviction, to a fine not exceeding level 3 on the standard scale.

(6) In any proceedings for an offence under this section, it is a defence for the accused to show that, even though at the time of the alleged offence the taxi conformed with those provisions of the taxi accessibility regulations with which it was required to conform, it would not have been possible for the wheelchair in question to be carried in safety in the taxi.

(7) If the licensing authority is satisfied that it is appropriate to exempt a person from the duties imposed by this section—

(*a*) on medical grounds, or

(*b*) on the ground that his physical condition makes it impossible or unreasonably difficult for him to comply with the duties imposed on drivers by this section,

it shall issue him with a certificate of exemption.

(8) A certificate of exemption shall be issued for such period as may be specified in the certificate.

(9) The driver of a regulated taxi is exempt from the duties imposed by this section if—

(*a*) a certificate of exemption issued to him under this section is in force; and

(*b*) the prescribed notice of his exemption is exhibited on the taxi in the prescribed manner.

37. Carrying of guide dogs and hearing dogs (1) This section imposes duties on the driver of a taxi which has been hired—

(*a*) by or for a disabled person who is accompanied by his guide dog or hearing dog, or

(*b*) by a person who wishes such a disabled person to accompany him in the taxi.

(2) The disabled person is referred to in this section as 'the passenger'.

(3) The duties are—

(*a*) to carry the passenger's dog and allow it to remain with the passenger; and

(*b*) not to make any additional charge for doing so.

(4) A driver of a taxi who fails to comply with any duty imposed on him by this section is guilty of an offence and liable, on summary conviction, to a fine not exceeding level 3 on the standard scale.

(5) If the licensing authority is satisfied that it is appropriate on medical grounds to exempt a person from the duties imposed by this section, it shall issue him with a certificate of exemption.

(6) In determining whether to issue a certificate of exemption, the licensing authority shall, in particular, have regard to the physical characteristics of the taxi which the applicant drives or those of any kind of taxi in relation to which he requires the certificate.

(7) A certificate of exemption shall be issued—

(*a*) with respect to a specified taxi or a specified kind of taxi; and
(*b*) for such period as may be specified in the certificate.

(8) The driver of a taxi is exempt from the duties imposed by this section if—

(*a*) a certificate of exemption issued to him under this section is in force with respect to the taxi; and
(*b*) the prescribed notice of his exemption is exhibited on the taxi in the prescribed manner.

(9) The Secretary of State may, for the purposes of this section, prescribe any other category of dog trained to assist a disabled person who has a disability of a prescribed kind.

(10) This section applies in relation to any such prescribed category of dog as it applies in relation to guide dogs.

(11) In this section—

'guide dog' means a dog which has been trained to guide a blind person; and

'hearing dog' means a dog which has been trained to assist a deaf person.

38. Appeal against refusal of exemption certificate (1) Any person who is aggrieved by the refusal of a licensing authority to issue an exemption certificate under section 36 or 37 may appeal to the appropriate court before the end of the period of 28 days beginning with the date of the refusal.

(2) On an appeal to it under this section, the court may direct the licensing authority concerned to issue the appropriate certificate of exemption to have effect for such period as may be specified in the direction.

(3) 'Appropriate court' means the magistrates' court for the petty sessions area in which the licensing authority has its principal office.

SI 1979/1379
Taximeters (EEC Requirements) Regulations 1979

Made - - - 30th October 1979

Part I
General

1. Citation and commencement These Regulations may be cited as the Taximeters (EEC Requirements) Regulations 1979 and shall come into operation on 1st December 1979.

2. Interpretation (1) In these Regulations—

'the Directive' means Council Directive No 77/95/EEC on the approximation of the laws of the member States relating to taximeters;

'inspector' means a person authorised in writing by the Secretary of State to be an inspector for the purposes of these Regulations;

'the relevant limits of error' means the range of permissible errors laid down by item 5.1 and 5.2 of the Annex to the Directive;

'manufacturer', where more than one person is responsible for the manufacture of an instrument, means the person responsible for the final stage of manufacture;

['the principal Regulations' means the Measuring Instruments (EEC Requirements) Regulations 1988];

'taximeters' means instruments which, according to the characteristics of the vehicle in which they are installed and the tariffs for which they have been set, calculate automatically and indicate constantly when in use the fares to be paid by the users of taxi-cabs on the basis of the distance covered, and, below a certain speed, the time for which the vehicle is occupied, exclusive of various surcharges which may be authorised by local regulations in force in member States.

(2) These Regulations shall extend to Northern Ireland.

Notes

Amendment
Para (1): definition 'the principal Regulations' substituted by SI 1988/1128, reg 5(*a*).

3. Application These Regulations apply to taximeters not containing an electronic device in the measuring sequence; and references to instruments in these Regulations are references to such taximeters.

4. Pattern approval and partial verification: the EEC signs and marks (1) The EEC signs and marks referred to in these Regulations are the following signs and marks—

    (*a*) The sign of EEC pattern approval described in paragraph 1 of Schedule 1 to the principal Regulations;

    (*b*) The sign of EEC limited pattern approval described in paragraph 2 of the said Schedule 1; and

(c) The mark of EEC partial verification described in paragraph 6 of the said Schedule 1.

In these Regulations references to the United Kingdom version of a sign or mark referred to in paragraph (1) above are references to the sign or mark appropriate, in accordance with the provisions of the said Schedule, for an EEC pattern approval granted in, or an EEC partial verification carried out in, the United Kingdom.

Part II
EEC Pattern Approval and Partial Verification in the United Kingdom

5. Introductory This part of the Regulations contains provisions with respect to the grant, extension and revocation of EEC pattern approval in the United Kingdom and the carrying out of EEC partial verification in the United Kingdom and generally with respect to the application in the United Kingdom of the EEC signs and marks in relation to instruments to which these Regulations apply.

6. EEC Pattern Approval (1) [Regulations 8 to 12] (which contain amongst other things provision with respect to the grant, extension and revocation of EEC pattern approval in the United Kingdom) of the principal Regulations, and Schedule 2 to those Regulations (which regulates the conduct in the United Kingdom of EEC pattern approval), shall so far as applicable apply in relation to the pattern approval of instruments to which these Regulations apply as they apply in relation to the pattern approval of instruments to which those Regulations apply.

(2) Where an EEC pattern approval (whether granted under these Regulations or by any member State other than the United Kingdom) is in force in respect of any pattern of instrument, the manufacturer shall cause the sign of EEC pattern approval, or where the pattern approval is a limited pattern approval, the sign of EEC limited pattern approval, to be affixed to instruments conforming to the approved pattern on the dial or on a sealed plate, and the sign must be easily visible and legible under normal conditions of installation.

Notes

Amendment
Para (1): amended by SI 1988/1128, reg 5(b).

7. EEC partial verification (1) An application for consideration of any instrument for EEC partial verification shall be made to the Secretary of State in such manner as he may direct.

(2) The Secretary of State shall determine whether an EEC pattern approval is in force in respect of the instrument and, if so, whether it conforms to the approved pattern.

(3) Where the Secretary of State is satisfied—

(a) that the instrument conforms to the requirements of the Directive; and
(b) that an EEC pattern approval is in force in respect of the instrument and that the instrument conforms to the approved pattern, and bears the sign required by Regulation 6 (2) above;

he shall cause to be affixed to the instrument the United Kingdom mark of EEC partial verification.

(4) If the Secretary of State refuses to cause any mark of EEC partial verification to be affixed to an instrument he shall give to the applicant a statement in writing of his reasons for the refusal.

(5) Where an EEC pattern approval is subject to a condition limiting the number of instruments which may be submitted for partial verification by reference to the pattern in question, a person who makes an application, or causes or permits the making of an application, which if granted would contravene the condition shall be guilty of an offence unless it is shown that he did not know, and had no reason to believe, that it would or might contravene the condition.

Part III
Whole Measuring Systems

8. (1)   Whole measuring systems for use in the United Kingdom shall be adjusted in such a way that the relevant limits of error are asymmetric in relation to the zero error and that all errors are in favour of the hirer.

(2)   In this Regulation 'whole measuring system' means the vehicle and the taximeter bearing an EEC mark which is installed in it.

Part IV
Supplementary Provisions

9. Enforcement of conditions applicable to EEC limited pattern approval
Where an EEC limited pattern approval is subject to a condition limiting the use of instruments of the pattern in question a person who, knowing that any such condition applies to any instrument, disposes of the instrument to any other person in a state in which it could be used without informing that other person of the condition, shall be guilty of an offence, and the instrument shall be liable to be forfeited.

10. Effect of revocation of EEC pattern approval   (1)   Where an EEC pattern approval is revoked, whether under these Regulations or by any member State other than the United Kingdom, any person who, knowing that the pattern approval has been revoked, disposes of an instrument of the pattern in question bearing any EEC sign or mark related to that pattern approval to any other person in a condition in which it could be used without informing that other person of the revocation, shall be guilty of an offence and the instrument shall be liable to be forfeited.

(2)   Paragraph (1) above does not apply if any such sign or mark on the instrument has been obliterated under Regulation 13 below.

(3)   For the purposes of this Regulation and Regulations 11 and 13 below, an EEC sign or mark shall be regarded as related to a pattern approval if it is a sign framed by reference to that pattern approval or a mark of EEC partial verification which was affixed by reference to conformity to the pattern which was the subject of that pattern approval.

(4)   A certificate by the Secretary of State stating that an EEC pattern approval granted by any member State other than the United Kingdom has been revoked and thereby ceased to have effect on a date specified shall be conclusive as to the matters certified in any proceedings for an offence under this Regulation.

11. Effect of non-extension of EEC pattern approval   Where an EEC pattern approval, whether granted under these Regulations or by any member State other than the United Kingdom, is not extended—

    (*a*)   these Regulations shall, in relation to any instrument of the pattern in question which was used before the pattern approval ceased to have effect, apply as if the pattern approval had continued in force;

(*b*) the manufacturer of any instrument of the pattern in question, bearing any EEC sign or mark related to that pattern approval, which has not been so used shall be guilty of an offence, if, after the pattern approval has ceased to have effect, he disposes of the instrument to any other person, and the instrument shall be liable to be forfeited.

12. Temporary prohibition of sale (1) Where the Secretary of State is satisfied that instruments constructed according to a pattern in respect of which an EEC pattern approval granted by a member State other than the United Kingdom is in force reveal in service a defect of a general nature which makes them unsuitable for their intended use, he may issue a prohibition notice under this Regulation with respect to instruments of that pattern.

(2) Regulation 10 above shall apply, with the necessary modifications, so long as a prohibition notice issued under this Regulation is in force with respect to instruments of any pattern, as it applies in a case where pattern approval is revoked by the Secretary of State.

(3) A prohibition notice under this Regulation shall give particulars of the pattern to which it relates.

(4) The Secretary of State may withdraw a prohibition notice at any time.

(5) If the Secretary of State issues a prohibition notice under this Regulation he shall give a statement in writing of his grounds for doing so to any person appearing to him to be concerned.

(6) The Secretary of State shall cause to be published—

(*a*) any prohibition notice issued under this Regulation; and
(*b*) notice of withdrawal of any such prohibition notice.

13. Obliteration of EEC signs and marks (1) An inspector may obliterate any EEC sign or mark affixed to an instrument not incorporated in a vehicle if he is satisfied—

(*a*) that the instrument bearing the sign or mark falls outside the relevant limits of error, or
(*b*) that the instrument does not comply in any other respect with the requirements of the Directive.

(2) Without prejudice to paragraph (1) above, an inspector may, at the request of any person appearing to him to be the owner of an instrument, obliterate any EEC sign or mark on the instrument which is related to an EEC pattern approval (whether granted under these Regulations or by any member State other than the United Kingdom) which the inspector is satisfied has ceased to have effect.

(3) Subject to paragraph (4) below, obliteration under this Regulation shall be carried out by an inspector by means of punches or pincers of a six-pointed star design as shown in the following illustration—

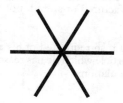

(4) Paragraph (3) above shall not apply where in the opinion of the inspector it would be impossible to obliterate any EEC sign or mark by the method there specified; and in any such case obliteration shall be carried out in such other manner as the Secretary of State may direct, whether generally or in relation to signs or marks of any particular description.

14. Unauthorised application of EEC signs and marks, etc (1) Subject to paragraph (2) below, any person who, in the case of any instrument—

(*a*) not being an inspector or a person acting under the authority of an inspector, marks in any manner any plug, seal or plate used or designed for use for the reception of any EEC mark; or

(*b*) not being a manufacturer authorised or required to do so under any provision of these Regulations, or the duly authorised agent of any such manufacturer, marks any such instrument with any EEC sign; or

(*c*) forges, counterfeits or, except in accordance with Regulation 13 above, in any way alters or defaces any EEC sign or mark; or

(*d*) removes any EEC sign or mark and inserts it into any instrument; or

(*e*) makes any alteration in the instrument after any EEC sign or mark has been applied to it in accordance with these Regulations, so that it no longer complies with the requirements of the Directive;

shall be guilty of an offence.

(2) A person shall not be guilty of an offence under paragraph (1) above by reason solely of the destruction or obliteration of any sign, mark, plug, seal or plate in the course of the adjustment or repair of any instrument by, or by the duly authorised agent of, a person who is the manufacturer of, or regularly engaged in the business of repairing, instruments.

(3) Any person who sells or exposes or offers for sale any instrument which to his knowledge—

(*a*) bears any EEC sign or mark which is a forgery or counterfeit, or which has been transferred from another instrument, or which has been altered or defaced otherwise than under Regulation 13 above, or as permitted by virtue of paragraph (2) above, or

(*b*) does not comply with the requirement of the Directive by reason of any alteration made in the instrument after any EEC sign or mark was applied to it in accordance with these Regulations;

shall be guilty of an offence.

(4) Any instrument in respect of which an offence under this Regulation was committed, and any implement used in the commission of the offence, shall be liable to be forfeited.

15. Powers of inspection and entry (1) Subject to the production if so requested of his authority, an inspector may, at all reasonable times—

(*a*) inspect and test any instrument not incorporated in a vehicle;

(*b*) enter any premises at which he has reasonable cause to believe any such instruments are manufactured or stored, not being premises used only as a private dwelling house.

(2) Subject to the production if so requested of his authority, an inspector may at any time seize and detain any article which he has reasonable cause to believe is liable to be forfeited under these Regulations.

(3) If a justice of the peace, by information on oath—

(*a*) is satisfied that there is reasonable ground to believe that any such instrument or article as is mentioned in paragraph (1) or (2) above is manufactured or stored on any premises, or that any offence under these Regulations has been, is being or is about to be committed on any premises; and

(*b*) is also satisfied either—

  (i) that admission to the premises has been refused, or a refusal is apprehended, and that notice of the intention to apply for a warrant has been given to the occupier, or

  (ii) that an application for admission, or the giving of such a notice, would defeat the object of the entry, or that the case is one of urgency, or that the premises are unoccupied or the occupier is temporarily absent;

the justice may by warrant under his hand, which shall continue in force for a period of one month, authorise an inspector to enter the premises, if need be by force. In the application of this paragraph to Scotland, the expression 'a justice of the peace' shall be construed as including the sheriff. In the application of this paragraph to Northern Ireland, for the word 'information' there shall be substituted the word 'complaint'.

(4) An inspector entering any premises by virtue of this Regulation may take with him such other persons and such equipment as may appear to him necessary; and on leaving any premises which he has entered by virtue of a warrant under paragraph (3) above, being premises which are unoccupied or the occupier of which is temporarily absent, he shall leave them as effectively secured against trespassers as he found them.

(5) If any inspector or other person who enters any work-place by virtue of this Regulation discloses to any person any information obtained by him in the work-place with regard to any secret manufacturing process or trade secret, he shall, unless the disclosure was made in the performance of his duty, be guilty of an offence.

16. Obstruction of inspectors (1) Any person who—

(*a*) wilfully obstructs an inspector acting in the execution of any provision of these Regulations; or

(*b*) without reasonable cause fails to give any inspector acting as aforesaid any assistance or information which the inspector may reasonably require of him for the purposes of the performance by the inspector of his functions under these Regulations;

shall be guilty of an offence.

(2) If any person, in giving an inspector any such information as is mentioned in paragraph (1) above, gives any information which he knows to be false, he shall be guilty of an offence.

(3) Nothing in this Regulation shall be construed as requiring any person to answer any question or give any information if to do so might incriminate him.

17. Offences by corporations Regulation 24 of the principal Regulations (offences by corporations) shall apply in relation to offences under these Regulations as it applies in relation to offences under those Regulations.

18. Prosecution and punishment of offences Proceedings for any offence under these Regulations shall not—

(*a*) in England and Wales, be instituted except by or on behalf of the Secretary of State or the chief officer of police for a police area; or

(*b*) in Northern Ireland, be instituted except by or on behalf of the Department of Commerce for Northern Ireland or the Director of Public Prosecutions for Northern Ireland.

19. Any person guilty of an offence under Regulation 14, 15 or [16] above shall be liable on summary conviction to a fine not exceeding [£2000], and any person guilty of an offence under any other provision of these Regulations shall be liable on summary conviction to a fine not exceeding [£400].

Notes

Amendment
Amended by SI 1985/306, reg 5.

SI 1981/400
Hackney Carriage Fares (Amendment of Byelaws) Order 1981

Made - - - 14th March 1981

1. (1)   This Order may be cited as the Hackney Carriage Fares (Amendment of Byelaws) Order 1981 and shall come into operation on 25th March 1981.

2. (1)   If it appears to a local authority having power to amend any taxi fare byelaws that the charges permitted by such byelaws should be increased with a view to off-setting an addition to the costs of operating hackney carriages which is attributable to any of the variations of duty specified in paragraph (2) below affecting those costs, they may, for that purpose but subject to the provisions of this Order, at any time before 31st May 1981 or at their first meeting on or after that date, by resolution amend those byelaws so as to increase those charges.

(2)   The variations of duty mentioned in paragraph (1) above are—

(*a*)   the increases, with effect from 10th March 1981, in the rates of excise duty on hydrocarbon oils; and

(*b*)   the increases, with effect from 11th March 1981, in the rates of vehicle excise duty.

3. An increase in charges made in pursuance of this Order shall be a surcharge of a single sum, not exceeding 5p, in respect of each hiring and in any amendment of taxi fare byelaws permitting such surcharge there shall be included a provision requiring that a notice setting out the amount of the surcharge be prominently displayed in each hackney carriage in such a manner as to be clearly legible by the hirer throughout the hiring.

4. (1)   Where a local authority pass a resolution in pursuance of this Order they shall cause to be published, in two consecutive weeks in at least one local newspaper circulating in the area to which the taxi fare byelaws apply, a notice setting out the terms of the resolution.

(2)   A copy of the resolution shall be deposited at the offices of the local authority and shall at all reasonable hours be open to public inspection without payment, and a copy thereof shall, on application and without payment, be furnished to any person.

(3)   A resolution passed in pursuance of this Order shall not require confirmation by the Secretary of State.

Note

Amendment
This Order has not been revoked. However, the power conferred by the Order would appear to be spent by virtue of the dates specified in it. (Note by the DETR, Buses and Taxis Division.)

SI 1986/567
Local Services (Operation by Taxis) Regulations 1986

Made - - - 20th March 1986

1. Citation and commencement   These Regulations may be cited as the Local Services (Operation by Taxis) Regulations 1986 and shall come into operation on 16th April 1986.

2. Interpretation   (1)   In these Regulations—

'the 1847 Act' means the Town Police Clauses Act 1847;

'the 1976 Act' means the Local Government (Miscellaneous Provisions) Act 1976;

'the 1985 Act' means the Transport Act 1985;

'local service' has the meaning given by section 2 of the 1985 Act;

'local taxi area' means the area in which a vehicle is licensed to ply for hire under section 37 of the 1847 Act;

'special licence' means a restricted PSV operator's licence granted by virtue of section 12 of the 1985 Act;

'licensed taxi' and 'taxi code' have the meanings given by section 13(3) of the 1985 Act; and

'taximeter' has the meaning given by section 80(1) of the 1976 Act.

(2)   Any reference in these Regulations to the 1847 Act is a reference to that Act as it applies in relation to a vehicle as a part of the taxi code (and accordingly as it so applies as incorporated, extended or applied by or under any enactment).

3. Application   These Regulations apply to a licensed taxi which is licensed under section 37 of the 1847 Act, at any time when that vehicle is being used to provide a local service under a special licence.

4. Prescribed provisions   (1)   The provisions specified in the first column of the Table to the extent that they are part of the taxi code, subject to the exceptions and modifications specified in the second column thereof, are hereby prescribed as applying in relation to a vehicle to which these Regulations apply.

(2)   Where any part of the taxi code is contained in provisions made by or under any local Act, then any such provisions which have substantially similar purpose and effect to those provisions prescribed by paragraph (1) of this regulation are hereby prescribed as applying in relation to a vehicle to which these Regulations apply.

(3)   The provisions so prescribed shall apply—

    (*a*)   whether or not the use of the vehicle to provide a local service is within the local taxi area for that vehicle, and accordingly any limitation in those provisions to that area shall have no effect when the vehicle is being so used; and

    (*b*)   subject to the modification that any reference to a hackney carriage includes a reference to a vehicle to which these Regulations apply.

TABLE

Column 1	Column 2
Provisions Prescribed	**Modifications**
The 1847 Act, sections 37–65	Section 52 is modified by the omission of the words from 'or if the driver' to 'or any less number'; and sections 53–59, 62 and 64 are excepted.
Public Health Act 1875, section 251	None
The 1976 Act, Part II	Sections 63, 65–67, 69, and 75 are excepted Section 64(1) is modified by the omission of the words 'other than a hackney carriage'.
Any byelaws made under section 68 of the 1847 Act or conditions attached to a licence under section 47 of the 1976 Act with the purpose in either case of regulating:	None

    a. the display of the licence number on the vehicle;

    b. the number of persons that may be carried in the vehicle;

    c. the wearing of a badge by the driver;

    d. the safe custody and redelivery of any property accidentally left in the vehicle;

    e. the reporting of accidents

    f. the tampering with any taximeter with which the vehicle is provided;

    g. the civil and orderly behaviour of the driver and the precautions to be taken by him in regard to the safety of passengers; and

    h. the equipment and fittings of the vehicle;

and any byelaws prescribing penalties for breach of the above-mentioned byelaws

5. The holder of a special licence shall during such time as the vehicle is being used to provide a local service cause—

    (*a*)   to be displayed on the vehicle a notice clearly legible from the front which includes the word 'BUS' in letters at least 60 millimetres high and indicates either the destination of the vehicle, or its route, or the nature of the service being provided;

(*b*)   any notice which the vehicle is required to display to indicate that it is available for exclusive hire (including any such notice which bears any of the words 'hire', 'taxi' or 'cab') not to be illuminated by any light forming part of the equipment of the vehicle;

(*c*)   a fare table to be displayed in the vehicle in a manner clearly legible by passengers, and containing sufficient information for any passenger to ascertain the fare for his journey or the manner in which that fare is computed.

SI 1998/1946
Deregulation (Taxis and Private Hire Vehicles) Order 1998

Made 8th August 1998
Coming into force in accordance with Article 1

1. Citation and commencement   This Order may be cited as the Deregulation (Taxis and Private Hire Vehicles) Order 1998 and shall come into force 28 days after the day on which it is made.

Notes

Initial Commencement

Specified date
Specified date: 5 September 1998: see above.

2. Qualifications for drivers of private hire vehicles   In section 51 of the Local Government (Miscellaneous Provisions) Act 1976 (licensing of drivers of private hire vehicles), in subsection (1) as inserted by the Driving Licences (Community Driving Licence) Regulations 1996, in paragraph (*b*) after 'section 99A(1)' there shall be inserted 'or section 109(1)'.

Notes

Initial Commencement

Specified date
Specified date: 5 September 1998: see art 1.

3. Qualifications for drivers of taxis   In section 59 of the Local Government (Miscellaneous Provisions) Act 1976 (qualifications for drivers of hackney carriages), in subsection (1A) as inserted by the Driving Licences (Community Driving Licence) Regulations 1996, in paragraph (*b*) after 'section 99A(1)' there shall be inserted 'or section 109(1)'.

Notes

Initial Commencement

Specified date
Specified date: 5 September 1998: see art 1.

Circulars

Joint Circular from the DOT Circular 3/85, 4 December 1985

Scottish Development Department Circular 32/85 WO Circular 64/85

TRANSPORT ACT 1985

INTRODUCTION

1. This circular describes the provisions of the Transport Act 1985 as they affect local authorities in Great Britain though it does not purport to provide an interpretation of the law. It also explains the steps by which it is intended to bring in the new arrangements. Separate circulars, DTp 4/85 (WO 63/85) for England and Wales and SDD 30/85 for Scotland, describe the provisions about local authority and Passenger Transport Executive ('PTE') bus undertakings and their transfer to public transport companies and contain the statutory advice of the Secretary of State under sections 59, 68 and 69. The Departments will also be issuing shortly a Code of Practice on Tendering, and further guidance on concessionary fare schemes. A list of these and other proposed Departmental publications about the Act is at Annex 1.

Interpretation

2. References throughout this circular to county councils should be read as meaning non-metropolitan councils in Scotland. 'The Act' means the Transport Act 1985 and references to sections are to sections of that Act 1985 and references to sections are to sections of that Act unless otherwise stated. 'London' means the present administrative area of Greater London. 'The 1968 Act' means the Transport Act 1968 and 'the 1981 Act' means the Public Passenger Vehicles Act 1981.

Main provisions of the Act

3. The purpose of the Act is to establish the disciplines of a competitive market in the provision of local bus services. To achieve this the Act—

(1) in Parts I and II abolishes road service licensing everywhere in Great Britain outside London and replaces it with a system of registration; and reduces the barriers between bus and taxi operations;

(2) in Part III provides for the reorganisation and privatisation of the National Bus Company and its subsidiaries;

(3) in Part IV revises the public transport powers and responsibilities of local authorities and PTEs to suit competitive conditions; and provides for the transfer of existing local authority and PTE bus undertakings to public transport companies at arms length from their parent authorities;

(4) in Part V sets out new requirements for co-operation between social services, education and public transport authorities, and for tendering for subsidised local services; and contains provisions about travel concession schemes, and about certain grants;

(5) in Part VI applies to the bus industry various provisions of existing competition law and covers various miscellaneous matters;

(6) in schedule 6 sets out the arrangements for the transition from the old system to the new. The transitional period will run from 6 January to 25 October 1986.

This Act does not weaken the existing requirements for PSV operator licences and driver licences for vehicles and maintenance standards; these essential quality controls remain intact. Indeed, the Act contains some additional powers to control the behavior of operators of local services.

Implementation
4. Authorities with public transport responsibilities have a heavy programme of work throughout 1986 to implement the Act. Many are already well-advanced in their planning. Authorities' attention is particularly drawn to two matters on which very prompt action will need to be taken. The first is the preparation of new public transport policies and consultation on those policies, including specific consideration of the scope for co-ordination with education and social services transport. The requirements are set out in paragraphs 43–50, 65–70 and 81–86; these affect PTAs and county councils. Only when those policies are settled, can these authorities proceed to secure the particular services which require subsidy through a process of open tendering. The tendering is to be completed by 26 October 1986. Authorities will no doubt wish to complete the policy formulation stage by Easter 1986 at the latest. The second area needing quick action is the publication by 8 April 1986 of proposed concessionary fare schemes, for those authorities who wish to have power to compel operators to participate in them. This is set out in paragraphs 114 and 115.

PART I: GENERAL PROVISIONS RELATING TO ROAD PASSENGER TRANSPORT

Note Paragraphs 5–18 are not relevant to hackney carriage and private hire licensing.

Taxis and hire cars
19.   Sections 10 to 17 deal with taxis and hire cars. Apart from section 12, this circular is concerned only with those provisions as they affect taxi and hire car operation in England and Wales. The Scottish Development Department will be issuing a separate circular for Scotland in due course.

Sharing of taxis & hire cars in England and Wales
20.   Sections 10 and 11 provide for the sharing of taxis and hire cars in England and Wales by passengers paying separate fares. Section 10 provides for taxi sharing schemes and section 11 allows pre-booked passengers to be carried at separate fares in licensed taxis and licensed hire cars. These sections will be brought into force in early Summer 1986 with the necessary regulations and orders. Discussions are already taking place with the Association of District Councils and Association of Metropolitan Authorities about the future advice to be given to taxi licensing authorities about taxi sharing schemes made under section 10.

Taxis providing local services: special licences
21.   Section 12 lays down conditions under which taxis may be used to provide local services throughout Great Britain. In line with the other provisions relating to local services, this section will be brought into force on January 6. Vehicles operated under section 12 will be subject to hybrid controls. Vehicle quality and safety standards will continue to be the responsibility of the district council, as the taxi licensing authority. The service will, like any other local service, be subject to regulation by the traffic commissioner. Since such control may be exercised by means of conditions attached to the operator's licence, this section makes provision for a taxi proprietor to obtain a 'special licence' under conditions which recognise that he has already satisfied his district council of his suitability to operate passenger-carrying services. The object of this section is, therefore, to put a taxi proprietor wishing to operate local services on the same footing as a bus operator—making him subject to equivalent but not identical controls.

22.   The holder of a taxi licence will from 6 January be able to apply to the traffic commissioner for a special PSV operator's licence which will enable him to register

local services (whether those provided without subsidy or ones to be provided under a contract for service subsidies with a local authority or PTE). A local authority can consider a tender from a taxi proprietor who has not yet obtained his special licence but will not be able to award a contract until he has done so. During the transitional period, a holder of a special PSV operator's licence will be able to apply for a road service licence just like any other PSV operator's licence holder. Regulations governing the operation of vehicles under section 12 will be in place by 1 March 1986 to permit service to be provided under road service licences from that date.

Taxis providing local services in London
23.   Similar arrangements will apply in London, where the Assistant Commissioner of the Metropolitan Police, as the taxi licensing authority, will be responsible for ensuring quality control of taxis used to provide local services. Holding a special PSV operator's licence will enable the holder of a London taxi licence to operate local services from 1 March 1986 under agreement with London Regional Transport or under a London local service licence granted under Part II of the Act.

Section 13
24.   Section 13 will be brought into force on 6 January in order to provide the definitions required by section 12. Regulations made under section 13 will modify the taxi and hire car codes as they apply to vehicles operated under sections 10 and 11. These regulations will be brought into force with those sections.

Extension of taxi licensing in England and Wales
25.   Section 15 extends taxi licensing to all districts and parts of districts in England and Wales where there is no such licensing at present. The section will be brought into force later. District councils which license taxis in part of parts only of their area may wish to reconsider their policy on this matter with a view to rationalising their arrangements for taxi licensing before this section is brought into force. This would be achieved by resolution made under paragraph 25 of schedule 14 to the Local Government Act 1972 and, if appropriate, section 45 of the Local Government (Miscellaneous Provisions) Act 1976. The Department is willing to advise any district council on the procedure necessary and on the way in which they might implement taxi licensing.

Grant of taxi licences: vehicles with 8 passenger seats
26.   Section 16 will also be brought into effect on 6 January. This section qualifies the power which district councils now have under the Town Police Clauses Act 1847 to refuse to grant taxi licences in support of a policy of limiting the number of taxis in their area. Under the section a district may refuse an application for a licence in order to limit the number of taxis if, but only if, they are satisfied that there is no significant unmet demand for taxi services within the area to which the licence would apply. An applicant whose licence is refused by a district council has a right of appeal to the Crown Court. The section does not require district councils to limit the number of taxis licences they issue for this reason; it forbids them to restrict numbers for any other reason. The powers of district councils to refuse licences or put conditions on them, relating to the fitness of the applicant or his vehicle are undiminished. In view of the fact that these vehicles may now be authorised to carry passengers at separate fares, district councils may wish to review the conditions of fitness laid down for these vehicles and the enforcement of maintenance standards. The attention of district councils is drawn to the provisions of paragraph 1 of schedule 7, which establishes that taxis may be licensed with up to eight passenger seats.

Advice on the grant of taxi licences
27.   District councils may wish to review their policy on the control of taxi numbers in the light of the section. Limitation of taxi numbers can have many undesirable effects—an insufficiency of taxis, either generally or at particular times or in partic-

ular places; insufficient competition between the providers of taxi services, to the detriment of their customers; and prices for the transfer of taxi licences from one person to another which imply an artificial restriction of supply. Under the section a district council may refuse a licence to restrict numbers only if *satisfied* that there is not significant unmet demand for taxis in the relevant area. If there is an appeal, it will be for the council to convince the court that they had reasonable grounds for being so satisfied. It will not, in general, be sufficient for a district council to rely on the assertion of existing taxi licence holders that the demand is already catered for. They have evidence only of the demand which they satisfy and it will be for the council themselves to seek for and examine the evidence of unmet demand. There may be those who have given up trying to use taxis because of the inadequacy of the service and there may be latent demand in parts of a district that have not been adequately served—where those who wish to use taxis may not have demonstrated their demand since there had been no opportunity of having it satisfied. Moreover, if the applicant for a new taxi licence proposed to use it to provide a new service—for instance under section 12—and had reasonable grounds to believe that there would be demand for his service if he provided it, a council which wished to refuse a licence would have to satisfy themselves that that demand would not be forthcoming. Overcrowding at taxis ranks is not of itself evidence that there is no unmet demand. It may be that the provision of ranks has hitherto been too limited and the council should look actively for sites for further ranks.

28. There are a number of district councils which already exercise no control on the number of taxis in their areas without causing problems of over-supply. However, the Department accepts that in some areas the total abandonment of quantity control could lead to an initial over-supply of taxis before market forces could bring about an equilibrium between supply and demand. In order to avoid possible disruption, a district council faced with a large number of new applicants, could, in the Department's view, reasonably grant a proportion of the applications, deferring consideration of the remainder until the effects of granting the first tranche could be assessed.

DOT Circular 7/86, 18 December 1986

TRANSPORT ACT 1985: THE SHARING OF TAXIS AND HIRE CARS

Contents   **Paragraph**

INTRODUCTION

1.   This Circular contains guidance for local authorities in England (outside London) and Wales on the provisions contained in the Transport Act 1985 'the 1985 Act' under which licensed taxis or hire cars may be used to carry passengers at separate fares. It has no legal force. Whilst every care has been taken in composing the descriptions of the various legislative provisions, those descriptions should not be taken as authoritative interpretations of the provisions. Authorities should seek their own advice on the precise interpretation of the legislation. The arrangement applying in Scotland are the subject of a separate circular (No 25/1986) issued by the Scottish Development Department.

2.   Prior to the 1985 Act, the sharing of taxis and hire cars was permitted under the conditions laid down in Part I of Schedule I to the Public Passenger Vehicles Act 1981 ('the 1981 Act'). These permitted a group of people travelling together to agree among themselves to contribute to a single fare for the hire of the vehicle but, in particular, prohibited the driver from initiating the arrangement. Sharing was also permitted under an arrangement approved by a County Council (or Metropolitan District Council) for the provision of services designed to meet the social and welfare needs of one or more communities. The relevant paragraphs of Schedule 1 to the 1981 Act have not been repealed and taxis and hire cars may continue to be shared in accordance with those conditions. These are set out at Annex A.

3.   Taxi and hire car sharing could also be authorised by county councils under the provisions of Sections 47 to 49 of the 1981 Act. These provided for the authorisation of individual services in specially designated 'Experimental Areas'. In view of the more general provisions of the 1985 Act, Sections 47 to 49 of the 1981 Act were repealed with effect from 26 October 1986.

4.   The effect of the 1985 Act was to extend greatly the circumstances under which taxis and hire cars may be used to provide shared services. For England and Wales, three new forms of service were permitted—

(a)   under Section 12, a licensed taxi may be used to provide local 'bus' services;

(b)   under Section 11, a licensed taxi or licensed hire car may be used to carry pre-booked passengers at separate fares;

(c)   under Section 10, taxi licensing authorities are empowered to set up schemes under which licensed taxis may be used to stand for shared hire only or for either shared or exclusive hire (at the discretion of the first hirer).

333

5.   The legal provisions which apply to each of these forms of sharing are described in Parts I to III of this Circular. A feature that is common to them all is that they apply only to licensed vehicles. This requirement was imposed in order that the vehicles should be subject to the quality control of a licensing authority. For this purpose, the vehicle and driver remain subject to the same regime as would apply to them if they were used for exclusive hire.

6.   The vehicle operating regime differs according to the type of service involved. Pre-booked hiring of taxis and hire cars under the provisions of Section 11 is the simplest form of shared operation and no special provision is made to regulate the manner or circumstances under which this service may be offered. Local services operated under the provisions of Section 12 are subject to the same control by the Traffic Commissioner as any other local service. The use of taxis to stand for shared hire under the provisions of Section 10 is regulated according to a local taxi sharing scheme set up by the taxi licensing authority, (the district council). District councils are given wide discretion to control the extent of taxi sharing in their area and the manner in which the service is to be provided. The Department's advice on the making of taxi sharing schemes is given in Part IV and model provisions are set out in Annex C of this Circular.

7.   This Circular is concerned with the implementation of the 1985 Act. The financial and manpower effects for local authorities of the Act as a whole are described in paragraphs 188 to 191 of Department of Transport Circular 3/85 (Welsh Office Circular 64/85).

PART I. SECTION 12—THE USE OF TAXIS IN PROVIDING LOCAL SERVICES

8.   Section 12 of the 1985 Act was brought into force on 6 January 1986. It lays down the conditions under which taxis may be used to provide local services throughout Great Britain. Taken together with the regulations made under Sections 12(9) and (10)[1] the provisions of the section define the legislative framework within which such vehicles operate. The principle underlying these provisions is that the service has to be registered with the Traffic Commissioner in the same way as any other local bus service, but that vehicle quality and safety standards continue to be the responsibility of the authority that licensed the taxi. This is achieved by making the vehicle subject to the selective application of public service vehicle and taxi legislation.

1   The Local Services (Operation by Taxis) Regulations 1986 SI 1986/567. The Local Services (Operation by Taxis) (London) Regulations 1986 SI 1986/566.

Public service vehicle controls
9.   When used to provide a local service, a taxi becomes a public service vehicle, subject to most of the provisions of the 1981 Act. The most significant modification of these provisions is made in Section 12(1) of the 1985 Act which provides that the holder of a taxi licence has a right to be granted a restricted public service vehicle operator's licence under Part II of the 1981 Act (a 'special licence') for use in providing a local service with his licensed taxi. Since operating standards will remain the responsibility of the taxi licensing authority he is not required to meet the conditions laid down in Section 14 of the 1981 Act.

10.   Section 12(4) of the 1985 Act requires the Traffic Commissioner on granting a special licence, to attach the conditions mentioned in Section 12(5). These conditions provide that only licensed taxis may be used under a special licence and limit such use to the provision of a local service that is not an excursion or tour. (This second condition does not prevent the vehicle from being used, for example, to

provide a normal, exclusive taxi service since the vehicle would not then be being used under the special licence). The third condition that must be attached to a special licence requires that every local service operated under the licence must have at least one stopping place (defined in Section 137 of the 1985 Act as a point where passengers are taken up or set down) in the taxi licensing area in which the vehicle is licensed. This condition does not prevent such a service from also having stopping places in other taxi licensing areas.

11. Section 1(2) of the 1981 Act is disapplied by Section 12(8) of the 1985 Act, with the result that the vehicle ceases to be a public service vehicle at any time when it is not being used to provide a local service. The disapplication of this section permits a licensed taxi to alternate between providing local services and operating as an exclusive taxi or a taxi shared under the provisions of Section 10 or 11 of the 1985 Act. Furthermore, a number of other provisions of the 1981 Act are disapplied by Section 12(13) of the 1985 Act. These are as follows—

(a) *Sections 16(1A) and (2) of the 1981 Act,* which limit to two the number of vehicles which may be operated under a restricted operator's licence and empower the Traffic Commissioner to attach conditions to an operator's licence specifying different maximum numbers for different descriptions of vehicles. These provisions are replaced by those of Section 12(7) of the 1985 Act, there being only one description of vehicle which may be operated under a special licence: namely one for which the holder of the licence has a taxi licence. As many vehicles may be operated under a special licence as the holder holds taxi licences.

(b) *Section 17(3)(d) of the 1981 Act,* which empowers the Traffic Commissioner to revoke or suspend a restricted public service vehicle operator's licence if it appears to him that the holder no longer satisfies the requirements of good repute or financial standing. These requirements do not apply to a special licence (see paragraph 9 above).

(c) *Section 18 of the 1981 Act,* which requires all vehicles operated under a public service vehicle operator's licence to exhibit an operator's disc showing particulars of the operator of the vehicle and of the public service vehicle operator's licence under which it is being used. Instead, the vehicle remains subject to any requirements of the taxi code[1] regarding the display of information concerning its taxi licence.

(d) *Sections 19 and 20 of the 1981 Act,* which impose duties on the holder of a public service vehicle operator's licence to give to the Traffic Commissioner certain information including information about conditions relevant to good repute and about the vehicles operated under that licence. This is not required since quality control of special licence holders and their vehicles remains the responsibility of the taxi licensing authority.

(e) *Section 22 of the 1981 Act,* which requires that the driver of a public service vehicle shall be licensed for the purpose under that section. These vehicles remain licensed taxis and, under the taxi code, may be driven only by the holder of a taxi driver's licence. It was therefore not necessary to retain duplicate driver licensing requirements under the 1981 Act.

(f) *Section 26 of the 1981 Act,* which makes provision for regulations to be made with respect to the number of persons who may be carried in a public service vehicle and the mark to be carried on the vehicle showing that number. These matters are regulated under the taxi code.

(g) *Subsections (5) and (6) of Section 26 of the 1985 Act,* which make provision for the Traffic Commissioner to attach to an operator's licence a condition restricting to specified vehicles the vehicles which may be used under that licence. The vehicles used under a special licence are restricted to those for which the holder has a taxi licence and their fitness is regulated under the taxi code. The further provisions of Section 26(4) and (5) are not therefore required. It should be noted, however, that the Traffic Commissioner retains the power to attach conditions to a special licence under Section 26(1) of the 1985 Act (for failing to operate a local service in a satisfactory manner) or under Section 8 of that Act (for the purpose of enforcing traffic regulation conditions).

1 'Taxi code' is defined in Section 13 of the 1985 Act as 'those provisions made by or under any enactment which would apply (to a licensed taxi) if the vehicle were plying for hire and were hired by a single passenger or is exclusive use'.

Controls under the taxi code

12.   Section 12(10) of the 1985 Act provides a power for the Secretary of State to make regulations prescribing those provisions of the taxi code that are to apply to a licensed taxi when it is being used to provide a local service under a special PSV operator's licence. Since there are in Great Britain three different licensing regimes for taxis, three sets of Regulations have been made. The Local Services (Operation by Taxis) Regulations 1986, SI 1986/567, apply to vehicles licensed under Section 37 of the Town Police Clauses Act 1847 (that is, to taxis licensed in England (outside London) and Wales). The Local Services (Operation by Taxis) (London) Regulations 1986, SI 1986/566, apply to vehicles licensed in London under Section 6 of the Metropolitan Public Carriage Act 1869, and the Local Services (Operation by Taxis) (Scotland) Regulations 1986, SI 1986/1239/S.106, apply to vehicles licensed in Scotland under section 10 of the Civic Government (Scotland) Act 1982. These regulations have the common purpose of providing that the quality, safety and enforcement aspects of vehicle operation continue to be regulated by the authority that licensed the taxi.

13.   For England (outside London) and Wales, the regulations apply to these vehicles the greater part of the taxi code that is contained in the 1847 Act and in the Local Government (Miscellaneous Provisions) Act 1976 (the 1976 Act) where Part II of that Act has been adopted. In particular—

(a)   *Section 46 of the 1847 Act* provides that these vehicles may be driven only by a licensed taxi driver;

(b)   *Section 50 of the 1847 Act and Section 60 of the 1976 Act* provide a power to suspend or revoke the vehicle licence; and

(c)   *Section 68 of the 1976 Act* provides a power for vehicles to be inspected and tested by authorised officers and for the licences of defective vehicles to be suspended.

14.   The provisions of the taxi code which are not applied to these vehicles are those which conflict with their use to carry passengers at separate fares. In particular—

(a)   *Section 53 of the 1847 Act* under which the driver of a taxi may be compelled to accept a hiring;

(b)   *Sections 54 to 58 of the 1847 Act and byelaws made under Section 68 of that Act* which serve to control the fares which may be charged. As with any other local service, the operator of a taxi used to provide a local service is free to determine what fares to charge.

(c)   *Section 52(Part) and 59 of the 1847 Act and Section 69 of the 1976 Act* which specify certain rights of the exclusive hirer of a taxi providing a conventional service.

15.   These Regulations also contain provisions made under Section 12(9) of the 1985 Act requiring that when a taxi is being used to provide a local service—

(a)   it must carry a sign which includes the word 'BUS' and which indicates the service being provided;

(b)   any 'taxi' or 'for hire' sign must not be illuminated; and

(c)   a fare table must be displayed in the vehicle.

PART II. SECTION 11—ADVANCE BOOKING OF TAXIS AND HIRE CARS AT SEPARATE FARES

16.   Section 11 of the 1985 Act, which applies only to England and Wales, was brought into force on 1 July 1986. It makes provision for the carriage at separate fares in licensed taxis and hire cars of passengers who have booked their journeys in advance. This form of shared operation does not involve standing or plying for hire on the street and is therefore open to hire cars as well as taxis. The primary purpose is to permit taxi radio circuits and hire car operators to offer a prospective passenger the choice of either an exclusive service, as at present, or a shared service at a lower fare. They are not required to offer a shared service but, where the travel needs of a prospective passenger can be accommodated on a vehicle which has been previously booked, they may, subject to the consent of the first passenger, combine what would otherwise be two or more separate journeys. Such a service may be offered only if all passengers have booked their journey in advance and consented to the sharing of the vehicle on the basis of separate fares.

17.   Such services may be provided only by licensed taxis or licensed hire cars. When providing such a service the vehicle does not become a public service vehicle for the purposes of the 1981 Act, but continues to be subject to regulation as a taxi or hire car. There is nothing in the hire care code[1] which conflicts with the provision of these services and, for them, no further regulations are required. There are, however, provisions of the taxi code that are incompatible with the provision of shared services. These are disapplied in two Orders[2] made under Section 13 of the 1985 Act. These Orders apply also to taxis available for immediate hiring at separate fares under the provisions of Section 10 of the 1985 Act and are discussed at greater length in Part III of this Circular. However, one aspect of the Orders which is particularly relevant to services provided under Section 11 is the disapplication of taxi fares control. There is no power under Section 11 for the taxi licensing authority to exercise this control over pre-booked services and consequently the Orders have the effect of putting pre-booked shared taxis on the same footing as shared hire cars providing a similar service.

1   'hire car code' is defined in section 13 of the 1985 Act as 'those provisions made by or under any enactment which would apply (to a licensed hire car) if it were hired by a single passenger for his exclusive use'.

2   Licensed Taxis (Hiring at Separate Fares) Order 1986, SI 1986/1386. The Licensed Taxi (Hiring at Separate Fares) (London) Order 1986, SI 1986/1387.

PART III. SECTION 10—IMMEDIATE HIRING OF TAXIS AT SEPARATE FARES

18.   Section 10 of the 1985 Act applies only to England and Wales and lays down the conditions under which a taxi may be hired at separate fares for a journey commencing there and then. The principal conditions are that—

    (*a*)   all passengers board the vehicle at the same place;

    (*b*)   the boarding place has been authorised by the authority responsible for licensing taxis in the area in which that place is situated;

    (*c*)   the hiring is in accordance with any other requirements laid down by that authority; and

    (*d*)   the vehicle is licensed as a taxi by the same authority.

19.   Provided the conditions are met, the vehicle is exempt from being a public service vehicle for the purposes of the 1981 Act or related enactments. When offering or providing such a service the vehicle does not cease to be subject to the taxi code (except as provided for by Order made under Section 13 of the 1985 Act).

20.   That the vehicle must be a licensed taxi and remains subject to the taxi code ensures that both the vehicle and driver are subject to the quality control of the taxi licensing system. That it must be licensed by the same authority that designates the place at which shared services may be offered restricts this form of service to the same vehicles as may offer exclusive taxi services in that area. That all passengers must board the vehicle at the same place prevents the vehicle from picking up passengers in the course of the journey. (This restriction does not, of course, apply to a local service operated under the provisions of Section 12 of the 1985 Act or to a vehicle booked in advance to pick up passengers at several places under the provisions of Section 11).

Application of the taxi code
21.   The taxi code applies to vehicles used to provide these shared services as modified by two Orders[1] made under Section 13 of the 1985 Act. These Orders disapply parts of the taxi code which are incompatible with the provision of shared services. These include—

(a)   the right of the hirer to demand to be carried to any place within the compellable distance;

(b)   the right of the hirer to determine which or how many people should be carried, or to require luggage to be carried;

(c)   conditions which require the driver of an unhired taxi to drive to the nearest taxi stand—he may instead go to a place authorised by the licensing authority for the provision of shared services;

(d)   regulations which prohibit the driver from seeking further passengers to share the vehicle; and

(e)   regulations governing exclusive fares.

1   The Licensed Taxis (Hiring at Separate Fares) Order 1986, SI 1986/1386. The Licensed Taxi (Hiring at Separate Fares) (London) Order 1986, SI 1986/1387.

Taxi sharing schemes
22.   Central to the legal framework for the operation of these shared services is the making of a scheme by the taxi licensing authority. The authority has discretion over whether or not to make a scheme except that it is required under Section 10(4) to do so if requested by the holders of at least 10% of current taxi licences, (not 10% of licenceholders). Irrespective of whether the scheme is made as a result of such a request, it is for the licensing authority to decide the form and nature of the scheme.

23.   Every scheme must—

(a)   designate the places in the area from which shared taxis may be hired (the 'authorised places');

(b)   specify the requirements to be met in relation to the hiring of taxis at separate fares;

(c)   include any provision that the Secretary of State requires by regulations to be included;

(d)   not include any provision that the Secretary of State by regulations prohibits from being included; and

(e)   be made in accordance with the prescribed procedures.

Procedure for making a scheme
24.   The procedures to be followed by a district council in making a taxi sharing scheme are laid down in the Taxis (Schemes for Hire at Separate Fares) Regulations 1986, SI 1986/1779. These require the authority to obtain the consent of the highway authority in respect of any authorised place and of the landowner in respect of any such place that is not on the highway. The authority is required to consult the chief constable, the county council (or in the case of a metropolitan district, the

Passenger Transport Authority) and the local taxi owners and drivers (or their representatives). It is then required to publish the proposed scheme and invite representations. After considering such representations, the scheme may be made with or without modification but, if significant modification is made, the council is required to consult again on the modified aspects of the scheme. A similar procedure must be followed in varying a scheme.

Obligatory provisions

25. The description of the provisions required by the Secretary of State to be included in all schemes are prescribed in the Taxis (Schemes for hire at Separate Fares) Regulations 1986. These are as follows—

  (a) any vehicle licensed by the licensing authority to ply for hire in an area where a scheme is in operation may at the option of the holder of the licence be used for the carriage of passengers at separate fares under the terms of the scheme;

  (b) the provisions of the scheme shall apply to any part of a shared journey outside the area in which the scheme is in operation as well as to the part within that area; and

  (c) any vehicle standing for hire under the terms of the scheme at an authorised place shall display (in addition to any sign, mark or notice which it is required to display by the taxi code) a notice indicating that the vehicle is available for shared hire.

26. The first of these provisions is intended to ensure that the scheme is open to all taxis in the area but that no proprietor may be compelled to participate. The second provides that a vehicle leaving its licensing area in the course of a shared hiring remains subject to its own local scheme (it cannot of course be used to ply for hire—whether shared or exclusive—outside its own area). The third condition is designed to ensure that vehicles used under a scheme carry a clear indication of the service available, for the benefit of travellers and enforcement officials.

27. The Secretary of State has not at present used his powers under Section 10(5) of the 1985 Act to prescribe provisions which may not be included in a local authority scheme. He will, however, treat this as a reserve power to be used if, for instance, there is evidence that licensing authorities are imposing conditions against the interests of the travelling public.

Authorised places

28. Subject to the consultations and consents provided for by the Taxis (Scheme for Hire at Separate Fares) Regulations 1986—any place may be designated as a place from which taxis may be hired at separate fares. Such places may form part of an existing taxi rank, or may be separate from the facilities for exclusive taxis.

Signing of authorised places

29. For authorised places on the highway the local authority should place a road marking in the form of diagram 1028.1 in Schedule 2 to the Traffic Signs Regulations and General Directions 1981, SI 1981/859 to indicate the extent of the authorised place to both taxi drivers and other road users. The legend 'TAXIS' should be used where the place is for both exclusive and shared taxis. Where the place is to be used only by shared taxis the legend should be varied to 'SHARED TAXIS' (See drawing WM1028.1 at Annex B).

30. An informatory sign WBM(R)857.1 is available to indicate how many taxis may use the stand and also to provide prospective passengers with information on the operation of a shared taxi scheme such as fare tables, times of operation or other relevant details. This information may be changed as necessary from time to time.

Three variants of the sign are available headed 'TAXIS', 'SHARED TAXIS' and 'TAXIS AND SHARED TAXIS'. Details of the designs are given in Annex B.

31. Designation of a taxi rank under Section 64 of the Local Government (Miscellaneous Provisions) Act 1976 automatically prohibits the stopping of all other vehicles on the rank and this should be indicated by signs in the form of diagrams 642 and 642.1 in the Traffic Signs Regulations or in the form of WBM(R)650.1. (See drawing at Annex B). Where problems are likely to be experienced with other vehicles waiting or loading on a place authorised for use by shared taxis only, a parking place order should be made under Section 32 of the Road Traffic Regulation Act 1984 to restrict the use of the place to shared taxis. The order may either just prohibit waiting by other vehicles (which will still allow them to load or unload goods or passengers) or prohibit the stopping of all other vehicles for any purpose including loading or unloading. The restriction should be signed by the appropriate variant of the regulatory sign WBM(R)650.1. In all cases where this sign is used the diagram 1028.1 road marking should be coloured yellow, notwithstanding the provisions of Regulation 24(4) of the Traffic Signs Regulations.

32. In all cases the highway authority (when different from the taxi licensing authority) should be consulted before any road markings or signs are installed. Furthermore all the signs and road markings referred to above, except the diagram 1028.1 road marking with the legend 'TAXIS', coloured in accordance with the provisions of Regulation 24(4), and the signs in diagrams 642 and 642.1, require authorisation by the appropriate Department of Transport Regional Office or by the Welsh Office before they are installed. Any further advice on signing should also be sought from the Regional Office or the Welsh Office.

Other requirements of the scheme
33. Section 12(6) of the 1985 Act contains a list, which is not exhaustive, of matters for which a scheme may make provision. These are—

(*a*) fares;
(*b*) the signs to be carried on vehicles used under the scheme and those used to mark authorised places;
(*c*) the manner in which arrangements are to be made for the carriage of passengers at separate fares; and
(*d*) the conditions to apply to the use of a taxi on a shared hiring.

34. The effect of the Licensed Taxis (Hiring at Separate Fares) Order 1986, is to disapply any provision of the taxi code which, in its existing form, is incompatible with taxi sharing. It is open to the licensing authority to replace or reinstate in a suitable form any such provision as part of its scheme, (provided these do not conflict with the obligatory provisions described in paragraph 25*)*. The Department's guidance on the additional requirements of the scheme is contained in Part IV of this Circular.

PART IV. GUIDANCE ON THE MAKING OF TAXI SHARING SCHEMES

35. Guidance is given in Part III on the statutory requirements governing the form and content of taxi sharing schemes and the procedure by which they are to be made. This part of the Circular sets out the Department's guidance on the options open to a licensing authority in formulating its scheme. A model taxi sharing scheme is given in Annex C. This is not intended to provide a blueprint for local schemes. Rather, having decided what provisions are required, a district council may find certain of the model provisions helpful in drafting its scheme.

General

36.   In preparing their local schemes district councils should bear in mind the general principles that lay behind the Government's promotion of the idea of taxi sharing and its approval by Parliament. Taxi sharing was seen as providing district councils with the opportunity to improve the public transport facilities available in their areas and to permit the taxi trade to widen its market and share in the new opportunities opened up by the 1985 Act. A shared taxi journey should give the taxi proprietor a greater return while being significantly less expensive for each passenger. This will bring travel by taxi within the reach of many more people.

37.   It was decided not to set up a new class of vehicle authorised to offer only a shared service. In order to make the most efficient use of the vehicles available, the driver should be free to switch between exclusive and shared operations according to demand. In practice, although the making of the scheme is entirely the responsibility of the licensing authority, vehicles will be made available for shared hire only to the extent that the provisions of the scheme are acceptable to the taxi trade and, equally, there will be enough customers to make a scheme a success only if the provisions of the scheme are attractive to a significant proportion of the travelling public.

38.   Taxi drivers and proprietors will need to be reassured that taxi sharing will not reduce the earnings or size of the taxi trade by combining existing passengers into fewer journeys. Shared taxis, with their lower fares, offer the prospect of attracting more passengers, so increasing total taxi revenue as well as benefiting the travellers. The trade will wish to put this to the test and licensing authorities may adopt an incremental approach, starting with a relatively limited scheme that can be extended once experience has been gained.

39.   A second benefit of this approach is that it would be possible initially to provide for sharing where it is likely to cause few problems. The level of control which will need to be exercised on the operation of shared taxi services will depend very much on the type of scheme being set up. A service from an out-of-town shopping centre to residential estates is unlikely to raise the same problems as one operating from a city centre late at night. Licensing authorities will find no shortage of possible problems which could be dealt with only by extensive regulation. Rather than seeking to provide for these at the outset, the initial scheme might be restricted to locations or times of day when difficulties would not be expected to occur and the operation of the scheme could be subject to minimal regulations. As experience is gained, the scheme could be extended and regulations added to deal with any particular problems as they arise.

Authorised places

40.   The designation of authorised places will generally involve two types of decision: where in the licensing area the authorised places should be located and whether they should be combined with exclusive taxi ranks or segregated from them. It is suggested that the licensing authorities should first determine where shared facilities would provide maximum benefit to travellers in the area. They may wish to look first to the provision of services at out-of-town shopping centres, hospitals, railway stations, airports or other facilities that attract relatively large numbers of passengers. The scheme could later be varied to include, for example, night services from a city centre.

41.   In rural areas and small towns there may be few places where there is a particularly high demand for taxis. Equally taxi sharing is likely to cause few problems and the authorities for such areas are advised to consider designating all taxi ranks as authorised places.

42.   In larger conurbations authorities may initially wish to specify the destinations to be served by shared taxis from each of the authorised places. For instance, shared taxis from a shopping centre might initially be limited to serving one or two residential estates. Shared taxis from the railway station might be authorised to operate only to the city centre. Such an arrangement would avoid, at the outset, any problems associated with assembling groups of passengers to share, and it is amenable to a simple flat rate or zonal fare tariff. Again, once experience has been gained, the scheme might be extended to additional destinations.

43.   Whether authorised places should be combined with exclusive taxi ranks must to some extent depend on the space available. Where space is limited, as in many city and town centres, the best use of available space is likely to be achieved by combining shared and exclusive ranks. Except at the busiest ranks in the larger cities it should be enough simply to designate the entire rank as being available for both shared and exclusive services. However, where there may be confusion at, for example, an airport or busy railway terminus it may be preferable to divide the rank, reserving some spaces for the use of shared taxis only, so that both the drivers and prospective passengers choose in advance whether to go to the shared or exclusive part of the rank.

Exclsive and shared compellability
44.   'Exclusive compellability' is the existing right of the hirer of a taxi to demand an exclusive service and to be carried to any place in the licensing area. 'Shared compellability' would be the right of the first passenger who wished to share the vehicle to require the driver to take him to his chosen destination if at least one further passenger could be found.

45.   The disapplication of Section 53 of the 1847 Act provided for in the Licensed Taxis (Hiring at Separate Fares) Order has the effect of disapplying exclusive compellability. Unless this is reinstated or replaced by shared compellability as part of the scheme, it will be open to the driver of a taxi operating under the scheme to refuse to accept a hiring, either exclusive or shared.

46.   Whether exclusive compellability should be reinstated will depend on the way in which the scheme is to operate. There can be no case for allowing a taxi driver to refuse a hiring if his vehicle is standing at a place from which exclusive taxis may be hired. Thus, at a combined shared/exclusive rank, irrespective of whether a driver is offering a shared service, he should be deemed also to be available for exclusive hire by providing in the scheme for exclusive compellability. Where shared and exclusive taxis are segregated (even if only at different parts of the same taxi rank) or where there is an exclusive service available nearby, a passenger should probably not be given the right to demand such a service from a taxi standing for shared hire.

47.   A special case might be where an authorised place has been designated for the provision of a shared service to a particular destination—for example into a city centre in the morning peak hours. The driver of a taxi offering such a service may be doing so only because he wishes to travel in that particular direction and he would offer no service at all rather than risk being compelled to accept a hiring in the wrong direction. In this case it would be reasonable not to reinstate exclusive compellability but instead to give the passenger the right to be carried to the specified destination at a discounted fare, even if no other passenger can be found to share the vehicle.

48.   As a general feature of schemes, licensing authorities may wish to provide for shared compellability in support of passengers wanting to share the vehicle to a destination which is unpopular with taxi drivers (perhaps because there is difficulty in obtaining a return fare). There should then be no circumstance in which a passenger

is unable to make his journey, although he cannot always be guaranteed a shared service at a discounted fare.

Signs on vehicles and at authorised places

49.   As described in paragraph 25 every scheme must contain provision for a sign to be carried on a vehicle standing for hire under the scheme. The form and wording of this sign and the manner in which it is to be displayed are left to the discretion of the licensing authority. It is advised to avoid complex and expensive requirements that might act as a barrier to taxi proprietors wishing to participate in the scheme. In many cases a simple but uniform sign displayed in the windscreen of the vehicle will be adequate. If the desired operational flexibility is to be achieved, the sign should be capable of being easily removed and replaced.

50.   The wording of the sign will depend on the type of service permitted under the scheme and authorities are advised to use a form of words that conveys as precisely as possible what is on offer. For example if the scheme provides generally for exclusive compellability a sign such as that used in Queensland Australia may be appropriate; this reads, 'This vehicle may be shared at the free choice of the first hirer'. A similar message is conveyed more briefly but less precisely by signs reading 'Shared or exclusive hire', 'Available for shared hire' or 'Shared hirings accepted'. Where the scheme does not provide for exclusive compellability, this might be made clear by a sign reading 'Shared hire only'. Although some of these signs might be rather large it should be noted that they are required to be displayed only when the vehicle is stationary.

51.   Details of the signing arrangements at authorised places are given in paragraphs 29 to 32.

Operation

52.   As suggested earlier, it may not be necessary at the outset to regulate every aspect of the arrangements for sharing and the conditions under which a taxi may be so hired. Much can be left to the goodwill and commonsense of those involved, with the power to introduce additional regulations kept in reserve. Moreover, the way in which sharing will operate will depend on other aspects of the scheme, such as whether combined or separate ranks have been designated and whether exclusive or shared compellability has been instated.

53.   All schemes will need to make clear the respective roles of the passengers and the driver in the arrangements for sharing. It is suggested that the driver should be made responsible for deciding whether the destination of subsequent passengers can reasonably be accommodated on a journey serving that of the first passenger. Under this arrangement, the first passenger, having elected to share the vehicle, would not have the right to choose or reject fellow passengers but any passenger should be allowed to decide not to travel without incurring a financial penalty.

54.   The driver should also be made responsible for determining the route of the vehicle and the order in which passengers are set down, subject to the condition that he should not unreasonably prolong the journey of any passenger.

55.   Licensing authorities may also wish to specify in the scheme the manner in which the arrangements to share the vehicle are to be made. This would include regulating such aspects as the period for which the driver must wait for further passengers to the same or similar destination and determining what may happen if no further passengers come forward.

Fares

56.   Any scheme for shared fares should offer an incentive both to the taxi proprietor and to the intending passengers. The driver should receive more in fares than for

an exclusive hire and, each passenger should pay less. However, care has to be taken to strike a balance between these incentives. If shared fares are set too high, passengers will not make use of the service; if the margin for the driver is set too low, there will be no incentive for him to participate in the scheme. How these margins should be set will be a matter for the judgement of the licensing authority; but if they are not balanced both the taxi trade and their passengers will be denied the benefits of a properly operating system for shared fares.

57.   However the fare is to be calculated it should be made apparent to the passengers that the specified shared fare is to be paid by each person and is not the fare for the hire of the vehicle. It should also be made clear that sharing is an additional facility. Thus a group of people travelling together may continue to hire as a whole a taxi available for exclusive hire, paying the exclusive fare plus the permitted extra charge for additional passengers. If however, they chose to hire the vehicle on a shared basis they will each pay the shared fare.

58.   There are four basic ways in which shared fares might be charged by taxi drivers, though there are many possible variations. The four methods are—

  (*a*)   a flat fare system;
  (*b*)   a zonal system;
  (*c*)   modified use of existing meters; or
  (*d*)   use of special (or specially adapted) meters.

Flat fare systems
59.   These systems have two major advantages: they are easily understood and passengers know in advance how much their journey will cost. They will be particularly applicable where all passengers travel much the same distance. An obvious example would be airport taxis: all passengers would be coming from (or going to) the airport and the other end of their journey will usually be close to the town centre. So a large part of the journey will be common for all passengers. Other examples where a flat fare system might be appropriate would be where a common taxi journey is from a close group of small towns and villages into a neighbouring city centre (and back) or even for all journeys made entirely within a small town. But licensing authorities will be best placed to identify for their own areas trips for which a flat charge would be appropriate.

60.   A flat fare system does not necessarily mean that the fare should be like a bus fare, ie not dependent on the number of passengers travelling. It could readily be provided that the more passengers who are sharing the taxi the less each would pay. Such an arrangement might be necessary to maintain the correct balance between the interests of the passengers and the driver, without introducing too complicated a fare system.

Zonal systems
61.   The simplest extension of a flat fare system would be to introduce destination zones by, for example, treating different residential estates as separate fare zones for journeys from a shopping centre. At its most comprehensive, a zonal system involves dividing the licensing area into zones and laying down the fare per passenger for journeys between each pair of zones. This may be done in a fare table (to be displayed in the vehicle together with the zonal map) or by specifying the fare according to the number of different zones through which the passenger is carried. Such a system might be appropriate for larger towns.

62.   The major disadvantage of a zonal system is that, unless there are very few zones, it is too complex for the fare to vary according to the number of passengers carried and so the last passenger left in the vehicle receives an exclusive service at the shared rate. In consequence, zonal fares tend to be pitched at a relatively high level.

63.   It is worth noting that a zonal system may be used to compute both shared and exclusive fares (as is done in Washington DC). Consequently, where a full zonal system is introduced for the purpose of calculating shared fares, it might also be applied to exclusive fares, so dispensing with the need for taxi meters.

Metered systems
64.   Although they do not permit passengers to know their fare in advance, taxi meters are familiar and give the public confidence that they are not being over-charged. Meters are available which are capable of computing shared fares where passengers board and alight at different points on the route. However, the form of sharing permitted under Section 10 of the 1985 Act requires that all passengers must board the vehicle at the same place. It follows that full shared metering is not essen-tial for the schemes to be set up under the 1985 Act. Moreover, time has to be allowed for the public to become used to shared taxis, for the trade to test whether such a service is worthwhile commercially and for more meter manufacturers to be persuaded that there is a large enough potential market for a shared taxi meter.

65.   Because all passengers must board the vehicle at the same authorised place it is possible to use an unmodified taxi meter to compute shared fares. The fare shown on a normal taxi meter when each passenger alights is directly related to the distance that he has been carried. And it would be possible to provide that each passenger should pay a stipulated proportion of the fare shown on the meter when he leaves the taxi. However, no matter how that proportion is defined, such schemes have a number of drawbacks. First, there may be arguments over the arithmetic, even if the percentages are kept simple; and as the scheme becomes more complex so does the scope for argument. Secondly, where each passenger pays the same proportion of the metered fare, the return to the driver shows enormous variation. He stands to lose money where the last passenger left in the taxi gets off long after the others, and so enjoys a long exclusive ride at the discounted rate. The use of an unmodified taxi meter is therefore best suited to the case where all passengers travel to the same destination.

Metered systems—modified existing meters
66.   The problem outlined above would be overcome if the meter could be adapted to run at a rate that was dependent on the number of people using the vehicle at that particular time. It is understood that most modern meters are capable of holding 4 separate tariffs. So they can be programmed to run at a rate appropriate to the number of people of sharing—
  Tariff 1—Exclusive rate
  Tariff 2—Two people sharing
  Tariff 3—Three people sharing
  Tariff 4—Four or more people sharing.

67.   Tariff I would therefore be 100% of the exclusive rate, and Tariff 2, 3 and 4 would represent progressively smaller percentages (in that order) of the exclusive rate. If, for example, four people boarded a shared taxi the meter would be set at Tariff 4. When the first passenger left it would be stopped (not set to zero) and he would pay the amount shown on the meter, which would then be set to run at Tariff 3. This sequence would be repeated until the last passenger remained, when the meter would be set to run at the exclusive rate. In this way, most existing meters could be used to operate as a full shared meter for the type of sharing provided for in the Act.

68.   The main limitation on using existing meters in this way is that they are gen-erally capable of holding only 4 tariffs. If taxi sharing proves popular it may well be more efficient to use larger vehicles (a taxi may be licensed with up to 8 passenger seats) and the Government would not wish to see the method of regulating fares

inhibit what might otherwise be a beneficial change. This, however, is unlikely to be a problem at the outset when few vehicles are licensed to carry more than 5 passengers. More seriously, many licensing authorities require the use of two or more metered tariffs for the metering of exclusive fares. For example, different tariffs may be laid down for immediate and pre-booked hirings or, as in London, a second tariff may be brought in automatically on long journeys. In some cases these problems may be overcome by the simple expedient of employing Tariff 3 for three or more people sharing; in others it may preclude the use of adapted taxi meters.

Metered systems—special meters

69.   It is understood that most meter manufacturers intend developing fully shared meters capable of storing in separate memories the fare so far for each passenger (and incrementing them in accordance with the fare scheme in operation), and perhaps of displaying them simultaneously or in rotation. Such meters will be capable of handling up to 8 tariffs and, if sharing proves popular, they will almost certainly become the standard for the next generation of taxi meters. Licensing authorities are, however, cautioned against prematurely requiring their taxi trades to invest in new meters.

Tariff structure

70.   In fixing the shared tariff it will be necessary for licensing authorities to decide—

   (*a*)   whether there should be any initial hiring charge and if so how it should be treated;
   (*b*)   whether the shared tariff should include waiting time;
   (*c*)   how 'extras' should be handled; and
   (*d*)   the level of discount.

Although each of these matters may be decided separately, they will, in combination, determine the balance that is struck between the interests of the passengers and the drivers.

71.   The *initial hiring charge* could be retained, with every passenger paying the charge at the exclusive rate. Alternatively, it could be discounted at the same rate as the distance tariff or abandoned altogether.

72.   So far as *waiting time* is concerned, it is suggested that this should be metered in exactly the same way as for the existing exclusive tariff. It would not be possible to share a *luggage charge* since it would not apply to all passengers and it is suggested that this charge should be dropped. It would also be simpler to drop '*extras*' that depend on the time of day or day of operation but these could be treated in the same way as the initial hiring charge. Charges for *additional passengers* should be dropped.

73.   It is recommended that licensing authorities adopt the simplest arrangements for the above elements of the tariff and, in discussion with their taxi trade, use the *discount rates* to set fares which apportion the benefits of sharing fairly between them and their passengers.

Publicity

74.   Licensing authorities will wish to ensure that potential users of shared service are aware of the scheme and have some understanding of how to use it. Publication of the scheme, as well as fulfilling a statutory requirement, will provide an opportunity of explaining how the scheme will operate. This is likely to create considerable interest and generate publicity in the local press and radio. Newspaper articles might be made available and a press release issued at little cost. In some circumstances the printing and distribution of an explanatory leaflet might be appropriate, possibly as a joint venture with the taxi trade.

PUBLIC PASSENGER VEHICLES ACT 1981,   ANNEX A
SCHEDULE 1, PART 1
(As amended by the Transport Act 1985)

SHARING OF TAXIS AND HIRE-CARS

1.   The making of the agreement for the payment of separate fares must not have been initiated by the driver or by the owner of the vehicle, by any person who has made the vehicle available under any agreement, or by any person who receives any remuneration in respect of the arrangements for the journey.

2.—(1) The journey must be made without previous advertisement to the public of facilities for its being made by passengers to be carried at separate fares, except where the local authorities concerned have approved the arrangements under which the journey is made as designed to meet the social and welfare needs of one or more communities, and their approvals remain in force.

(2) In relation to a journey the local authorities concerned for the purposes of this paragraph are those in whose area part of the journey is to be made; and in this sub-paragraph 'local authority' means—

   (a)   in relation to England and Wales, the council of a county, metropolitan district or London borough and the Common Council of the City of London;
   (b)   in relation to Scotland, a regional or islands council.

Note See Annex B overleaf.

MODEL TAXI SHARING SCHEME   ANNEX C

The District Council of   [1], in exercise of the powers conferrred by Section 10(4) of the Transport Act 1985 and having obtained the consents and carried out the consultations required by the Taxis (Schemes for Hire at Separate Fares) Regulations 1986[2] hereby resolve to make the following scheme.

Citation and Commencement
1.   This scheme may be cited as the   [1] (Taxi Hire at Separate Fares) Scheme 19— and shall come into operation on
   19 .

Interpretation
2.   In this scheme, unless the context otherwise requires—
   'the Act' means the Transport Act 1985;
   'the Council' means the district council of   [1];
   'taxi' means a vehicle licensed by the Council under Section 37 of the Town Police Clauses Act 1847;
   'authorised place' has the meaning given by Section 10(5) of the Act; 'designated area' means   [3]
   'exclusive service' means a service other than at separate fares; and 'shared service' means a service at separate fares.

Application
3 .—(1) Any taxi licensed by the Council to ply for hire in the designated area may at the option of the holder of the licence be used for the carriage of passengers at separate fares under the terms of this scheme.

TRAFFIC SIGNS AT TAXI RANKS

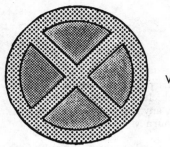

WM 642

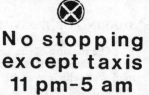

WBM 650.1

On taxi rank

WM 642.1

TAXIS AND
SHARED TAXIS
Stand for 3 taxis

WBM (R) 857.1
Variants

SHARED TAXIS
Stand for 3 taxis

EDGE OF CARRIAGEWAY

SHARED   TAXIS

WM 1028.1
Variant

SHARED TAXIS   SHARED TAXIS

SHARED   TAXIS   SHARED   TAXIS

(2) When a taxi is hired in accordance with this scheme, the provisions of the scheme applying to the journey for which it is hired shall apply to any part of that journey outside the designated area as they apply to any part within that area.

Authorised places
4.   The places listed in Schedule 1 to this scheme, are authorised places [at the times and for the journeys indicated in that Schedule].

Signs on vehicles
5.   There should be displayed on any taxi available for hire under the terms of this scheme at an authorised place (in addition to any other sign, mark or notice which is required to be displayed on the taxi) a notice containing the sign described [illustrated] in Schedule 2 to this scheme[4].

1   Add name of Council.

2   SI 1986/1779.

3   Describe here the licensing area for taxis under Section 37 of the Town Police Clauses Act 1847. If the Council licenses taxis in part only of the district the designated area will comprise only that part of the district. If the Council licenses taxis in two or more parts of the district, the designated area will comprise one only of those parts and separate schemes will be necessary for each licensing area.

4   This is the minimum requirement for the display on the notice. The Council may, if it considers necessary, impose additional requirements relating to the manner in which the notice is constructed and displayed.

Fares
6.   The fare payable by each passenger for a journey made under this scheme shall be calculated in accordance with Schedule 3 to this scheme.

7.   The fare table specified in Schedule 4 to this scheme shall be displayed in a manner that is clearly legible to passengers, in any vehicle standing for hire or hired under this scheme.

Taxi meters
8[1].—(1) Any taxi standing for hire or hired under this Scheme shall be fitted with a taxi meter capable of displaying a fare calculated in accordance with Schedule 3 to this Scheme.

(2) The meter shall be set in motion only when the taxi leaves the authorised place and shall display the fare calculated in accordance with Schedule 3 to this scheme and appropriate to the number of passengers in the taxi at that time.

(3) When any passenger leaves the taxi, the meter shall be stopped (but not returned to zero) and shall be restarted at the tariff appropriate to the number of passengers remaining in it when the taxi continues the journey for which it is hired under this scheme.

Operation
9.   A taxi shall be available for hire under this scheme when it is standing at an authorised place and displaying the sign specified in paragraph 5 hereof.

10[2]. If—

    (*a*)   a person at any time seeks to hire for an exclusive service a taxi available for hire under this scheme; and—

    (*b*)   the driver and a person seeking a shared service are not waiting for another person to offer to share the taxi; and

(c) the driver either

    i. would, apart from the Licensed Taxis (Hiring at Separate Fares) Order 1986, be required to accept the hiring; or

    ii. accepts the hiring although not required to do so,

then that taxi shall thereupon cease to be available for hire under this scheme until the expiry of that hiring.

10^2. If—

(a) a person at any time seeks to hire for an exclusive service a taxi available for hire under this scheme; and

(b) the driver and a person seeking a shared service are not waiting for another person to offer to share the taxi; and

(c) the driver accepts the hiring although not required to do so,

then that taxi shall thereupon cease to be available for hire under this scheme until the expiry of that hiring.

1 Paragraph 8 would apply only if metered fares are specified in Schedule 3.

2 The two versions of paragraph 10 are alternatives; the first provides for 'exclusive compellability', the second does not.

11. If a person seeks to hire for a shared service a taxi available for hire under this scheme and the driver is unable to find at least one other person to share the hiring within [. . . minutes] [a reasonable time] then, no fare shall be payable and, subject to paragraph 10 of this scheme, the driver shall be free to seek an alternative hiring, provided that the driver and that person may continue to wait for another person to offer to share the taxi for so long as they both agree to do so.

12^1. The driver of a taxi available for hire under this scheme shall not unreasonably refuse a hiring to two or more persons seeking a shared service to any destination within the designated area [indicated in Schedule 1].

1 Paragraph 12 provides for 'shared compellability' and should be omitted if that is not required.

13. Before a taxi has left an authorised place for the purpose of a shared service, any person may decide not to be carried as a passenger (notwithstanding any earlier agreement) and no fare shall be payable by him.

14. The driver may decline to accept as a passenger any person on the grounds that his intended destination could not be reached without an excessive or unreasonable addition to the journey distance of any passenger previously accepted for a journey, or that his luggage could not be accommodated safely within the luggage compartment of the taxi, but shall not refuse to carry a person already accepted by him as a passenger because his destination or luggage are not on such grounds compatible with those of a person who subsequently seeks a service.

15. The driver shall not refuse to carry luggage in his taxi provided that the luggage can be accepted safely within the luggage compartment of the taxi having regard to the luggage of other passengers.

16. The route taken by the taxi and the order in which passengers are set down shall be determined by the driver, but he shall not unreasonably prolong the journey of any passenger.

SCHEDULE 1—AUTHORISED PLACES

The places listed in column 1 are designated as places from which taxis may be hired under the scheme.

[For each authorised place, passengers may be carried at separate fares to the corresponding places shown in column 2. Where there are no places listed in column 2 against a particular authorised place, passengers may be carried to any destination, without limitation.]

[The times at which the scheme shall operate at each authorised place are listed in column 3. Where no times are listed against an authorised place, the scheme shall operate at all times from that place.]

Column 1	Column 2	Column 3
Market Place (Hackney Carriage Stand)		
[Named] Shopping Centre	[Named] residential estates	
Railway Station Forecourt		Monday to Friday 5pm to 8pm

SCHEDULE 2—SIGNS ON VEHICLES

1. This appendix should contain a description or drawing of the sign prescribed for the purpose of paragraph 5 of the scheme.

SCHEDULE 3—FARES

The fare to be charged to each person for services provided under the scheme shall be based on the distance and time elements of the fare for an exclusive service as contained in [byelaw no   ] [the table of fares made by the Council under Section 65 of the Local Government (Miscellaneous Provisions) Act 1976] as amended or replaced and in force from time to time.

The following tariffs shall apply—
    4 people sharing: for each person X% of the exclusive tariff
    3 people sharing: for each person Y% of the exclusive tariff
    2 people sharing: for each person Z% of the exclusive tariff

No additional charge shall be made for the carriage of luggage.

No fare shall be charged for children under the age of 5 unless they occupy a separate seat which would otherwise have been taken by a farepaying passenger.

SCHEDULE 4—FARE TABLE

In every vehicle used under the scheme there shall be displayed in a manner that is clearly legible to passengers the following sign—

'FARE TABLE FOR SHARED SERVICES'

1.   The taxi meter on this vehicle is capable of metering shared fares.

2.   During any time that the vehicle is shared the meter will record the separate fare payable by each of the passengers.

3.   The rate at which the fare increases depends on the number of passengers sharing in accordance with the following table—
     4 people sharing: X% of normal tariff
     3 people sharing: Y% of normal tariff
     2 people sharing: Z% of normal tariff

4.   The normal tariff is shown on the second fare table displayed in this vehicle.

5.   No additional charge shall be made for the carriage of luggage.

6.   No fare shall be charged for children under the age of 5 years unless they occupy a separate seat which would otherwise have been taken by a farepaying passenger.

Note: The above provisions would apply to metered fares. For zonal fares a faretable and map would be required. For flat fares between authorised places and specified destinations a faretable would be required together with a definition of the destinations to be served.

DOT Circular 8/86, 17 November 1986

TRANSPORT ACT 1985: SECTION 15:
EXTENSION OF TAXI LICENSING THROUGHOUT
ENGLAND AND WALES

INTRODUCTION
1. This Circular applies to England (outside London) and Wales. It provides guidance to local authorities on the effect of Section 15 of the Transport Act 1985 ('the 1985 Act'), though it does not purport to provide an interpretation of the law. Section 15 has the effect of extending taxi licensing throughout England and Wales. Provision is made in the Transport Act 1985 (Commencement Number 6) Order 1986, SI 1986/1794 (c. 63) to bring this section into force with effect from 1 January 1987.

THE PURPOSE OF SECTION 15
2. The 1985 Act contains provisions under which taxis may be used to carry passengers at separate fares. (These are described in Departmental Circular 7/86). These vehicles are not subject to all of the controls exercised under public service vehicle legislation. In order to safeguard quality and safety standards these provisions extend only to vehicles which are subject to controls under a taxi licensing system.

3. Shared taxi services are thought likely to be of particular benefit in rural areas where conventional bus services may be uneconomic and smaller vehicles can cope with the demand. However, in many such areas there is at present no taxi licensing, with the result that taxi proprietors are prevented from offering this wider range of services in areas where they might be of great benefit.

4. Section 15 extends to previously uncontrolled areas the consumer protection afforded by the licensing of taxis and taxi drivers. Moreover, with the extension of taxi licensing throughout England and Wales all taxi proprietors will be able to benefit from the opportunity to provide shared services and no area will be deprived of such services by the absence of a licensing system.

THE PRESENT ARRANGEMENTS
5. In England (outside London) and Wales, taxis may be licensed by district councils under the hackney carriage provisions of the Town Police Clauses Act 1847 ('the 1847 Act'). By virtue of Section 171(4) of the Public Health Act 1875 ('the 1875 Act') these provisions were applied to the urban districts which were formed under the 1875 Act. Part II of Schedule 14 to the Local Government Act 1972 ('the 1972 Act') provided that Section 171(4) of the 1875 Act should apply to those areas, and only those, to which it applied immediately before 1 April 1974. However, under paragraph 25 of that Schedule, district councils were empowered to resolve that section 171(4) of the 1875 Act should apply throughout their area or should cease to apply throughout their area (whether or not it previously applied only to part of their area). A resolution disapplying this provision had to be passed before 1 April 1975 but no time limit was placed on the extension of taxi licensing throughout a local authority area.

6. The cumulative effect is that there are areas of England and Wales where taxis are licensed under the provisions of the 1847 Act either because they were urban districts in 1875 or because an extension resolution has been passed by the district council under the provisions of the 1972 Act. Conversely, there are areas where there is no taxi licensing under the 1847 Act either because they were not urban districts in 1875 or because licensing has been disapplied by a resolution passed before 1 April 1975.

7. Such areas may be combined in a single district with the result that there may be districts with the following licensing arrangements—

(a)   taxis licensed throughout the district as a single taxi licensing area (this would arise where the district was formed from a single 1875 urban district or where an extension resolution has been passed under the 1972 Act);

(b)   taxis licensed throughout the district, but in two or more distinct taxi licensing areas (this would arise where the district was formed from two or more 1875 urban districts);

(c)   taxis licensed in part or parts only of the district (this would arise where the district was formed from one or more 1875 urban districts but also contained some area that was not such a district); or

(d)   taxis licensed in no part of the district (this would arise where the district contained no 1875 urban districts or where licensing had been disapplied by a resolution passed under the 1972 Act).

8. There are some 260 districts in categories (a) and (b) which license taxis throughout their areas. These will not be affected by Section 15 of the 1985 Act. There are about 50 districts in each of categories (c) and (d) with partial licensing or none at all, and it is these which will be affected by Section 15.

THE EFFECT OF SECTION 15

9. Section 15 of the 1985 Act applies the taxi licensing provisions of the 1847 Act to all districts and parts of districts in England (outside the Metropolitan Police District) and Wales. By virtue of Section 15(1)(a), where there is at present no area of a district in which taxis are licensed (category (d) of paragraph 7 above), the 1847 Act will apply throughout the district. Where taxis are already licensed in part or parts of the district (category (c) of paragraph 7 above), Section 15(1)(b) creates an additional licensing area comprising so much of the district as is not already subject to the provisions of the 1847 Act (or of the Metropolitan Public Carriage Act 1869).

10. Except as described below, from 1 January 1987 it will be an offence for a vehicle to be used to stand or ply for hire in a street or public place in England or Wales unless it is licensed for that purpose in accordance with the provisions of the 1847 Act.

11. The exceptions to paragraph 10 are—

(a)   a public service vehicle operated under the provisions of the Public Passenger Vehicles Act 1981; or

(b)   a vehicle standing or plying for hire in the Metropolitan Police District (which must be licensed in accordance with the provisions of the Metropolitan Public Carriage Act 1869); or

(c)   a a vehicle to which the saving provision of the Commencement Order applies (see paragraph 13 below).

12. It follows that the councils for those districts affected by Section 15 should be prepared from 1 January 1987 to consider applications for taxi licences. An applicant who is refused such a licence or whose application is not considered within a reasonable time would have a right of appeal to a Crown Court by virtue of the Public Health Act 1875 and the Public Health Acts Amendment Act 1890.

TRANSITIONAL PROVISIONS

13. The Order commencing Section 15 of the 1985 Act makes two transitional provisions. The first is a saving provision permitting existing taxi proprietors and drivers to continue until 1 April 1987 to provide a service without holding the necessary licences. This will apply to taxi proprietors and drivers who before 1 January 1987 were operating without a licence in an area affected by Section 15.

It will also apply to proprietors and drivers who were licensed in an adjacent area but were similarly providing a service in the new licensing area.

14.   The second transitional provision empowers a district council to resolve before 1 January 1987 to adopt Part II of the Local Government (Miscellaneous Provisions) Act 1976 (see paragraphs 19 and 20). This modifies taxi licensing under the 1847 Act and also provides for the licensing of hire cars. It cannot normally be adopted unless the 1847 Act is already in place. This transitional provision permits those councils that wish to adopt these provisions to bring them into force at the same time as the 1847 Act.

ZONING
15.   Where a district contains two or more 1875 urban districts (and an extension resolution has not been made under the 1972 Act) each of those areas will be separate zones for the purpose of taxi licensing. That is, a taxi licence granted for one such area does not permit the vehicle to be used to stand or ply for hire in another. A council may resolve to amalgamate such zones and so licence taxis throughout its district as a single taxi licensing area but there is no statutory power under which a council may choose to divide its district into zones for the purpose of taxi licensing.

16.   Where a district council has no taxi licensing controls, the effect of Section 15 will be to make the entire district a single licensing area. Where there are already taxi controls in part or parts of a district, Section 15 will create an additional licensing area. Existing licensing zones will be unaffected unless and until the council passes an extension resolution.

17.   The benefits or otherwise of retaining licensing zones are closely related to the question of taxi quantity control, in that zoning serves to support limitation of taxi numbers in urban areas. The Government's guidance on quantity control is contained in paragraphs 26 to 28 of Departmental Circular 3/85 (Welsh Office Circular 64/85) in relation 'to Section 16 of the 1985 Act. In considering whether to support quantity control by the retention of licensing zones councils will wish to take account of the reduced efficiency resulting from requiring a taxi arriving in one zone from another to return empty. Furthermore, since zones are totally independent licensing areas, the council will be required to exercise separate control for each area. This could involve increased administrative costs in preparing licensing conditions and making byelaws, regulations and taxi sharing schemes for each area.

18.   It will remain open to councils with more than one licensing zone to pass an extension resolution to combine these into a single licensing area. For the reasons given in the previous paragraph, the Government recommends this.

THE LOCAL GOVERNMENT (MISCELLANEOUS PROVISIONS) ACT 1976
19.   Part II of this Act provides for the licensing of hire cars and modifies the licensing of taxis under the 1847 Act. This legislation is adoptive and may be brought into force by council resolution only for those areas in which the 1847 Act is in force. Section 15 has no effect on the application of these provisions. However, a transitional provision is made in the commencement of Section 15 to enable a district council to resolve in advance of the coming into force of the 1847 Act, to adopt Part II of the 1976 Act (see paragraph 14).

20.   The 1976 Act provides additional powers for ensuring that vehicles are suitable for use as taxis and that they are maintained in a satisfactory condition. In particular, sections 50 and 68 contain specific powers to inspect and test taxis and section 60 provides the power to suspend, revoke or refuse to renew a licence. In addition, the 1976 Act permits taxi fares to be set by council resolution rather than byelaw. However, in considering whether to adopt these provisions, councils will wish to be

aware that Part II of the 1976 Act must be adopted in its entirety, including the provision for licensing hire cars.

THE METROPOLITAN POLICE DISTRICT

21.   Section 15 of the 1985 Act does not apply to the Metropolitan Police District where the licensing of taxis and taxi drivers is done under the Metropolitan Public Carriage Act 1869. As the Metropolitan Police District is not precisely the same as the administrative area of Greater London there are a few districts which have the 1869 Act in force in part of their area. Section 15 'extends the application of the 1847 Act to those parts of such districts which are not covered by the 1869 Act.

CONTROLS

22.   The 1847 Act *requires* a district council that licenses taxis to accept and consider applications for taxi and taxi drivers' licences and to maintain a register of licences granted. In addition it *empowers* such an authority to make bylaws for the purposes of—

- (*a*)   specifying how licence plates are to be carried on the vehicle;
- (*b*)   laying down requirements for vehicle construction and fitting;
- (*c*)   regulating the fares to be charged and the use of an approved taxi meter,
- (*d*)   regulating the behaviour of taxi proprietors and drivers;
- (*e*)   fixing taxi stands; and
- (*f*)   securing the safe custody and re-delivery of lost property.

The Home Office issued a set of model byelaws in 1974 and these are annexed.

23.   It will be for each council to decide on the level of control appropriate to local circumstances. It has been open to councils since 1972 to resolve to extend taxi licensing throughout their district. Consequently, none of the areas affected by Section 15 are those for which the responsible council has seen a compelling need to apply taxi licensing. In view of this the Government does not recommend the setting up of an extensive or burdensome licensing system. The application of taxi licensing to previously uncontrolled areas was provided for in the 1985 Act in order to protect the safety of passengers. While regulating vehicle and driver standards the Council may not consider it necessary to control the way in which the taxi service is operated. In particular, the Government can see no reason why a council should seek to limit the number of taxis licensed to operate in these areas. There may be no need to control taxi fares; in the past these have been set by the operators, and councils may wish to allow this to continue. On the same basis, the imposition of exacting constructional requirements for vehicles is unlikely to be justified: such regulatory requirements impose a cost on the taxi trade which must ultimately be borne by taxi passengers.

VEHICLE STANDARDS

24.   The only vehicle requirement imposed by national legislation (other than those governing the fitness of any road vehicle) is in respect of seating capacity. A vehicle adapted to carry more than eight passengers that is used for hire or reward is a public service vehicle. Consequently, a taxi may have no more than eight passenger seats. Historically, taxis have been saloon cars licensed to carry four or five passengers and the attention of licensing authorities is drawn to the higher legal seating limit. Vehicles adapted to carry seven or eight passengers may be particularly suitable for the provision of shared taxi or 'bus' services and their use should not be precluded by vehicle licensing pre-conditions. Such pre-conditions may be laid down in order to ensure that a vehicle is suitable in type and design for use as a taxi. In deciding whether there is a need to prescribe such conditions councils will wish to consider whether their absence has resulted in this operation of unsuitable vehicles or is likely to do so.

25.   A council will wish to ensure that the vehicles that it licenses are mechanically sound, road worthy and safe. This is normally achieved by granting licences for one

year subject to the vehicle passing an annual test. Testing may be delegated to suitable garage companies in the area or other local agents or, where the council has its own testing facilities, they may undertake this work themselves. The cost of vehicle testing may be recovered as part of the licence fee (see paragraph 29) and should not be charged separately.

26.   Some councils set advisory age limits on the vehicles they are prepared to licence. These cannot be rigidly enforced and if a vehicle proves to be in a satisfactory condition it should be licensed regardless of its age. It has recently come to the notice of the Department that some councils are proposing to insist that any vehicle submitted for initial licensing must be new. This is seen as an unwarranted restriction on entry to the trade for would-be taxi proprietors.

DRIVERS' STANDARDS

27.   A district council will wish to satisfy itself that an applicant for a taxi driver's licence is a fit and proper person. The Medical Commission on Accident Prevention has drawn up guidelines on medical fitness of applicants for the holders of vocational driving licences (Medical Aspects of Fitness to Drive, £3 inc p & p from 35–43 Lincolns Inn Fields, London WC2A 3PN).

28.   Many councils set a special driving test for taxi drivers and some test their geographical knowledge of the taxi licensing area. Neither of these tests are likely to be appropriate for the licensing of taxi drivers in an area to which Section 15 applies.

FINANCIAL AND MANPOWER EFFECTS

29.   This Circular is concerned with the implementation of the 1985 Act. The financial and manpower effects for local authorities of the Act as a whole are described in paragraphs 188 to 191 of Department Circular 3/85 (Welsh Office Circular 64/85). Under Section 35 of the Transport Act 1981, a district council may recover in the form of licensing fees the reasonable administrative or other costs incurred in connection with the licensing, control and supervision of taxis.

ANNEX

MODEL BYELAWS FOR HACKNEY CARRIAGES
(revised 1974)

[Note: When submitting draft byelaws for provisional approval it is Important that the required assurances should be given about the siting of stands [No 15, footnote (1)] the operation of taximeters [No 15, footnote (2) and No 4, footnote (1)(a)] and, where appropriate, about the custody of lost property [No 17, footnote (1).]

BYELAWS
Made under section 68 of the Town Police Clauses Act 1847, and section 171 of the Public Health Act 1875, by the[1]

with respect to hackney carriages in[2]

Interpretation

1.   Throughout these byelaws 'the Council' means the[1] and 'the district' means[2].

Provisions regulating the manner in which the number of each hackney carriage corresponding with the number of its licence, shall be displayed

2.
   (*a*)   The proprietor of a hackney carriage shall cause the number of the licence granted to him in respect of the carriage to be legibly painted or marked on the outside and inside of the carriage, or on plates affixed thereto,

   (*b*)   A proprietor or driver of a hackney carriage shall—

      i. not wilfully or negligently cause or suffer any such number to be concealed from public view while the carriage is standing or plying for hire;

      ii. not cause or permit the carriage to stand or ply for hire with any such painting, marking or plate so defaced that any figure or material particular is illegible.

Provisions regulating how hackney carriages are to be furnished or provided

3.   The proprietor of a hackney carriage shall—

   (*a*)   provide sufficient means by which any person in the carriage may communicate with the driver,

   (*b*)   cause the roof or covering to be kept water-tight;

   (*c*)   provide any necessary windows and a means of opening and closing not less than one window on each side;

   (*d*)   cause the seats to be properly cushioned or covered;

   (*e*)   cause the floor to be provided with a proper carpet, mat, or other suitable covering;

   (*f*)   cause the fittings and furniture generally to be kept in a clean condition, well maintained and in every way fit for public service;

   (*g*)   provide means for securing luggage if the carriage is so constructed as to carry luggage;

   (*h*)   provide an efficient fire extinguisher which shall be carried in such a position as to be readily available or use; and

   (*i*)   provide at least two doors for the use of persons conveyed in such carriage and a separate means of ingress and egress for the driver.

1 Insert 'District Council of

2 Insert name of district.

4. [1]The proprietor of a hackney carriage shall cause any taximeter with which the carriage is provided to be so constructed, attached, and maintained as to comply with the following requirements, that is to say—

   (*a*)   the taximeter shall be fitted with a key, flag, or other device the turning of which will bring the machinery of the taximeter into action and cause the word 'HIRED' to appear on the face of the taximeter,

   (*b*)   such key, flag, or other device shall be capable of being locked in such a position that the machinery of the taximeter is not in action and that no fare is recorded on the face of the taximeter;

   (*c*)   when the machinery of the taximeter is in action there shall be recorded on the face of the taximeter in clearly legible figures a fare not exceeding the rate or fare which the proprietor or driver is entitled to demand and take for the hire of the carriage by [time as well as for] distance in pursuance of the byelaw[2] in that behalf;

   (*d*)   the word 'FARE' shall be printed on the face of the taximeter in plain letters so as clearly to apply to the fare recorded thereon;

   (*e*)   the taximeter shall be so placed that all letters and figures on the face thereof are at all times plainly visible to any person being conveyed in the carriage, and for that purpose the letters and figures shall be capable of being suitably illuminated during any period of hiring; and

(f)   the taximeter and all the fittings thereof shall be so affixed to the carriage with seals or other appliances that it shall not be practicable for any person to tamper with them except by breaking, damaging or permanently displacing the seals or other appliances.

Provisions regulating the conduct of the proprietors and drivers of hackney carriages plying within the district in their several employments, and determining whether such drivers shall wear any and what badges

5.   The driver of a hackney carriage provided with a taximeter shall—

(a)   when standing or plying for hire, keep the key, flag or other device fitted in pursuance of the byelaw in that behalf locked in the position in which no fare is recorded on the face of the taximeter,

(b)   Before beginning a journey for which a fare is charged for distance [and time], bring the machinery of the taximeter into action by moving the said key, flag or other device, so that the word 'HIRED' is legible on the face of the taximeter and keep the machinery of the taximeter in action until the termination of the hiring; and

(c)   cause the dial of the taximeter to be kept properly illuminated throughout any part of a hiring which is during the hours of darkness as defined for the purposes of the Road Traffic Act 1972, and also at any other time at the request of the hirer.

1 (a)   An assurance should be given that proprietors of cabs already fitted with taximeters will have no difficulty in complying with the byelaws relating to taximeters, and, where the byelaws will require all cabs to be fitted with meters, that the other proprietors will be able to obtain and fit suitable meters and 'FOR HIRE' signs by the time the byelaws may be expected to come into operation.

(b)   Where the Council wishes to require all cabs to be fitted with a taximeter, the following form of words may be used;

'The proprietor of a hackney carriage shall cause the same to be provided with a taximeter so constructed, attached and maintained as to comply with the following requirements, that is to say,'

(c)   Where taximeters are not in use and their use cannot be foreseen, model byelaws 4, 5 and 6 may be omitted. If they are omitted, the heading preceding model byelaw 5 should remain.

2 On adoption of Local Government (Miscellaneous Provisions) Act 1976 'byelaw' should be deleted and 'tariff fixed by the Council' should be inserted.

6.   A proprietor or driver of a hackney carriage shall not tamper with or permit any person to tamper with any taximeter with which the carriage is provided, with the fittings thereof, or with the seals affixed thereto.

7.   The driver of a hackney carriage shall, when plying for hire in any street and not actually hired—

(a)   proceed with reasonable speed to one of the stands fixed by the byelaw in that behalf;

(b)   if a stand, at the time of his arrival, is occupied by the full number of carriages authorized to occupy it, proceed to another stand;

(c)   on arriving at a stand not already occupied by the full number of carriages authorized to occupy it, station the carriage immediately behind the carriage or carriages on the stand and so as to face in the same direction; and

(d)   from time to time when any other carriage immediately in front is driven off or moved forward cause his carriage to be moved forward so as to fill the place previously occupied by the carriage driven off or moved forward.

8.   A proprietor or driver of a hackney carriage, when standing or plying for hire, shall not, by calling out or otherwise, importune any person to hire such carriage and

shall not make use of the services of any other person for the purpose.

9.   The driver of a hackney carriage shall behave in a civil and orderly manner and shall take all reasonable precautions to ensure the safety of persons conveyed in or entering or alighting from the vehicle.

10.   The proprietor or driver of a hackney carriage who has agreed or has been hired to be in attendance with the carriage at an appointed time and place shall, unless delayed or prevented by some sufficient cause, punctually attend with such carriage at such appointed time and place.

11.   The driver of a hackney carriage when hired to drive to any particular destination shall, subject to any directions given by the hirer, proceed to that destination by the shortest available route[1].

12.   A proprietor or driver of a hackney carriage shall not convey or permit to be conveyed in such carriage any greater number of persons than the number of persons specified on the plate affixed to the outside of the carriage.

1   Where the Local Government (Miscellaneous Provisions) Act 1976 has been adopted, this byelaw will be replaced by the provisions of Section 69 of that Act.

13.   If a badge has been provided by the Council and delivered to the driver of a hackney carriage he shall, when standing or plying for hire, and when hired, wear that badge in such position and manner as to be plainly visible.

14.   The driver of a hackney carriage so constructed as to carry luggage shall, when requested by any person hiring or seeking to hire the carriage—
   (*a*)   convey a reasonable quantity of luggage;
   (*b*)   afford reasonable assistance in loading and unloading; and
   (*c*)   afford reasonable assistance in removing it to or from the entrance of any building, station, or place at which he may take up or set down such person.

Provisions fixing the stands of hackney carriages

15.   [1]Each of the several places specified in the following list shall be a stand for such number of hackney carriages as is specified in the list[2, 3]

1   Assurances are required that—
   (*a*)   the proposed stands are not situated on parking places provided by the Council under section 32 of the Road Traffic Regulation Act 1984, or an earlier similar provision;
   (*b*)   the police are in agreement with the siting of the stands, so far as traffic considerations are concerned; and
   (*c*)   i. the proposed stands are situated on roads for the maintenance of which the Council is responsible; or
   ii. where any other person or authority is responsible for the maintenance of the road, the consent of that authority or person has been obtained. (In the case of a stand on railway property such consent should, if possible, be in terms which relieve proprietors and drivers of the necessity to obtain permission individually to use the stand.)

2   Descriptions of the stands should be sufficient to enable them to be identified (eg against the kerb opposite nos 93 to 97 King Street.)

3   This byelaw will cease to have effect on adoption of Local Government (Miscellaneous Provisions) Act 1976 by virtue of Section 63(4) of that Act.

Provisions fixing the rates or fares to be paid for hackney carriages within the district, and securing the due publication of such fares[1]

16.   The proprietor or driver of a hackney carriage shall be entitled to demand and take for the hire of the carriage the rate or fare prescribed by the attached table[2][5], the rate or fare being calculated by distance unless the hirer express at the commencement of the hiring his desire to engage by time[3].

Provided always that where a hackney carriage furnished with a taximeter shall be hired by distance the proprietor or driver thereof shall not be entitled to demand and take a fare greater than that recorded on the face of the taximeter, save for any extra charges authorised by the attached table[5] which it may not be possible to record on the face of the taximeter[4].

1   The desirability of consultations with the local cab trade, whilst at the same time bearing in mind the interests of the cab using public, should not be overlooked when fares are being considered, in view of the possibility of objections being made at a later stage.

2   In compiling the table, care should be taken to ensure that no difficulties will arise as to the recording of the fares by taximeters. An assurance should be given that the fares will be capable of being recorded in the prescribed units by all taximeters likely to be employed on cabs in the district, or, alternatively, that no taximeters are in use in the district and that their use in the future is not foreseen.

3   When no fares for time are prescribed, hirings by time will be uncontrolled and the fare will be subject to individual contract in each case. In view of the difficulty of fixing fares for time which are reasonable to both parties, this is generally regarded as preferable.

4   This proviso should be included whether or not taximeters are introduced in case they are introduced on a voluntary basis before further byelaws are made.

5   On adoption of the Local Government (Miscellaneous Provisions) Act 1976 'attached table' should be deleted and 'Council' inserted.

17.
   (*a*)   The proprietor of a hackney carriage shall cause a statement of the fares fixed by byelaw[1] to be exhibited inside the carriage, in clearly distinguishable letters and figures.
   (*b*)   The proprietor or driver of a hackney carriage bearing a statement of fares in accordance with this byelaw shall not wilfully or negligently cause or suffer the letters of figures in the statement to be concealed or rendered illegible at any time while the carriage is plying or being used for hire.

Provisions securing the safe custody and re-delivery of any property accidentally left in hackney carriages, and fixing the charges to be made in respect thereof

18.   The proprietor or driver of a hackney carriage shall immediately after the termination of any hiring or as soon as practicable thereafter carefully search the carriage for any property which may have been accidentally left therein.

19.   The proprietor or driver of a hackney carriage shall, if any property accidentally left therein by any person who may have been conveyed in the carriage be found by or handed to him—

   (*a*)   carry it as soon as possible and in any event within 48 hours, if not sooner claimed by or on behalf of its owner, to[2] the office of the Council, and leave it in the custody of the officer in charge of the office on his giving a receipt for it; and
   (*b*)   be entitled to receive from any person to whom the property shall be re-delivered an amount equal to five pence in the pound of its estimated value (or the fare for the distance from the place of finding to the office of the Council, whichever be the greater) but not more than five pounds.

Penalties

20.   Every person who shall offend against any of these byelaws shall be liable on summary conviction to a fine not exceeding one hundred pounds and in the case of

a continuing offence to a further fine not exceeding five pounds for each day during which the offence continues after conviction therefor.

Repeal of byelaws[3]

21.   The byelaws relating to hackney carriages which were made by the Council[4] on the day of and which were confirmed by[5] on the day of are hereby repealed.

1   On adoption of the Local Government (Miscellaneous Provisions) Act 1976 'byelaw' should be deleted and 'council resolution' inserted.

2   It may be desired to substitute 'a police station in the district'. In this case an assurance will be required that the consent of the police has been obtained.

3   If there are no byelaws in force upon the subject, this should be stated and the clause struck out.

4   State names in full of all local authorities whose byelaws are to be repealed.

5   State the confirming authority, eg The Local Government Board; the Minister of Health; One of the Principal Secretaries of State of His Late Majesty King George VI; One of Her Majesty's Principal Secretaries of State.

Table of fares in relation to byelaw 16[1]

(i) Mileage	New pence
If the distance does not exceed one mile	
for the whole distance	V
If the distance exceeds one mile	
for the first mile	V
for each subsequent yards or uncompleted part thereof	W
(ii) Waiting time[2]	
For each period of minutes or uncompleted part thereof	W
(iii) Extra charges[3]	
a. For hirings begun between p.m./Midnight and a.m.	X% of the above rate or fare
b. For each article of luggage conveyed outside the passenger compartment of the carriage	Yp
c. For each person in excess of	Zp

1   On adoption of the Local Government (Miscellaneous Provisions) Act 1976 this table will be replaced by the 'Table of Fares' provided for by Section 65 of that Act.

2   Where taximeters are in use, or are likely to be brought into use, it will be necessary to permit *all* waiting time to be charged in order to prevent contravention of byelaw 4(c). Taximeters record all waiting, whether at the hirer's request or due to traffic congestion.

3   The 'extra charges' table is included only for the guidance of local authorities who wish to prescribe extra charges; it should not be taken as indicating that all or any of the extra charges should necessarily be prescribed.

DOT Circular 2/92; HO Circular 13/92

DISCLOSURE OF CRIMINAL RECORDS:
APPLICANTS FOR HACKNEY CARRIAGE & PRIVATE HIRE VEHICLE DRIVERS' LICENCES

SUMMARY

1. This circular advises local authorities on the procedures to adopt for checking with the police the criminal convictions of applicants for hackney carriage and private hire vehicle drivers' licences. They apply where—

- local authorities have responsibilities under the Local Government (Miscellaneous Provisions) Act 1976; or
- any local Act contains a provision requiring a local authority to be satisfied as to the fitness of an applicant to hold a licence to drive a hackney carriage or a private hire vehicle.

2. This facility does not apply to local authorities who have not adopted the Local Government (Miscellaneous Provisions) Act 1976 and therefore license hackney carriage drivers by virtue of the Town Police Clauses Act 1847 only.

Annex A—explains the procedure.
Annex B—sets out a model local policy statement.
Annex C—is a model request for a police check.
Annex D—contains example guidelines relating to the relevance of convictions.

ACTION

3. The procedure described in Annex A comes into effect on 1 April 1992. Local authorities responsible for the licensing of drivers of hackney carriages or private hire vehicles are asked to adopt it for gaining access to the police records described, and to nominate an officer to liaise with the police. The name of the nominated officer should be given to the police as soon as possible.

BACKGROUND

4. These arrangements stem from Section 47 of the Road Traffic Act 1991 which provides that a council may send to the chief officer of police for the police area in which the council is situated a copy of an application for a hackney carriage or private hire vehicle driver's licence and may request the chief officer's observations on it. The chief officer is required to respond to the request. The arrangements are intended to assist local authorities in satisfying themselves that applicants are fit and proper persons to hold driver licences. The arrangements do not apply to London.

5. This Circular has been drawn up in consultation with representatives of the local authority associations, the Association of Chief Police Officers and taxi trade associations.

ENQUIRIES

6. Contact points for enquiries are:

From local authorities:
Mrs K Turnbull
Department of Transport
Room S15/20
2 Marsham Street
LONDON SW1P 3EB
Tel:[020 7276 4896]

From the Police:
Mr F E Whittaker
F2 Division
Home Office
50 Queen Anne's Gate
LONDON SW1H 9AT
Tel: [020 7273 3716]

DISCLOSURE OF CRIMINAL RECORDS

APPLICANTS FOR HACKNEY CARRIAGE AND PRIVATE HIRE VEHICLE DRIVERS' LICENCES

Scope

1.   The legislation provides that local authorities with responsibilities under the Local Government (Miscellaneous Provisions Act 1976 (the Act)) or equivalent local legislation may ask the chief officer of police for their area for his observations on—

- any application for a licence to drive a hackney carriage;
- any application for renewal of a licence to drive a hackney carriage;
- any application for a licence to drive a private hire vehicle under Section 51 of the Act;
- any application for renewal of a licence to drive a private hire vehicle

where the application was received on or after 1 April 1992 or was under consideration at that date.

The police check

2.   In all cases the police check will be made against the index to the national collection of criminal records maintained on the Police National Computer (PNC). These records include details of persons convicted of all offences, broadly speaking, for which a term of imprisonment may be given.

3.   Hackney carriage and private hire vehicle (PHV) driver licences may run for up to three years, although many authorities re-grant them annually. Because of constraints on resources authorities should note that, in commenting on an application, the police will normally only conduct a criminal record check if the licence is being granted or re-granted for the first time under these arrangements, or if a period of three years has elapsed since the applicant was last subject to a criminal record check (but see also paragraphs 17 and 25).

Nominated officer

4.   An officer in each local authority to whom these arrangements apply should take responsibility for requesting checks from the police. Authorities should give their police force details of their nominated officer as soon as possible. He or she should be responsible for—

- overseeing the operation of the checking procedure within the authority;
- ensuring that requests fall within the terms of the legislation and this circular;
- ensuring that requests are made at the right time;
- ensuring that the provisions of the Rehabilitation of Offenders Act 1974 are observed;
- ensuring that information received from the police is released only to those who need to see it, and
- ensuring that records are kept securely and for no longer than is necessary.

Procedure

5.   Police checks should not take the place of normal licensing procedures. Other checks to establish a person's integrity and fitness to hold a licence to drive a hackney carriage or PHV should be carried out, and attempts made to account satisfactorily for any unexplained gaps in employment.

6. A police check should not be requested if an applicant is unsuitable for other reasons.

7. In considering applications from potential licence holders authorities should be aware that applicants do not have to reveal, and licensing authorities must not take into account, offences which are spent under the Rehabilitation of Offenders Act 1974, although these may be included in any record provided by the police. The nominated officer should take responsibility for identifying spent convictions and ensuring that those considering the application are not influenced by them.

8. An applicant should be informed in writing that a police check will be carried out.

9. Authorities should make every effort to confirm the identity of the applicant before the police are asked to process a check. Verification of identity, date of birth and any change of name should be obtained. Apart from checking any available documentation such as birth certificate, passport, driving licence etc, it is recommended that independent verification of the applicant's identity is sought, perhaps from a previous employer. Incomplete or incorrect identification details may invalidate the police check and lead to a failure to discover relevant convictions.

10. Authorities may wish to consider making a policy statement available to people who will be subject to a criminal records check under these arrangements. A model statement is offered at Annex B.

11. When a police check is desired, the request should be sent to the Chief Constable of the police force for the area in which the applicant has applied for a licence. Requests should be made in a form consistent with the model layout shown at Annex C.

12. The police will reply to the nominated officer either indicating that there is no trace on national police records of a record which matches the details provided, or that those details appear identical with the person whose record will be attached. The record will contain details of all convictions recorded nationally against that person.

13. It should be noted that the police record will not include details of motoring convictions. Such information may be obtained from the Driver and Vehicle Licensing Agency. This will be provided on receipt of a written request which must include the subject's driver number, or failing that, their full name and date of birth. A fee of £3.50 (for each individual enquiry) is payable at the time the request is made. The information given will include endorsement/disqualification details. Requests should be sent to—

DEU (Data Subject Enquiries)
Room C1/16
DVLA
Longview Road
Swansea 5A6 7JL.

14. Where

- the information provided by the police differs from that provided by the applicant, and is of significance, the nominated officer should discuss the discrepancy with the applicant before reaching any final decision in which the nature of the information received is a factor;

- there is disagreement, the person should have the opportunity to see the information provided by the police.

15. It should be noted that applicants themselves may reveal certain minor convictions or cautions which are not recorded in the national collection of criminal records and, therefore, not included in the convictions provided by the police. In general, corroboration of such convictions or cautions should not be sought from the police.

16. A person who believes the information provided by the police is incorrect and who wishes to make representations to the police should do so in the first place through the nominated officer. Authorities will want to ensure that cases of this kind are dealt with at an appropriate level.

Checks on persons already in possession of hackney carriage/phv drivers' licences

17. Checks should not normally be made on persons other than in connection with an application for grant or renewal of a licence. If, however, serious allegations are made against a driver, or previously unrevealed information comes to light and the nominated officer is satisfied that the information cannot be verified in any other way, a police check may be requested. This should not be done without the knowledge of the individual concerned who must be given an opportunity to discuss the outcome of the check.

Use of information

18. The fact that a person has a criminal record or is known to the police does not necessarily mean that he or she is unfit to hold a driver's licence. The authority concerned should make a balanced judgement about a person's suitability taking into account only those offences which are considered relevant to the person's suitability to hold a licence. A person's suitability should be looked at as a whole in the light of all the information available.

19. In deciding the relevance of convictions, authorities will want to bear in mind that offences which took place many years in the past may often have less relevance than recent offences. Similarly, a series of offences over a period of time is more likely to give cause for concern than an isolated minor conviction. In any event the importance of rehabilitation must be weighed against the need to protect the public.

20. In order to ensure consistent and fair treatment when determining whether or not criminal convictions render an applicant unsuitable to hold a licence, local authorities may find it very helpful to draw up detailed policy guidelines containing general criteria against which applications may be considered. The guidelines at Annex D are based on those used by the Metropolitan Police and are offered to local authorities as an example which they may wish to use or adapt.

21. Where it is discovered that a driver, licensed prior to implementation of section 47, had failed to disclose past convictions, local authorities will need to consider carefully whether they should now refuse to re-grant the driver licence. In most cases, if those convictions are such that they would now lead to the refusal of a licence, refusal should be considered. If, however, previously unrevealed convictions are discovered which would not now disqualify the individual from holding a licence, consideration should normally be given to granting it. It is possible that a significant proportion of drivers will be shown to have concealed previous convictions and it is recommended that local authorities develop a consistent and fair policy when dealing with them.

Appeals

22.   Any person who is aggrieved by the licensing authority's decision to refuse a driver's licence may appeal to a Magistrates' Court.

Storage and destruction of records

23.   Any information the police supply will be of a sensitive and personal nature. It must be used only in connection with the application which gave rise to the request for a check to be made. The nominated officer must ensure it is kept securely while the licensing process takes its course and that the information is not kept for longer than is necessary. An indication on the Authority's own record that a check with the police has been carried out may be made but should not refer to specific offences.

Checks on applicants from overseas

24.   Other than in exceptional circumstances, the police cannot—

* make enquiries about the antecedents of people from overseas; or
* establish details of convictions acquired outside the United Kingdom.

Applicants from certain EC countries may, however, be able to produce certificates of good conduct.

Police reporting of convictions as they occur

25.   If a police force is able to identify that the holder of a driver licence has acquired a relevant conviction, it will give details to the local nominated officer. This will occur only where the police are aware that a person is licensed under the Act and so will not mean that the nominated officer will automatically get information about all relevant convictions.

Police monitoring

26.   Where possible forces are asked to collate the following information in respect of each authority with which they deal:

* number of PNC checks requested,
* time taken to process checks,
* number of positive traces, and
* any apparent difficulties with these arrangements, including the resource implications.

27.   The results of this monitoring will be kept under review by the Home Office in conjunction with the Association of Chief Police Officers and the local authority associations.

ANNEX B

STATEMENT OF POLICY ABOUT RELEVANT CONVICTIONS

(See Annex A, paragraph 10)

When formulating their own policy, local authorities may wish to consider using the following statement, suitably adapted:

> 'When submitting an application for a licence to drive a hackney carriage or private hire vehicle you are requested to declare any convictions or cautions you may have,

unless they are regarded as "spent" under the Rehabilitation of Offenders Act 1974. The information you give will be treated in confidence and will only be taken into account in relation to your application.

You should be aware that the licensing authority is empowered in law to check with the police for the existence and content of any criminal record held in the name of an applicant. Information received from the police will be kept in strict confidence while the licensing process takes its course and will be retained for no longer than is necessary.

The disclosure of a criminal record or other information will not debar you from gaining a licence unless the authority considers that the conviction renders you unsuitable. In making this decision the authority will consider the nature of the offence, how long ago and what age you were when it was committed and any other factors which may be relevant. [Authorities may wish to refer to any guidelines to which they adhere.] Any applicant refused a driver's licence on the ground that he/she is not a fit and proper person to hold such a licence has a right of appeal to a Magistrates' Court.

If you would like to discuss what effect a conviction might have on your application you may telephone [A N Other on 012–345–6789] in confidence, for advice.'

ANNEX C

REQUEST FOR A POLICE CHECK IN RESPECT OF AN APPLICATION FOR GRANT OR RENEWAL OF A LICENCE TO DRIVE A HACKNEY CARRIAGE OR PRIVATE HIRE VEHICLE

Part A. To be completed by applicant.

I am aware that the grant of such a licence is subject to a police record check. This has been explained to me and I understand that spent convictions are not considered by the licensing authority. I hereby declare that the information given below is true.

Signature .... Date ....

Surname .... All Forenames ....

Maiden Name .... Previous surnames ....

Date of Birth .... Place of Birth .... Sex M/F

Present Address ....

....

Previous addresses in last 5 years   Date from .... to ....

....

Continue overleaf if necessary, giving dates.

HAVE YOU EVER BEEN CONVICTED AT A COURT OR CAUTIONED BY THE POLICE FOR ANY OFFENCE WHICH IS NOT NOW SPENT UNDER THE TERMS OFTHE REHABILITATION OF OFFENDERS ACT 1974? YES/NO

If yes provide details overleaf, including approximate date, the offence and the court or police force which dealt with you.

....

Part B. To be completed by the Nominated Officer

The person identified above satisfies the conditions of Joint Circular DTp 2/92 HO 13/92. The details provided have been verified and I am satisfied they are accurate.

The subject has not been checked previously/was last checked on....... /....... /........

(Signed) .... (Date) ....

....

Part C. For Police Use Only.   *Ref* ....

PNC/NIB Records only have been checked against the above details:

☐ No trace on details supplied   ☐ The subject appears identical with the person whose criminal record is attached

(Signed) .... (Date) ....

ALL FORMS TO BE RETURNED UNDER CONFIDENTIAL COVER

ANNEX D

It is recommended that local authorities adopt their own guidelines relating to the relevance of convictions for use in determining applications for hackney carriage and private hire vehicle (PHV) drivers' licences. The following is an example only and is based on criteria used by the Metropolitan Police.

GUIDELINES RELATING TO THE RELEVANCE OF CONVICTIONS

General policy

1. Each case will be decided on its own merits.

2. A person with a current conviction for serious crime need not be permanently barred from obtaining a licence but should be expected to remain free of conviction for 3 to 5 years, according to the circumstances, before an application is entertained. Some discretion may be appropriate if the offence is isolated and there are mitigating circumstances. However, the overriding consideration should be the protection of the public.

3. The following examples afford a general guide on the action to be taken where convictions are admitted.

(a) Minor traffic offences

Convictions for minor traffic offences, eg obstruction, waiting in a restricted street, speeding etc, should not prevent a person from proceeding with an application. If sufficient points have been accrued to require a period of disqualification of the applicant's driving licence then a hackney carriage or PHV licence may be granted after its restoration but a warning should be issued as to future conduct.

(b) Major traffic offences

An isolated conviction for reckless driving or driving without due care and attention etc, should normally merit a warning as to future driving and advice on the standard expected of hackney carriage and PHV drivers. More than one conviction for this type of offence within the last two years should merit refusal and no further application should be considered until a period of 1 to 3 years free from convictions has elapsed.

(c) Drunkenness

(i) With motor vehicle

A serious view should be taken of convictions of driving or being in charge of a vehicle while under the influence of drink. An isolated incident should not necessarily debar an applicant but strict warnings should be given as to future behaviour. More than one conviction for these offences should raise grave doubts as to the applicant's fitness to hold a licence. At least 3 years should elapse (after the restoration of the driving licence) before an applicant is considered for a licence. If there is any suggestion that the applicant is an alcoholic, a special medical examination should be arranged before the application is entertained. If the applicant is found to be an alcoholic a period of 5 years should elapse after treatment is complete before a further licence application is considered.

(ii) Not in motor vehicle

An isolated conviction for drunkenness need not debar an applicant from gaining a licence. However, a number of convictions for drunkenness could indicate a medical problem necessitating critical examination (see (i) above). In some cases, a warning may be sufficient.

(d) Drugs

An applicant with a conviction for a drug related offence should be required to show a period of at least 3 years free of convictions before an application is entertained, or 5 years after detoxification treatment if he/she was an addict.

(e) Indecency offences

As hackney carriage and PHV drivers often carry unaccompanied passengers, applicants with convictions for indecent exposure, indecent assault, importuning, or any of the more serious sexual offences, should be refused until they can show a substantial period (at least 3 to 5 years) free of such offences. More than one conviction of this kind should preclude consideration for at least 5 years. In either case if a licence is granted a strict warning as to future conduct should be issued.

(f) Violence

As hackney carriage and PHV drivers maintain close contact with the public, a firm line should be taken with applicants who have convictions for grievous bodily harm, wounding or assault. At least 3 years free of such convictions should be shown before an application is entertained and even then a strict warning should be administered.

(g) Dishonesty

Hackney carriage and PHV drivers are expected to be persons of trust. The widespread practice of delivering unaccompanied property is indicative of the trust that business people place in drivers. Moreover, it is comparatively easy for a dishonest driver to defraud the public by demanding more than the legal fare etc. Overseas visitors can be confused by the change in currency and became 'fair game' for an unscrupulous driver. For these reasons a serious view should be taken of any conviction involving dishonesty. In general, a period of 3 to 5 years free of conviction should be required before entertaining an application.

Hackney Carriage Byelaws:
Local Government Reorganisation (England)

1.   This note explains the Department of Transport's position in respect of hackney carriage byelaws submitted by those local licensing authorities affected by changes arising from the Local Government Act 1992. This advice concerns only England. Different considerations apply to Wales by virtue of the Local Government (Wales) Act 1994.

THE LOCAL GOVERNMENT ACT 1992
2.   Essentially, the 1992 Act allowed for three types of changes to be implemented—

- a structural change involving the replacement, in a non-metropolitan area, of the two principal tiers of local government with a single tier;
- a boundary change which may be made for the purposes of facilitating a structural change or independently of such a change. It may involve the alteration of a local government area, the constitution of a local government area by the amalgamation of more such areas or the abolition of an area and its distribution amongst other areas;
- electoral changes which are changes in the electoral arrangements for a local government area, whether made in consequence of any structural or boundary change or independently of any such change.

3.   So far as taxi licensing is concerned, structural changes are not in themselves a problem; where one tier of local government ceases to exist, without boundary changes, all the functions of local government in the area are exercisable by a single authority. Neither is there a problem in respect of electoral changes. The problems affecting taxi licensing are generated by the boundary changes that accompany structural changes.

DEVELOPMENT OF TAXI ZONES
4.   In considering the effect of boundary changes on taxi licensing, it is first appropriate to trace the history of the zoning concept up to the coming into force on 1st January 1987 of section 15 of the Transport Act 1985.

i. 1847–1974
5.   The Town Police Clauses Act 1847 refers to 'the prescribed distance' and defines the word 'prescribed' as referring to such matter as may be prescribed or provided for in the special Act. The prescribed distance is particularly relevant as the distance within which a hackney carriage may be licensed to ply for hire (section 37) and the distance within which the driver of the hackney carriage can be compelled to go (section 53). There are numerous other references to it.
6.   Section 5 (repealed) of the Public Health Act 1875 provided that England (except the metropolis) should consist of districts to be called urban sanitary districts and rural sanitary districts which were to be subject to the jurisdiction of local authorities, respectively called urban sanitary authorities and rural sanitary authorities, which were invested with various powers mentioned in the Act. Section 171 (which is still in force) dealt with the Town Police Clauses Act 1847. That Act was originally a clauses Act, that is to say it had no independent existence of its own and only applied to an area if there was a special Act so applying it. Section 171 of the 1875 Act applied the provisions of the 1847 Act with respect to hackney carriages and provided that, for the purposes of regulating hackney carriages in urban districts, those provisions should be incorporated with the 1875 Act; the expression 'within

the prescribed distance' was defined for the purposes of that Act as meaning within any urban district.

7.   At this point there was no concept of 'zoning'; a single urban authority licensed hackney carriages to ply for hire within the whole of the urban district.

8.   Under the Local Government Act 1894, urban sanitary authorities became urban districts and urban sanitary authorities urban district councils, except where the area consisted of a borough. Under the Local Government Act 1933 the relevant areas for taxi licensing were county districts, which could be either urban district councils or non-county boroughs, and county boroughs. In a few cases taxi licensing was extended to rural districts by virtue of orders under section 276 of the Public Health Act 1875.

ii Local Government Act 1974

9.   In 1974 effect was given to the reorganisation set out in the Local Government Act 1972. All local authorities inside England and Wales were abolished and a new two-tier system of county councils and district councils was constituted. They key provision of the 1972 Act is section 180. This provides that for the purposes of (inter alia) the Public Health Act 1875, the local authority and sanitary authority (whether urban or not) for a district is the district council. Section 180 introduced Schedule 14, Part II of which provided that section 171(4) of the Public Health Act 1875 should apply to those areas, and only those, to which it applied immediately before 1st April 1974. In the Department's view, it is this provision which established the concept of zoning.

10.   What it meant in practice was that the taxi licensing situation within new district councils effectively became 'frozen'; a prescribed distance before the change remained a prescribed distance after the change. Consequently, a new district council which, for example, incorporated two former urban districts (ie two district prescribed distances) would administer taxi licensing for those two districts or 'zones'. The new district council might also have inherited an area which was not a former urban district and where taxis had not been licensed; in the absence of any action on the part of the new district council, the effect of the 1972 Act was to leave that remaining area unlicensed.

11.   Paragraph 25 of Schedule 14, however, enabled a local authority after giving the requisite notice to resolve that section 171(4) should apply throughout their area or cease to apply throughout their area (whether or not, in either case the enactment applied only to part of their area). A resolution disapplying section 171(4) had to be passed before 1st April 1975, but a resolution that section 171(4) should apply throughout their area could be passed at any time. Such a resolution does not have effect unless approved by the Secretary of State.

12.   Consequently, a new district council, on coming into being under the 1972 Act, had three options in respect of taxi licensing—

(i)   it could do nothing, in which case taxis would be licensable in those of the areas included in the new district in which taxis were previously licensable. These would comprise separate taxi licensing zones. The remainder of the district would not be subject to taxi licensing.

(ii)   it could pass a resolution disapplying section 171(4) of the Public Health Act 1875 which meant that taxi licensing would cease in those urban districts where taxis had previously been licensed and there would be no taxi licensing at all within the new district council's area. Such a resolution had to be passed before 1 April 1975.

(iii) it could pass a resolution applying section 171(4) throughout the area, which meant that the former urban districts [and boroughs] where taxis had previously been licensed would merge with the remainder of the new district to create a single taxi licensing area comprising the whole of the new district council's area.

13.   At this point the legislation cuts adrift from the phrase 'within the prescribed distance', but that continues to be a key expression in the 1847 Act. In the Department's view it is clear that, so long as the hackney carriage provisions in the 1847 Act continue to apply after 1st April 1974 to an area where they applied immediately before that date the words 'within the prescribed distance' continue to refer to that area but, when a resolution that section 171(4) of the 1875 Act should apply throughout the district becomes effective, those words refer to the whole district.

iii Transport Act 1985

14.   The next significant legislative change affecting taxi licensing areas was the enactment of section 15 of the Transport Act 1985. This provides that where, immediately before the commencement of section 15, the provisions of the 1847 Act with respect to hackney carriages were not in force throughout the whole area of a district council in England and Wales those provisions (as incorporated by the 1875 Act) shall —

- if not then in force in part of the council's area, apply throughout that area; and
- if in force in part only of its area, apply also in the remainder of that area.

15.   Again the Act does not make specific reference to the prescribed distance. However, in the Department's opinion, the construction of section 15 certainly recognises that a district might have distinct prescribed distances or taxi licensing zones as a result of the changes generated by the Local Government Act 1972.

16.   The effect of the 1985 Act was explained in Circular 8/86 (copies available from Miss P Brown on 0171 271 5056). If taxi licensing had not previously applied at all in a district then section 15(1)(a) meant that it applied throughout that district and the whole of the district was 'within the prescribed distance' for the purposes of the 1847 Act. If, however, the 1847 Act only applied in part of the district (ignoring by virtue of section 15(2) any part of the district in the Metropolitan Police district) then the effect of section 15(1)(b) was that the 1847 Act 'applied also' in the remainder of the district; that remaining area constituted a separate zone, so that the words 'within the prescribed distance' referred to each of the zones and not to the district as a whole.

17.   Relating section 15 to the three options which a district council could have taken in 1974 (paragraph 12 above)—

- in case (i) (where taxis were licensed in one or more distinct zones within the district), the effect of section 15 would have been to create an additional taxi licensing zone comprising that part of the district which was not already subject to taxi licensing;
- in case (ii) (where taxis were not licensed at all in the district), the effect of section 15 would have been to create a single taxi licensing comprising the whole of the district; and
- in case (iii) (where the whole of the district comprised a single taxi licensing area by virtue of having passed an extension resolution) the effect of section 15 would have been nil; the intention of section 15 was to extend taxi licensing to those areas where taxis had not previously been licensed.

18.   If a council falling into the case (i) category wanted to turn the whole of its district into a single licensing zone, it could do so by passing a resolution under Schedule 14 of the Local Government Act 1972 ('an extension resolution') providing that the 1847 Act as to apply throughout the district.

19.   Two circumstances support the Department's position. One is the subtle difference of wording between paragraphs (a) and (b) of section 15(1) ('apply throughout' as against 'apply also'). The other is the fact that the references to section 171(4) of the 1875 Act in Part II of Schedule 14 to the 1972 Act were not repealed. Accordingly, after section 15 was enacted, Parliament left in force provisions of the 1972 Act enabling a district council to apply section 171(4) 'throughout their area'. There is little substance to the argument that Schedule 14 of the 1972

Act became redundant after the coming into force of section 15 of the 1985 Act. The 1985 Act neither repealed nor amended Schedule 14 of the 1972 Act.

The Effect of the Local Government Act 1992

20.   Any new area constituted by an order made under the 1992 Act will be an area within all of which taxi licensing applies. However, the new area may include the whole or parts of single zone districts and/or of multiple zone districts. The possible combinations of circumstances are numerous which is why it is important to be clear as to the underlying principles.

21.   The relevant provisions which impinge on taxi licensing areas are regulations 4 and 5 of the Local Government Changes for England Regulations 1994 (as amended by SI 1995/1748).

22.   The Department takes the view that the general effect of these provisions in regard to taxi licensing may be summarised as follows—

- As with the 1972 reorganisation, the taxi licensing situation is effectively 'frozen' until further action is taken. Licences granted by a transferor authority continue in force in the areas in relation to which they were granted. Thus a licence granted in respect of an area which is split between two district councils is treated as granted by each of those councils in relation to so much as that area as lies within each new local government area. When that licence comes to an end, the licensee will have to apply for a new licence to one or other or both of the successor authorities.
- Nothing in the reorganisation effects any byelaws. Thus, if a new area to which taxi byelaws apply, becomes split between two districts, the byelaws will continue in force in the areas in respect of which they were made and will be treated as made by the successor council in relation to the part of the original area falling within their local government area.
- The reorganisation will not affect taxi zones. Thus, if a new area comprises the whole or parts of existing taxi licensing areas, those areas will continue to be separate licensing areas unless and until the local authority passes a resolution under Schedule 14 to the 1972 Act to apply the 1847 Act throughout its area (referred to in Circular 8/86 as 'an extension resolution').

EXAMPLES

23.   A first example is a new unitary authority comprising the whole of two former districts, A and B, each of which was a single taxi licensing zone. Licences granted by the transferor councils will continue in force as respects the areas for which they were granted. Likewise byelaws will continue in force for the two areas. It follows that new taxi licences can only be granted for one or other area. There would be nothing, however, to prevent the council of the new unitary authority from granting an applicant a licence to ply for hire in zone A and a licence to ply for hire in zone B. If the Council wished to combine the two zones, it could do so by passing an extension resolution and making byelaws to apply throughout the district. Both would have to be approved by the Secretary of State.

24.   A second example is a unitary authority where the new area comprises the whole of one former district and parts of three districts contiguous with it. On the day when the unitary authority is formed, taxi licences granted by all four of the former councils will continue in force with respect to the areas for which they were granted. Thus, the unitary authority will, by default, comprise four separate taxi licensing zones – A being the whole of the former district which remains intact and B, C and D being parts of former neighbouring districts which have been surrendered to the new unitary authority. Four separate sets of byelaws would continue to apply. The licence for B would be valid not only in the relevant part of the new district but also in that part of the existing prescribed distance which lies outside the new unitary authority. The same applies to C and D.

25.   One the expiration of a licence relating to B, C and D, the holder will have to decide which council to apply to for a new licence. One option would be to apply to

the new unitary authority, which would mean that a driver could ply for hire within the relevant zone of the unitary authority, but not in the area of the council which had issued his expired licence. Another option would be for the licence holder to apply to the council which had issued his expired licence in which case his new licence would not permit him to ply for hire within the area of the new unitary authority.

26. Again, however, there would be nothing to prevent the unitary authority from granting to the same applicant separate licences to ply for hire within two or more of those zones.

27. Here too, as in the first example, the unitary authority concerned could combine its zones by passing an extension resolution and making a uniform set of byelaws, subject to the approval of the Secretary of State.

28. The second example would also apply mutatis mutandis, to cases of boundary changes involving two or more district councils, where a unitary authority was not involved.

CONCLUSION

29. A key consideration underpinning the local government reorganisation was the importance of maintaining continuity as far as practicable. This advice note suggests that continuity in terms of the area in which a taxi driver can ply for hire is the natural course when unitary authorities are created. A change in the area in which a driver could ply for hire would only come if the licensing authority chooses to amalgamate the prescribed distances which it inherits, or if a licence to ply for hire within a prescribed distance which has been split by the reorganisation expires and a decision has to be made about where to operate in future.

30. The Department takes the view that if a unitary authority wishes to amalgamate its taxi licensing zones and apply taxi licensing uniformly to its area, then it must pass a resolution under Schedule 14 of the Local Government Act 1972, and secure the approval of the Secretary of State. If it does not do so the Department will decline to confirm byelaws for the new district as a whole.

Department of Transport
Busses and Taxis Division
May 1997

Applications for the Secretary of State's approval to extension resolutions; and hackney carriage byelaws *in draft form* should be sent to—

Miss P A Brown
Buses and Taxis Division
3/12 Great Minster House
76 Marsham Street
LONDON
SW1P 4DR

[020 7271 5056]
[020 7271 5314] (fax)

Local Government Reorganisation (Wales)
Hackney Carriage Byelaws

1   This note explains the position of the Department of the Environment, Transport and the Regions (DETR) in respect of hackney carriage byelaws submitted by those local licensing authorities affected by changes arising from the Local Government (Wales) Act 1994. This advice concerns only Wales. A separate advice note has been prepared in respect of local government reorganisation in England.

THE LOCAL GOVERNMENT (WALES) ACT 1994

2.   In Wales, local government has been completely restructured by the 1994 Act. This Act replaced the county councils and district councils by new unitary principal areas known as counties and county boroughs. The existing communities are continued in being as are their councils. The 1994 Act allows for the making of changes to the boundaries and electoral arrangements of local government areas. A boundary change may involve the alteration of a local government area; the constitution of a new local government area by the amalgamation of more such areas or communities or by the aggregation of parts of such areas or by the separation of part of such an area; the abolition of an area or community and its distribution among other principal areas or communities and the constitution of a new community. The 1994 Act also allows a change in electoral arrangements for any local government area which is either consequential on any change in local government areas resulting from any boundary changes or is independent of a change in the boundaries of a particular area.

3.   So far as taxi licensing is concerned, structural changes are not in themselves a problem; the 1994 Act provides for the transfer of functions to the new unitary authorities. Electoral changes do not present any problems either. However, the problems affecting taxi licensing are generated by the boundary changes that accompany structural changes.

DEVELOPMENT OF TAXI ZONES

4. In considering the effect of boundary changes on taxi licensing, it is first appropriate to trace the history of the zoning concept up to the coming in to force on 1 January 1987 of section 15 of the Transport Act 1985.

i 1847–74

5.   The Town Police Clauses Act 1847 refers to 'the prescribed distance' and defines the word 'prescribed' as referring to such matter as may be prescribed or provided for in the special Act. The prescribed distance is particularly relevant as the distance within which a hackney carriage may be licensed to ply for hire (section 37) and the distance within which the driver of the hackney carriage can be compelled to go (section 53). There are numerous other references to it.

6.   Section 5 (repealed) of the Public Health Act 1875 provided that England and Wales (except the metropolis) should consist of districts to be called urban sanitary districts and rural sanitary districts which were to be subject to the jurisdiction of local authorities, respectively called urban sanitary authorities and rural sanitary authorities, which were invested with various powers mentioned in the Act. Section 171 (which is still in force) dealt with the Town Police Clauses Act 1847. That Act was originally a clauses Act, that is to say it had no independent existence of its own and only applied to an area if there was a special Act so applying it. Section 171 of the 1875 Act applied the provisions of the 1847 Act with respect to hackney carriages and provided that, for the purposes of regulating hackney carriages in

urban districts, those provisions should be incorporated with the 1875 Act; the expression 'within the prescribed distance' was defined for the purposes of that Act as meaning within any urban district.

7.   At this point there was no concept of 'zoning'; a single urban authority licensed hackney carriages to ply for hire within the whole of the urban sanitary district.

8.   Under the Local Government Act 1894, urban sanitary districts became urban districts and urban sanitary authorities urban district councils, except where the area consisted of a borough. Under the Local Government Act 1933, the relevant areas for taxi licensing were county districts, which could be either urban district councils or non-county boroughs, and county boroughs. In a few cases taxi licensing was extended to rural districts by virtue of orders under section 276 of the Public Health Act 1875.

ii Local Government Act 1972

9.   In 1974, effect was given to the reorganisation set out in the Local Government Act 1972. All local authorities inside England and Wales were abolished and a new two-tier system of county councils and district councils was constituted. So far as taxi licensing is concerned, the key provision of the 1972 Act is section 180. This provides that for the purposes of (inter alia) the Public Health Act 1875, the local authority and sanitary authority (whether urban or not) for a district is the district council. Section 180 introduced Schedule 14, Part II of which provided that section 171(4) of the Public Health Act 1875 should apply to those areas, and only those, to which it applied immediately before 1 April 1974. In the view of DETR, it is this provision which established the concept of zoning.

10.   What it meant in practice was that the taxi licensing situation within new district councils effectively became 'frozen' until the taking of action as mentioned in paragraph 11 below; a prescribed distance before the change remained a prescribed distance after the change. Consequently, a new district council which, for example, incorporated two former urban districts (ie two distinct prescribed distances) would administer taxi licensing for those two districts or 'zones'. The new district council might also have inherited an area which was not a former urban district and where taxis had not been licensed; in the absence of any action on the part of the new district council the effect of the 1972 Act was to leave that remaining area unlicensed.

11.   Paragraph 25 of Schedule 14, however, enabled a local authority after giving the requisite notice to resolve that section 171(4) should apply throughout their area or cease to apply throughout their area (whether or not, in either case, the enactment applied only to part of their area). A resolution disapplying section 171(4) had to be passed before 1 April 1975, but a resolution that section 171(4) should apply throughout their area could be passed at any time. Such a resolution does not have effect unless approved by the Secretary of State.

12.   Consequently, a new district council, on coming into being under the 1972 Act, had three options in respect of taxi licensing—

(i)   It could do nothing, in which case taxis would continue to be licensable in those of the areas included in the new district in which taxis were previously licensable. These would comprise separate taxi licensing zones. The remainder of the district would not be subject to taxi licensing; or

(ii)   it could pass a resolution disapplying section 171(4) of the Public Health Act 1875 which meant that taxi licensing would cease in those urban districts where taxis had previously been licensed and there would be no taxi licensing at all within the new district council's area. Such a resolution had to be passed before 1 April 1975; or

(iii) subject to the approval of the Secretary of State, it could pass a resolution applying section 171(4) throughout the area, which meant that the former urban districts (and boroughs) where taxis had previously been licensed would merge with the remainder of the new district to create a single taxi licensing area comprising the whole of the new district council's area.

13. At this point the legislation cuts adrift from the phrase 'within the prescribed distance', but that continues to be a key expression in the 1847 Act. In the view of DETR, it is clear that, so long as the hackney carriage provisions in the 1847 Act continue to apply after 1 April 1974 to an area where they applied immediately before that date, the words 'within the prescribed distance' continue to refer to that area but, when a resolution that section 171(4) of the 1875 Act should apply throughout the district becomes effective, those words refer to the whole district.

iii. Transport Act 1985
14. The next significant legislative change affecting taxi licensing areas was the enactment of section 15 of the Transport Act 1985. This provides that where, immediately before the commencement of section 15, the provisions of the 1847 Act with respect to hackney carriages were not in force throughout the whole of the area of a district council in England and Wales, those provisions (as incorporated by the 1875 Act) shall—

- if not then in force in part of the council's area, apply throughout that area; and
- if in force in part only of its area, apply also in the remainder of that area.

15. Again, the Act does not make specific reference to the prescribed distance. However, in the opinion of DETR, the construction of section 15 certainly recognises that a district might have distinct prescribed distances or taxi licensing zones as a result of the changes generated by the Local Government Act 1972.

16. The effect of the 1985 Act was explained in Circular 8/86 (copies available from Miss P Brown on 0171 271 5056). If taxi licensing had not previously applied at all in a district then section 15(1)(a) meant that it applied throughout that district and the whole of the district was 'within the prescribed distance' for the purposes of the 1847 Act. If, however, the 1847 Act only applied in part of the district (ignoring by virtue of section 15(2) any part of the district in the Metropolitan Police district) then the effect of section 15(1)(b) was that the 1847 Act 'applied also' in the remainder of the district; that remaining area constituted a separate zone, so that the words 'within the prescribed distance' referred to each of the zones and not to the district as a whole.

17. Relating section 16 to the three options which a district council could have taken in 1974 (paragraph 12 above)—

- in case (i) (where taxis were licensed in one or more distinct zones within the district), the effect of section 15 would have been to create an additional taxi licensing zone comprising that part of the district which was not already subject to taxi licensing;
- in case (ii) (where taxis were not licensed at all in the district), the effect of section 15 would have been to create a single taxi licensing comprising the whole of the district; and
- in case (iii) (where the whole of the district comprised a single taxi licensing area by virtue of having passed an extension resolution) the effect of section 15 would have been nil; the intention of section 15 was to extend taxi licensing to those areas where taxis had not previously been licensed.

18. If a council falling into the case (i) category wanted to turn the whole of its district into a single licensing zone, it could do so by passing a resolution under Schedule 14 of the Local Government Act 1972 ('an extension resolution') providing that the 1847 Act as to apply throughout the district.

19. Two circumstances support the position of DETR. One is the subtle difference of wording between paragraphs (a) and (b) of section 15(1) ('apply throughout' as against 'apply also'). The other is the fact that the references to section 171(4) of the 1875 Act in Part II of Schedule 14 to the 1972 Act were not repealed. Accordingly, after section 15 was enacted, Parliament left in force provisions of the 1972 Act enabling a district council to apply section 171(4) 'throughout their area'. There is

little substance to the argument that Schedule 14 of the 1972 Act became redundant after the coming into force of section 15 of the 1985 Act. The 1985 Act neither repealed nor amended Schedule 14 of the 1972 Act.

THE LOCAL GOVERNMENT (WALES) ACT 1994

20. Any new principal area under the 1994 Act will be an area within all of which taxi licensing applies. However, the new area may include the whole or parts of single zone districts or of multiple zone districts. The possible combinations of circumstances are numerous which is why it is important to be clear as to the underlying principles.

21. DETR takes the view that—

- as with the 1972 reorganisation, the taxi licensing situation is effectively 'frozen' until further action is taken. Licences granted by a transferor authority continue in force in the areas in relation to which they were granted. Thus a licence granted in respect of an area which is split between two unitary authorities is treated as granted by each of those authorities in relation to so much as that area as lies within each new authority area. When that licence comes to an end, the licensee will have to apply for a new licence to one or other or both of the successor authorities;
- nothing in the reorganisation affects any byelaws. Thus, if an area to which taxi byelaws apply, becomes split between two unitary authorities, the byelaws will continue in force in the areas in respect of which they were made and will be treated as made by the successor authority in relation to the part of the original area falling within their local government area; and
- the reorganisation will not affect taxi zones. Thus, if a new area comprises the whole or parts of existing taxi licensing areas, those areas will continue to be separate licensing areas unless and until with the approval of the Secretary of State for the Environment, Transport and the Regions, the unitary authority passes a resolution under Schedule 14 to the 1972 Act to apply the 1847 Act throughout its area (referred to in Circular 8/86 as 'an extension resolution').

EXAMPLES

22. A first example is a new unitary authority comprising the whole of two former districts, A and B, each of which was a single taxi licensing zone. Licences granted by the transferor authorities will continue in force as respects the areas for which they were granted. Likewise byelaws will continue in force for the two areas. It follows that new taxi licences can only be granted for one or other area. There would be nothing, however, to prevent the council of the new unitary authority from granting an applicant a licence to ply for hire in zone A and a licence to ply for hire in zone B. If the authority wished to combine the two zones, it could do so by passing an extension resolution and making byelaws to apply throughout the district. Both would have to be approved by the Secretary of State.

23. A second example is a unitary authority where the new area comprises the whole of one former district and parts of three districts contiguous with it. On the day when the unitary authority is formed, taxi licences granted by all four of the former authorities will continue in force with respect to the areas for which they were granted. Thus, the unitary authority will, by default, comprise four separate taxi licensing zones – A being the whole of the former district which remains intact and B, C and D being parts of former neighbouring districts which have been surrendered to the new unitary authority. Four separate sets of byelaws would continue to apply. The licence for B would be valid not only in the relevant part of the new district but also in that part of the existing prescribed distance which lies outside the new unitary authority. The same applies to C and D.

24. One the expiration of a licence relating to B, C or D, the holder will have to decide which authority to apply to for a new licence. One option would be to apply to the new unitary authority, which would mean that a driver could ply for hire

within the relevant zone of the unitary authority, but not in the area of the council which had issued his expired licence. Another option would be for the licence holder to apply to the authority which had issued his expired licence in which case his new licence would not permit him to ply for hire within the area of the new unitary authority.

25.   Again, however, there would be nothing to prevent the unitary authority from granting to the same applicant separate licences to ply for hire within two or more of those zones.

26.   Here too, as in the first example, the unitary authority concerned could combine its zones by passing an extension resolution and making a uniform set of byelaws, subject to the approval of the Secretary of State.

Conclusion

27.   A key consideration underpinning the reorganisation of local government in both England and Wales was the importance of maintaining continuity as far as practicable. This advice note suggests that continuity in terms of the area in which a taxi driver can ply for hire is the natural course when unitary authorities are created. A change in the area in which a driver could ply for hire would only come if the licensing authority chooses to amalgamate the prescribed distances which it inherits, or if a licence to ply for hire within a prescribed distance which has been split by the reorganisation expires and a decision has to be made about where to operate in future.

28.   DETR takes the view that if a unitary authority wishes to amalgamate its taxi licensing zones and apply taxi licensing uniformly to its area, then it must pass a resolution under Schedule 14 of the Local Government Act 1972, and secure the approval of the Secretary of State. If it does not do so, the Department of the Environment, Transport and the Regions will decline to confirm byelaws for the new district as a whole.

Applications for the approval of the Secretary of State for the Environment, Transport and the Regions to extension resolutions; and hackney carriage byelaws in draft form should be sent to—

Miss P A Brown
Buses and Taxis Division
Zone 3/12
Department of the Environment, Transport and the Regions
Great Minster House
76 Marsham Street
LONDON
SW1P 4DR

Department of the Environment, Transport and the Regions
Busses and Taxis Division
February 1998

Appendix III

Enforcement Concordat

The Principles of Good Enforcement:

Policy and Procedures

This document sets out what business and others being regulated can expect from enforcement officers. It commits us to good enforcement policies and procedures. It may be supplemented by additional statements of enforcement policy.

The primary function of central and local government enforcement work is to protect the public, the environment and groups such as consumers and workers. At the same time, carrying out enforcement functions in an equitable, practical and consistent manner helps to promote a thriving national and local economy. We are committed to these aims and to maintaining a fair and safe trading environment.

The effectiveness of legislation in protecting consumers or sectors in society depends crucially on the compliance of those regulated. We recognise that most businesses want to comply with the law. We will, therefore, take care to help business and others meet their legal obligations without unnecessary expense, while taking firm action, including prosecution where appropriate, against those who flout the law or act irresponsibly. All citizens will reap the benefits of this policy through better information, choice and safety.

We have therefore adopted the central and local government Concordat on Good Enforcement. Included in the term 'enforcement' are advisory visits and assisting with compliance as well as licensing and formal enforcement action. By adopting and concordat we commit ourselves to the following policies and, which contribute to best value, and will provide information to show that we are observing them.

Policy

STANDARDS

In consultation with business and other relevant interested parties, including technical experts where appropriate, we will draw up clear standards setting out the level of service and performance the public and business people can expect to receive. We will publish these standards and our annual performance against them. The standards be made available to business and others who are regulated.

OPPENNESS

We will provide information and advice in plain language on the rules that we apply and will disseminate this as widely as possible. We will be open about how we set, consulting business, voluntary organisations, charities, consumers and workforce representatives. We will discuss general issues, specific compliance failures or problems with anyone experiencing difficulties.

HELPFULNESS

We believe that prevention is better than cure and that our role therefore involves actively working with business, to advise on and assist with compliance.. We will provide a courteous and efficient service and our staff will identify themselves by name. We will provide a contact point and telephone number for further dealings with us and we will encourage business to seek advice/information from us. Applications for approval of establishments, licences, registrations etc, will be dealt with efficiently and promptly. We will ensure that, wherever practicable, our enforcement services are effectively co-ordinated to minimise unnecessary overlaps and time delays.

COMPLAINTS ABOUT SERVICE

We will provide well publicised, effective and timely complaints procedures easily accessible to business, the public, employees and consumer groups. In cases where disputes cannot be resolved, any right of complaint or appeal will be explained, with details of the process and the likely time-scales involved.

PROPORTIONALITY

We will minimise the costs of compliance for business by ensuring that any action we require is proportionate to the risks. As far as the law allows, we will take account of the circumstances of the case and the attitude of the operator when considering action.

We will take particular care to work with small businesses and voluntary and community organisations so that they can meet their legal obligations without unnecessary expense, where practicable.

CONSISTENCY

We will carry out our duties in a fair, equitable and consistent manner. While inspectors are expected to exercise judgement in individual cases, we will have arrangements in place to promote consistency, including effective arrangements for liaison with other authorities and enforcement bodies through schemes such as those operated by the Local Authorities Co-Ordinating Body on Food and Trading Standards (LACOTS) and the Local Authority National Type Approval Confederation (LANTAC).

Procedures

Advice from an officer will be put clearly and simply and will be confirmed in writing, on request, explaining why any remedial work is necessary and over what time-scale, and making sure that legal requirements are clearly distinguished from best practice advice.

Before formal enforcement action is taken, officers will provide an opportunity to discuss the circumstances of the case and, if possible, resolve points of difference, unless immediate action is required (for example, in the interests of health and safety or environmental protection or to prevent evidence being destroyed).

Where immediate action is considered necessary, an explanation of why such action was required will be given at the time and confirmed in writing in most cases within 5 working days and, in all cases, within 10 working days.

Where there are rights of appeal against formal action, advice on the appeal mechanism will be clearly set out in writing at the time the action is taken (wherever possible this advice will be issued with the enforcement notice).

March 1998
Better Regulation Unit,
Cabinet Office,
Horse Guards Road,
London SW1P 3AL
Telephone: [020 7270 6928]
Fax: [020 7270 6402]

Appendix IV

Model forms

<u>**PRIVATE AND CONFIDENTIAL**</u>

APPLICATION FOR A LICENCE TO DRIVE A HACKNEY CARRIAGE
IN THE DISTRICT OF [   ]

All applicants are required—

(a) To have held a full current driving licence for the last 12 months and to produce that licence.

(b) To produce on the prescribed form (supplied by the [   ] Council) a medical certificate of fitness to drive a licensed vehicle completed by your General Practitioner.

(c) To complete the Statutory Declaration sworn before a Solicitor.

(d) To provide a sealed print out of the information held on the Police National Computer against your name under the provisions of the Data Protection Act 1984.

(e) *To pass a test of competency in driving.* *

(f) *To pass a written and verbal knowledge test on the Council's Area and the surrounding Districts.* *

(g) To pay a licence fee of £........

(h) To produce four recent photographs of themselves of passport size and specification.

* Only applicable if the relevant Council has these requirements

NOTE: It is a criminal offence to drive a hackney carriage licensed by [   ] Council without a hackney carriage driver's licence issued by the [   ] Council.

All questions must be answered. Failure to do so will result in consideration of the application being delayed.

Please write in BLOCK LETTERS.

1. Full Name   (a) Last Name ....

                            (b) First Name and other names ....

                            (c) Date of Birth ....

                            (d) Telephone No. (if any) ....

2.   Present Address

_____

_____

_____

_____

3.   Present trade or occupation

_____

4.   Do you intend to work as a full-time or part-time driver?

_____

5.   Have you ever previously held a hackney carriage driver's licence, hackney carriage vehicle (proprietor's) licence, private hire driver's licence, private hire vehicle licence or private hire operator's licence, issued by this Council or any other council? If so, please state which council and date?

_____

_____

6.   Have you ever been refused a hackney carriage driver's licence, hackney carriage vehicle (proprietor's) licence, private hire driver's licence, private hire vehicle licence or private hire operator's licence or had such a licence suspended or revoked, by this council or any other council. If so, please state which council and the date?

_____

_____

I declare that to the best of my knowledge and belief the answers given above are true. If a licence is granted I undertake to comply with the hackney carriage byelaws and/or conditions* attached on the grant of the licence. Should I engage in other employment, I also agree to partake of sufficient rest and refreshment after finishing work before commencing driving for hire.

*Delete if the Council does not have Hackney Carriage Byelaws and/or Hackney Carriage Drivers Conditions

Date _____   Usual Signature of Applicant _____

APPLICANTS ARE ADVISED THAT TO MAKE, KNOWINGLY OR RECKLESSLY, A FALSE STATEMENT OR OMIT ANY INFORMATION FROM THIS APPLICATION IS A CRIMINAL OFFENCE.

This form, together with the Statutory Declaration duly sworn before a Solicitor/ Commissioner for Oaths, and the sealed Data Protection Act print out should be <u>brought in person</u> to the [address of Council].

Postal applications will not be accepted.

[Add Statutory Declaration and Rehabilitation of Offenders Act Notes: see pp 408–410]

APPLICATION TO RENEW A LICENCE TO DRIVE A HACKNEY CARRIAGE IN THE DISTRICT OF [   ]

All applicants are required—

(a) To produce a full current driving licence.

(b) To provide a sealed print out of the information held on the Police National Computer against your name under the provisions of the Data Protection Act 1984.

(c) To complete the Statutory Declaration sworn before a Solicitor.

(d) To complete the Department of Transport/Home Office Circular Form 13/92, which will be forwarded to the [*local police force name*] Police every three years.

(e) To pay a licence fee of £......

(f) To produce four recent photographs of themselves of passport size and specification.

NOTE: It is a criminal offence to drive a hackney carriage licensed by [   ] Council without a hackney carriage drivers licence issued by the [   ] Council.

I hereby apply to renew my hackney carriage driver's licence which expires on _____ and understand that if in giving the following information I knowingly or recklessly make a false statement or omit any material I shall be guilty of an offence.

All questions must be answered. Failure to do so will result in consideration of the application being delayed.

Please write in BLOCK LETTERS.

1. Full Name   (*a*) Last Name ....

(*b*) First Name and other names ....

(*c*) Date of Birth ....

(*d*) Telephone No. (if any) ....

(*e*) Badge No. ....

2.   Present Address

_____

_____

_____

3.   Name and address of employer within the trade OR (if applicable) state whether you are self-employed

_____

4.   Do you work as a full-time or part-time driver?

_____

I declare that to the best of my knowledge and belief the answers given above are true. If a licence is granted I undertake to comply with the hackney carriage byelaws and/or conditions* attached on the grant of the licence. Should I engage in other employment, I also agree to partake of sufficient rest and refreshment after finishing work before commencing driving for hire.

*Delete if the Council does not have Hackney Carriage Byelaws and/or Hackney Carriage Drivers Conditions

Date _____ Usual Signature of Applicant _____

APPLICANTS ARE ADVISED THAT TO MAKE, KNOWINGLY OR RECKLESSLY, A FALSE STATEMENT OR OMIT ANY INFORMATION FROM THIS APPLICATION IS A CRIMINAL OFFENCE.

This form, together with the Statutory Declaration duly sworn before a Solicitor/Commissioner for Oaths, and the sealed Data Protection Act print out should be <u>brought in person</u> to the [address of Council].

Postal applications will not be accepted.

[Add Statutory Declaration and Rehabilitation of Offenders Act Notes: see pp 408–410]

PRIVATE AND CONFIDENTIAL

APPLICATION FOR A HACKNEY CARRIAGE PROPRIETOR'S LICENCE FOR THE DISTRICT OF [   ]

All applicants are required to produce with this form—

(a) To pay a licence fee of £ _____ .

(b) A valid certificate or policy of insurance for the vehicle if any in force. If not yet arranged, a valid insurance policy must be produced before the licence will be handed to the applicant.

(c) 2 passport type photographs are required of the applicant.

(d) A Statutory Declaration sworn before a Solicitor entitled to administer Oaths, from each person named below. (Additional forms may be obtained on request).

(e) The Vehicle Registration Document (Log Book) must be produced with this application form. (If it is not available then other proof of ownership such as a legal bill of sale must be produced.)

PLEASE NOTE: **Only *[e.g. wheelchair accessible FX4s, Metro Cabs and TX1s will be licensed as hackney carriages]* ***

* Alter as applicable dependent upon the Council's policies

All questions must be answered. Failure to do so will result in consideration of the application being delayed.

Please write in BLOCK LETTERS.

1. Name of Applicant   Hackney Carriage Driver's badge No. (if applicable)

2. Make of Vehicle   Seating Capacity

3. Model

4. Colour   Year of Registration

5. Registration Number

6. Chassis No.   Engine No.

7. Is the vehicle licensed with any other council?   YES/NO

(In the event of the vehicle being licensed with another council, you **must** inform the licensing unit).

If so: (a) Which authority?
       (b) Licence Plate number for the vehicle
       (c) Date of vehicle licence expiring

390

8.   Fare meter number and make.

9.   Is the vehicle wheelchair accessible? If so, was it   Purpose Built
                                                                Converted (when and
                                                                 by whom)

9.   Where is the vehicle to be based when not in use?

10.   State the name and address of every person including any limited company who is a proprietor or part proprietor of the above vehicle, and every person who is concerned either solely or in partnership with any other person or as a Director or Secretary of a company in the renting, keeping, employing or letting for hire such vehicle.

Forename and Surname   **Address**   **Tel. No.**

I/We declare that to best of my/our knowledge and belief, the answers given above are true. If a licence is granted I/We undertake to comply with the conditions attached on the grant of the licence and/or the hackney carriage byelaws.

Date   _____   Usual Signature of Applicant(s)   _____

Date   _____   _____

APPLICANTS ARE ADVISED THAT TO MAKE, KNOWINGLY OR RECKLESSLY, A FALSE STATEMENT OR OMIT ANY INFORMATION FROM THIS APPLICATION IS A CRIMINAL OFFENCE.

This form, together with the Statutory Declaration duly sworn before a Solicitor/Commissioner for Oaths, should be <u>brought in person</u> to the [address of Council].

Postal applications will not be accepted.

[Add Statutory Declaration and Rehabilitation of Offenders Act Notes: see pp 408–410]

APPLICATION TO RENEW A HACKNEY CARRIAGE PROPRIETOR'S LICENCE FOR THE DISTRICT OF [   ]

All applicants are required to produce with this form—

(a)   To pay a licence fee of £_____ .

(b)   A valid certificate or policy of insurance for the vehicle.

(c)   2 passport type photographs are required of the applicant.

(d)   A Statutory Declaration sworn before a Solicitor entitled to administer Oaths, from each person named below. (Additional forms may be obtained on request.)

(e)   The Vehicle Registration Document (Log Book) must be produced with this application form. (If it is not available then other proof of ownership such as a legal bill of sale must be produced.)

PLEASE NOTE: **Only *[e.g. wheelchair accessible FX4s, Metro Cabs and TX1s* *will be licensed as hackney carriages]****

* Alter as applicable dependent upon the Council's policies

All questions must be answered. Failure to do so will result in consideration of the application being delayed.

Please write in BLOCK LETTERS.

1.   Name of Applicant   Hackney Carriage Driver's
                                                                    badge No. (if applicable)

2.   Hackney Carriage Plate Number

3.   Make of Vehicle   Seating Capacity

4.   Model

5.   Colour   Year of Registration

6.   Registration Number

7.   Chassis No.   Engine No.

8.   Fare meter number and make.

9.   Is the vehicle wheelchair accessible? If so, was it   Purpose Built
                                                                    Converted (when and
                                                                    by whom)

10.   Where is the vehicle to be based when not in use?

11. State the name and address of every person including any limited company who is a proprietor or part proprietor of the above vehicle, and every person who is concerned either solely or in partnership with any other person or as a Director or Secretary of a company in the renting, keeping, employing or letting for hire such vehicle.

Forename and Surname   **Address**   **Tel. No.**

I/We declare that to best of my/our knowledge and belief, the answers given above are true. If a licence is granted I/We undertake to comply with the conditions attached on the grant of the licence and/or the hackney carriage byelaws.

Date _____   Usual Signature of Applicant(s) _____

Date _____   _____

APPLICANTS ARE ADVISED THAT TO MAKE, KNOWINGLY OR RECKLESSLY, A FALSE STATEMENT OR OMIT ANY INFORMATION FROM THIS APPLICATION IS A CRIMINAL OFFENCE.

This form, together with the Statutory Declaration duly sworn before a Solicitor/Commissioner for Oaths, should be <u>brought in person</u> to the [address of Council].

Postal applications will not be accepted.

[Add Statutory Declaration and Rehabilitation of Offenders Act Notes: see pp 408–410]

PRIVATE AND CONFIDENTIAL

APPLICATION FOR A LICENCE TO DRIVE A PRIVATE HIRE VEHICLE IN THE DISTRICT OF [   ]

All applicants are required—

- (a) To have held a full current driving licence for the last 12 months and to produce that licence.

- (b) To produce on the prescribed form (supplied by the [   ] Council) a medical certificate of fitness to drive a licensed vehicle completed by your General Practitioner.

- (c) To complete the Statutory Declaration sworn before a Solicitor.

- (d) To provide a sealed print out of the information held on the Police National Computer against your name under the provisions of the Data Protection Act 1984.

- (e) *To pass a test of competency in driving.* *

- (f) *To pass a written and verbal knowledge test on the Council's Area and the surrounding Districts.* *

- (g) To pay a licence fee of £......

- (h) To produce four recent photographs of themselves of passport size and specification.

* Only applicable if the relevant Council has these requirements

NOTE: It is a criminal offence to drive a private hire vehicle licensed by [   ] Council without a private hire driver's licence issued by the [   ] Council.

All questions must be answered. Failure to do so will result in consideration of the application being delayed.

Please write in BLOCK LETTERS.

1. Full Name   (a) Last Name ....

                         (b) First Name and other names ....

                         (c) Date of Birth ....

                         (d) Telephone No. (if any) ....

2.   Present Address

_____

_____

_____

_____

3.   Present trade or occupation

_____

4.   Do you intend to work as a full-time or part-time driver?

_____

5.   Have you ever been previously held a private hire driver's licence, private hire vehicle licence, private hire operator's licence, hackney carriage driver's licence or hackney carriage vehicle (proprietor's) licence issued by this Council or any other council? If so, please state which council and date?

_____

_____

6.   Have you ever been refused a private hire driver's licence, private hire vehicle licence, private hire operator's licence, hackney carriage driver's licence or hackney carriage vehicle (proprietor's) licence or had such a licence suspended or revoked, by this council or any other council. If so, please state which council and the date?

_____

_____

I declare that to the best of my knowledge and belief the answers given above are true. If a licence is granted I undertake to comply with the conditions attached on the grant of the licence. Should I engage in other employment, I also agree to partake of sufficient rest and refreshment after finishing work before commencing driving for hire.

Date   _____   Usual Signature of Applicant _____

APPLICANTS ARE ADVISED THAT TO MAKE, KNOWINGLY OR RECKLESSLY, A FALSE STATEMENT OR OMIT ANY INFORMATION FROM THIS APPLICATION IS A CRIMINAL OFFENCE.

This form, together with the Statutory Declaration duly sworn before a Solicitor/ Commissioner for Oaths, and the sealed Data Protection Act print out should be brought in person to the [address of Council].

Postal applications will not be accepted.

[Add Statutory Declaration and Rehabilitation of Offenders Act Notes: see pp 408–410]

<u>**PRIVATE AND CONFIDENTIAL**</u>

APPLICATION TO RENEW A LICENCE TO DRIVE A PRIVATE HIRE VEHICLE IN THE DISTRICT OF [   ]

All applicants are required—

(a) To produce a full current driving licence.

(b) To provide a sealed print out of the information held on the Police National Computer against your name under the provisions of the Data Protection Act 1984.

(c) To complete the Statutory Declaration sworn before a Solicitor.

(d) To complete the Department of Transport/Home Office Circular Form 13/92, which will be forwarded to the [*local police force name*] Police every three years.

(e) To pay a licence fee of £......

(f) To produce four recent photographs of themselves of passport size and specification.

NOTE: It is a criminal offence to drive a private hire vehicle licensed by [   ] Council without a private hire drivers licence issued by the [   ] Council.

I hereby apply to renew my private hire driver's licence which expires on and understand that if in giving the following information I knowingly or recklessly make a false statement or omit any material I shall be guilty of an offence.

All questions must be answered. Failure to do so will result in consideration of the application being delayed.

Please write in BLOCK LETTERS.

1.   Full Name   (a) Last Name ....

(b) First Name and other names ....

(c) Date of Birth ....

(d) Telephone No. (if any) ....

(e) Badge No. ....

2. Present Address

_____

_____

_____

_____

3. Name and address of employer within the trade OR (if applicable) state whether you are self-employed

_____

4. Do you work as a full-time or part-time driver?

_____

5. Which Operator is your current licence deposited with?

_____

I declare that to the best of my knowledge and belief the answers given above are true. If a licence is granted I undertake to comply with the conditions attached on the grant of the licence. Should I engage in other employment, I also agree to partake of sufficient rest and refreshment after finishing work before commencing driving for hire.

Date _____ Usual Signature of Applicant _____

APPLICANTS ARE ADVISED THAT TO MAKE, KNOWINGLY OR RECKLESSLY, A FALSE STATEMENT OR OMIT ANY INFORMATION FROM THIS APPLICATION IS A CRIMINAL OFFENCE.

This form, together with the Statutory Declaration duly sworn before a Solicitor/Commissioner for Oaths, and the sealed Data Protection Act print out should be <u>brought in person</u> to the [address of Council].

Postal applications will not be accepted.

[Add Statutory Declaration and Rehabilitation of Offenders Act Notes: see pp 408–410]

APPLICATION FOR A LICENCE TO OPERATE PRIVATE HIRE VEHICLES IN THE DISTRICT OF [   ]

All applicants are required to produce with this form—

    (a)   A licence fee of £........ per year

    (b)   A Statutory Declaration duly sworn and completed before a Solicitor entitled to administer Oaths, if necessary by more than one person.

    (c)   Current certificate of insurance for employer's Liability Policy

All questions must be answered. Failure to do so will result in consideration of the application being delayed.

Please write in BLOCK LETTERS.

1.   Full name and address of person(s) or limited company wishing to operate private hire vehicle

_____

_____

1(a)   Trading name of person(s) or limited company _____

1(b)   Registered Office address of limited company if different from 1 above.

_____

2.   If the applicant is a partnership or limited company the full names and addresses of all partners or directors and secretary.

_____   _____

_____   _____

_____   _____

_____   _____

3.   Address at which you intend to carry on business as an operator.

_____

4.   Has any person in 1 or 2 above ever applied for an operator's licence before, to this Council or any other Council? If so, when and where did you apply?

_____

_____

_____

5.   Does any person in 1 or 2 above hold any of the following—private hire driver's licence, private hire vehicle licence, hackney carriage driver's licence or hackney carriage vehicle (proprietor's) licence—issued by this Council or any other Council? If so, give full details including the Council name, badge numbers, date of grant and expiry. Continue on a separate sheet of paper if required.

_____

_____

6.   Has any person in 1 and 2 above ever been refused a private hire driver's licence, private hire vehicle licence, private hire operator's licence, hackney carriage driver's licence or hackney carriage vehicle (proprietor's) licence or had any such licence suspended or revoked? If so, give full details including the name of the Council and the date.

7.   What trade, business or profession has each person named in 1 and 2 carried on over 5 years prior to applying for this licence and where?

_____

_____

8.   Do you intend to fit radio phones in vehicles you operate?   YES/NO

  If YES state—

  (a)   make and model _____

  (b)   the frequency on which the radios broadcast _____

  (c)   address where radio transmitter is based _____

9.   Do you have or intend to have a waiting room at the premises mentioned in question 3 for members of the public?   YES/NO

10.   How many telephone lines will you have which will be available for public telephone bookings?

  _____

10(a)   Please state Telephone Number (if known) ....

10(b)   If any of the above are 'FREEPHONES' please state the location(s) of the freephones

_____

_____

11.   How many private hire vehicles do you intend to operate from your base?

_____

12.   If any person in 1 or 2 above is or has been a director or secretary of any other limited company the following information must be provided about each of those companies.

  (a)   Name and Registered Office

(b) Trade or business activities carried on by each company.

_____

(c) Previous applications made by each company for an operator's licence, to this council or any other council.

_____

(d) Any revocation or suspension of any operator's licence issued by this council or any other council previously held by any company.

_____

(e) All convictions in relations to any offence recorded against any company.

_____

I/We declare that to best of my/our knowledge and belief, the answers given above are true. If a licence is granted I/We undertake to comply with the conditions attached on the grant of the licence.

Date _____ Usual Signature of Applicant(s) _____

_____   _____

APPLICANTS ARE ADVISED THAT TO MAKE, KNOWINGLY OR RECKLESSLY, A FALSE STATEMENT OR OMIT ANY INFORMATION FROM THIS APPLICATION IS A CRIMINAL OFFENCE.

This form, together with the Statutory Declaration duly sworn before a Solicitor/ Commissioner for Oaths, should be <u>brought in person</u> to the [address of Council].

Postal applications will not be accepted.

[Add Statutory Declaration and Rehabilitation of Offenders Act Notes: see pp 408–410]

APPLICATION TO RENEW A LICENCE TO OPERATE PRIVATE HIRE VEHICLES IN THE DISTRICT OF [   ]

All applicants are required to produce with this form—

(a)   A licence fee of £....... per year

(b)   A Statutory Declaration duly sworn and completed before a Solicitor entitled to administer Oaths, if necessary by more than one person.

(c)   Current certificate of insurance for employer's Liability Policy

All questions must be answered. Failure to do so will result in consideration of the application being delayed.

Please write in BLOCK LETTERS.

1.   Full name and address of person(s) or limited company wishing to operate private hire vehicle

_____

_____

1(a)   Trading name of person(s) or limited company _____

1(b)   Registered Office address of limited company if different from 1 above.

_____

2.   If the applicant is a partnership or limited company the full names and addresses of all partners or directors and secretary.

_____   _____

_____   _____

_____   _____

_____   _____

3.   Address from which you operate.

_____

4.   Has any person in 1 or 2 above ever applied for an operator's licence before, other than the existing licence which you are applying to renew, to this Council or any other Council? If so, when and where did you apply?

_____

_____

_____

401

5. Does any person in 1 or 2 above hold any of the following—private hire driver's licence, private hire vehicle licence, hackney carriage driver's licence or hackney carriage vehicle (proprietor's) licence—issued by this Council or any other Council? If so, give full details including the Council name, badge numbers, date of grant and expiry. Continue on a separate sheet of paper if required.

---

6. Has any person in 1 and 2 above ever been refused a private hire driver's licence, private hire vehicle licence, private hire operator's licence, hackney carriage driver's licence or hackney carriage vehicle (proprietors) licence or had any such licence suspended or revoked? If so, give full details including the name of the Council and the date.

7. What trade, business or profession has each person named in 1 and 2 carried on over 5 years prior to applying for this licence and where?

---

8. Do the vehicles you operate have radio phones?   YES/NO

    If YES state—

    (a) make and model

    (b) the frequency on which the radios broadcast

    (c) address where radio transmitter is based

9. Do you have a waiting room at the premises mentioned in question 3 for members of the public?   YES/NO

10. How many telephone lines are there available for public telephone bookings?

10(a) Please state Telephone Number(s) ....

10(b) If any of the above are 'FREEPHONES' please state the location(s) of the freephones

---

---

11. How many private hire vehicles are you operating from your base?

---

12. If any person in 1 or 2 above is or has been a director or secretary of any other limited company the following information must be provided about each of those companies.

Application to renew a licence to operate private hire vehicles

(a)   Name and Registered Office

_____

(b)   Trade or business activities carried on by each company.

_____

(c)   Previous applications made by each company for an operator's licence, to this council or any other council.

_____

(d)   Any revocation or suspension of any operator's licence issued by this council or any other council previously held by any company.

_____

(e)   All convictions in relations to any offence recorded against any company.

_____

I/We declare that to best of my/our knowledge and belief, the answers given above are true. If a licence

is granted I/We undertake to comply with the conditions attached on the grant of the licence.

Date _____   Usual Signature of Applicant(s) _____

_____

APPLICANTS ARE ADVISED THAT TO MAKE, KNOWINGLY OR RECKLESSLY, A FALSE STATEMENT OR OMIT ANY INFORMATION FROM THIS APPLICATION IS A CRIMINAL OFFENCE.

This form, together with the Statutory Declaration duly sworn before a Solicitor/Commissioner for Oaths, should be <u>brought in person</u> to the [address of Council].

Postal applications will not be accepted.

[Add Statutory Declaration and Rehabilitation of Offenders Act Notes: see pp 408–410]

PRIVATE AND CONFIDENTIAL

APPLICATION FOR A PRIVATE HIRE VEHICLE PROPRIETOR'S LICENCE FOR THE DISTRICT OF [   ]

All applicants are required to produce with this form—

(a) To pay a licence fee of £ _____ .

(b) A valid certificate or policy of insurance for the vehicle if any in force. If not yet arranged, a valid insurance policy must be produced before the licence will be handed to the applicant.

(c) 2 passport type photographs are required of the applicant.

(d) A Statutory Declaration sworn before a Solicitor entitled to administer Oaths, from each person named below. (Additional forms may be obtained on request.)

(e) The Vehicle Registration Document (Log Book) must be produced with this application form. (If it is not available then other proof of ownership such as a legal bill of sale must be produced.)

PLEASE NOTE: **FX4s, Metro Cabs and TX1s** will **NOT** be licensed as private hire cars.

All questions must be answered. Failure to do so will result in consideration of the application being delayed.

Please write in BLOCK LETTERS.

1. Name of Applicant   Private Hire Driver's
                                          badge No. (if applicable)

2. Make of Vehicle   Seating Capacity

3. Model

4. Colour   Year of Registration

5. Registration Number

6. Chassis No.   Engine No.

7. Is the vehicle licensed with any other council?   YES/NO

(In the event of the vehicle being licensed with another council, you **must** inform the licensing unit).

If so:

(a) Which authority?

(b) Licence Plate number for the vehicle

(c) Date of vehicle licence expiring

404

8. Please state the name of the Private Hire Operator who will operate the vehicle.

9. Where is the vehicle to be based when not in use?

10. State the name and address of every person including any limited company who is a proprietor or part proprietor of the above vehicle, and every person who is concerned either solely or in partnership with any other person or as a Director or Secretary of a company in the renting, keeping, employing or letting for hire such vehicle.

Forename and Surname   **Address**   **Tel. No.**

I/We declare that to best of my/our knowledge and belief, the answers given above are true. If a licence is granted I/We undertake to comply with the conditions attached on the grant of the licence.

Date _____ Usual Signature of Applicant(s) _____

_____   _____

APPLICANTS ARE ADVISED THAT TO MAKE, KNOWINGLY OR RECKLESSLY, A FALSE STATEMENT OR OMIT ANY INFORMATION FROM THIS APPLICATION IS A CRIMINAL OFFENCE.

This form, together with the Statutory Declaration duly sworn before a Solicitor/ Commissioner for Oaths, should be <u>brought in person</u> to the [address of Council].

Postal applications will not be accepted.

[Add Statutory Declaration and Rehabilitation of Offenders Act Notes: see pp 408–410]

PRIVATE AND CONFIDENTIAL

**APPLICATION TO RENEW A PRIVATE HIRE VEHICLE
PROPRIETOR'S LICENCE FOR THE DISTRICT OF [   ]**

All applicants are required to produce with this form—

(a)   To pay a licence fee of £_____ .

(b)   A valid certificate or policy of insurance for the vehicle.

(c)   2 passport type photographs are required of the applicant.

(d)   A Statutory Declaration sworn before a Solicitor entitled to administer Oaths, from each person named below. (Additional forms may be obtained on request.)

(e)   The Vehicle Registration Document (Log Book) must be produced with this application form. (If it is not available then other proof of ownership such as a legal bill of sale must be produced.)

PLEASE NOTE: **FX4s, Metro Cabs and TX1s** will **NOT** be licensed as private hire cars.

All questions must be answered. Failure to do so will result in consideration of the application being delayed.

Please write in BLOCK LETTERS.

1.   Name of Applicant   Private Hire Driver's badge No.
                                                                    (if applicable)

2.   Private hire plate number

3.   Make of Vehicle   Seating Capacity

4.   Model

5.   Colour   Year of Registration

6.   Registration Number

7.   Chassis No.   Engine No.

8.   Please state the name of the Private Hire Operator who will operate the vehicle.

9.   Where is the vehicle to be based when not in use?

10. State the name and address of every person including any limited company who is a proprietor or part proprietor of the above vehicle, and every person who is concerned either solely or in partnership with any other person or as a Director or Secretary of a company in the renting, keeping, employing or letting for hire such vehicle.

406

Application to renew a private hire vehicle proprietor's licence

Forename and Surname   **Address**   **Tel. No.**

I/We declare that to best of my/our knowledge and belief, the answers given above are true. If the licence is renewed I/We undertake to comply with the conditions attached on the grant of the licence.

Date _____ Usual Signature of Applicant(s) _____

_____   _____

APPLICANTS ARE ADVISED THAT TO MAKE, KNOWINGLY OR RECKLESSLY, A FALSE STATEMENT OR OMIT ANY INFORMATION FROM THIS APPLICATION IS A CRIMINAL OFFENCE.

This form, together with the Statutory Declaration duly sworn before a Solicitor/ Commissioner for Oaths, should be <u>brought in person</u> to the [address of Council].

Postal applications will not be accepted.

[Add Statutory Declaration and Rehabilitation of Offenders Act Notes: see pp 408–410]

STATUTORY DECLARATION

(See over for Explanatory Notes)

I (full name), _____

Of (address) _____

Date of Birth _____ state:

1. I have never been convicted for any offence.

OR

2. I have been convicted for an offence or offences and I list below every offence for which I have been convicted, whether or not it is spent within the terms of the Rehabilitation of Offenders Act, 1974, together with the date and place where the offence was committed, the court which dealt with the matter, the date the sentence was imposed and the sentence imposed by the Court. I have not been convicted for any other offences.

STATUTORY DECLARATION 1 AND 2 ABOVE RELATES TO **ALL OFFENCES INCLUDING** ANY MOTORING OFFENCES

Date and Place Offence Committed	Court which dealt with the matter (type of Court and Town)	Date of Court Hearing	Date Sentence imposed (if different from date of hearing)	Sentence Imposed

And I make this solemn declaration conscientiously believing the same to be true and by virtue of the provisions of the Statutory Declarations Act 1835, and section 5 of the Perjury Act 1911.

Declared at _____ This _____ day of _____

In the County of _____

Signature of Applicant _____

Before me _____ Solicitor/Commissioner for Oaths

Office Address/Stamp _____

EXPLANATORY NOTES ON THE REHABILITATION OF OFFENDERS ACT, 1974

This Act provides that after a certain lapse of time, convictions for criminal offences are to be regarded as 'spent' for certain purposes. However, all criminal convictions are relevant for hackney carriage and private hire licensing purposes and must be declared. The Council will consider the offence committed and the time elapsed since conviction for that offence.

The following is a guide to the periods of time that have to elapse before the offence is spent for other purposes.

Sentences of imprisonment exceeding 30 months' duration can never be treated as spent.

Sentence	Rehabilitation period Adult	Rehabilitation period Under 18
A sentence of imprisonment, detention in a young offender institution or youth custody or corrective training for a term exceeding 6 months but not exceeding 30 months.	10 Years	5 Years
A sentence of imprisonment, detention in a young offender institution or youth custody for a term not exceeding 6 months.	7 Years	3½ Years
A fine, probation order, or community service order.	5 Years	2½ Years
A sentence of cashiering, discharge with ignominy or dismissal with disgrace from Her Majesty's service.	10 Years	As for adult
A sentence of dismissal from Her Majesty's service.	7 years	As for adult
Conditional discharge or binding over	1 year from conviction or when period expires (whichever is longer)	
Disqualification/Prohibition	To the end of the disqualification or prohibition	
Absolute discharge	6 months	6 months
Mental Health Act order	5 years or 2 years after hospital order ends (whichever is longer)	

The periods of time which must elapse in other cases before the conviction becomes spent vary considerably according to the nature of the offence and other circumstances. The rehabilitation period may be extended by the commission of a further offence during the rehabilitation period.

As a result of this, the summarised provisions above are intended only as a general guide.

Further guidance on this may be obtained from the Home Office publication 'A Guide to the Rehabilitation of Offenders Act, 1974' or from a Solicitor or the Citizens Advice Bureau.

APPLICANTS SHOULD NOTE THAT TO MAKE A FALSE STATUTORY DECLARATION IS A SERIOUS CRIMINAL OFFENCE, PUNISHABLE UPON CONVICTION BY IMPRISONMENT FOR A TERM NOT EXCEEDING TWO YEARS OR TO A FINE TO BE DECIDED BY THE COURT OR BOTH. THIS STATUTORY DECLARATION MAY IN CERTAIN CIRCUMSTANCES BE FORWARDED TO THE POLICE FOR EXAMINATION.

Index